Uncertainty, Production, C

The State-Contingent Approach

This book demonstrates that the state-contingent approach provides the best way to think about all problems in the economics of uncertainty, including problems of consumer choice, the theory of the firm, and principal–agent relationships. The authors demonstrate that dual methods apply under uncertainty and that the dual representations can be developed for stochastic technologies. Moreover, proper exploitation of the properties of alternative primal and dual representations of preferences allows analysts to generalize and extend the results of the existing literature on preferences under uncertainty, thus making expected-utility theory largely superfluous for many decisions. These insights open the way for developments in the basic theory of production under uncertainty, the theory of hedging behavior, the analysis of agency problems, and the theory of production insurance.

Robert G. Chambers is Professor and Chair in the Department of Agricultural and Resource Economics at the University of Maryland, where he has served on the faculty since 1979. Professor Chambers has also taught or lectured at the Ohio State University, the University of Helsinki, and several European universities. He served as senior staff economist for agriculture at the U.S. President's Council of Economic Advisers in 1985–6. Professor Chambers has published more than 100 articles, books, and book chapters on production economics, agricultural economics, public economics, microeconomic theory, and agricultural policy analysis. His book *Applied Production Analysis: A Dual Approach* (Cambridge University Press, 1988) continues to be a leading reference in the field. He was named a Fellow of the American Agricultural Economics Association (AAEA) in 1999 and has received numerous research awards from the AAEA and other professional associations.

John Quiggin is an Australian Research Council Senior Fellow in Economics based at the Australian National University (ANU), Canberra. He has also taught at the University of Maryland, the University of Sydney, and held other positions at ANU and the Australian Bureau of Agricultural and Resource Economics. Professor Quiggin is prominent as both a research economist and a commentator on Australian economic policy. He has published more than 300 research articles, books, and reports in fields such as risk analysis, production economics, and the theory of economic growth, as well as on policy topics including unemployment, microeconomic reform, privatization, competitive tendering, and the economics of education. Professor Quiggin received the Australian Social Science Academy Medal for 1993 and was elected Fellow of the Academy of the Social Sciences in Australia in 1996.

Advance Praise for *Uncertainty, Production, Choice, and Agency*

"By adopting the state-contingent approach and developing an analytical framework in which producers can explicitly respond to uncertainty, this book fundamentally departs from the traditional 'black-box' treatment of production under uncertainty. Among many advantages of the new approach is the transparency with which one can analyze the effects of changes in each of the underlying sources of uncertainty on decision variables, thereby enabling one to gain useful policy insights. This book makes an important and timely contribution to literature on production and choice under uncertainty, and no serious student, researcher, or policy analysts in this area can afford to miss it."

– Y. Hossein Farzin, *University of California, Davis*

Uncertainty, Production, Choice, and Agency

The State-Contingent Approach

ROBERT G. CHAMBERS
University of Maryland

JOHN QUIGGIN
Australian National University

CAMBRIDGE
UNIVERSITY PRESS

PUBLISHED BY THE PRESS SYNDICATE OF THE UNIVERSITY OF CAMBRIDGE
The Pitt Building, Trumpington Street, Cambridge, United Kingdom

CAMBRIDGE UNIVERSITY PRESS
The Edinburgh Building, Cambridge CB2 2RU, UK http://www.cup.cam.ac.uk
40 West 20th Street, New York, NY 10011-4211, USA http://www.cup.org
10 Stamford Road, Oakleigh, Melbourne 3166, Australia
Ruiz de Alarcón 13, 28014 Madrid, Spain

First published 2000

Printed in the United States of America

Typeface Times Roman 10.5/13 pt. *System* QuarkXPress [BTS]

A catalog record for this book is available from the British Library.

Library of Congress Cataloging in Publication Data
Chambers, Robert G.
Uncertainty, production, choice, and agency : the state-contingent approach / Robert G. Chambers, John Quiggin.
p. cm.
Includes bibliographical references.
ISBN 0-521-62244-1 (hb) – ISBN 0-521-78523-5 (pbk.)
1. Uncertainty. 2. Production (Economic theory). 3. Consumer behavior. 4. Microeconomics. I. Quiggin, John. II. Title.
HB615 .C52 2000
338.5 – dc21 99-052880

ISBN 0 521 62244 1 hardback
ISBN 0 521 78523 5 paperback

To:

Christopher
Daniel
Geoffrey
Leigh
Timothy

Contents

List of Symbols

$\mathbf{0}_{M\times S}$:	$M \times S$ matrix with all elements equal to zero
$\mathbf{1}^s$:	S-dimensional unit vector
$Af(\underline{u})$:	landlord's cost of reducing reservation utility
$\mathbf{a}_{[]}$:	increasing rearrangment of the vector **a** with elements satisfying $a_{[1]} \le a_{[2]} \le \cdots \le a_{[S]}$
$B(w, \mathbf{y})$:	benefit function for **y** relative to the welfare level w
$\mathbf{b}^k$:	vector of basis risk with typical element $f_s^k - q^k$
$c(\mathbf{w}, \mathbf{z})$:	effort-cost function under linear input pricing
$c^c(\mathbf{w}, z)$:	minimum cost of producing a scalar nonstochastic output z
$c(\mathbf{z})$:	effort-cost function
$C(\mathbf{r}, \mathbf{p})$:	revenue-cost function
$C(\mathbf{w}, \mathbf{r}, \mathbf{p})$:	revenue-cost function under linear input pricing
$\hat{C}(\mathbf{w}, \mathbf{T}(\mathbf{r}, \mathbf{p}, \mathbf{w}), \mathbf{p})$:	revenue-cost function for technology exhibiting constant absolute riskiness
$\overline{C}(\mathbf{w}, \overline{\mathbf{T}}(\mathbf{r}, \mathbf{p}, \mathbf{w}), \mathbf{p})$:	revenue-cost function for technology exhibiting constant relative riskiness
$C(\mathbf{z})$:	private effort-cost function
$D(\mathbf{y}, w)$:	distance function for **y** relative to the welfare level w
$e(\mathbf{y})$:	certainty equivalent for **y**
$e^c(\mathbf{r}, \mathbf{p})$:	cost certainty equivalent revenue
$f(\mathbf{x}, \theta)$:	stochastic production function
F:	set of probability distributions for random variables associated with Y
$F(t; \mathbf{y}, \boldsymbol{\pi})$:	cumulative distribution function for t relative to **y** and $\boldsymbol{\pi}$

$\mathbf{f}^k$:	vector of state-contingent spot prices for commodity in which the kth futures contract is traded
$g(\mathbf{x})$:	producer's effort evaluation function
h:	amount hedged in a forward contract
h^k:	amount hedged in kth futures market
$h(u)$:	inverse of utility function
I^*:	subset of $\Re^S_{++}$ consisting of vectors with all elements equal to one another
I_s:	net indemnity in state s
$\mathbf{I}$:	vector of state-contingent net indemnities
$\Xi(\mathbf{w}, \mathbf{p})$:	efficient set
$\overline{\Xi}(\mathbf{w}, \mathbf{p})$:	efficient frontier
$l(I_s)$:	loading factor for net indemnity in state s
$m(n)$:	environmental damage function
M:	number of outputs
$\preceq_m$:	majorization ordering
$n(\mathbf{z})$:	private cost-minimizing pollution level
n:	pollution level
N:	number of inputs
$O(\mathbf{z}, \mathbf{x})$:	state-contingent output-distance function
$p(\mathbf{r}, \mathbf{p})$:	production-risk premium
$\mathbf{p}$:	matrix of state-contingent output prices
$\mathbf{P}$:	vector of state-contingent net premiums
π_s^*:	loaded probability in state s
π_s:	probability of state s occurring
$\boldsymbol{\pi}^*$:	vector of loaded probabilities
$\boldsymbol{\pi}$:	probability vector
Π:	set of all probability vectors
$\preceq_\pi$:	π-majorization (Rothschild–Stiglitz) riskiness ordering
q:	forward price of a commodity
q^k:	futures price in kth futures market
$r(\mathbf{y})$:	absolute risk premium for $\mathbf{y}$
$r(\mathbf{r}, \mathbf{p})$:	relative production-risk premium
r_s:	revenue in state s
$\mathbf{r}$:	vector of state-contingent revenues
$\Re_{++}$:	strictly positive real numbers
$\Re_+$:	positive real numbers
$\Re$:	real numbers
S:	number of states of nature

$T(\mathbf{r}, \mathbf{p})$: revenue aggregate satisfying the translation property in revenues

$T(\mathbf{r}, \mathbf{p}, \mathbf{w})$: revenue aggregate satisfying the translation property in revenues under linear input pricing

$\overline{T}(\mathbf{r}, \mathbf{p})$: revenue aggregate satisfying positive linear homogeneity in revenues

$\overline{T}(\mathbf{r}, \mathbf{p}, \mathbf{w})$: revenue aggregate satisfying positive linear homogeneity in revenues under linear input pricing

$\underline{u}$: reservation utility

$\mathbf{u}$: state-contingent utility vector

u_s: utility in state s

$u(y)$: ex post utility function for an expected-utility maximizer

$\mathbf{u}(\mathbf{z})$: optimal state-contingent utility vector for second-best agency cost problem

$v(\mathbf{y})$: relative risk premium for $\mathbf{y}$

$V(\boldsymbol{\pi}, \underline{u})$: principal's second-best objective function under moral-hazard

$V(\underline{u}, p, \boldsymbol{\pi})$: principal's indirect objective function under expected-utility taking for agrarian exploitation problem

$V_{FB}(\boldsymbol{\pi}, \underline{u})$: principal's first-best indirect objective function under moral-hazard

Ω: set of states of nature

$W(p, \boldsymbol{\pi}; A)$: principal's indirect objective function for agrarian exploitation problem

$W(\mathbf{y})$: function giving the producer's evaluation of state-contingent income or revenue

W^p: principal's expected return

$\mathbf{w}$: vector of input prices

$\preceq_W$: riskiness ordering induced by W

$X(\mathbf{z})$: input set

$X^*(\mathbf{z})$: input set dual to $c(\mathbf{w}, \mathbf{z})$

$\mathbf{x}$: input vector

y_s: income in state s

Y: set of available state-contingent outcomes

$Y(z_1, z_2; \pi, \underline{u})$: second-best agency-cost function

$Y_{FB}(z_1, z_2; \pi, \underline{u})$: first-best agency-cost function

$\mathbf{y}$: vector of state-contingent incomes (or, more generally, a state-contingent vector of elements of Y)

$\mathbf{y}_{[]}$: increasing rearrangement of $\mathbf{y}$
$Z(\mathbf{x})$: state-contingent output set
$\overline{Z}(\mathbf{x})$: frontier of $Z(\mathbf{x})$
$\mathbf{z}$: matrix of state-contingent outputs

Acknowledgments

Perhaps the most logical place for us to start is by thanking one another. By and large, we are two very different individuals with two very different sets of skills and personal peculiarities. But in our case, the fortunate consequence of the differences is a synergy that has led us to develop in tandem in ways that wouldn't have been possible in isolation.

After that self-congratulatory note, we need to turn to the more serious business of thanking individuals who have contributed either directly or indirectly to the work that we have reported in the chapters that follow. Most importantly, several individuals have read either the whole book or portions of the book while making important comments that have helped us in many different ways. We are particularly indebted to Rolf Färe and Marc Nerlove. Rolf Färe read several drafts of the chapters that lay out the basic theory of state-contingent production correspondences. He has saved us from making a number of errors, and we greatly appreciate his efforts on our behalf. A simple note in an Acknowledgments isn't enough to properly recognize his contribution to this work. Marc Nerlove was kind enough to read the entire penultimate draft of the book. We thank him for a number of substantive comments on the contents of the book, but we most acknowledge his comments about what was missing from the book at that stage. The introductory chapter owes much to his guidance and suggestions. We deeply appreciate and are honored by the contributions these two individuals have made to the material that follows.

Others to whom we are obliged for reading parts of the book include Jean-Marc Bourgeon, Simon Grant, Arne Hallam, John Horowitz, Erik Lichtenberg, and Lars Olson. We also thank Scott Parris and the staff of Cambridge University Press who encouraged us with this project, three reviewers who forced us to improve the book in a number of important ways, and Nancy Wallace, who read the final text and made numerous editorial improvements.

Over the years, several generations of students in applied microeconomics at the University of Maryland were exposed to draft versions of the first five chapters of the book. Their reactions, both adverse and positive, led to a number of important changes, especially in the final versions of Chapter 3. We also thank Liesl Koch and Lien Trieu for assistance in preparing several drafts of the book and Jeff Cunningham for skillfully preparing the camera-ready illustrations.

In addition to these joint thanks, each of us owes a debt of gratitude to individuals whose support and friendship have nourished and sustained us in the years during which we developed and refined the ideas that are presented below. John Quiggin would like to thank Jock Anderson for support and encouragement to pursue this topic over many years, and his wife and colleague, Nancy Wallace, whose help and support have been crucial in many dimensions, and their two sons, Leigh and Daniel, who have borne yet another big project with good grace and love.

Bob Chambers, at the cost of being redundant, recognizes the fruits of his collaboration and friendship with Rolf Färe. Much of Chambers's contribution to the book reflects a number of lessons that were learned either in collaboration with or directly from Rolf. He also thanks Rulon Pope for years of productive conversations and joint effort. On a more personal level, Bob also thanks his three sons, Christopher, Geoffrey, and Timothy, his father, and his wife Michelle for their love, support, help, and forbearance.

Introduction

A particularly compelling insight that arises in studying economics is the formal equivalence between the seemingly disparate problems of consumers deciding what to buy and of firms deciding what to produce. Personally, we both recall clearly the moment that this insight flashed across our consciousnesses, and the many additional insights that came with it. Chief among them was the recognition that lessons learned in one area of economics can be readily applied in others.

This perspective is broadened and deepened by the study of duality theory. The natural symmetry between the consumer's expenditure function and the producer's cost function provides just one example of the way in which tools developed in one context can be straight-forwardly applied in another. But, even more generally, one realizes early on in the study of economics that virtually all economic decision making can be characterized by a tangency between a preference set and a constraint set. As the adage goes, economics always boils down to equating marginal benefits with marginal costs. The visual simplicity of this representation is instilled in the economist's psyche from first principles on, and forms the core of the economic heuristic.

The situation, however, seems to change drastically when uncertainty is introduced. Radically different representations of prefer-

We would like to thank Marc Nerlove for insightful comments that were of great help in writing this Introduction.

ences and of problems involving production and consumption are required. Individual preferences under uncertainty are characterized by a range of competing models, including mean-variance, expected-utility, and generalized expected-utility models. Each of these bears only a limited resemblance to the representations of preferences used in the study of consumption under certainty.

The analysis of problems of production under uncertainty requires yet another set of new concepts and techniques. Typically, such problems are represented in terms of a stochastified production function that responds in a rather crude fashion to (typically unspecified) sources of uncertainty and that has no axiomatic foundation. Whereas modern nonstochastic production theory is characterized by its elegance, generality, and clear axiomatic basis, stochastic production theory hasn't advanced past the most basic representation of a technology – the production function. Ultimately, however, even the primitive stochastic production function approach proves unworkable in many instances. In its place, one finds a *parametrized distribution formulation* in which decisions, such as the choice of a scalar level of effort, are represented as the choice of one member of a family of distributions parametrized by the effort level. Here, instead of affecting productive outcomes, changes in inputs shift probability distributions specified over a fixed set of possible outcomes. Gone is the recognition of the physical roles that inputs and outputs play in productive processes and with it the appealing symmetry between producer and consumer problems. Gone, too, are the visual aids so familiar to economists. Even the most elementary treatments of production under uncertainty are devoid of the preference curves, isoquant maps, and transformation curves so familiar from nonstochastic theory. In their place, one finds a veritable jungle of partial derivatives and integrals that are so daunting that virtually all theorists operating in this area confine themselves to the implausible single output and single- or two-input cases. Intuition is cast to the winds, to be replaced with brute computation. As a result, production under uncertainty is definitely not a subject to be broached with novice economists.

This is a highly unsatisfactory situation. It is made worse by the dogma that the standard methods of modern production and consumer theory have no role to play in the analysis of problems involving uncertainty. A folk wisdom has emerged that holds that "duality does not apply under uncertainty." Indeed, some point out, as a "failing of duality," the supposed inability to deal with uncertainty using dual concepts. This implies a precarious status for the economics profession and the science of economics in general. After all, the reason for studying nonstochastic production processes is that, by the principle of abstraction, we hope to learn something about the real world, which is highly uncertain. If the basic tools developed in this abstract world don't even approximately apply in the real world, then one must question the value of this abstraction.

Unfortunately as a consequence of the mistaken belief that standard methods do not apply, the economics of uncertainty now relies on a ragbag of special-purpose models, which have little in common with one another, and, in most cases, even less with standard microeconomic theory. Around each of these models (adverse selection, moral hazard, the firm under uncertainty, price stabilization, and so on), a sophisticated, highly specialized, and often almost impenetrable, literature has developed. Experts on one model may know little or nothing about the models applied to closely related problems.

It did not have to be this way. When economists were first embarking on the study of problems involving uncertainty, Arrow (1953) and Debreu (1952, 1959) developed the elegantly simple idea of state-contingent commodities. The project of developing a rigorous general equilibrium theory had already led to the notion of differentiating commodities by their time and place of delivery. It was a relatively small step to deal with uncertainty through the notion of state-contingent commodities, that is, commodities whose delivery is contingent on the occurrence of a particular state of nature. Once this connection was made, all the tools developed for a nonstochastic world could be applied almost effortlessly to decision making under uncertainty. In Debreu's words, the notion of a state-contingent commodity "allows one to obtain a theory of uncertainty free from any probability concept and formally identical with the theory of certainty . . ." (1959, p. 98). Yaari (1969) developed this point further showing how notions of comparative risk aversion could be developed in a state-contingent framework, without any necessary reliance on probability distributions.

This should have been welcome news to economists. It means that tools honed in other areas can be used to analyze decision making under uncertainty. Even more force was added to the argument by Hirshleifer's (1965) demonstration of the analogy between the insights obtained from a state-contingent interpretation of uncertainty and the way in which Irving Fisher's treatment of time preference had demystified the concept of production and consumption over time. Unfortunately, except in fairly restricted areas of economic theory, this pathbreaking insight was ignored in the analysis of production decisions under uncertainty.

If the approach set out by Arrow, Debreu, Hirshleifer, and Yaari had been systematically pursued, we are confident that the development of the theory of choice under uncertainty would have proceeded in parallel with the rest of modern microeconomics instead of lagging so far behind. Unfortunately, initial analyses of the firm under uncertainty were largely undertaken using what was, in effect, a stochastic production-function approach. This approach appeared to be simpler than the general state-contingent approach and to allow exploitation of the analogy between production problems involving uncertainty and portfolio allocation problems. In fact, however, the apparent simplicity of the approach can be preserved only if attention is restricted to scalar choice sets.

Even greater difficulties arose from attempts to give a state-contingent interpretation to the restrictive technology implicit in the stochastic production-function approach. Attempts to model agency problems in a state-contingent framework failed because the underlying production technology was represented in an inconsistent fashion. This led to the belief that, while intuitively appealing, the state-contingent model was not applicable to such problems. As a result, the state-contingent approach has been abandoned in the analysis of agency problems, while remaining dominant in general equilibrium theory and finance theory (Milne 1995). The ultimate effect is to add to the proliferation of competing representations of problems involving uncertainty, all of which must be dealt with by anyone wishing to read and understand the literature on the topic.

Our intention in writing this book is to show that the state-contingent approach provides the best way to think about all problems involving uncertainty, including problems of consumer choice, the theory of the firm, and principal–agent relationships. In doing so, we demonstrate that the folk beliefs that "duality does not apply under uncertainty" and that "uncertainty is a failing of duality" are wrong. On the contrary, *the modern theory of production, including tools of duality theory like the cost function, is fully applicable under uncertainty.* Moreover, proper exploitation of the properties of alternative primal representations of preferences, such as the distance and benefit functions familiar from the dual approach, allows us to generalize and extend the results of the existing literature on preferences under uncertainty, such as those based on the concepts of absolute and relative risk aversion. Furthermore, the natural symmetry between production and consumption means that the same properties have a natural and meaningful interpretation in terms of the absolute and relative riskiness of production technologies. More generally, our main assertion reiterates Debreu's much earlier one that decision making under uncertainty is formally identical to decision making under certainty. The immediate corollary is that tools and techniques developed in the latter, including its widely used visual aids, can be applied directly to productive decision making under uncertainty.

These insights open the way for a whole host of developments in the basic theory of production under uncertainty, the theory of hedging behavior, and the theory of production insurance, all based on state-contingent technologies and preference structures general enough to subsume all existing preference representations as special cases. One of the clearest implications of the state-contingent approach is that in many instances, the expected-utility model, long maligned for its inconsistency with observed behavior but lauded for its apparent tractability, is superfluous. Another outcome is a demonstration that agency problems can be modeled in a state-contingent framework and that the resulting models are more tractable, and yield more plausible results, than existing models based on an outcome-state representation. We claim that this is only the beginning of what can be done with state-contingent models.

OVERVIEW OF THE BOOK

This book has 10 chapters that fall naturally into two parts. Chapters 1 to 5 are devoted to a thorough examination of state-contingent models, starting from first principles. So in Chapter 1, we introduce the notions of a state of nature and of a state-contingent commodity. We then compare and contrast the state-contingent approach to decision making under uncertainty with the more familiar parametrized distribution approach and the closely related result-state approach. And in particular, we show that the more familiar parametrized distribution approach, the direct intellectual descendant of the stochastic production function, suffers from an inherent "identification" problem that circumscribes its usefulness for comparative-static analysis.

In Chapter 2, we turn to an examination of a proper state-contingent production technology using the modern axiomatic approach to production pioneered by Shephard (1970). Our starting point is the state-contingent technology associated with a stochastic production function. We first show that, as usually written, it is a degenerate technology that doesn't allow the decision maker any leeway to arrange state-contingent outputs in response to economic phenomena. Using these observations as a foundation, we then develop, following Arrow, Debreu, and Shephard, an axiomatic representation of a state-contingent technology in terms of state-contingent input and output correspondences. We show how the more familiar stochastic production function approach is a badly behaved polar case of the state-contingent approach that corresponds closely to a Leontief-in-outputs multioutput technology. We also offer a truly axiomatic development of the stochastic production function from basic axioms on the general state-contingent technology. The chapter closes with an examination of an array of different restrictions on the technology that prove analytically useful at later points in the book.

As is apparent from the preceding paragraph, Chapter 2 represents a distinct break with the stochastic production-function model familiar to most economists. And as such, it represents the fundamental point of departure of the book. Therefore, its material is essential to almost all the arguments made later in the book. Because most of this material had not been previously developed, we felt bound to present a complete treatment of the basic model. At times, this means going considerably beyond the simple graphical arguments that suffice to communicate the essential core of our ideas. Although we have tried to keep the argument as intuitive and as visually accessible as possible, the going may be tough at times, especially for those readers not familiar with the modern set-theoretic approach to production problems. Early reviewers of this Chapter roughly split into two camps – production economists and nonproduction economists. The production economists have reacted enthusiastically to Chapter 2, as we had hoped they would. However, the response from nonproduction economists was considerably more querulous, and more along the lines, "Why are we boring the reader with all this production detail?" Our reasons are two. First, virtually everything that is introduced in Chapter 2 will be used repeatedly in later chapters. Second, to our knowledge, no thorough development of an axiomatic approach to stochastic production exists. Arrow and Debreu presented the basic idea of a state-contingent output set, and glimpses of a more fully developed analysis can be found in Luenberger (1995), but there is nothing approaching the level of completeness that Shephard (1970), McFadden (1978), and Färe (1988) have achieved for nonstochastic technologies. We hope that we have succeeded in raising the theory of stochastic technologies toward that level.

We emphasize, however, that Chapter 2 is not intended exclusively for production economists. We hope it will prove accessible to all readers who are willing to devote some effort to mastering the basics of state-contingent technologies. Readers not familiar with the more modern approach to production analysis might wish to consult a more accessible book at various points throughout this chapter. Possible references that might help the reader over some of the tougher spots would be Chambers (1988, especially Chapter 7) and Luenberger (1995).

Chapter 3 focuses on objective functions. Without doubt, the preference representation that dominates the analysis of economic choice under uncertainty is expected-utility theory. However, as popular as the expected-utility approach is, it is just as widely recognized that actual choices are often inconsistent with its basic tenets. Therefore, we have devoted the entire chapter to developing a general representation of preferences over state-contingent outcomes, which subsumes the mean-variance, the expected-utility, and the generalized expected-utility models as special cases. This representation of preferences is based on the most rudimentary notion of risk aversion and allows us to deduce subjective probabilities directly from an individual's preference structure. We have chosen this model because it works extremely well with the Arrow–Debreu state-contingent technology and because it corresponds heuristically with traditional notions of preferences from nonstochastic decision making. This allows us to illustrate virtually all our arguments with indifference contours and transformation curves or isoquant maps that should be familiar to even intermediate undergraduates. (More than one of the results contained in Chapter 3 and elsewhere in the book have their origins in intuition originally gleaned from such simple two-dimensional diagrams.)

Among other things, we show how to characterize the certainty equivalent and absolute and relative risk premiums for general preferences using Luenberger's (1992) benefit function and the Shephard–Malmquist distance function. The facility of representing preferences in terms of these functions also lets us fully characterize families of preferences exhibiting constant relative risk aversion, constant absolute risk aversion, as well as the conjunction of these two properties for general preferences. By using these developments, whole families of preference functions exhibiting these properties can be easily specified.

Chapter 3 also examines various definitions of increases in risk, including multiplicative spreads, simple-mean preserving spreads, and Rothschild–Stiglitz increases in risk, for general preferences. We use the Rothschild–Stiglitz notion of an increase in risk to generalize the notion of majorization, familiar from the literature on income inequality measurement, to account for unequal weighting of outcomes. This generalization leads us to a characterization of preferences, which we call *generalized Schur-concavity*, that yields a total ordering of risky outcomes. Generalized Schur-concavity subsumes among others the mean-variance, the expected-utility, the rank-dependent expected utility, and the maximin preference structures as special cases.

Chapter 4 is our first real foray into economic analysis proper. There, we use the building blocks of the state-contingent approach developed in the first three chapters to examine producer decision making in the face of a state-contingent technology. Specifically, we examine the properties of two cost functions: the effort-cost function and the revenue-cost function. This chapter's primary contribution is a conclusive demonstration that well-behaved cost functions exist for the state-contingent technology, and that in the presence of linear input pricing, these cost functions are dual to the state-contingent technology. This discussion, we hope, will finally bury the surprisingly prevalent belief that the requirements for cost minimization are more restrictive for stochastic technologies than for nonstochastic technologies. As we have already shown elsewhere (Chambers and Quiggin 1998a), this belief is wrong even for technologies characterized by continuously distributed random components. As long as increases in cost depress a producer's objective function, he will act to minimize cost.

After showing that well-behaved cost functions exist, we then show how these same cost functions, in conjunction with Shephard's Lemma, can be used to examine the issue of how input utilization responds to changes in risk. The stochastic production-function literature has institutionalized a notion of *risk-increasing inputs*. We use the input demand functions developed in this chapter to develop a clear and graphically intuitive method for characterizing input variation associated with changes in the riskiness of the state-contingent output. To emphasize the difference between our notion and the more common notion in the literature, we introduce a new, and we hope, more descriptive, terminology in terms of risk substitutes and risk complements.

At the outset, we stressed that lessons learned in one arena can frequently be usefully applied in other areas. In Chapter 4, we apply this dictum and use the analogy between state-contingent preferences and state-contingent technologies to characterize the inherent physical riskiness of a state-contingent production technology. The argument is completely parallel to that used in Chapter 3 and is based on the simple notion that it is typically costly to remove uncertainty from physical technologies. On this basis, we develop notions of cost-certainty equivalents and production-risk premiums that enable us to characterize whole families of state-contingent technologies much in the same fashion that absolute and relative risk premiums were used to characterize preferences in Chapter 3. In latter chapters, particularly Chapters 5, 6, and 7, these characterizations permit us to develop a number of new comparative static results. We close Chapter 4 by examining the consequences of the restrictions imposed on the state-contingent technology in the closing section of Chapter 2.

Chapter 5, the final chapter in the first part of the book, examines production decisions under uncertainty using the state-contingent technology developed in Chapter 2, the general state-contingent preference structure from Chapter 3, and the revenue-cost function developed in Chapter 4. The focus is on determining the optimal mix of state-contingent revenues by risk-averse and risk-neutral decision makers. Hence, it is best viewed as the culmination of the preceding four chapters and includes (along with Chapter 4) what we hope is a reasonably thorough treatment of the firm under uncertainty. One of the key contributions of Chapter 5 is an examination of the consequences of various restrictions on the structure of the revenue-cost function developed in Chapter 4 for risk-averse and risk-neutral decision makers. An important new result is an arbitrage condition depending only on cost monotonicity. At an optimum, the marginal cost of raising revenue by one unit in every state of the world must be equal to one. With knowledge of the production technology, this result helps to characterize a risk-aversely efficient frontier on which all firms must operate.

An important contrast between Chapter 5 and previous analyses of which we are aware is that there is no reliance on any specific functional representation of preferences under uncertainty, such as the expected-utility or mean-variance representations. Our results apply to these special cases and to any preferences satisfying specified conditions on risk aversion along with standard properties of monotonicity, continuity, and so on. This illustrates our claim that, whatever the normative and descriptive status of expected-utility theory, the separability assumption characterizing the theory is largely redundant in modeling economic choices such as the production decisions of the firm under uncertainty.

The second part of the book, Chapters 6 through 10, comprises a series of applications of the state-contingent models developed in Chapters 1 through 5 to several different economic problems centered around different tools for risk management and agency problems. In particular, Chapter 6 examines productive decision making in the presence of futures and forward markets for the class of generalized Schur-concave objective functions developed in Chapter 3. It represents an extension and generalization of our earlier work (Chambers and Quiggin 1997) on this problem in the expected-utility framework. Because much of the existing literature in this area focuses on producers using nonstochastic technologies and facing uncertain prices, we pay particular attention to the state-contingent generalization of a nonstochastic technology developed in Chapters

2 and 4 – the generalized Schur-convex technology. Besides developing a complete theory of producer behavior in the presence of futures and forward markets, this chapter also develops a number of striking results. The arbitrage result derived in Chapter 5 is applied to derive "separation" results that apply to stochastic and nonstochastic technologies. Second, we show that even risk-averse producers will not generally choose a nonstochastic technology when they face stochastic prices. (The intuitive reason is that they use the stochastic technology as a self-insurance tool.)

Chapter 7 considers the effect that another risk-management tool, competitive production insurance, has on producers facing both price and production risk. Working in a more general preference framework than previous production-insurance studies, we develop a complete theory of producer behavior in two separate informational frameworks. In the first, the insurer has enough information to be able to offer and enforce an actuarially fair insurance contract, whereas in the second, lack of such information forces insurers to offer actuarially unfair insurance contracts. In the first case, the informational structure is rather unrealistic; it is assumed that everything the producer can observe is also observable by the insurer. In such cases, it is well known that expected-utility maximizers facing a competitive insurance market will fully insure and will produce in the same fashion as a risk-neutral individual facing the same state-contingent technology. We confirm this result for our more general preference structure while examining a number of other issues. In the second case, we offer a theoretical explanation for the observed phenomenon of risk-averse producers fully insuring in the presence of actuarially unfair production insurance. This part of the chapter, for the first time, broaches some of the incentive-based agency problems that form the core of the final three chapters. In particular, we show that an insurer who can only base his indemnification scheme on observed production cannot profitably offer an actuarially fair insurance contract. If an insurer tried to do so, he would encourage the farmer to optimally exert the lowest amount of productive effort possible.

An important feature of Chapter 7 is an analysis of the significance of smoothness in preferences. We have already argued that the stochastic production function is analogous to a Leontief technology, in which isocost curves are characterized by a kink at the efficient production point. Preferences with a kink at the point corresponding to a certain outcome display what has been described as "first-order" risk aversion (Segal and Spivak 1990). We generalize the observation of Segal and Spivak that individuals with first-order risk-aversion may seek full insurance at actuarially unfair prices.

Chapters 8 through 10 examine the contracting problems that arise as a result of one party to an economic contract (the principal) not being able to fully observe the actions of another party to a contract (the agent) in a uncertain world where the actions of the agent directly impinge on the stochastic outcomes realized by the principal. We examine three different informational structures in these three chapters. In Chapter 8, which generalizes our earlier work on nonpoint-source pollution (Chambers and Quiggin 1996) in several directions, we examine a situation in which the principal can observe everything about the world that the agent can, except for the agent's choices of his state-contingent outputs and a nonstochastic output about which the principal cares. For the sake of concreteness, the discussion is cast in the context of an agricultural nonpoint-source pollution problem in which the principal is a governmental authority who cannot feasibly monitor the farmer's realized output and the amount of runoff pollution that the farmer's activity incurs. The main contribution of this chapter is an analytical algorithm for dealing with this generic class of problems. It turns out that the optimal design of the farmer's remuneration scheme depends closely on whether the runoff pollution can be characterized as either a risk complement or a risk substitute for the farmer's crop output. This represents a substantial extension of the idea that crop insurance will tend to reduce usage of inputs such as pesticides, treated in the stochastic production-function literature as *risk-reducing*.

Chapter 9, based on Quiggin and Chambers (1998b), examines the principal–agent problem most familiar to economists; a risk-neutral principal is designing an incentive contract, based only on observed output, so as to get the agent to act in a fashion as consonant as possible with the principal's objectives. We spend a lot of time discussing the existing literature on this problem and our approach to it. Our reasons are several. First, the existing literature is based on faulty axiomatic foundations. It is impossible to reason axiomatically from a general state-contingent production technology to the typical specification of the principal–agent problem without invoking a degree of irrational behavior on the part of the agent. Second, in the light of early failures to develop moral–hazard models in a state-space setting, it has been claimed that the state-contingent framework is incapable of handling principal–agent problems. We argue that these failures resulted from a combination of the axiomatically faulty specification of the technology and the implausible stochastic production–function model, which completely circumscribes the agent's ability to respond to output-based incentive schemes. Since the early days of principal–agent models, when theorists struggled with the state-contingent approach to the principal–agent problem, this approach has received little or no attention. Completely developing a method for dealing with it consumes a fair amount of space. The central product of this chapter is an algorithm for dealing with such problems that can be usefully applied in a number of areas. We present a number of results characterizing the properties of the agency–cost function and the equilibrium contract, but clearly recognize that further work remains to be done in this area.

The final chapter is cast in the same informational framework as Chapter 9, but its goal is to initiate the examination of the equilibrium determination of the agent's reservation utility. In the typical principal–agent model (and in Chapters 8 and 9), the agent's reservation utility is taken as given. Chapter 10 uses the conceptual model developed in Chapter 9 to examine how a principal who has the power to affect the agent's reservation utility might do so. We use the metaphor of a landlord (the principal) contracting with a peasant farmer (the agent) over the peasant farmer's production practices on a plot of land owned by the landlord. The landlord is assumed to be able to affect the agent's reservation utility through extra-contract means. Here we identify a number of results on the optimal determination of the peasant's reservation utility in response to changes in market phenomena.

I The Theory

1 States of Nature

This book is about state-contingent production. Its central claim is that insight into problems involving production under uncertainty is best gained by consistent use of the concept of states of nature and of actions having different consequences in different states of nature. Production decisions are thus best viewed as choices between bundles of state-contingent goods. This way of looking at production under uncertainty contrasts with competing approaches in which decisions are modeled as choices between random variables indexed by input (effort) levels or between probability distributions over a finite set of possible outcomes, often confusingly referred to as *states*. In what follows, these alternative approaches are referred to generically as the *parametrized distribution formulation* and the *outcome-state formulation* of production under uncertainty.

This chapter starts by developing the idea of a set of states of nature and then shows how an analysis based on a state-space framework contrasts with the alternative (and more complex) parametrized distribution formulation and outcome-state approach. Elements of the standard decision-theoretic framework associated with the state-contingent approach are presented and discussed. We describe similarities and differences with the approach adopted here.

1.1 STATES OF NATURE

What precisely is a state of nature? Ideally, a comprehensive set of states of nature is a mutually exclusive and exhaustive set of possible descriptions of the state of the world. Of course, a complete description is impossibly complex as a simple thought experiment illustrates. Try to elaborate, in detail, all the possibilities for tomorrow's weather including the degree of clarity of the atmosphere, the temperature, the amount of precipitation and all other physical phenomena that we refer to with the catch-all term, *weather*. Therefore, in any practical analytical representation, we must abstract from those features that are irrelevant to the problem at hand and include only those features that are relevant. For example, in a problem concerning lightning insurance and self-protection against lightning damage, the states of nature might be "lightning strike" and "no lightning strike." Or, in a problem concerning agricultural production, the states might be "rain" and "no rain."

We can elaborate the description of the states of nature in at least two ways. Instead of a simple binary split into "rain" and "no rain" states, for example, we might specify a more finely graded range of precipitation, say {drought, drier than average, average, above average, wet, flood}. By going further, a partition into a finite set of states of nature may be replaced with a continuum in which, for example, the states of nature are given by an interval in the real line corresponding to all possible annual rainfall levels. Alternatively, if we wish to consider more than one possible characteristic, we might think in terms of a Cartesian product space that elaborates all possible combinations of multiple characteristics. Our original "no rain"–"rain" and "no lightning strike"–"lightning strike" examples illustrate the two–characteristic cases. The possible states of nature arising from these two–separate sets of characteristics are {rain with lightning strike, rain with no lightning strike, no rain with lightning strike, and no rain with no lightning strike}, which we denote by Weather. If we denote the set {no rain, rain} by P (for precipitation) and the set {lightning strike, no lightning strike} by E (for electricity), then this finer description of the states of nature is formally given by the expression

$$\text{Weather} = P \times E$$

We can also collapse multiple states of nature into one if the outcome for any action the decision maker might take is the same for all the states of nature under consideration. For example, the return to the crop-planting decisions of an Australian wheat grower is likely to be the same whichever horse wins the Kentucky Derby in the relevant year. It might, however, be affected by whether the Republicans or Democrats win congressional elections and, therefore, gain influence over U.S. agricultural trade policy. So, in our elaboration of the states of nature, when we are considering a problem involving the decisions of an Australian wheat grower, we would probably want to include information on the outcome of the congressional elections, but not on the outcome of the Kentucky Derby. However, if we were elaborating the set of states of nature relevant to forecasting the chance of any particular horse winning the Triple Crown, we would include whichever horse wins the Kentucky Derby, but we would probably not want to include the outcome of congressional elections. To be a bit more specific, suppose that the states of the world are given by the mythical pairs:

Republicans win, Phar Lap wins.	Republicans win, Secretariat wins.
Republicans lose, Phar Lap wins.	Republicans lose, Secretariat wins.

Then, in the consideration of the possible states facing an Australian wheat farmer, we might safely collapse this to {Republicans win, Republicans lose}.

A fundamental presumption of the state-space approach is that *the decision maker can do nothing to determine which state of nature will occur*. This is an important point that bears emphasizing. Which state of nature occurs is beyond the scope of the decision maker's choice. This does not mean, however, that the decision maker is impotent when it comes to the future. Instead of her decisions affecting which state of nature occurs, they affect the outcome realized if a given state of nature occurs. Our lightning-strike example illustrates the point. The decision maker cannot affect whether lightning occurs in her area or not. However, if the decision maker installs a lightning conductor, she will bear the fixed cost of installing it in both states of nature. But if she chooses not to install the lightning conductor, she bears no cost in the "no lightning strike" state, but incurs the consequence "house burns down" in the "lightning-strike" case. Her choices have affected the outcomes that can be realized in either state but have not affected the actual states that may or may not occur.

This exogeneity property is crucial in deciding how to represent the state space. If we are modeling the choices of an individual producer in a competitive market, it is a reasonable extension of standard microeconomic assumptions to regard stochastic prices faced by the producer as exogenous and, therefore, to define one state of the world for each possible price level. If, however, we want to discuss industry equilibrium, the price level will be determined within the model and the state space is more appropriately represented in terms of the underlying variables affecting demand and the production possibility set.

An example of a variable that is almost never exogenous is yield (whether of crops or of fault-free silicon chips). Yields are determined by interaction between the underlying state of nature and the actions of the decision maker. In the expanded agricultural example discussed earlier, the drought state may result in low yields for a farmer relying on natural rainfall but above-average yields for a farmer relying on irrigation. In a state-space representation of production under uncertainty, it is always desirable to refer to the states of nature that result in low or high yields rather than to the yields themselves.

The distinction between states of nature and the outcomes that are experienced in those states is crucial to the state-space approach, but is ignored in competing approaches. The parametrized distribution formulation and the outcome-state approach represent production uncertainty directly in terms of yields. To make things more explicit: In the precipitation example, the state-space approach specifies probabilities of occurrence for drought and the other gradations of precipitation. These probabilities would be taken as given (perhaps believed is better here) by the farmer. The parametrized distribution formulation on the other hand would specify probabilities of occurrence for different yield levels with the probabilities being at least partially determined by the amount of input that the farmer applies.

A representation in terms of the underlying variables is preferable whenever it does not unduly complicate the analysis because it conserves the information content of the model. However, even within the state-space approach, sometimes it makes sense to leave certain informational aspects out of the model. For example, the use of prices as state variables in the analysis of the competitive firm facing price uncertainty is justifiable because the firm's net profit is related in a simple way to the stochastic prices it faces and only indirectly, through prices, to the underlying state of demand for outputs and supply of inputs.

1.1.1 State Ordering

In some cases, the states of nature may have a natural ordering from worst to best. For example, the state in which lightning strikes will generally be less favorable than that in which it does not. Mostly, "rain" will be preferable to "no rain" for farmers. However, there is rarely a preference ordering of the states that is the same for all possible actions a decision maker might undertake. A farmer who chooses to rely totally on irrigation water from distant watersheds might find local rainfall an unwelcome obstacle to production and a possible source of damage from waterlogging.

Even unambiguously "bad" events like lightning strikes might be beneficial to the decision maker under certain social arrangements. Suppose, for example, that the decision maker has a house insured for more than its true value. She might then welcome lightning strikes and take actions (for example, storing drums of gasoline in the cellar) designed to ensure that the outcome associated with the "lightning strike" state of nature was total loss of the house.

An analogy with the distribution of production over physical space may help sort out ideas here. Let's think for the moment in terms of our set of states being given by 50 states of the United States of America instead of the states of nature. Some states (those with warm, predictable climates) are more suited to growing oranges than others, and we normally expect to see more oranges produced in those areas. However, this is a matter of choice. It is technically possible, using greenhouses, to grow oranges in Alaska. So the choice set open to society certainly includes allocations in which more oranges are produced in Alaska than in Florida. Furthermore, it is perfectly possible to design tax-subsidy régimes under which it would be individually rational for orange growers to locate their operations in Alaska. It is difficult to envisage a situation under which such an allocation would be socially beneficial. However, the relative importance of, say, Florida and California in a socially optimal allocation of orange production will vary depending on such variables as the cost of water, the opportunity cost of land, transport costs, and the demand for different varieties of orange. Hence, no unambiguous ordering of the states of the Union exists for orange production. Similarly, there is, in general, no unambiguous ordering of the possible states of nature. Under some choices of production technology, cloudless days and cold nights may lead to high yields. Under other choices, such states of nature may be associated with large-scale frost damage.

Even when an unambiguous ordering of the states exists, it is normally possible for decision makers to choose activities that enhance the outcome in good states or mitigate the outcome in bad states. (This is the key premise underlying the concept of moral hazard.) There is always a trade-off between state-contingent outcomes. And, in most cases, this trade-off between state-contingent outcomes is the subject of economic choice, so that ignoring it brings the cost of ignoring important economic decisions that determine outcomes under uncertainty. Unfortunately, however, the trade-off between state-contingent outcomes is almost universally ignored in models of economic decision making under production uncertainty, where a bundle of inputs applied uniquely determines the outcome in every state of nature. In models of this kind, the effect of an increase in this bundle of inputs is to increase returns in every state of nature. The model provides the decision maker with no capacity to trade off an increased return in one state for a lower return in another. We return to this point in Chapters 2, 4, and 5.

1.2 THE PARAMETRIZED DISTRIBUTION FORMULATION

Any given choice generates a state-contingent vector of outcomes, which may be described by a random variable.[1] Many researchers, therefore, have chosen to disregard the underlying state space, and analyze problems purely in terms of choices over random variables. Working in these terms is what we are referring to when we talk about the parametrized distribution approach.

The relationship between the parametrized distribution formula-

1. As will be shown in Chapter 3, this statement depends on the existence of well-defined subjective probabilities and is, therefore, valid subject to some relatively weak assumptions about preferences.

tion and the state-space representation of the problem is analogous to that between reduced forms and structural models in econometrics. The state-space representation, which contains all the relevant information about the possible states of nature, the input choices of the producers, and the possible range of outcomes, corresponds to the structural form. The parametrized distribution formulation, which confounds all these relationships into a simple relationship between possible outcomes and inputs, corresponds to the reduced form. As with the identification problem in econometrics, it is always possible to derive a parametrized distribution formulation from any state-space representation, but the reverse does not apply. In particular, as a general rule, most parametrized distribution formulations may correspond to several different state-space representations. (A specific example, in which a single parametrized distribution formulation corresponds to an infinity of state-space representations, is presented at the end of the next section.) This certainly achieves some economy in representation and analysis just as reduced-form estimation achieves some economy in econometric estimation. Unfortunately, the economy generally is a false one because it is purchase at the cost of confounding causal factors for any economic phenomena that may emerge in such models. As a result, only limited comparative-static analysis can be undertaken in the parametrized distribution formulation. Other problems emerge with the parametrized distribution formulation. For example, when specified in state-contingent terms, an uncertain production technology may have reasonable properties, but when captured in its reduced form, it may have unreasonable properties.

To illustrate this latter problem, suppose that there are two states of nature, each occurring with probability 1/2 and let Y be the set of available state-contingent outcomes represented by Figure 1.1(a). The state-contingent vectors (y_1^0, y_2^0) and (y_2^0, y_1^0) are distinct elements of Y, but they have the same probability distribution $(y_1^0, y_2^0; 1/2, 1/2)$ in which each of the outcomes y_1 and y_2 occurs with probability 1/2. Denote by F the set of probability distributions for random variables associated with Y. Then $(y_1, y_2; 1/2, 1/2) \in F$ if either $(y_1, y_2) \in Y$ or $(y_2, y_1) \in Y$.

Now the associated set of feasible outcomes represented as random variables may be represented as in Figure 1.1(b). The choice set of random variables is formed by "folding" the state-contingent

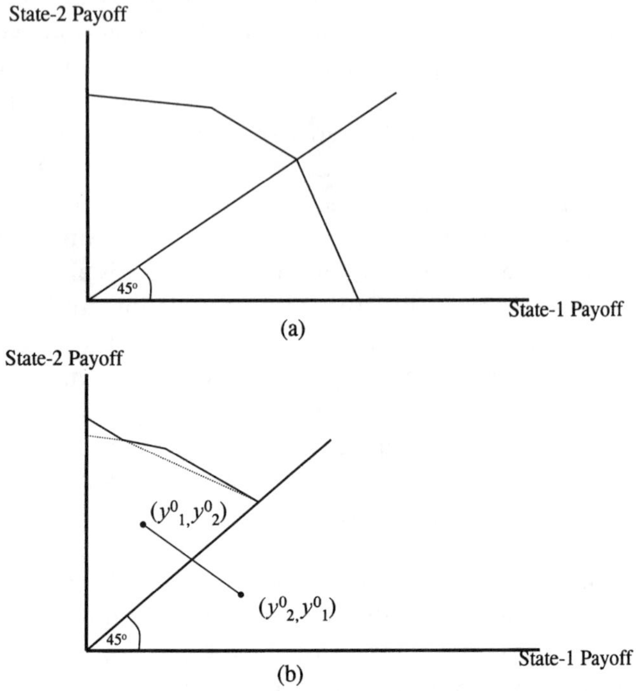

Figure 1.1 (a) A state-contingent choice set (equal probabilities). (b) Random-variable representation of choice set in (a).

choice set over the 45° line bisecting the positive quadrant. So, for example, this folding transformation maps the point (y_2^0, y_1^0) into the point (y_1^0, y_2^0), which lies above the bisector. The boundary of the choice set, now viewed as random variables, is formed as the maximum of the boundaries of the set $(y_1, y_2) \in Y, y_1 \leq y_2$ lying above the bisector and of the image of $(y_1, y_2) \in Y, y_1 \geq y_2$ under the folding transformation.

Note that whereas the original choice set is smooth and convex, the derived set of random variables is not. Thus, in the state-space representation, we can immediately observe that, provided preferences are quasi-concave, there will exist a unique optimal element. Superficially, it would appear that the same is not true for F. However, since any preference ordering over F induces a symmetric ordering over Y, we can observe that, provided the induced preferences over Y are quasi-concave, a unique optimum must exist. Expressing this condition in terms of the original preferences over F is not straightforward.

In economics, as elsewhere, an inappropriate choice of problem representation usually leads to a complex and confusing analysis. By diverting attention from the underlying state space and the richer information structure available therein, the parametrized distribution formulation has been an obstacle to progress. In particular, in problems involving production under uncertainty, it has further widened the gap between the theory of asymmetric information and the general equilibrium tradition going back to Arrow and Debreu.

As we shall see in later chapters, even where the state-space formulation apparently proved unworkable in moral-hazard problems, the unworkability actually indicated fundamental problems with the technology specification. The basic difficulty was referred to in the previous section – the models in question did not allow any trade-off between state-contingent outcomes. These problems were not resolved, but merely papered over, by the shift to a parametrized distribution formulation of the problem.

1.3 PROBABILITY DISTRIBUTIONS OVER FINITE SETS OF OUTCOMES

Although the state–act terminology that we shall employ in this book is standard in decision theory, a nonstandard terminology (at least in terms of decision theory) is adopted by many users of the parametrized distribution formulation. This is particularly true in the literature on principal–agent problems. There the term "state," or sometimes "event," is used to refer to an outcome, and the acts are regarded as defining probability distributions over these "states." Most frequently, the set of "states" is finite and the set of acts may be parametrized by a positive scalar, usually interpreted as "effort," with the probability distribution of the "states" being determined by a continuous mapping from effort space (or input space) to the unit simplex whose dimension equals the number of "states." This special case of the parametrized distribution formulation is what we refer to as the "outcome-state" representation.

Although the underlying state space (and here we mean state in our sense) is suppressed completely in the outcome-state representation of the problem, you can always represent outcome-state problems in terms of the state-space approach. Hirshleifer and Riley (1992) have already made this observation, and their discussion contains a treatment of how to go from one approach to the other. Because of the inherent identification problems, however, to be able to resurrect the required set of acts, the state space must be a continuum (the unit interval is the obvious choice) with the outcome space being the discrete set usually referred to as "states."

The lightning-strike example illustrates the difference between the two approaches. In the parametrized distribution formulation, the outcomes "house burns down" and "house doesn't burn down" would be referred to as "states" and the agent's action of installing a lightning conductor would be conceived of as shifting the probability distribution over these two "states." Here, the term "states" specifically refers to the perceived outcome that results from the conjunction of what we would refer to as the act, installing the lightning conductor, and the occurrence of a particular state of nature. For that reason, we shall refer to these states in the rest of the book by the term *outcome states* to distinguish them from states of nature.

Suppose for the sake of argument that if no lightning conductor is installed and the state of nature "lightning strikes" occurs, the decision maker's house will always burn down while it will never burn down if a lightning conductor is installed. Thus, if a lightning conductor is not installed and lightning strikes, the outcome state is "house burns down." If the states of nature "lightning strikes" and "no lightning strikes" both occur with probability 1/2, then the probability of the outcome state "house burns down" is 1/2 if no lightning conductor is installed and zero if a lightning conductor is installed. This illustrates how the act shifts the probability distribution of the outcome states and how the outcome states are derived from the conjunction of the act and the state of nature.

To illustrate the identification problem we described earlier, consider the closely related (and unrealistic but still illustrative) state-space problem depicted in Table 1.1 where the state space is a bit

Table 1.1. *Specification of the State Space for Modified Lightning Strike Example*

		Lightning Strike	
		Yes	No
Lightning Conductor	Works	Yes, Work	No, Work
	Fails	Yes, Fail	No, Fail

richer because it admits the possibility that a lightning conductor may or may not be effective in preventing a house from burning down if lightning strikes. In this table, four possible states are represented, each corresponding to a different combination of the events {lightning strike, no lightning strike} and {lightning conductor works, lightning conductor fails}.

Table 1.2(a). *Specification of Probabilities for Modified Lightning Strike Example: Case 1*

		Lightning Strike	
		Yes	No
Lightning Conductor	Works	1/4	1/2
	Fails	0	1/4

The outcome states remain the same as before {house burns down, house doesn't burn down}. Suppose the respective probabilities are given by Table 1.2(a).

Then if no lightning conductor is installed, the probability of the outcome state "house burns down" is 1/4, and if a lightning conductor is installed, the probability of the outcome state "house burns down" is zero. Notice, however, that if the probabilities were given by Table 1.2(b), installing a lightning conductor still results in a prob-

Table 1.2(b). *Specification of Probabilities for Modified Lightning Strike Example: Case 2*

		Lightning Strike	
		Yes	No
Lightning Conductor	Works	1/4	1/4
	Fails	0	1/2

ability of the outcome state "house burns down" of zero, whereas not installing a lightning conductor still results in a probability of the outcome state "house burns down" of 1/4, the same as before. So the outcome-state representation would be incapable of differentiating between these two distinct economic structures. In fact, it is easy to see that an infinity of state-space representations correspond to this particular reduced form.

Viewed from a state-contingent perspective, the outcome-state representation has a number of features in addition to the identification problem that render it unsatisfactory. Most notably, a marginal increase in effort leaves output unchanged with probability 1. This happens because the range of outputs is fixed {house burns down, house doesn't burn down} and applying inputs or effort only affects the probability of either outcome state occurring and does not affect the actual level of the outcome. To some extent, this worry can be glossed over by a finer specification of outcome states, but the problem remains: committing additional effort has no direct effect on the stochastic output. More formally, the entire impact of such an increase in effort or in the application of inputs is concentrated on the set of measure zero where output makes a discrete jump from one level to the next. This may be a realistic representation of some real-world problems where the production process itself is unimportant and can be safely abstracted from, but it is entirely unsatisfactory for those real-world problems (for example, agricultural production, silicon-chip production) in which the production process is an important component of the economic environment that the producer or decision maker faces.

1.4 CHOICE UNDER UNCERTAINTY

The standard decision-theoretic representation of choice under uncertainty was originated by Savage (1954), and developed further in an economic context by Hirshleifer (1966), Hirshleifer and Riley (1992), and others. It assumes the existence of a set of *states* $\Omega = \{1, 2, \ldots, S\}$, with elements or states denoted s, from which a force exogenous to the economic problem chooses. Typically, the exogenous force is referred to as *Nature* so that the elements of Ω are usually referred to as "states of nature" or "states of the world" to emphasize the fact that they are exogenous to the decision maker. A subset of Ω is referred to as an *event*.

Decision makers choose between *acts*, which yield for each state s an outcome $\mathbf{y}$, which is an element of a space of consequences $Y \subseteq \Re^M$. A generic act, therefore, generates a range of outcomes that varies according to the realized state of nature. Hence, we can denote acts by mappings $A: \Omega \to \Re^M$. Each act defines a state-contingent outcome vector $\mathbf{y}(A) \in \Re^{M \times S}$. More generally, we will define a *random variable* as a mapping $\theta: \Omega \to \Re^M$, which defines a vector of realizations $\theta \in \Re^{M \times S}$. The vector notation is most useful in discussion of scalar-valued random variables that are simply elements of $\Re^S$.

To clarify the distinction between acts, random variables, and consequences, it may be useful to consider a simple example. Suppose an individual is allocating a fixed sum of wealth, w, between cash (defined to have a payoff of 1 in every state of the world) and a security having a payoff $(1 + r_s)$ in state $s, s = 1, \ldots, S$. Denote the amount allocated to the risky asset by a and define the return in state s as

$$y_s(a) = (w - a) + a(1 + r_s) = w + ar_s.$$

With these definitions, $r = (r_1, r_2, \ldots, r_S)$ is a random variable. Each possible choice of a is an available act, yielding consequence $y_s(a)$ if state s occurs. The consequences of act a therefore may be summarized by the state-contingent outcome vector $\mathbf{y}(a) = (y_1(a), y_2(a), \ldots, y_S(a))$.

The choice set in this simple case is easily illustrated graphically for the case of two states of nature, that is, $\Omega = \{1, 2\}$. For the sake of illustration, assume that the return on the security is positive in state

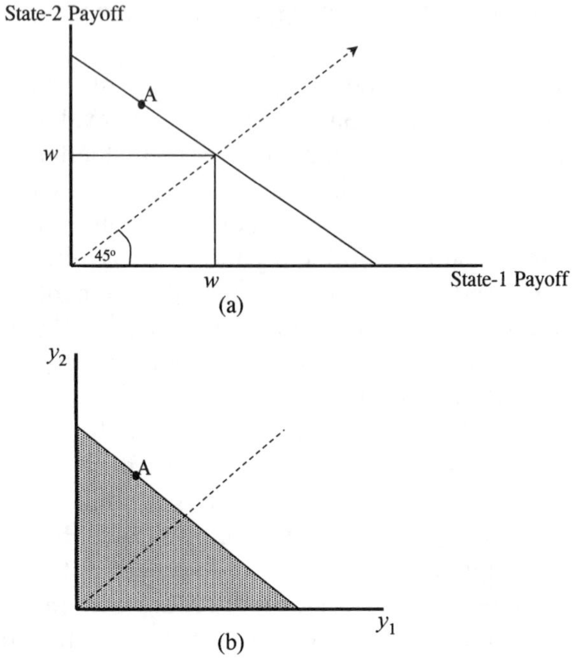

Figure 1.2 (a) Choice set for simple portfolio problem. (b) Choice set for a simple portfolio problem with free disposal.

2 and negative in state 1, $r_2 > 0 > r_1$. The vector of state-contingent outcomes from an all-cash portfolio is given in Figure 1.2(a) by the point (w, w) on the 45° line bisecting the positive quadrant. We shall frequently refer to the 45° line as the *bisector*. The payoff from setting $a = w$ is given by point A. The negatively-sloped line segment through A indicates outcomes that may be obtained by short-selling or by buying on margin [Figure 1.2(a)]. For simplicity, we are only looking at the case in which contracts generating negative wealth in any state of nature are not permissible; the presumption is that the individual can do no more than lose his initial wealth. Notice, in particular, the similarity between this choice set and the budget line facing a consumer with a fixed income in a two-commodity world. The pictorial analogy is made complete when one interprets consumption in distinct states of nature as being consumption of distinct commodities.

A more realistic representation of the choice set would allow for a number of different securities and allow free disposal of wealth in all states, that is, the individual may consume less than his entire wealth in any given state. In this representation, the choice set in Figure 1.2(a) would be redrawn to be the shaded area in Figure 1.2(b). If one imposes a convex preference structure (see Chapter 3) over wealth in the different states of nature, the problem of choosing between uncertain acts is then completely analogous to a standard consumer choice problem, except that the "goods" are now state-contingent outcomes. Therein lies the power of the state-preference approach to decision making under uncertainty. The state-preference approach permits the application of standard choice theory and all of the results inherited therefrom to the analysis of decision making under uncertainty. Unfortunately, this strength has been almost entirely ignored in the literature that involves production under uncertainty. A primary goal of the present book is to exploit that strength systematically.

2 State-Contingent Production

So far, we have discussed state-contingent commodities and actions with state-contingent consequences. There are two ways to proceed. One is to adopt the metaphor of consumer choice and focus on preferences over state-contingent consumption bundles. The other is to adopt the metaphor of production and focus on the transformation of inputs (or, more fundamentally, factor endowments) into state-contingent outputs. The general tendency of economic theorists has been to take the first path, sometimes to the point of confining attention to pure-exchange economies.

This book unashamedly puts the primary emphasis on production. This is not to say that we neglect consumption and consumer preferences. On the contrary, a major advantage of the state-contingent approach is that the symmetry between models of consumer choice and models of producer choice, a salient feature of modern microeconomics which has been ignored to date in models of choice under uncertainty, can be usefully exploited in a state-contingent framework. Throughout the book, this symmetry is developed and extended. In particular, in Chapter 3, we use this symmetry to analyze preferences under uncertainty in what we feel is a new and informative fashion.

Nevertheless, our fundamental contention is that changes in technology rather than changes in tastes are typically the primary determinants of changes in the allocation of resources and of changes in human welfare. When we consider economies subject to uncertainty, differences in the set of possibilities for allocating resources between different state-contingent outputs often provide the main sources of differences in performance.

It is unfortunate, then, that the issue of production has been treated so casually in the economics literature. One need only contrast the complex treatment of equilibrium concepts in the game-theoretic literature on oligopoly problems with the simplistic treatment of technology in the same literature to obtain a feeling for the inadequate attention that the profession has paid to the conditions of production. That is not to say that production has been entirely ignored. The work of modern duality theorists, beginning with the pathbreaking contributions of Shephard (1953, 1970) to the axiomatization of production technologies and duality relationships, would give the lie to that assertion. But all too often these advances have been ignored in the analysis of interesting economic problems.

The situation is, if anything, worse in the analysis of production under uncertainty. That literature lacks the axiomatic treatment of production problems found in the work of Shephard and his successors. There the usual approach is to take the most rudimentary notion of a technology, the production function, and stochastify it in a seemingly plausible way.

Excellent examples are offered by the literatures on stochastic-efficiency measurement and principal–agent analysis. In the former, stochastic-frontier technologies are specified simply by adding a stochastic error term to a nonstochastic technology. Sophisticated econometric methods for analyzing the resulting specification are developed. A similar approach is followed in principal–agent analyses. A sophisticated analysis of informational issues is applied to models based on simple, indeed simplistic, specifications of stochastic technology. But here the consequences have been more extreme. Attempts to develop even the simplest and most intuitive relationships have foundered not because of their ultimate economic implausibility, but because of what turns out to be an intractable specification of the production technology.[1]

This process culminates in the use of parametrized distribution formulations, which assume what is, in effect, a technology with fixed-output proportions. Where this has led to implausible results, the general tendency has not been to relax the assumption of fixed-

1. A detailed consideration of these issues is addressed in Chapters 8, 9, and 10.

output proportions, but to impose even more stringent and implausible restrictions on the technology in an attempt to paper over fundamental problems of specification.

This chapter shows that most analyses of production under uncertainty have been based on models that involve implausible restrictions on the technology, when considered in Arrow–Debreu terms as a set of feasible transformations of state-contingent commodities. Our starting point is an exposition of the stochastic production-function approach, which demonstrates its inherent restrictions concerning the set of feasible production possibilities. We show how even a moderate relaxation of these assumptions, allowing multiple activities that each display fixed-output proportions, leads rapidly to a general technology of state-contingent production. A particularly compelling analytical merit of state-contingent production under uncertainty, like production of commodities differentiated in time and space, is that it can be interpreted as a special kind of a general multi-input, multi-output production technology. Hence all of the duality tools developed for the latter apply automatically to the former as we shall see in Chapter 4.

2.1 THE STOCHASTIC PRODUCTION FUNCTION

A natural place to initiate the discussion of state-contingent production technologies is the stochastic-production function model that has been the foundation of most studies of production under uncertainty. Suppose we let $\mathbf{x} \in \Re_+^N$ denote a vector of nonstochastic inputs that are committed prior to the resolution of uncertainty, $\theta \in \{1, 2\}$, a random input that assumes two mutually exclusive values, and $f: \Re_+^N \times \{1, 2\} \to \Re_{++}$, the production function. For example, one might envision an agricultural technology where $\mathbf{x}$ represents the inputs that the producer can control and θ represents the randomly occurring events "rain" and "no rain." The stochastic-production function model is based on the presumption that the random output $z \in \Re_+$ is determined by

$$z = f(\mathbf{x}, \theta).$$

So, for example, if $\mathbf{x}$ is committed, and the random input assumes the value 1, then ex post, or realized, output is $f(\mathbf{x}, 1)$. If the random

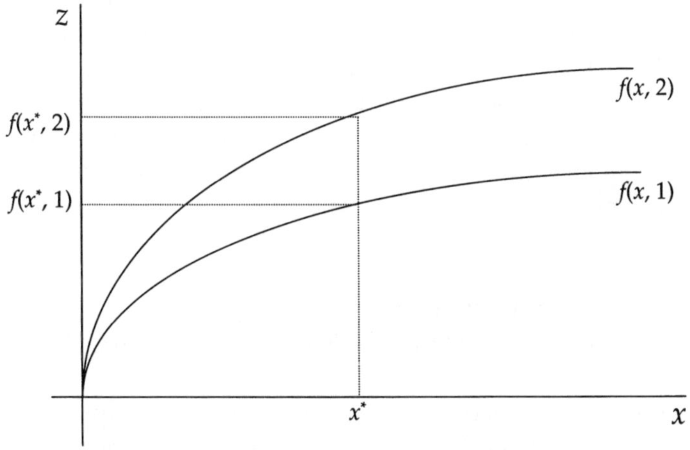

Figure 2.1 A stochastic production function for scalar x.

input assumes the value 2, then the realized output is $f(\mathbf{x}, 2)$. This representation incorporates several implicit assumptions. Most importantly, the resolution of uncertainty only serves to shift the production function up or down, depending on whether it is increasing or decreasing in θ. This is illustrated in Figure 2.1 by two separate production contours emanating from the origin. The higher one graphs output against input commitment $\mathbf{x}$ and traces out what happens when $\theta = 2$, and the lower traces out what happens when $\theta = 1$. All the resolution of uncertainty does is to increase or decrease the productivity of a given bundle of nonstochastic inputs. In a very real sense, therefore, *the effect of uncertainty on technology is disembodied*. The analogy is made complete when one recognizes that if θ were indexing technical change and not a stochastic input, the production function depicted in Figure 2.1 would be consistent with the traditional notion of disembodied technical change.

Second, because the technology is modeled by a production function, the implicit presumption is that all variable inputs, $\mathbf{x}$, are used efficiently in the production process. That is, given a realized value of θ, the producer always achieves the highest possible output for a given bundle of inputs. This removes the possibility that producers may be deliberately inefficient. One might ask: "Why would a rational producer ever choose to produce inefficiently?" "After all," the argument would run, "that means the producer is intentionally throwing away output that she could consume without increasing effort." This logic is unassailable given the implicit assumption that the producer is also the residual claimant, that is, has the sole right to consume or dispose of the output produced. But without this assumption, the argument is generally false. If the producer is not the residual claimant, rationality would dictate that the producer choose an inefficient production pattern whenever it is to her advantage.

2.2 THE BEGINNINGS OF A STATE-CONTINGENT TECHNOLOGY

Suppose that instead of graphing output against input commitment as in Figure 2.1, we hold the level of $\mathbf{x}$ fixed, and graph the output when $\theta = 2$ occurs against the output when $\theta = 1$ occurs. For a fixed input commitment, say, $\mathbf{x}^*$ in Figure 2.1, the result is portrayed in Figure 2.2 as the single point $(f(\mathbf{x}^*, 1), f(\mathbf{x}^*, 2))$, where $f(\mathbf{x}^*, 2) > f(\mathbf{x}^*, 1)$. This point is the *state-contingent output set* given $\mathbf{x}^*$: It gives the range of outputs in states $\theta = 1$ and $\theta = 2$ when input vector $\mathbf{x}^*$ is committed.

Figure 2.2 clearly illustrates the two implicit assumptions of the stochastic production-function approach that we have already discussed: the role that inputs play remain fundamentally the same regardless of whether $\theta = 1$ or $\theta = 2$ occurs; and no technical inefficiency is allowed. Let us consider relaxing the latter assumption first. To relax the assumption of technical efficiency, all we need do is to require that $f(\mathbf{x}^*, 2)$ represents the upper bound on production given $\mathbf{x}^*$ and $\theta = 2$ while admitting the possibility that the producer, if she so chooses, can always produce less than this upper bound once $\mathbf{x}^*$ is committed. This assumption, known formally as *free disposability of state-contingent output*, allows us to include all levels less than or equal to $f(\mathbf{x}^*, 2)$ as producible when $\theta = 2$. Visually, this allows us to include everything on the line segment perpendicular to the horizontal axis, which lies below the point $(f(\mathbf{x}^*, 1), f(\mathbf{x}^*, 2))$, and no lower than the horizontal axis. If we admit the same possibility when $\theta = 1$ occurs, the resulting state-contingent production possibilities set changes from the single point in Figure 2.2 to the rectangle in Figure 2.3. Everything within the rectangle is producible given the assumption of free disposability of output and the commitment of

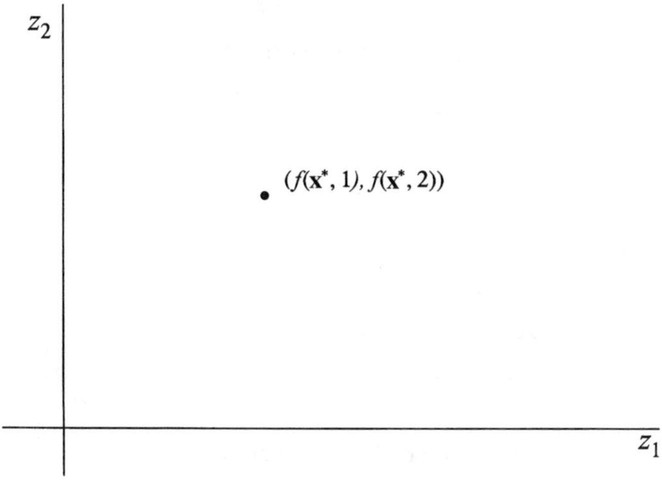

Figure 2.2 State-contingent output set for a stochastic production function.

$\mathbf{x}^*$. The producer will locate at the outer vertex of this rectangle only if it is to her advantage. If it isn't, she'll locate elsewhere within the rectangle.

Figure 2.3 is reminiscent of the pictorial representation of a non-stochastic multi-output technology characterized by fixed coefficients or zero substitutability between outputs. Perhaps more intuitively, it's analogous to a technology that behaves as though it were Leontief in outputs (see, e.g., Chambers 1988, Chapter 7). Why does this extreme form emerge from the stochastic production-function approach? The answer lies in the first implicit assumption that we discussed. Because the fundamental role that inputs play remains the same regardless of which θ occurs, the stochastic-production-function approach does not allow for the possibility of substituting one state-contingent output for another; the way that inputs are applied and the effect that they have on ex post output is severely circumscribed in this approach. Notice, in particular, that each state-contingent output, $f(\mathbf{x}^*, 2)$ and $f(\mathbf{x}^*, 1)$, depends on the total bundle of inputs committed, $\mathbf{x}^*$. Hence, as long as this bundle remains unchanged, the producer's decidion to lower output when $\theta = 1$ does not bring with it the ability to increase output when $\theta = 2$. *Inputs are completely nonstate-specific*. This is,

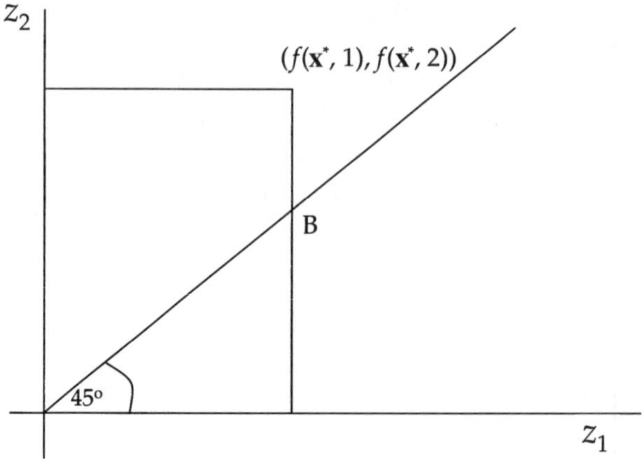

Figure 2.3 Free disposability of state-contingent output.

perhaps, best illustrated by an exaggerated, but not entirely unrealistic, example. Suppose again that the stochastic production function corresponds to an agricultural commodity and that the random input θ corresponds to possible levels of rainfall: too little rainfall for any crop growth ($\theta = 1$); and rainfall adequate for crop growth, but too much for optimal growth ($\theta = 2$). So under the stochastic production-function approach, $f(\mathbf{x}, 1) = 0$ and $f(\mathbf{x}, 2) > 0$, implying that our single point in Figure 2.2 now lies somewhere on the vertical axis.

Now suppose, for the sake of argument, that $\mathbf{x}$ is a scalar variable called "effort," and that effort can be devoted to either of two precautionary activities carried out prior to the realization of θ: developing and applying irrigation activities or building flood-control and water-catchment facilities.[2] If all precautionary effort were applied to the latter activity, zero output would be realized if no rain occurred. Naturally, flood-control and water-catchment facilities would have zero ex post marginal productivity if it did not rain. Would the same be true of effort devoted to irrigation? The stochastic production-function approach, quite implausibly, would imply "yes." Regardless of how much effort we devoted to irrigation, we would remain on the

2. Our thanks to Colin Carter for suggesting this example to us.

vertical axis at that single point if $\theta = 1$. Of course, reality says "no." If it doesn't rain, effort devoted to irrigation activity would have a large and positive ex post marginal product.

Does our generalization of the technology obtained by introducing free disposability of state-contingent outputs improve the situation? Here it only serves to include everything below $f(\mathbf{x}, 2)$ in the technology. When rain does not occur, and all effort is still devoted to irrigation, the ex post marginal product of effort is the same as if everything had been devoted to digging flood catchments – zero. Free disposability of state-contingent output only allows for the possibility of inefficient production.

One way to circumvent this type of problem is to allow effort to be allocated to differing activities. Reconsider our current example, but modify it by assuming that output when $\theta = 2$ occurs only depends on the amount of effort committed to the construction of flood-control and water-catchment facilities ($\mathbf{x}^2$), whereas output when $\theta = 1$ occurs only depends on effort committed to irrigation activities ($\mathbf{x}^1$), where $\mathbf{x}^1 + \mathbf{x}^2 = \mathbf{x}$. (We shall refer to this as the *state-allocable input technology*.) That state-contingent outputs are now capable of substituting for one another is easily illustrated with the "beaker" diagram presented in Figure 2.4. The horizontal dimension of the "beaker" measures available effort. Effort committed to irrigation facilities is measured from left to right, and effort committed to flood control is measured from right to left. The left vertical axis measures the output produced when $\theta = 1$, and the right vertical axis measures the output produced when $\theta = 2$. Plotted against the respective vertical axes are the ex post production functions, $f(\mathbf{x}^1, 1)$ and $f(\mathbf{x}^2, 2)$, which exhibit diminishing marginal productivity of effort.

Suppose to start that $\mathbf{x}^{1*}$ is applied to irrigation facilities, with the residual committed to flood control. Then output when $\theta = 1$ occurs is $f(\mathbf{x}^{1*}, 1)$ and $f(\mathbf{x} - \mathbf{x}^{1*}, 2)$ when $\theta = 2$. The corresponding point in state-contingent output space is *A* in Figure 2.5. Now divert a small amount of irrigation effort toward flood control. Output when $\theta = 2$ goes up, whereas output when $\theta = 1$ goes down. In Figure 2.5, this is represented by the movement from A northwesterly to B. If this experiment is repeated, that is, the same amount of effort is reallocated from irrigation to flood control, the state-contingent produc-

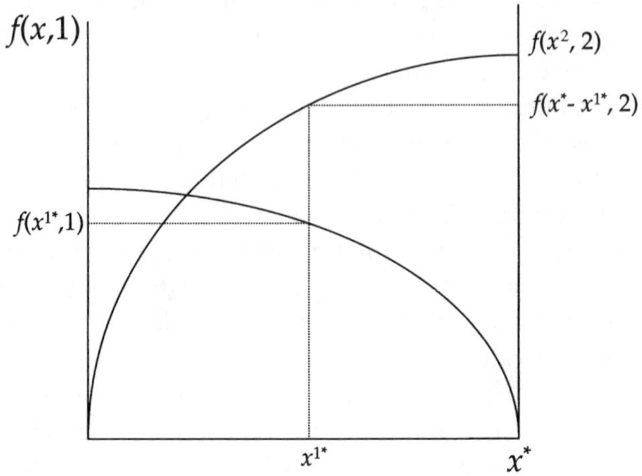

Figure 2.4 Effort allocable across states.

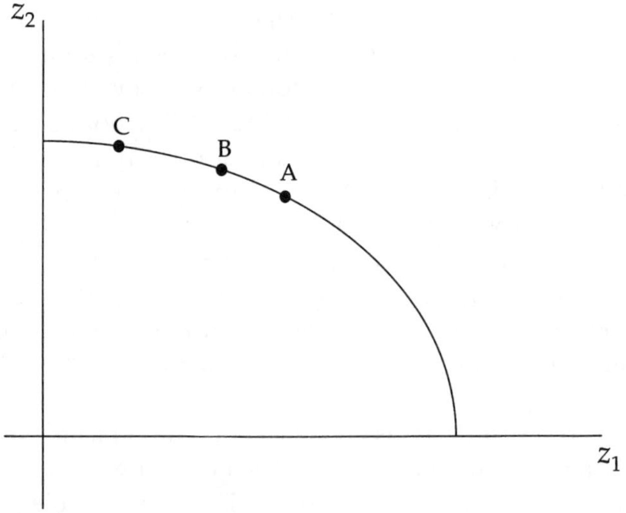

Figure 2.5 State-contingent product transformation curve.

tion pair moves from B toward the northwest again. But now, because of the diminishing marginal productivity of effort, the output increment when $\theta = 2$ is smaller than previously, whereas the output decrement when $\theta = 1$ is larger. Hence, the new state-contingent production point lies more to the west and less to the north, say, at point C. If this thought experiment is repeated continuously in both directions, a surface similar to the one depicted by the curve that passes through A, B, and C is obtained.

The curve in Figure 2.5 depicts how output when $\theta = 2$ trades off against output when $\theta = 1$ as a result of effort being reallocated from irrigation to flood control. As such, it might be thought of as a *state-contingent product-transformation curve*. Its negative slope, which can be thought of as a state-contingent marginal rate of transformation, and its shape (concave to the origin) reflect the presumption that increasing one state-contingent output can only be achieved at increasing cost in terms of the other state-contingent output.

If, in addition to the modification in the stochastic production functions depicted in Figure 2.4, technical inefficiency is permitted, technical possibilities in this stochastic world are represented by everything on or below the curve in Figure 2.5.

2.3 A STATE-CONTINGENT PRODUCTION TECHNOLOGY

Recall from Chapter 1 that uncertainty is modeled by "Nature" making a choice from a finite set of mutually exclusive alternatives, $\Omega = \{1, 2, 3, \ldots, S\}$. Each alternative is called a "state," and once the state is known, uncertainty is removed. As noted in Chapter 1, we abstract from the infinite complexity of a description of all possible states of nature, using Ω to index only those uncertain aspects that impinge on production decisions.

Our present goal is to specify a stochastic technology that is sufficiently general and flexible to include as special cases those depicted in Figures 2.2 and 2.5, but that does not limit attention to those special cases. This technology transforms vectors of inputs, $\mathbf{x} \in \Re_{+}^{N}$, committed by the producer prior to Nature making a draw from Ω into a matrix of state-contingent outputs, $\mathbf{z} \in \Re_{+}^{M \times S}$. The typical element of $\mathbf{z}$, z_{ms}, corresponds to the amount of output m that would be produced if state s occurs. $\mathbf{z}$, therefore, is a matrix of ex ante or potential outputs. Ex post, only one column of $\mathbf{z}$ actually occurs – the one with the same index as Nature's draw from Ω. The s column of $\mathbf{z}$, corresponding to state s, is denoted by $\mathbf{z}_s \in \Re_+^M$. Its domain is $\Re_+^M$ to allow for multiple outputs.

The technology is modeled by two correspondences. The first, the *state-contingent output correspondence*, generalizes Figures 2.2 and 2.5 and gives the matrices of state-contingent outputs that can be produced using a given vector of inputs.[3] Formally, it is defined by

$$Z(\mathbf{x}) = \{\mathbf{z} \in \Re_+^{M \times S} : \mathbf{x} \in \Re_+^N \text{ can produce } \mathbf{z}\}.$$

To illustrate, in Figures 2.2 and 2.5, $S = 2$, as there are only two possible outcomes for the random input (which plays the same role there as Ω here), and $M = 1$, because a single stochastic output is considered. Therefore, for the stochastic production-function technology, $Z(\mathbf{x}^*)$ is portrayed in Figure 2.2 as the single point, $(f(\mathbf{x}^*, 1), f(\mathbf{x}^*, 2))$. If we permit inefficiency, then $Z(\mathbf{x}^*)$ is given by all possible pairs of contingent outputs lying to the southwest of $(f(\mathbf{x}^*, 1), f(\mathbf{x}^*, 2))$. More formally,

$$Z(\mathbf{x}^*) = Z_1(\mathbf{x}^*) \times Z_2(\mathbf{x}^*),$$

where $Z_1(\mathbf{x}^*) = \{z_1 : z_1 \leq f(\mathbf{x}^*, 1)\}$, and $Z_2(\mathbf{x}^*) = \{z_2 : z_2 \leq f(\mathbf{x}^*, 2)\}$. And finally, in Figure 2.5, $Z(\mathbf{x})$ is everything on or below the curve passing through A, B, and C. $Z(\mathbf{x})$ will be referred to interchangeably as a *state-contingent output set* or more simply as an *output set*.

An alternative, but equivalent, representation of the state-contingent technology is the *input correspondence*, which converts a matrix of state-contingent outputs into sets of inputs that can produce that state-contingent output matrix. Formally, it is defined by

$$X(\mathbf{z}) = \{\mathbf{x} \in \Re_+^N : \mathbf{x} \text{ can produce } \mathbf{z} \in \Re_+^{M \times S}\}.$$

Intuitively, $X(\mathbf{z})$, which we refer to as the *input set*, is everything on or above an isoquant for the state-contingent technology. The stochastic production-function technology illustrates: because there are two states and only one output, $\mathbf{z} \in \Re_+^2$, and $X(\mathbf{z})$ is given by

3. Our notion of a state-contingent output correspondence and its image, the output set, is thus different from the state-contingent "production set" discussed by Hirshleifer and Riley (1992, pp. 135–8). Although their graphical depiction of their production set corresponds closely to our graphical depiction of state-contingent output sets, it's easy to show that the state-contingent output set for their technology is, in fact, what we shall come to refer to as output cubical.

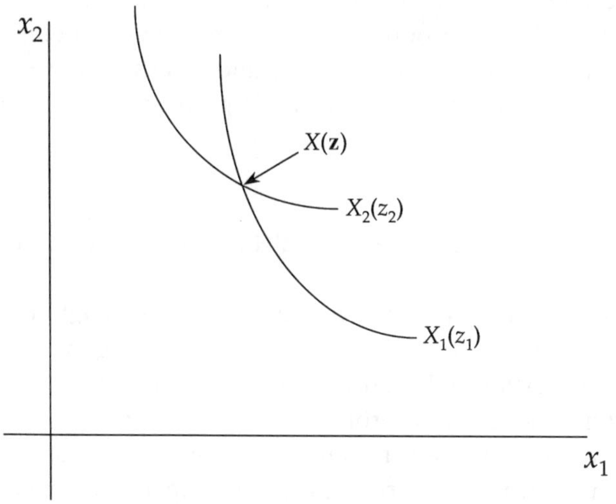

Figure 2.6 Input correspondence for stochastic production function.

$$X(\mathbf{z}) = \{\mathbf{x} : \mathbf{z}_1 = f(\mathbf{x}, 1), \mathbf{z}_2 = f(\mathbf{x}, 2)\}.$$

Letting $X_1(\mathbf{z}_1)$ and $X_2(\mathbf{z}_2)$ represent the isoquants for $f(\mathbf{x}, 1)$ and $f(\mathbf{x}, 2)$, respectively:

$$X(\mathbf{z}) = X_1(\mathbf{z}_1) \cap X_2(\mathbf{z}_2).$$

This case is depicted in Figure 2.6, where the isoquants for each of the realized stochastic production functions are drawn: $X(\mathbf{z})$ is the point of intersection between these two isoquants.

By their definitions, the following relationship holds between the input set and the output set:

$$\mathbf{x} \in X(\mathbf{z}) \Leftrightarrow \mathbf{z} \in Z(\mathbf{x}),$$

or, in words, if **x** can produce the matrix of state-contingent outputs **z**, the matrix of state-contingent outputs **z** is producible by **x**, and vice versa. Thus, the input set and the output set give equivalent, but alternative, representations of the technology. The fact that we have several alternatives for looking at the state-contingent technology turns out to be very useful when it comes to analyzing economic decisions made subject to the state-contingent technology.

Unfortunately, we need more than just the notions of the input and output sets to discuss production under uncertainty intelligently. So, in the next few sections, we present and discuss some reasonable properties that one might expect to impose on a state-contingent technology.

2.4 PROPERTIES OF THE OUTPUT SET

This section introduces a set of properties that one might reasonably impose on a state-contingent output set. Our strategy will be to first list these properties and then to discuss their intuitive content and possible limitations. These properties are not cast in iron. At times, we shall find it convenient to impose certain of them and, at times, others. Which properties are appropriate depends crucially on the characteristics of the problem to be studied. Thus, what follows is perhaps best viewed as a menu of alternative assumptions on the technology from which the individual researcher can select. (Most of these properties are borrowed directly from the axiomatic approach to nonstochastic technologies for which Shephard [1970] and Färe [1988] provide complete treatments.)

Properties of the Output Set (Z)

Z.1. $\mathbf{0}_{M\times S} \in Z(\mathbf{x})$ for all $\mathbf{x} \in \Re^N_+$, $\mathbf{z} \notin Z(\mathbf{0}_N)$ for $\mathbf{z} \neq \mathbf{0}_{M\times S}$

Z.2. $\mathbf{z}' \leq \mathbf{z} \in Z(\mathbf{x}) \Rightarrow \mathbf{z}' \in Z(\mathbf{x})$ (free disposability of outputs)

Z.2.W. $\mathbf{z} \in Z(\mathbf{x}) \Rightarrow \lambda\mathbf{z} \in Z(\mathbf{x})$ for $0 < \lambda < 1$ (weak disposability of output)

Z.3. $\mathbf{x}' \geq \mathbf{x} \Rightarrow Z(\mathbf{x}) \subseteq Z(\mathbf{x}')$ (free disposability of inputs)

Z.3.W. $Z(\mathbf{x}) \subseteq Z(\lambda\mathbf{x})$ for $\lambda > 1$ (weak disposability of inputs)

Z.4. $Z(\mathbf{x})$ is bounded for all $\mathbf{x} \in \Re^N_+$ (boundedness)

Z.5. $Z(\mathbf{x})$ is convex for all $\mathbf{x} \in \Re^N_+$

Z.6. $Z(\mathbf{x}) \cap Z(\mathbf{x}') \subseteq Z(\mu\mathbf{x} + (1 - \mu)\mathbf{x}')$ for $\mu \in [0, 1]$ and all $\mathbf{x}$, $\mathbf{x}' \in \Re^N_+$ (quasi-concavity)

Z.7. $\mu Z(\mathbf{x}) + (1 - \mu)Z(\mathbf{x}') \subseteq Z(\mu\mathbf{x} + (1 - \mu)\mathbf{x}')$ for $\mu \in [0, 1]$ and all $\mathbf{x}, \mathbf{x}' \in \Re^N_+$ (concavity)

Z.8. $Z(\mathbf{x})$ is a closed correspondence[4]

4. The correspondence Z is closed if, when $\mathbf{x}^k \rightarrow \mathbf{x}^o$, $\mathbf{z}^k \rightarrow \mathbf{z}^o$ and $\mathbf{z}^k \in Z(\mathbf{x}^k)$ for all k, $\mathbf{z}^o \in Z(\mathbf{x}^o)$.

2.4.1 No Fixed Costs and No Free Lunch

Z.1 comes in two parts. The first, $\mathbf{0}_{M\times S} \in Z(\mathbf{x})$ for all $\mathbf{x} \in \Re_{+}^{N}$, says that all input bundles can produce nothing. Or put another way, output inaction is always possible. Formally, this ensures that all output sets are nonempty, because each at least contains the origin. The second part of Z.1 means that failure to commit a strictly positive amount of at least one input cannot be consistent with the production of a positive amount of any state-contingent output. Traditionally, the second part of Z.1 is referred to in Friedmanesque terms – there is no "free lunch." Together, the components of Z.1 imply that $Z(\mathbf{0}_N) = \{\mathbf{0}_{M\times S}\}$: the only state-contingent output bundle that can be produced without applying some inputs is the one with no state-contingent output in it. Therefore, Z.1 in essence says the technology is long run in the sense that "doing nothing" is always possible.

2.4.2 Disposability of State-Contingent Outputs

Z.2 represents one of the two main departures made from the stochastic-production-function approach. It says that a producer can choose to operate inefficiently. In pictorial terms, it's the formal assumption that allows us to move from Figure 2.2 to Figure 2.3. To see why, return to Figure 2.2 and consider $(f(\mathbf{x}^*, 1), f(\mathbf{x}^*, 2))$. When cast in these terms, Z.2 says that all output bundles to the southwest of $(f(\mathbf{x}^*, 1), f(\mathbf{x}^*, 2))$ are also producible using $\mathbf{x}^*$. We often refer to Z.2 as *free disposability of outputs* or *output-free disposability*.

A glance at Figure 2.3, however, reveals that free disposability of state-contingent outputs has other important implications for decision making under production uncertainty. Output free disposability implies that the producer can always, at appropriate cost in terms of foregone output, make production nonstochastic. Consider the ray emanating from the origin in Figure 2.3 with a slope of 1. This ray bisects state-contingent output space, and, typically, we refer to it as the *bisector*. On any point above the bisector, output in state 2 is higher than output in state 1, whereas below the bisector, the reverse is true. Along the bisector, output in state 1 equals output in state 2, that is, *there is no production uncertainty*. Geometrically, it's easy to see that the bisector will intersect any nonempty output set exhibiting free disposability of output. The important economic implication is that, if free disposability of output is imposed, production uncertainty is a choice that the producer makes and not something that is dictated to him or her.

In Figure 2.3, for example, the producer can always opt to produce at a point like B (or at any point between B and the origin on the bisector) that involves no production uncertainty but that requires the producer to forego some output in state 2. If the producer is the residual claimant of the output produced, this appears irrational (and, in fact, a rational producer regardless of his or her degree of risk aversion would never produce at B if he or she were the residual claimant). But when the producer is not the residual claimant, it's possible to construct examples in which an inefficient production plan like that at B is not only plausible but the best that a producer can do.

In the agricultural production example considered before, one sees that improperly designed crop insurance arrangements can give farmers an incentive to adopt a technically inefficient production plan. In many such cases, eligibility for assistance is contingent on the farmer suffering a sufficiently large loss to trigger relief provisions. Suppose that, with inputs $\mathbf{x}^*$, a farmer producing at point $(f(\mathbf{x}^*, 1), f(\mathbf{x}^*, 2))$ would not receive assistance in state 2, which we take to be the "Rain" state, because $f(\mathbf{x}^*, 2)$ would be too large an output to trigger insurance relief, but that a farmer producing at point B would be eligible for assistance of value greater than $f(\mathbf{x}^*, 2) - f(\mathbf{x}^*, 1)$. Then the technically inefficient B would be preferred.

Making production uncertainty an economic choice is not the only important implication of output-free disposability. Output-free disposability means exactly what it says: producers can dispose of outputs they may not desire for free. Although probably a harmless assumption when outputs are goods with a positive market value, it isn't so obviously harmless when one of the outputs is a "bad," for example, pollution in the form of fertilizer and pesticide runoff from agricultural land or smoke and carbon emissions in the case of a factory.

Suppose, in fact, that there are two outputs produced in each state of nature with one being a crop and the other being fertilizer and pesticide runoff. Figure 2.7, which draws the output set between these two outputs in a given state, holding all other states' outputs constant,

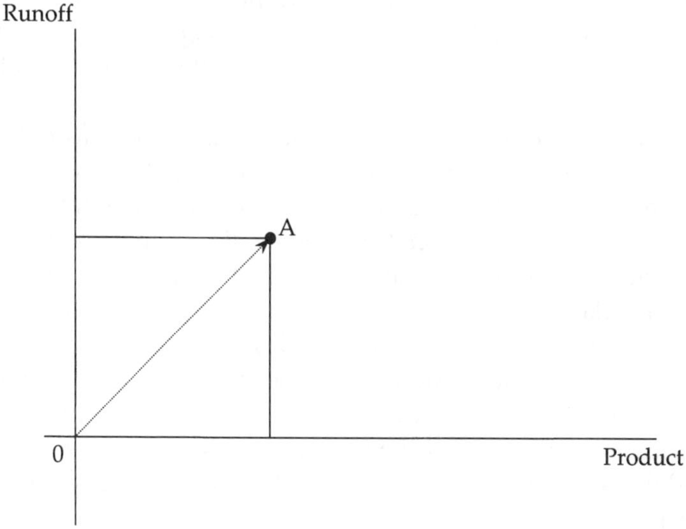

Figure 2.7 Free disposability of output.

illustrates what output-free disposability implies about these two products. (We emphasise that Figure 2.7 is drawn for a particular state of nature and does not reflect what happens across states of nature.) Assume that point A is technically feasible. Output-free disposability implies that all points in the rectangle, whose outermost vertex is given by A and whose innermost vertex is given by the origin, also are feasible. As apparently first noted by Shephard (1970), this seems implausible when one of the products is a bad.

In our example, if the producer wants to diminish runoff pollution in the current state without altering her overall input commitment, resources currently allocated to producing the crop in the current state or outputs in other states must be diverted to preventing the runoff. That means she will have to lower outputs in other states (in Figure 2.7, these are implicitly held fixed) or produce less of the crop. On the other hand, she might choose to increase the application of some inputs (for example, technology to deliver chemical inputs more precisely and with less runoff) to prevent runoff. Figure 2.7, however, suggests that the producer can rid herself of pollution at no cost. Indeed, if accurate, Figure 2.7 raises the question of why producers would ever operate anywhere except on the horizontal axis unless they derive some direct benefit from pollution. Because runoff pollution is unlikely to have a direct positive benefit to the producer, its presence is probably explained by the fact that removing pollution is costly.

A similar argument may be made with respect to outputs of a given commodity in different states of nature. If a given output is a "good" in one state of nature, but a "bad" in a closely related state of nature, it may be difficult to produce the good without generating the bad. For example, a smoke alarm that produces the desirable output "alarm sounds" in the state of nature "house fire" is likely to produce the same output, now undesirable, in the state of nature "burnt toast." There would be a positive cost in redesigning the system to discriminate between the two states of nature, producing the alarm in one but not the other, or, better still, a discreet warning in the case of burnt toast and a loud alarm in the case of a dangerous fire.

So for some applications, Z.2 may be too strong. Therefore, it's convenient to have a weaker assumption to fall back on. Z.2.W, where W stands for "weak," is that axiom: we shall typically refer to it as *weak disposability of output* or *output-weak disposability*. Instead of requiring all output combinations in the rectangle whose outer vertex is A in Figure 2.7 to be producible if A is producible, weak disposability of outputs only implies that outputs can be costlessly disposed of along the ray between the origin and A. It implies that to costlessly reduce one output, the other output must also be reduced proportionately. (This must happen across states as well.) The reasoning here is that if, for example, one of the outputs is an industrial good and the other is pollution, the resources that are required to abate pollution are liberated by the radial reduction in the good outputs that occurs across all states of nature. Hence, disposing of bad outputs like pollution no longer carries a zero opportunity cost. Instead, it bears a positive opportunity cost (for a fixed input bundle) in terms of foregone "good" outputs.

2.4.3 Input Disposability and Input Congestion

Z.3, *free disposability of inputs* or *input-free disposability*, generalizes the concept of positive marginal productivities of variable inputs. In Figure 2.2, Z.3 implies that, if any element of the input vector were increased, $(f(\mathbf{x}^*, 1), f(\mathbf{x}^*, 2))$ would remain producible with the now larger (in at least one element) input bundle. For most economists, positive marginal productivity of an input is easy to accept. Certainly, rational producers would not apply more of costly inputs for which they bear the cost and which have a negative marginal productivity. However, our present task is to describe physical characteristics of the state-contingent technology, and there are many real-world examples that indicate that some inputs may have negative marginal products. Typically, this happens when too much of a variable input is applied to a fixed bundle of nonvariable inputs for the additional variable input to find fixed inputs with which to cooperate (stage 3 of the production process). In a word, the variable input becomes congested. Fertilizers provide one of the best-known examples of input congestion. Applied at low rates, chemical fertilizer increases yield, but at excessive rates of application, the resultant chemical burning reduces yields. Another is the old saw, "Too many cooks spoil the broth."

Allowing for input congestion requires a weaker version of Z.3. Our candidate is Z.3.W, weak input disposability, which only requires that radial expansion of an input vector capable of producing a given state-contingent output matrix can also produce that same state-contingent output matrix. Here the reasoning is simple. If all inputs are expanded proportionately, the crowding phenomenon that arises from increasing amounts of a variable input being applied to a fixed input bundle will not occur. Again, chemical fertilizers are a good real-world example. If fertilizer and acreage are expanded proportionately, chemical burn is unlikely to emerge.

2.4.4 Bounds on Output Sets

Z.4 is a technical assumption that implies that the output set always has an upper bound for any potential combination of inputs. In a very real sense, it's a "free" assumption because it cannot be contradicted by any body of data generated from real-world observations. For Z.4 to be violated, one would have to observe unboundedly large combinations of state-contingent outputs. Although it cannot be contradicted by real-world observations, that doesn't mean that Z.4 isn't important to our purposes. It's the formal assumption that allows us to write down well-defined maximization problems for much of the economic analysis that follows.

2.4.5 Curvature Properties of Output Sets

Conditions Z.5 through Z.7 are all *curvature* conditions in the sense that they imply something about the shape of the output set. Notice that, generally, they are not equivalent. It's easy to show, however, that Z.7 implies both Z.5 and Z.6. However, neither Z.5 nor Z.6 imply Z.7, nor one another. Thus, these axioms represent different curvature conditions to impose on the output sets. But fundamentally, the rationale for each is some version of the *law of diminishing marginal returns*.

Z.5, convexity of the output set, says that output sets assume the same basic shape as the one illustrated in Figure 2.5 by everything on or below the curve. Thus, it contains several important assumptions. First, state-contingent outputs as well as different outputs within a single state of nature can be substituted for one another, given a fixed bundle of inputs. Second, this substitution occurs at increasing marginal cost, that is, successively more and more of a given output must be sacrificed in order to raise production of another output by equal increments. Thus, in Figure 2.5, output in state 2 can be transformed into output in state 1, but as we move toward either of the axes, it becomes increasingly hard to do so. Again, the state-allocable input agricultural technology illustrates. As effort is diverted from irrigation toward flood control, the marginal gains one realizes decrease as flood control gets better and better. Third, both state-contingent and within-state outputs are not lumpy, but perfectly divisible. That is, if any combination of state-contingent outputs can be produced then any weighted average of these state-contingent outputs can be produced using the same bundle of inputs.

The capacity to reallocate effort from one state of nature to another that underlies this substitutability between state-contingent outputs reduces the likelihood that producers will choose a technically inefficient state-contingent production vector. As long as there is a positive return to increased output in any state and effort can be reallocated between states, reallocation will be preferred to the choice of a technically inefficient output vector. In the two-state example, as long as the state-contingent marginal rate of transfor-

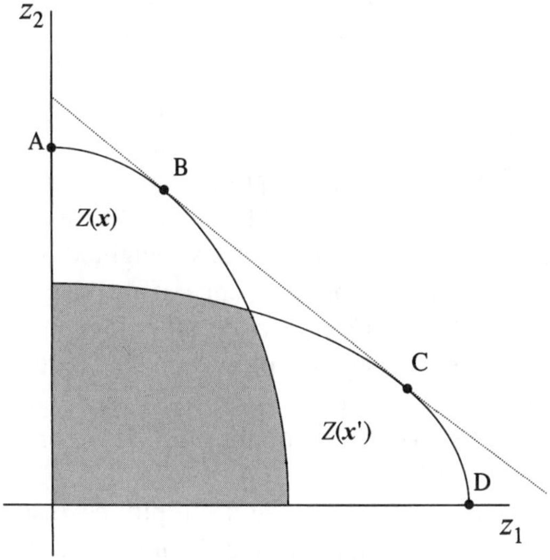

Figure 2.8 Properties Z.6 and Z.7.

mation is finite and nonzero, a movement around the frontier will be a preferred alternative to the adoption of a technically inefficient point inside the frontier.

Return to our agricultural example and consider public or private provision of drought relief. If drought relief provisions imply a negative return to increased output in the "no rain" state of nature, farmers will divert effort from activities such as irrigation toward alternatives such as flood control. Reductions in drought-state output will continue until either: (i) drought-state output is reduced to zero or (ii) the marginal return to drought-state output is positive (with an interior equilibrium where the ratio of marginal values of output is equal to the state-contingent marginal rate of transformation).

Z.6, as we later demonstrate, implies that input sets are convex, that is, isoquants are shaped in their normal fashion and exhibit a diminishing marginal rate of technical substitution between all inputs. (Formally, Z.6 implies that the state-contingent output correspondence $Z(\mathbf{x})$ is *quasi-concave.*) The intuition for output sets is a bit less obvious, but still clear. Figure 2.8 illustrates Z.6 in terms of two output sets $Z(\mathbf{x})$ and $Z(\mathbf{x}')$, defined by two distinct input bundles. As Figure

2.8 is drawn, the intersection of these two output sets is nonempty; Z.6 implies that any state-contingent output bundle in the shaded area denoting the intersection of the two sets also can be produced by using any arbitrary convex combination of $\mathbf{x}$ and $\mathbf{x}'$. But this makes sense if inputs can be substituted for one another in the usual way. Any point in the intersection corresponds to a state-contingent output bundle that can be produced by both $\mathbf{x}$ and $\mathbf{x}'$. Isolate such a point: Z.6 says that all convex combinations, weighted averages, of $\mathbf{x}$ and $\mathbf{x}'$ can also produce that point. Hence, if we visualize a line segment connecting $\mathbf{x}$ and $\mathbf{x}'$ in input space, all points on it must be able to produce the state-contingent output bundle. Isoquants being convex to the origin imply precisely that. All weighted averages of two input combinations on the isoquant must lie on or above the isoquant.

Z.7, concavity of the state-contingent output correspondence, implies, among other things, that both Z.5 and Z.6 are satisfied. Heuristically, concavity of the output correspondence imposes the strict notion of diminishing marginal returns. Geometrically, it implies that any state-contingent output bundle lying in the convex hull of the set $\{Z(\mathbf{x}) \cup Z(\mathbf{x}')\}$ is also producible by using some convex combination of $\mathbf{x}$ and $\mathbf{x}'$. (The convex hull of a set is the smallest convex set containing all elements of the set.) In Figure 2.8, this implies that the output set whose outer boundary is given by the outer boundary of $Z(\mathbf{x})$ from point A to point B, by the dashed-line segment connecting points B and C, and the outer boundary of $Z(\mathbf{x}')$ between C and D lies within $Z(\mu\mathbf{x} + (1 - \mu)\mathbf{x}')$ for $\mu \in [0, 1]$. Any state-contingent output bundle lying below this frontier is producible using some convex combination of $\mathbf{x}$ and $\mathbf{x}'$. The stochastic production function illustrates. Suppose that $f(\mathbf{x}, \theta)$ is strictly concave in the variable inputs. The law of diminishing marginal returns applies in its usual sense and further:

$$f(\mu\mathbf{x}+(1-\mu)\mathbf{x}',\theta) \geq \mu f(\mathbf{x},\theta)+(1-\mu)f(\mathbf{x}',\theta).$$

Consequently,

$$\begin{aligned}\mu Z(\mathbf{x})+(1-\mu)Z(\mathbf{x}') &= \mu[f(\mathbf{x},1),f(\mathbf{x},2)]+(1-\mu)[f(\mathbf{x}',1),f(\mathbf{x}',2)]\\ &\leq [f(\mu\mathbf{x}+(1-\mu)\mathbf{x}',1),f(\mu\mathbf{x}+(1-\mu)\mathbf{x}',2)]\\ &= Z(\mu\mathbf{x}+(1-\mu)\mathbf{x}').\end{aligned}$$

2.4.6 Output Sets Are Closed

Z.8 is a mathematical requirement that is useful in establishing the existence of minima and maxima. It should be noted that, as with Z.4, it is impossible to contradict Z.8 based solely on the observation of any finite data set. (Put another way, for any observed body of production data, one could construct a closed output set consistent with it.)

2.4.7 An Example

We close this section with an extended example that illustrates how these properties might be usefully deployed. Readers are encouraged to endure this example because we believe it to contain the first axiomatic development of a stochastic production function. As such, it illustrates that the state-contingent technology we have developed subsumes the stochastic production function as a special case.

Example 2.1: *Earlier we demonstrated that in the stochastic production-function case illustrated in Figure 2.3, the output set could be written as the Cartesian product of two output sets,* $Z(\boldsymbol{x}) = Z_1(\boldsymbol{x}) \times Z_2(\boldsymbol{x})$. *In this example, we show how to go the other way: how to develop axiomatically a state-contingent production function using the properties Z.*

Our starting point is the assumption that the output set assumes the natural generalization of the form illustrated in Figure 2.3, that is, $Z(\boldsymbol{x}) = \times_{s=1}^{S} Z_s(\boldsymbol{x})$, *where each* $Z_s \subseteq \Re_+$ *satisfies Z.1, Z.2.W, Z.3, Z.4, Z.6, and Z.8. Notice, in particular, that each* $Z_s(\boldsymbol{x})$ *depends on the same bundle of inputs. Figure 2.9 illustrates pictorially for the case where* $S = 3$. *There the state-contingent output set is given by all vectors lying within the depicted cube. The productively efficient point lies at the outer vertex of the cube. Moreover, decreasing any single state-contingent output, holding the input vector fixed, does not bring with it the ability to raise other state-contingent outputs. We shall, therefore, refer to the corresponding technology as involving nonsubstitutability between state-contingent outputs or more simply (and reflecting the geometric intuition of Figure 2.9) as being output-cubical. (It's the fact that each* $Z_s(\boldsymbol{x})$ *depends on the same input bundle that leads to the cubical shape. Luenberger (1995) contains a specific functional representation of an output-cubical technology.) Our claim*

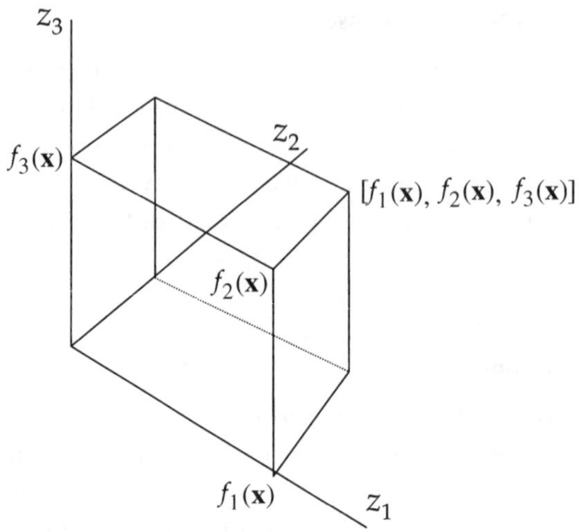

Figure 2.9 Output-cubical output set.

is that in the output-cubical case, there exist nondecreasing and quasi-concave state-contingent production functions $f_s(\boldsymbol{x})$, $s = 1, 2, 3, \ldots, S$, *such that*

$$Z(\boldsymbol{x}) = \{\boldsymbol{z} : z_s \le f_s(\boldsymbol{x}), s = 1, 2, \ldots, S\}.$$

The first step in proving this assertion is to note that by Z.1, each $Z_s(\boldsymbol{x})$ *is nonempty because each contains the origin. Z.4 and Z.8 imply that each* $Z_s(\boldsymbol{x})$ *is compact, that is, closed and bounded. Therefore, by the Weierstrass theorem (the real reason for imposing Z.4 and Z.8), the following maximal-value function exists and is well-defined for each* Z_s:

$$f_s(\boldsymbol{x}) = max\{Z_s(\boldsymbol{x})\}.$$

By weak disposability of output (which for scalar output is the same as free disposability) and Z.1, it then follows immediately that each $Z_s(\mathbf{x})$ *can be summarized by*

$$Z_s(\boldsymbol{x}) = \{z_s : z_s \le f_s(\boldsymbol{x})\}.$$

Now by Z.3, free disposability of input, $\boldsymbol{x}' \ge \boldsymbol{x}$ *implies that* $max\{Z_s(\boldsymbol{x}')\} \ge max\{Z_s(\boldsymbol{x})\}$ *so that each* $f_s(\boldsymbol{x})$ *is nondecreasing over* $\Re^N_+$. *Pictorially, therefore, the* $\mathbf{Z}_s(\boldsymbol{x})$ $(s = 1, 2, 3)$ *are represented in*

Figure 2.9, respectively, by everything lying below $f_1(\boldsymbol{x})$ *on the* z_1 *axis, everything lying below* $f_2(\boldsymbol{x})$ *on the* z_2 *axis, and everything lying below* $f_3(\boldsymbol{x})$ *on the* z_3 *axis.* $Z(\boldsymbol{x})$ *is given by the illustrated cube that is the Cartesian product of these output sets. By imposing weak disposability of output on each of the individual* Z_s*, we automatically impose free disposability of output on* Z.

So far, we have established that $Z(\boldsymbol{x})$ *can be completely described by* $\{\boldsymbol{z}: z_s \leq f_s(\boldsymbol{x}), s = 1, 2, \ldots, S\}$*, where each* f_s *is nondecreasing. All that remains to establish our assertion is to show that each of these state-contingent production functions are in fact quasi-concave, that is, possess isoquants that are convex to the origin and thus exhibit a diminishing marginal rate of substitution. But this follows easily from Z.6 because for Z.6:*

$$\begin{aligned} f_s(\mu\boldsymbol{x}+(1-\mu)\boldsymbol{x}') &= max\{Z_s(\mu\boldsymbol{x}+(1-\mu)\boldsymbol{x}')\} \\ &\geq max\{Z_s(\boldsymbol{x}) \cap Z_s(\boldsymbol{x}')\} \\ &= min\{f_s(\boldsymbol{x}), f_s(\boldsymbol{x}')\}, \end{aligned}$$

which is one definition of a quasi-concave function on $\Re^N_+$*. Another definition of quasi-concavity of a production function is that its input sets are convex. In the next section, we show that this is a consequence of Z.6. Finally, we should comment that if Z.7 had been substituted for Z.6, we would have been able to show that the state-contingent production functions were concave instead of only quasi-concave. (The verification of this fact is left for the reader.)*

2.5 PROPERTIES OF INPUT SETS

This section is devoted to examining the consequences of axioms Z.1 to Z.8 for the input correspondence and the associated input sets. The properties that follow for input sets are equivalent to those developed earlier for output sets. Our main reason for developing them is that it is often more convenient to work with input sets rather than with output sets. Moreover, the more different ways one can look at something, the better the chance that it will be understood. The following discussion is somewhat discursive and is not intended to represent formal proofs of the correspondences claimed. Less effort here will be devoted to developing the intuition behind results. However, the reader can be assured that these correspondences between the properties of input and output sets exist. In fact, they are simply the state-contingent extension of well-known results in the axiomatic approach to production. Those wanting formal proofs can refer to either Shephard (1970) or Färe (1988).

The easiest way to deduce the consequences of axioms Z.1 to Z.8 for $X(\mathbf{z})$ is to recall that the input correspondence and the output correspondence are mutual inverses of one another. Therefore, in most instances, deriving the properties of $X(\mathbf{z})$ only amounts to a simple rewriting of Z.1 to Z.8 in terms of input sets.

2.5.1 No Fixed Cost and No Free Lunch

The first part of Z.1 implies that the state-contingent output matrix with all zero entries (zero produced in all states for each different output) can be produced using any nonnegative combination of inputs. Hence, it immediately follows that the input set for $\mathbf{0}_{M\times S}$ equals the domain of the output correspondence, and thus $X(\mathbf{0}_{M\times S}) = \Re^N_+$. Intuitively, therefore, the first part of Z.1 says that the isoquant for $\mathbf{0}_{M\times S}$ is given by the axes in $\mathbf{x}$ space. The second part of Z.1 says that a zero commitment of inputs cannot be responsible for producing any positive output in any state; that is, the origin in input space cannot be in any input set for a state-contingent output matrix that has some nonzero entries. Symbolically, we write this in terms of input sets as $\mathbf{0}_N \notin X(\mathbf{z})$ for $\mathbf{z} \geq \mathbf{0}_{M\times S}$ and $\mathbf{z} \neq \mathbf{0}$.

2.5.2 Disposability of State-Contingent Outputs

Output-free disposability, Z.2, implies that, if an input bundle, $\mathbf{x}$, can produce a given state-contingent output matrix, $\mathbf{z}$, then $\mathbf{x}$ is always capable of producing any state-contingent output matrix that is no larger than $\mathbf{z}$. In other words, the producer can always choose to produce less if she wants. In mathematical terms, Z.2 means that if $\mathbf{x} \in X(\mathbf{z})$ (read $\mathbf{x}$ can produce $\mathbf{z}$), then $\mathbf{x} \in X(\mathbf{z}')$ for any $\mathbf{z}' \leq \mathbf{z}$. So $X(\mathbf{z}')$ must contain every element of $X(\mathbf{z})$, or $\mathbf{z}' \leq \mathbf{z} \Rightarrow X(\mathbf{z}) \subseteq X(\mathbf{z}')$.

As discussed, Z.2 may be too strong an assumption in certain cases. In these circumstances, Z.2 will be replaced by Z.2.W (weak disposability of output). Z.2.W implies a slightly different, but parallel, property for the input correspondence than Z.2, namely, $X(\mathbf{z}) \subseteq X(\lambda\mathbf{z})$ for $0 \leq \lambda \leq 1$. In words, any input combination that can

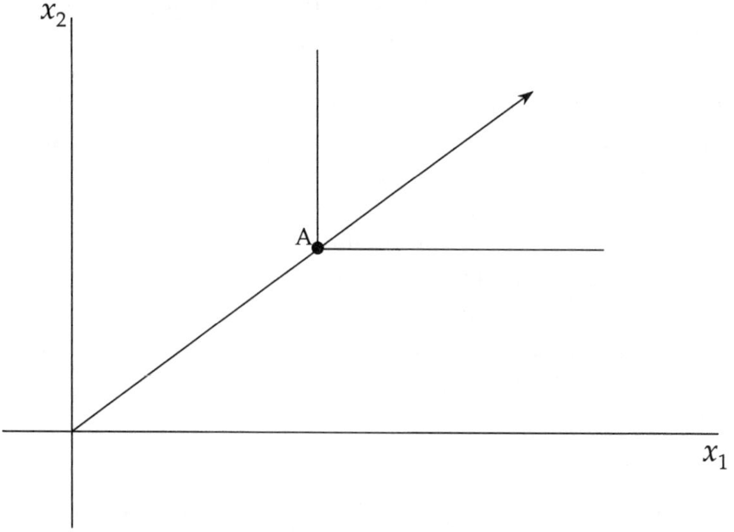

Figure 2.10 Free and weak input disposability.

produce a given state-contingent output matrix can always produce a suitably scaled-down (radially contracted) state-contingent output matrix.

2.5.3 Input Disposability and Input Congestion

Z.3, input-free disposability, says that if $\mathbf{x}$ can produce $\mathbf{z}$, then any larger bundle of inputs can also produce $\mathbf{z}$, that is, $\mathbf{x}' \geq \mathbf{x} \in X(\mathbf{z}) \Rightarrow \mathbf{x}' \in X(\mathbf{z})$. Graphically, input-free disposability is illustrated in Figure 2.10 by noting that if point A lies in $X(\mathbf{z})$, all points to the northeast of A are also in $X(\mathbf{z})$. As we have already noted, this may be an overly strong assumption, particularly if there is the possibility of congestion among the inputs. Z.3.W weakens this assumption to only requiring that points lying to the northeast of A and on the same ray from the origin as A also fall in $X(\mathbf{z})$.

2.5.4 Bounds on Output Sets

If $Z(\mathbf{x})$ is bounded for $\mathbf{x} \in \Re_+^N$, then, for any $\mathbf{x} \in \Re_+^N$, there cannot exist any producible state-contingent output matrix $\mathbf{z}$ with any "infinitely large" elements. Geometrically, this implies in the single-product case that any well-behaved output set cannot contain any vector of state-contingent outputs of infinite (Euclidean) length. In the multiproduct case, it means that the column vectorization of any producible **z** (A matrix is column vectorized by taking its columns and stacking them on one another to form in this case an $M \times S$–dimensional column vector.), which we denote by vec **z**, cannot be of infinite (Euclidean) length. In terms of input sets, this implies that any unbounded vec **z** can only have one input set corresponding to it – the empty set. Formally, this can be expressed in terms of unbounded sequences of vec **z** as: if $\|\text{vec } \mathbf{z}^k\| \to \infty$ as $k \to \infty$, then $\cap_{k\to\infty} X(\mathbf{z}^k) = \emptyset$. In other words, no **x** can produce an unbounded state-contingent output matrix.

2.5.5 Curvature Properties of Output and Input Sets

Z.5, convexity of the state-contingent output sets, implies that if **z** and **z**′ both belong to a particular output set, call it $Z(\mathbf{x})$, then any convex combination of **z** and **z**′ also belongs to $Z(\mathbf{x})$. Mathematically, $\mathbf{z} \in Z(\mathbf{x})$ and $\mathbf{z}' \in Z(\mathbf{x})$ implies that $\lambda\mathbf{z} + (1 - \lambda)\mathbf{z}' \in Z(\mathbf{x})$ for $\lambda \in [0, 1]$. Expressed in terms of input sets, this implies that, if $\mathbf{x} \in X(\mathbf{z})$ and $\mathbf{x} \in X(\mathbf{z}')$, then **x** also belongs to $X(\lambda\mathbf{z} + (1 - \lambda)\mathbf{z}')$. This, in turn, means that any element common to $X(\mathbf{z})$ and $X(\mathbf{z}')$, that is, any element of their intersection, must also be capable of producing arbitrary convex combinations of **z** and **z**′. More formally, $X(\mathbf{z}) \cap X(\mathbf{z}') \subseteq X(\lambda\mathbf{z} + (1 - \lambda)\mathbf{z}')$.

Property Z.6, quasi-concavity of the output correspondence, says that if $\mathbf{z} \in Z(\mathbf{x})$ and $\mathbf{z} \in Z(\mathbf{x}')$, then **z** must also belong to $Z(\mu\mathbf{x} + (1 - \mu)\mathbf{x}')$ for $\mu \in [0, 1]$. So if both **x** and **x**′ can produce **z**, that is, if $\mathbf{x} \in X(\mathbf{z})$ and $\mathbf{x}' \in X(\mathbf{z})$, then any weighted average of them (any $(\mu\mathbf{x} + (1 - \mu)\mathbf{x}')$ for $\mu \in [0, 1]$) must also be able to produce **z**, that is, $\mu\mathbf{x} + (1 - \mu)\mathbf{x}' \in X(\mathbf{z})$. This, however, is the definition of a convex set. As promised, we have shown that Z.6 implies that input sets are convex. Now recall Example 2.1, in which we showed that the state-contingent production function is quasi-concave in **x**. A defining characteristic of quasi-concave functions is that their upper contour sets, here the input set for the production function, be convex. The economic consequence is that inputs exhibit a diminishing marginal rate of technical substitution.

Z.7 implies both Z.6 and Z.5, as already noted. Rewriting it in an obvious fashion shows that it also implies $\lambda X(\mathbf{z}) + (1 - \lambda)X(\mathbf{z}') \subseteq X(\lambda\mathbf{z} + (1 - \lambda)\mathbf{z}')$, which implies both that input sets are convex (take $\mathbf{z} = \mathbf{z}'$), and that the intersection of the input sets for $\mathbf{z}$ and $\mathbf{z}'$ is a subset of $X(\lambda\mathbf{z} + (1 - \lambda)\mathbf{z}')$. However, in neither case does the converse apply.

2.5.6 Input Sets Are Closed

Finally, Z.8, which again is a mathematical requirement that will prove convenient in maximization and minimization problems, but that cannot be contradicted by real-world observations, implies that the input correspondence is closed.

2.5.7 List of Properties of Input Sets

This completes our discussion of the properties of input sets for state-contingent technologies. For later convenience, we shall list these properties separately as follows:

Properties of the Input Set (X)

X.1. $X(\mathbf{0}_{M\times S}) = \Re^N_+$, and $\mathbf{0}_N \notin X(\mathbf{z})$ for $\mathbf{z} \geq \mathbf{0}_{M\times S}$ and $\mathbf{z} \neq \mathbf{0}_{M\times S}$
X.2. $\mathbf{z}' \geq \mathbf{z} \Rightarrow X(\mathbf{z}) \subseteq X(\mathbf{z}')$
X.2.W. $X(\mathbf{z}) \in X(\lambda\mathbf{z})$ for $0 \leq \lambda \leq 1$
X.3. $\mathbf{x}' \geq \mathbf{x} \in X(\mathbf{z}) \Rightarrow \mathbf{x}' \in X(\mathbf{z})$
X.3.W. $\mathbf{x} \in X(\mathbf{z}) \Rightarrow \lambda\mathbf{x} \in X(\mathbf{z})$ for $\lambda > 1$
X.4. If $|\text{vec } \mathbf{z}^k| \to \infty$ as $k \to \infty$, then $\cap_{k\to\infty} X(\mathbf{z}^k) = \emptyset$
X.5. $X(\mathbf{z}) \cap X(\mathbf{z}') \subseteq X(\lambda\mathbf{z} + (1 - \lambda)\mathbf{z}')$, $0 < \lambda < 1$
X.6. $X(\mathbf{z})$ is a convex set for all $\mathbf{z} \in \Re^M_+$
X.7. $\lambda X(\mathbf{z}) + (1 - \lambda)X(\mathbf{z}') \subseteq X(\lambda\mathbf{z} + (1 - \lambda)\mathbf{z}')$, $0 \leq \lambda \leq 1$
X.8. $X(\mathbf{z})$ is closed for all $\mathbf{z} \in \Re^M_+$

2.5.8 Another Extended Example

We close this section with another extended example that is based on the state-allocable input model illustrated in Figures 2.4 and 2.5.

Example 2.2: *Earlier we showed that* $X(z_1, z_2) = X_1(z_1) \cap X_2(z_2)$ *in the two-state, stochastic-production-function case. From Example 2.1, it should now be obvious that in the more general* S

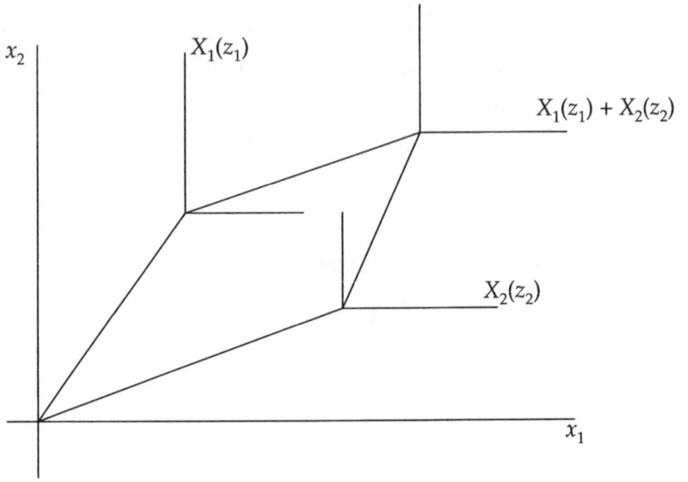

Figure 2.11 Input set for state-allocable technology.

state case that $X(\boldsymbol{z}) = \cap_{s=1}^{S} X_s(z_s)$, *where* $X_s(\boldsymbol{z}_s) = \{\boldsymbol{x}: z_s \leq f_s(\boldsymbol{x})\}$. *Consider now the input set for the state-allocable input model illustrated in Figures 2.4 and 2.5. There the input set corresponds to the sum of the inputs needed for deploying irrigation and water-catchment facilities. If we now (in a slight abuse of notation) use* $X_s(z_s)$ *to denote* $\{\boldsymbol{x}^s: z_s \leq f(\boldsymbol{x}^s, s)\}$, *it is immediate in the case of* S *states of nature that for the state-allocable input model* $X(\boldsymbol{z}) = \Sigma_{s=1}^{S} X_s(z_s)$.

Graphically, this is perhaps easiest to see in the case where the production function for each state exhibits fixed coefficients. When there are two states and two inputs, the situation is as depicted in Figure 2.11. The minimal amount of inputs that can be committed to production in each state is given by the vectors defining the lower vertices of $X_1(z_1)$ *and* $X_2(z_2)$. *Hence, the minimal amount of inputs that can produce both* z_1 *and* z_2 *is given by the vector arrived at by summing the vectors defining these vertices. This operation defines a fixed-coefficients technology, as illustrated in Figure 2.11.*

Building on the discussion in Example 2.1 and the formal relationship between input and output sets, the reader should be able to establish that if $X(\boldsymbol{z}) = \Sigma_{s=1}^{S} X_s(z_s)$ *with each* $X_s(z_s) \subseteq \Re_+^N$ *and satisfying X.1, X.2, X.3.W, X.4, X.5, and X.8, the state-contingent technology can be completely described by a set of nondecreas-*

ing and quasi-concave state-contingent production functions $f_s(\boldsymbol{x}^s)$*, and* $X(z) = \Sigma_{s=1}^{S}\{\boldsymbol{x}^s : z_s \le f_s(\boldsymbol{x}^s)\}$.

2.6 A FUNCTIONAL REPRESENTATION OF THE STATE-CONTINGENT TECHNOLOGY: THE STATE-CONTINGENT OUTPUT-DISTANCE FUNCTION

Most economists are used to thinking of technologies in terms of production functions or, in the multiproduct case, in terms of product-transformation functions. Our specification of the technology, however, has relied almost completely on input and output correspondences and their resulting input and output sets. This follows in the tradition established by Arrow and Debreu in specifying state-contingent technologies. In many instances, however, it's convenient to have a summary of the technology that is expressible as a scalar-valued function. In what follows, we focus on state-contingent output-distance functions. However, in passing, we note that it is also easy to characterize the technology using the technological equivalents of the benefit functions that will be used to characterize preference functionals in Chapter 3.

Distance functions represent maximal contractions of input or output bundles that are consistent with production feasibility. The *state-contingent output-distance function*, $O:\Re_{+}^{M\times S} \times \Re_{+}^{N} \to \Re_{+}$, gives the maximal expansion of a given state-contingent output matrix, alternatively the largest contraction of the state-contingent output set, consistent with the state-contingent output matrix being producible for the given input bundle. This distance function is defined by

$$O(\mathbf{z},\mathbf{x}) = \inf\left\{\theta > 0 : \frac{\mathbf{z}}{\theta} \in Z(\mathbf{x})\right\}.$$

Heuristically, it is easiest to understand the state-contingent output distance function in terms of its pictorial representation. Consider Figure 2.12, in which we have depicted, for the single-output, two-state case, an output set consistent with weak output disposability and convexity of the output set but not with free output disposability. For the point $\mathbf{z}^*$, the state-contingent output-distance function is given by

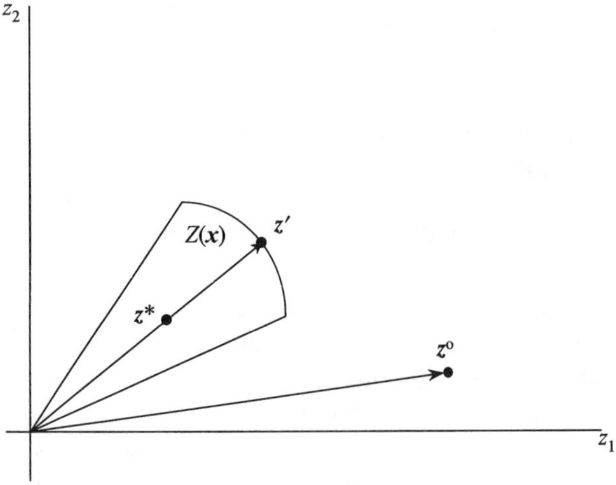

Figure 2.12 State-contingent output-distance function.

$|\mathbf{z}^*|/\|\mathbf{z}'\|$. Dividing $\mathbf{z}^*$ by this amount expands it radially to the frontier of $Z(\mathbf{x})$. Or, alternatively, multiplying $Z(\mathbf{x})$ by this amount shrinks the output set so that $\mathbf{z}^*$ just lies on its frontier. Notice that $O(\mathbf{z}^o, \mathbf{x}) = +\infty$ in Figure 2.12 because there is no way to radially shrink $\mathbf{z}^o$ and make it technically feasible.

The main properties of the state-contingent output-distance function are discussed in the Appendix. But, for our purposes, the most important property is that under weak disposability of output $O(\mathbf{z}, \mathbf{x})$ fully characterizes $Z(\mathbf{x})$, and, hence, $X(\mathbf{z})$ in the following sense:

$$O(\mathbf{z}, \mathbf{x}) \leq 1 \Leftrightarrow \mathbf{z} \in Z(\mathbf{x}).$$

The fact that the state-contingent output-distance function summarizes output sets under weak output disposability can be used to advantage. Define the frontier of $Z(\mathbf{x})$, which we denote as $\overline{Z}(\mathbf{x})$ by

$$\overline{Z}(\mathbf{x}) = \{\mathbf{z} : O(\mathbf{z}, \mathbf{x}) = 1\}.$$

Intuitively, this is just the state-contingent product-transformation curve.

When the state-contingent output-distance function is smoothly differentiable, the curvature of $\overline{Z}(\mathbf{x})$ in state-contingent output space, *the state-contingent marginal rate of transformation*, can be expressed always in terms of partial derivatives of $O(\mathbf{z}, \mathbf{x})$ in the state-contingent outputs. As we now illustrate, the state-contingent output-distance function is not always smoothly differentiable.

Example 2.3: *Consider the output-cubical technology:* $Z(\boldsymbol{x}) = \times_s Z_s(\boldsymbol{x})$, *with each* $Z_s(\boldsymbol{x}) \subseteq \Re_+$ *satisfying weak output disposability (Z.2.W). Its state-contingent output-distance function is given by*

$$O(z, \boldsymbol{x}) = inf\left\{\theta > 0 : \frac{z}{\theta} \in \times_s Z_s(\boldsymbol{x})\right\}$$
$$= inf\left\{\theta > 0 : \frac{z_s}{\theta} \in Z_s(\boldsymbol{x}), s = 1, 2, \ldots, S\right\}.$$

This last step implies that $O(z, \boldsymbol{x}) \geq O_s(z_s, \boldsymbol{x})$ *for each* s, *where* $O_s(z_s, \boldsymbol{x})$ *is now the output-distance function corresponding to* $Z_s(\boldsymbol{x})$. *Thus,* $O(z, \boldsymbol{x}) = max\{O_s(z_s, \boldsymbol{x}), s = 1, 2, \ldots, S\}$. *In this case, the state-contingent distance function is at best piecewise differentiable. The nondifferentiability of the output-distance function for the output-cubical case is the mathematical reflection of the inability of state-contingent outputs to substitute for one another as it implies that the state-contingent marginal rate of transformation is zero. Also, by recalling our definition of the state-contingent production functions as* $f_s(\boldsymbol{x}) = max\{Z_s(\boldsymbol{x})\}$, *it follows immediately that* $O_s(z_s, \boldsymbol{x}) = z_s/f_s(\boldsymbol{x})$, *so that*

$$O(z, \boldsymbol{x}) = max\{z_s/f_s(\boldsymbol{x}), s = 1, 2, \ldots, S\}.$$

Example 2.4: *Now suppose that* $M = 1$, $S = 2$, *and that* $O(z, \boldsymbol{x})$ *is differentiable everywhere. Then the rate at which* z_1 *is transformed into* z_2 *is given by*

$$\frac{\partial z_2}{\partial z_1} = -\frac{\partial O(z, \boldsymbol{x})/\partial z_1}{\partial O(z, \boldsymbol{x})/\partial z_2}. \quad (2.1)$$

Also suppose that the individual producer is the residual claimant of the production process and risk-averse, with her attitudes toward risk being determined by the expected-utility function:

$$\pi_1 u(z_1) + \pi_2 u(z_2),$$

where $u : \Re \to \Re$ *is a strictly increasing and strictly concave differentiable utility function. As we will illustrate in Chapter 3, her*

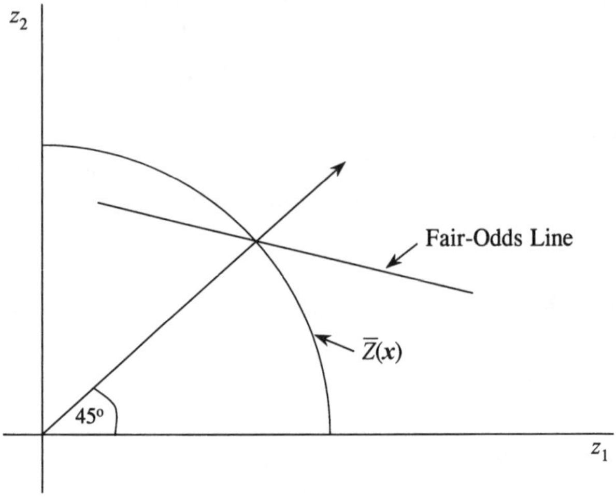

Figure 2.13 Good and bad states of nature.

indifference curves in state-contingent output space have slopes equalling $-\pi_1 u'(z_1)/\pi_2 u'(z_2)$, *which always equals* $-\pi_1/\pi_2$, *the slope of the fair-odds line, along the bisector.*

Suppose further that along the bisector:

$$\frac{\pi_1}{\pi_2} > \frac{\partial O(\boldsymbol{z}, \boldsymbol{x})/\partial z_1}{\partial O(\boldsymbol{z}, \boldsymbol{x})/\partial z_2},$$

as illustrated in Figure 2.13. In this case, points on $\overline{Z}(\boldsymbol{x})$ *immediately above the bisector will be strictly preferred by the producer (for a given commitment of* $\boldsymbol{x}$*) to points immediately below the bisector. Hence, the producer adopts a production pattern where* $z_2 \geq z_1$ *because the producer can always increase expected utility without incurring any additional cost. Loosely speaking, therefore, state-2 is perceived by risk-averse individuals as the "good" state of nature and state-1 is perceived by risk-averse individuals as the "bad" state, because, for given* $\boldsymbol{x}$*, a risk-averse producer will always choose to have more output produced in the second than in the first state.*

This example illustrates at least two important points. First, the state-contingent marginal rate of transformation offers a method of measuring the inherent local riskiness of the technology. (We will have more to say about the inherent riskiness of technologies in Chapter 4.) And second, whether a risk averter prefers any particular combination of state-contingent outputs depends both on her attitudes toward risk and on the production technology. Moreover, in general, there is no reason to expect that, for all levels of input commitment, a producer will always choose the same states of nature in which to produce relatively high and low outputs. To visualize this last point, perform a simple thought experiment. Imagine for the moment that engaging a strictly larger input bundle shifts $\overline{Z}(\mathbf{x})$ in Figure 2.13 outward in a nonneutral fashion so that for the now higher input bundle, $\mathbf{x}^*$, we have along the bisector

$$\frac{\pi_1}{\pi_2} \leq \frac{\partial O(\mathbf{z},\mathbf{x})/\partial z_1}{\partial O(\mathbf{z},\mathbf{x})/\partial z_2}. \tag{2.2}$$

For an input commitment of $\mathbf{x}^*$, a risk-averse producer would always choose to be immediately below the bisector rather than immediately above the bisector.

2.7 THE STRUCTURE OF STATE-CONTINGENT TECHNOLOGIES

So far, the only assumptions that we have placed on the technology are those summarized by Z.1 to Z.8 (alternatively, X.1 to X.8). In many instances, these restrictions will enable us to say a lot about producer decision making under uncertainty. In other circumstances, however, we need specific functional forms if we are to make analytical or empirical progress. In earlier Examples 2.1 and 2.2, we have already seen that when

$$Z(\mathbf{x}) = \times_s Z_s(\mathbf{x}),$$

where each $Z_s \subseteq \Re_+$, we can always rewrite the state-contingent technology in terms of state-contingent production functions, each depending on the entire vector of inputs committed. Similarly, when

$$X(\mathbf{z}) = \textstyle\sum_s X_s(z_s),$$

with each $X_s(z_s) \subseteq \Re_+^N$, we can always rewrite the state-contingent technology in terms of state-contingent production functions, each depending only on the vector of inputs committed, for example, to state s production. The first structural restrictions that we consider on the state-contingent technology are the natural multiple-output generalizations of these special cases.

2.7.1 Output-Cubical Technologies

The state-contingent technology described by either $Z(\mathbf{x})$ or $X(\mathbf{z})$ is said to be *output-cubical* or *nonsubstitutable in state-contingent outputs* if

$$Z(\mathbf{x}) = \times_s Z_s(\mathbf{x}),$$

where each $Z_s \subseteq \Re^M_+$. When the technology is output-cubical, the input set can be written

$$X(\mathbf{z}) = \cap_s X_s(\mathbf{z}_s),$$

with each $X_s(\mathbf{z}_s) \subseteq \Re^N_+$, and where we remind the reader that $\mathbf{z}_s \in \Re^M_+$ denotes an M-dimensional vector of outputs produced when state s occurs.

The important thing to remember about the output-cubical formulation is that it need not restrict the range of substitutability between separate outputs in the same state, but it does restrict interstate substitutability. For example, the producer deciding to uniformly decrease all outputs produced in a single state has no impact on the ability to produce any vector of outputs in other states as long as the total endowment of inputs is fixed. The output-cubical technology can be viewed heuristically as the state-contingent technology that is obtained by the simple expedient of stochastifying output sets (more appropriately output correspondences) in the same fashion that the stochastic-production-function approach stochastifies scalar-valued production functions. (Krug [1976] contains a measure-theoretic treatment of this type of stochastified output correspondence. Färe and Primont [1995] also consider this type of technology.)

2.7.2 State-Allocable Inputs

The state-contingent technology exhibits state-allocable inputs if

$$X(\mathbf{z}) = \sum_{s \in \Omega} X_s(\mathbf{z}_s),$$

where each $X_s(\mathbf{z}_s) \subseteq \Re_+^N$. (The state-allocable input model in the scalar-output single-state case is formally equivalent to the input nonjoint nonstochastic-production model. See, for example, Chambers [1988], Chapter 7.) Alternatively, the state-allocable input technology can be represented in terms of its state-contingent output set as

$$Z(\mathbf{x}) = \left\{ \times_s Z_s(\mathbf{x}^s) : \sum_{s \in \Omega} \mathbf{x}^s \leq \mathbf{x} \right\},$$

with each $Z_s(\mathbf{x}^s) \subseteq \Re_+^M$. The state-contingent output distance function with state-allocable inputs can be written

$$O(\mathbf{z}, \mathbf{x}) = \inf\left\{ \max\{O_s(\mathbf{z}_s, \mathbf{x}^s), s = 1, 2, \ldots, S\} : \sum_{s \in \Omega} \mathbf{x}^s \leq \mathbf{x} \right\}.$$

The state-allocable input model encompasses substitutability between state-contingent outputs both across states of nature and within states of nature. Once the inputs allocated to a given state of nature are determined, one can represent the range of outputs that may occur in that state of nature by a multiple-output correspondence that is specific to the state. As with the input nonjoint production model, it is the competition for allocable inputs across states that gives rise to production substitutability across states of nature. Uniformly decreasing all outputs in any given state of nature frees some inputs that can be reallocated to other states of nature, so it is possible to increase production in other states of nature while still committing the same total bundle of inputs. The reader, perhaps, can visualize this substitution process by returning to Figure 2.9. For any fixed allocation of inputs with scalar outputs in each state, the state-contingent output set is the S-dimensional generalization of the cube depicted in Figure 2.9. However, as inputs are reallocated between the various states, the base, width, and height of the cube will change in response to the input reallocation. As all possible reallocations are considered, one can then imagine the "point" of the cube shifting through S-space to trace out a production possibilities curve in response to the changing input allocations.

2.7.3 Output-Homothetic, State-Contingent Output Correspondences

Under the stochastic production-function formulation of uncertain production, it is usual to assume that the production function is strictly monotonic (usually strictly increasing) in the random input or random variable. In Figure 2.1, this is reflected in the production function for $\theta = 2$ always being higher than the production function for $\theta = 1$. Intuitively, therefore, one might be excused for thinking of $\theta = 2$ reflecting a "good" state of nature and $\theta = 1$ reflecting a "bad" state of nature. In state-contingent output space, for example, Figures 2.2 and 2.3, this property of the stochastic production function translates into the vertex of the output set always lying above the bisector. However, as we demonstrated in Examples 2.3 and 2.4, whether a particular state of nature is a good or bad state of nature depends critically on the producer's attitudes toward risk, as well as on the properties of state-contingent output sets. In particular, changing the endowment of inputs committed to production can have important implications for whether one state is a good or bad state. It is, therefore, important to examine technological structures in which whether a state of nature is good or bad is independent of the level of inputs committed. Such an example is given by a technology that is state-contingent output-homothetic (Färe and Primont 1995), that is,

$$Z(\mathbf{x}) = z(\mathbf{x})\mathbf{Z}',$$

where $z : \Re_+^N \to \Re_{++}$, and $\mathbf{Z}' \subseteq \Re_+^{M \times S}$ is an output set for a fixed (reference) bundle of inputs. State-contingent output-homotheticity thus implies that all state-contingent output sets can be described as radial expansions of $\mathbf{Z}'$. Accordingly, the choice of the reference bundle of state-contingent inputs is essentially arbitrary.

For the state-contingent output-homothetic case, it follows easily that

$$\begin{aligned} O(\mathbf{z}, \mathbf{x}) &= \inf\left\{\theta > 0 : \frac{\mathbf{z}}{\theta} \in z(\mathbf{x})\mathbf{Z}'\right\} \\ &= z(\mathbf{x})^{-1} \inf\left\{\theta z(\mathbf{x}) > 0 : \frac{\mathbf{z}}{\theta} \in z(\mathbf{x})\mathbf{Z}'\right\} \\ &= \frac{\hat{O}(\mathbf{z})}{z(\mathbf{x})}, \end{aligned}$$

where $\hat{O}(\mathbf{z})$ is the state-contingent output distance function for $\mathbf{Z}'$. From this representation, it follows immediately that the state-contingent marginal rate of transformation,

$$\frac{\partial \hat{O}(\mathbf{z})/\partial z_r}{\partial \hat{O}(\mathbf{z})/\partial z_s},$$

is independent of the level of inputs committed.

2.7.4 Input-Homothetic Input Correspondences

A technology is input-homothetic (Färe and Mitchell 1992) if its input sets can be written as

$$X(\mathbf{z}) = x(\mathbf{z})\mathbf{X}',$$

where $x:\Re_+^{M\times S} \to \Re_{++}$, and $\mathbf{X}' \subseteq \Re_+^N$ is an input set for a reference bundle of state-contingent outputs. Thus, input homotheticity implies that the input correspondence is defined as the product of a reference input set and a scalar-valued function of the outputs. Geometrically, it means that input sets for differing state-contingent output matrices are all radial expansions of a common reference set. Under weak disposability of inputs, the state-contingent output-distance function for an input-homothetic input correspondence can be written

$$O(\mathbf{z}, \mathbf{x}) = O^*(\mathbf{z}, h(\mathbf{x})),$$

where h is a positively linearly homogeneous and concave function of $\mathbf{x}$, and O^* is defined by $O^*(\mathbf{z}, h) = \inf\{\theta > 0 : x(\mathbf{z}/\theta) \leq h\}$. Because h is positively linearly homogeneous in inputs, the state-contingent output-distance function for an input-homothetic input correspondence will always be homothetic in inputs.

2.7.5 Completely (Inversely) Homothetic Technologies

A technology is completely (inversely) homothetic (Shephard 1970) if it is has both input-homothetic input correspondences and output-homothetic output correspondences. A technology is completely homothetic if and only if it is input-homothetic and output-homothetic and $x(\mathbf{z})$, as defined before, is a homothetic function of $\mathbf{z}$ and $z(\mathbf{x})$, as defined before, is a homothetic function of $\mathbf{x}$. The state-contingent output-distance function for a completely homothetic technology is expressible in the same form as one for an output-homothetic technology with the appropriate restriction on $z(\mathbf{x})$.

2.7.6 Homogeneous Technologies

A condition that encompasses both input homotheticity and output homotheticity is homogeneity. A state-contingent technology is homogeneous if its output correspondence is homogeneous. That is, a technology is homogeneous if $Z(\mu\mathbf{x}) = \mu^k Z(\mathbf{x})$ for all $\mu > 0$. The state-contingent output-distance function for such a technology satisfies:

$$O(\mathbf{z}, \mu\mathbf{x}) = \mu^{-k} O(\mathbf{z}, \mathbf{x}).$$

2.7.7 Output Translation Homotheticity

A state-contingent technology is said to be output translation-homothetic (Chambers and Färe 1998) if all output sets can be represented as appropriate translations of a reference output set. It is to be compared directly to output homotheticity where all output sets can be represented as radial expansions or contractions of a reference output set. More formally, a technology is output translation-homothetic if

$$Z(\mathbf{x}) = z(\mathbf{x}, \mathbf{g})\mathbf{g} + Z',$$

where $\mathbf{g} \in \Re_+^{M \times S}$, $z : \Re_+^N \times \Re_+^{M \times S} \to \Re_{++}$, and $\mathbf{Z}' \subseteq \Re_+^{M \times S}$ is an output set for a reference bundle of inputs.

2.7.8 Eliminating Uncertainty

Economists usually perceive randomness in output as something that can be avoided only at significant cost. For example, if we consider the traditional example of stochastic production – agriculture – we can easily conceive of costly production practices that are devoted to controlling the degree of randomness. Examples include greenhouses and irrigation equipment. However, one of the main strengths of the state-contingent approach that we are advocating is that *the degree of randomness of production is ultimately the subject of producer choice*. Only rarely has the literature on production under uncertainty admitted this basic characteristic of real-world production practices. More commonly, it has contented itself with examining two polar cases: no uncertainty in production and uncontrollable uncertainty. Neither case is particularly realistic.

Producers faced with a general state-contingent technology will rarely choose to generate a nonstochastic output, that is, to equalize outputs across states. Even so, it would seem useful, if only for comparative purposes, to have a notion of a technology where avoiding uncertainty is feasible, but where production also need not be certain.

We have already observed that if Z.2 (free disposability of output) is satisfied, the producer can always achieve certainty by discarding the "excess" output from high-output states. That is, given any feasible $(\mathbf{z}, \mathbf{x})$, free disposability of output implies that it is always possible to produce $(\mathbf{zmin}, \mathbf{x})$ where $\mathbf{zmin}$ is the vector with every entry equal to $\min\{\mathbf{z}_s\}$. However, in any situation where the producer is the residual claimant, or any agency situation in which payments are monotonic in output, this possibility is not very interesting.

A more interesting case arises when we strengthen Z.5 to require that $Z(\mathbf{x})$ be strictly convex for all $\mathbf{x} \in \Re_+^N$. In this case, it is evident that, contingent on a given $\mathbf{x}$, there is always a positive marginal rate of substitution between state-contingent outputs. In particular, this will be true in a neighborhood of any certain output, that is, along the bisector. Hence, under appropriate conditions on the relative valuation of different state-contingent outputs, a producer with monotonic preferences may rationally choose to equalize outputs across states.

2.7.9 Schur-Convex Technologies

Under fairly weak conditions on the technology, the producer can achieve a certain (that is, equal across states) output at some cost. However, since there is no reason to suppose, in general, that producers will choose to equalize state-contingent outputs, the existence of this possibility does not, in itself, provide an analog for the certainty case in the traditional analysis. For that, what is needed is a case in which, assuming outputs in different states of nature are valued equally, producers will choose to equalize outputs across states. Observationally, in the absence of incentives to vary outputs across states, technologies of this kind will appear to be certain. However, the technology will be more flexible than that considered in the standard analysis, since producers can vary state-contingent outputs if outputs are differentially valued or if preferences are nonconvex.

Such a case is given by what we shall refer to as Schur-convex input correspondences. *When we consider Schur-convex input correspondences, we shall always restrict attention to the case where $M = 1$*, that is, there is a single stochastic output.

An input correspondence is Schur-convex if $X: \Re_+^S \to \Re_+^N$ satisfies

$$\mathbf{z}' \preccurlyeq_m \mathbf{z} \Rightarrow X(\mathbf{z}) \subseteq X(\mathbf{z}'),$$

where $\mathbf{a} \preccurlyeq_m \mathbf{b}$ (stated as $\mathbf{a}$ is majorized by $\mathbf{b}$) means that the elements of vectors $\mathbf{a}$ and $\mathbf{b}$ sum to the same amount but that, in a sense we shall formalize, $\mathbf{a}$ is less dispersed than $\mathbf{b}$. Several equivalent definitions of majorization (Marshall and Olkin 1979) are available:

$$\sum_{i=1}^{s} a_{[i]} \geq \sum_{i=1}^{s} b_{[i]}, \qquad s = 1, \ldots, S,$$

and

$$\mathbf{a} = \mathbf{b}P$$

for some doubly stochastic matrix[5] P. Here $a_{[k]}$, for example, denotes the kth element of the increasing rearrangement of $\mathbf{a}$, which we label $\mathbf{a}_{[]}$.[6] In the equal probability case, $\mathbf{a} \preccurlyeq_m \mathbf{b}$ means that vectors $\mathbf{a}$ and $\mathbf{b}$ have the same expectation but that $\mathbf{a}$ is less risky than $\mathbf{b}$ in the Rothschild–Stiglitz sense (Chapter 3, Section 3.4.2).

Schur convexity implies that if $\mathbf{x}$ can produce $\mathbf{z}$, it can always produce any other S-dimensional state-contingent output vector that is majorized by $\mathbf{z}$. It thus follows immediately that a state-contingent technology is Schur-convex if $\mathbf{z}' \preccurlyeq_m \mathbf{z} \in Z(\mathbf{x})$ implies that $\mathbf{z}' \in Z(\mathbf{x})$.

5. A matrix is doubly stochastic (bistochastic) if all its elements are positive and all its rows and columns sum to 1.
6. That is, the element of vector $\mathbf{a}$ is rank-ordered so that $\mathbf{a}_{[1]} \leq a_{[2]} \leq \ldots \leq a_{[S]}$.

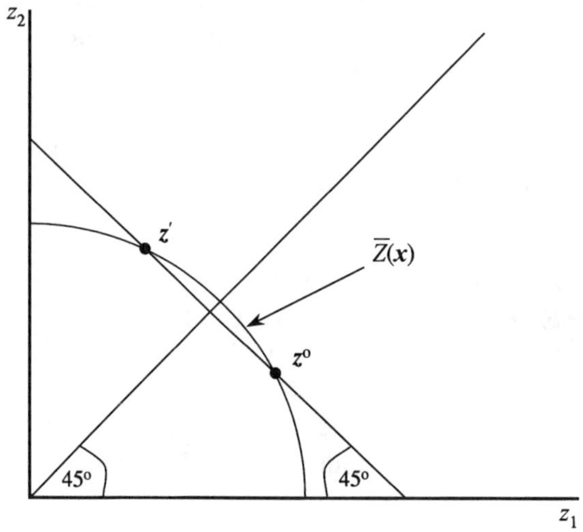

Figure 2.14 A Schur-convex output set.

Now because the ordering $\preccurlyeq_m$ is preserved by multiplying all elements of $\mathbf{z}'$ and $\mathbf{z}$ by the same positive scalar, it follows immediately by the definition of the state-contingent output-distance function and Schur convexity that $\mathbf{z}' \preccurlyeq_m \mathbf{z}$ implies

$$\frac{\mathbf{z}'}{O(\mathbf{z}, \mathbf{x})} \preccurlyeq_m \frac{\mathbf{z}}{O(\mathbf{z}, \mathbf{x})} \in Z(\mathbf{x}),$$

whence

$$\mathbf{z}' \preccurlyeq_m \mathbf{z} \Rightarrow O(\mathbf{z}', \mathbf{x}) \leq O(\mathbf{z}, \mathbf{x}).$$

Geometrically, it is easiest to see what Schur convexity implies by considering the case in which $S = 2$. Consider a single point $\mathbf{z}^o$ in Figure 2.14. All points on the negatively-sloped line segment, with slope equaling minus one, running through $\mathbf{z}^o$ in the figure have the same sum. Notice, however, that all points lying on the line segment to the southeast of $\mathbf{z}^o$ have the same sum but are more dispersed than $\mathbf{z}^o$. However, all points to the northwest of $\mathbf{z}^o$ but lying no farther to the northwest than the permutation of $\mathbf{z}^o$ (labeled $\mathbf{z}'$) also have the same sum and are less dispersed than $\mathbf{z}^o$. Thus, if the state-contingent output correspondence is Schur-convex and $\mathbf{z}^o$ is producible using $\mathbf{x}$, all points lying between $\mathbf{z}^o$ and $\mathbf{z}'$ must also be producible. Thus, an output correspondence is Schur-convex if it generates output sets that are symmetric around the bisector. (The reader might note that an extreme form of Schur convexity is given by a state-contingent production function exhibiting weak disposability of output with $f_2(\mathbf{x}) = f_1(\mathbf{x})$ for all $\mathbf{x}$, that is, certainty.)

2.8 APPENDIX: PROPERTIES OF THE STATE-CONTINGENT OUTPUT-DISTANCE FUNCTION

The most important property of the output-distance function is that, under weak disposability of output, it fully characterizes $Z(\mathbf{x})$, and hence $X(\mathbf{z})$.

This property is summarized by

$$O(\mathbf{z}, \mathbf{x}) \leq 1 \Leftrightarrow \mathbf{z} \in Z(\mathbf{x}),$$

if $Z(\mathbf{x})$ satisfies Z.2.W. Demonstrating this fact is easy. First, suppose that $\mathbf{z} \in Z(\mathbf{x})$, but that $O(\mathbf{z}, \mathbf{x}) > 1$. Because $\mathbf{z}/O(\mathbf{z}, \mathbf{x}) \in Z(\mathbf{x})$, this violates the definition of the state-contingent output-distance function as the minimal scalar by which the output set can be shrunk radially. Hence, $\mathbf{z} \in Z(\mathbf{x}) \Rightarrow O(\mathbf{z}, \mathbf{x}) \leq 1$. Now, on the other hand, suppose that $O(\mathbf{z}, \mathbf{x}) \leq 1$. It follows by weak disposability of state-contingent outputs that $\mathbf{z} \leq \mathbf{z}/O(\mathbf{z}, \mathbf{x}) \in Z(\mathbf{x})$, $\mathbf{z}$ must be closer to the origin on a state-contingent output ray than another state-contingent output matrix that belongs to $Z(\mathbf{x})$. Hence, $O(\mathbf{z}, \mathbf{x}) \leq 1 \Rightarrow \mathbf{z} \in Z(\mathbf{x})$ by weak output disposability.

Besides the fact that under weak disposability of state-contingent outputs, $O(\mathbf{z}, \mathbf{x})$ provides a summary measure of the state-contingent technology, $O(\mathbf{z}, \mathbf{x})$ also satisfies the following set of properties (Färe [1988]) that correspond to Z.1 to Z.8:

Properties of the state-contingent output-distance function (Z′)

Z′.1. $O(\mathbf{0}_{M\times S}, \mathbf{x}) = 0$; $\mathbf{x} \in \Re_+^N$; $O(\mathbf{z}, \mathbf{0}_N) = +\infty$, for all $\mathbf{z} \geq \mathbf{0}_{M\times S}$
Z′.2. For all $\mathbf{x} \in \Re_+^N$, $\mathbf{z}' \geq \mathbf{z} \Rightarrow O(\mathbf{z}', \mathbf{x}) \geq O(\mathbf{z}, \mathbf{x})$
Z′.2.W. For all $\mathbf{x} \in \Re_+^N$, $O(\mathbf{z}, \mathbf{x}) \geq O(\lambda\mathbf{z}, \mathbf{x})$ for $0 < \lambda < 1$
Z′.3. For all $\mathbf{z} \in \Re_+^{M\times S}$, $\mathbf{x}' \geq \mathbf{x} \Rightarrow O(\mathbf{z}, \mathbf{x}') \leq O(\mathbf{z}, \mathbf{x})$

Z′.3.W. For all $\mathbf{z} \in \Re_+^{M\times S}$, $O(\mathbf{z},\lambda\mathbf{x}) \leq O(\mathbf{z},\mathbf{x})$ for $\lambda > 1$
Z′.4. For all $\mathbf{x} \in \Re_+^N$, $O(\lambda\mathbf{z},\mathbf{x}) = \lambda O(\mathbf{z},\mathbf{x})$ for $\lambda > 0$
Z′.5. For all $\mathbf{x} \in \Re_+^N$, $O(\mathbf{z},\mathbf{x})$ is convex on $\Re_+^{M\times S}$
Z′.6. For all $\mathbf{z} \in \Re_+^{M\times S}$, $O(\mathbf{z},\mathbf{x})$ is quasi-convex on $\Re_+^N$
Z′.8. $O(\mathbf{z},\mathbf{x})$ is lower semicontinuous on $\Re_+^{M\times S} \times \Re_+^N$

The natural dual to the state-contingent output-distance function is the state-contingent input-distance function, defined as

$$I(\mathbf{z},\mathbf{x}) = \sup\left\{\mu > 0 : \frac{\mathbf{x}}{\mu} \in X(\mathbf{z})\right\},$$

which fully characterizes $Z(\mathbf{x})$ and $X(\mathbf{z})$ under weak disposability of inputs. We shall not have occasion to use the state-contingent input-distance function in what follows, but readers can refer to Färe (1988) for a general discussion of such functions for nonstochastic technologies.

3 Risk Aversion, Preferences, and Probability

There is a natural symmetry between producer choices over state-contingent production sets and consumer choices over state-contingent consumption sets. Tools developed for the analysis of production choices have natural analogs in the analysis of consumption choices and vice versa. An approach that exploits this symmetry entails a distinctive treatment of consumer preferences under uncertainty and, particularly, a distinctive interpretation of the concepts of risk aversion and probability. The distinction between technology and preferences is drawn differently in the state-contingent approach than in the parametrized distribution and outcome-state representations. This divergence is particularly evident in the treatment of the concept of probability.

In the parametrized distribution and outcome-state representations, the probabilities associated with the different states are treated as objectively given (although amenable to manipulation by altering the action or input vector). The critical question is: How can these objective probabilities be defined and observed?

Of the many answers that have been offered to this question, the most plausible, considered as a basis for an objective notion of probability, is based on relative frequency. The *frequentist* answer restricts the definition of probability to situations that may be regarded as draws from an infinite sample and defines the probability of any event as the limit to which its frequency of occurrence converges in an infinite series of draws. Apart from logical difficulties associated with this definition, it cannot be usefully applied to a wide range of economic problems involving uncertain choices in situations that are unique or will only be repeated a few times.

Our view, which may be traced back to the work of de Finetti (1974) and Savage (1954), is that probabilities used in economic decision making are inherently *subjective*. Consequently, probabilities can only be inferred from the observed behavior of decision makers, and are inseparably tied to beliefs and preferences. A logical consequence of this position is the recognition that any statement about subjective probabilities is ultimately a statement about the decision maker's beliefs and preferences. Therefore, intermingling probabilities with the technology of production, as is done in the parametrized distribution formulation, represents an important logical confusion. We argue that it also leads to analytical difficulties.

In this chapter, we first discuss the general problem of evaluating state-contingent outcomes. After that, we review the leading candidates for objective functions that currently exist in the literature. Then we turn to a discussion of our notion of risk aversion and its implication for decision making under uncertainty. After examining the notions of the certainty equivalent and risk premiums in our framework, we discuss increases in risk and the related notions of generalized Schur-concave preferences.

3.1 UTILITY AND THE FORM OF THE OBJECTIVE FUNCTION

The Arrow–Debreu analysis of uncertain markets places relatively weak restrictions on preferences over state-contingent commodities. All that's really required is that demand functions have their usual properties. Using standard assumptions about production sets and endowments, the existence of a competitive equilibrium in the presence of a full set of state-contingent markets can be established, provided that consumer preferences can be described by a quasi-concave mapping (that is, one having convex-to-the-origin indifference surfaces) $W: Y^S \to \Re$, where Y denotes a generic outcome space with typical element y. In general, we'll be considering cases where state-contingent markets are much more restricted. Therefore, we'll generally need stronger assumptions about preferences.

Suppose, for example, that there are two states of nature. For the purpose of demonstrating the existence of competitive equilibrium, there is no need to consider whether there is a closer substitution relationship between, say, butter in state 1 and margarine in state 1 than between butter in state 1 and margarine in state 2. But given that state 1 occurs, one's demand for butter is likely affected much more by one's actual consumption of margarine in state 1 than by the margarine that would have been consumed had state 2 occurred. In more familiar economic terms, one might argue that, in an individual's preference structure, state-1 consumption is *separable* from state-2 consumption.

Taking this argument a little further, it seems reasonable that attitudes about the relative desirability of different outcomes in a given state of nature will be, in some sense, independent of what might have happened in a different state of nature. Furthermore, with an appropriate specification of the output space, it's frequently reasonable to suppose that decision makers care only about the outcome they receive and not about the state of nature per se.[1] This seems especially true when the decision makers involved are producers. An example: Suppose the decision maker is a farmer and that the state of nature is determined by differing weather and market conditions. If any two distinct states of nature yield the same return for the farmer's crop (for example, good weather but low prices and bad weather and high prices), it's unlikely that the farmer would inherently prefer one state to the other. Ex post, he or she is left with the same return.

We are, therefore, led to focus on the case when outcomes can be expressed in monetary terms, so that our generic outcome space can be narrowed to $Y \subseteq \Re$, and the associated vector of state-contingent outcomes, $\mathbf{y}$, is an element of $\Re^S$. In the state-contingent production framework, however, producers choose elements of $(\mathbf{z}, \mathbf{x})$ subject to their being feasible. Given that state s has been realized, the variables relevant to the decision maker's welfare in the production problem are the committed inputs $\mathbf{x}$ and the realized vector of outputs $\mathbf{z}_s \in \Re^M_+$. The committed inputs are the same in every state of nature while the outputs are state-specific. We uniformly assume that the state-contingent utility function exhibits a degree of separability

1. Hirshleifer and Riley (1992) contain a thorough discussion of state-dependent utility structures.

between the effort $\mathbf{x}$ committed prior to the realization of the state of nature and the returns $r_s(\mathbf{z}_s) \in \Re_+$ received when the state of nature s is realized.

If outputs are sold in a competitive market, $r_s(\mathbf{z}_s)$ takes a particularly natural and convenient form as the producer's gross revenue in state s. Let $\mathbf{p} \in \Re_{++}^{M \times S}$ denote a matrix of state-contingent output prices that the producer takes as given. The interpretation of $\mathbf{p}$ parallels that of $\mathbf{z}$. If state s occurs, then prices for the M commodities are given by the vector $\mathbf{p}_s \in \Re_{++}^M$. Revenue in state s is then given by

$$r_s(\mathbf{z}_s) = \sum_{m=1}^{M} p_{ms} z_{ms}.$$

Two special cases are of particular interest. We refer to them as the *net-returns model* and the (additively) *separable-effort model.* In the net-returns model, the presumption is that the producer's concern is with his or her ex post profit. Net return in state s, y_s, is given by the difference between revenue in state s and the producer's evaluation of the cost of producing that vector of state-contingent revenues. Notationally,

$$y_s = r_s - g(\mathbf{x}),$$

where $g: \Re_+^n \to \Re$ is an effort-evaluation function giving the producer's evaluation of the input vector. The most familiar example, of course, is a producer purchasing inputs in a market where all inputs are in perfectly elastic supply. That is, a vector of strictly positive input prices, $\mathbf{w} \in \Re_{++}^N$, exists at which the producer can purchase as much of each input as desired. We shall refer to this special case as *linear input pricing*. More generally, however, we want to allow for the case in which the producer's marginal evaluation of each input can respond nonlinearly to the amount of the inputs used. This generalization is particularly relevant for studying problems where $\mathbf{x}$ contains some nonpurchased, but still scarce and valuable, inputs. Examples here might include problems involving the allocation of family labor or personal time to production. The producer's evaluation of the vector of state-contingent net returns, $\mathbf{y} \in \Re^S$, is then given by a continuous, nondecreasing function $W: \Re^S \to \Re$,

$$W(y_1, y_2, \ldots, y_S).$$

The separable-effort model assumes that the producer is still concerned with both state-contingent revenue and the cost of the input vector, but that the producer's joint evaluation of revenue and effort is given by the additively separable form:

$$W(\mathbf{r}) - g(\mathbf{x}),$$

where now $W: \Re_+^S \to \Re$ is a continuous nondecreasing function giving the producer's evaluation of the vector of state-contingent revenues. To conserve on notation, we do not introduce separate notation for the function evaluating state-contingent incomes in the net returns case and the function evaluating state-contingent revenues in the separable-effort case.

Separable effort is a natural representation, for example, of peasant agricultural production, where the labor of the producer (an individual or household), for which there may not exist a well-functioning market, is the main input to production. Newbery and Stiglitz (1981, 1982), and many subsequent writers, have adopted this formulation in the analysis of price stabilization, and the separable-effort model has become the model of choice in the literature on moral hazard and incentives because of its analytical tractability.

Both in the net-returns specification and the separable-effort model, the function W provides an evaluation of state-contingent vectors, which implies that it makes interstate comparisons of outcomes.

3.2 EXAMPLES OF PREFERENCE FUNCTIONS

Most analysis of choice under uncertainty is based on the assumption that preferences may be described by the expected-utility model. This assumption implies strong restrictions on preferences, analogous to an assumption that the production technology is characterized by state-allocable inputs. There is a lively debate about the appropriateness of expected-utility theory as a description of observed preferences and as a normative guide to behavior. Regardless of one's position in this debate, it seems preferable to present and analyze a general model of state-contingent choices, and then to consider the implications of particular special cases, rather than to focus on a special case from the outset.

We now present some examples of preference functions $W: Y^S \to \Re$ that have been used in studies of choice under uncertainty. The simplest case, often assumed by default when uncertainty is disregarded, is that of risk neutrality or expected-value maximization.

Example 3.1: *Risk Neutrality*

$$W(\mathbf{y}) = \sum_{s \in \Omega} \pi_s y_s$$

for some probability vector $\boldsymbol{\pi}$ *in the unit simplex* $\Pi = \{\boldsymbol{\pi} \in \Re^S_{++}: \Sigma_{s \in \Omega}\pi_s = 1\}$.

In nonstochastic producer and consumer theory, linear and Leontief functions are polar cases reflecting extreme assumptions about commodity or factor substitutability. Having noted that linearity corresponds to risk neutrality, it is therefore no surprise that Leontief preferences reflect extreme risk aversion.

Example 3.2: *Leontief or Maximin Preferences*

$$W(\mathbf{y}) = \min\{y_1, y_2, \ldots, y_s\}.$$

Maximin preferences imply an exclusive focus on the worst possible outcome. This makes sense in the context of a zero-sum game (von Neumann and Morgenstern 1944). Modified versions of maximin, such as safety-first rules, have been proposed as normative decision rules.

Most economic analysis of choice under uncertainty has been based on the expected-utility model, which allows for a range of risk attitudes.

Example 3.3: *Expected Utility*

$$W(\mathbf{y}) = \sum_{s \in \Omega} \pi_s u(y_s)$$

for some probability vector π *in the unit simplex* $\Pi = \{\boldsymbol{\pi} \in \Re^S_{++}: \Sigma_{s \in \Omega}\pi_s = 1\}$ *and utility function* $u: \Re \to \Re$. *Risk neutrality is the special case of expected utility with linear* u. *However, maximin preferences cannot be represented by an expected-utility function.*

Until the 1980s, the only important alternative to expected utility was the mean-variance model.

Example 3.4: *Mean Variance*

$$W(\mathbf{y}) = v(\mu[\mathbf{y}], \sigma^2[\mathbf{y}]),$$

where $\mu[\mathbf{y}] = \Sigma_{s\in\Omega} \pi_s y_s, \sigma^2[\mathbf{y}] = \Sigma_{s=1}^{S} \pi_s (y_s - \Sigma_{s\in\Omega} \pi_s y_s)^2$, $v: \Re^2 \to \Re$. *The mean-variance model is consistent with expected utility only for the case of a quadratic utility function, which has some unattractive properties. In particular, a concave, quadratic utility function is decreasing for sufficiently large values of* y. *However, there are a wide range of mean-variance preference functions that are not consistent with expected utility, but are otherwise well-behaved. More generally, the variance* $\sigma^2[\mathbf{y}]$ *may be replaced by any index of riskiness.*

Machina's (1982) seminal article showed that many of the desirable properties of expected-utility preferences carried over to more general preferences under plausible conditions. A wide variety of generalized expected-utility models have been developed since the early 1980s. Much attention, in particular, has been focused on rank-dependent models (Quiggin 1982; Yaari 1987; Schmeidler 1989). As the name implies the rank-dependent model is applied to the increasing rearrangement $\mathbf{y}_{[]}$ of $\mathbf{y}$, which satisfies $y_{[1]} \leq y_{[2]} \leq \ldots \leq y_{[S]}$.

Example 3.5: *Rank-Dependent Expected Utility*

$$W(\mathbf{y}) = \sum_{s\in\Omega} h_{[s]}(\boldsymbol{\pi}) u(y_{[s]})$$

where $\boldsymbol{\pi} \in \Pi$, $u: \Re \to \Re$, *and* $h_{[s]}(\boldsymbol{\pi})$ *is a probability weight such that*

$$h_{[s]}(\boldsymbol{\pi}) = q\left(\sum_{t=1}^{s} \pi_{[t]}\right) - q\left(\sum_{t=1}^{s-1} \pi_{[t]}\right)$$

for a transformation function $q: [0,1] \to [0,1]$ *with* $q(0) = 0$, $q(1) = 1$. *Note that*

$$\sum_{s\in\Omega} h_{[s]}(\boldsymbol{\pi}) = q\left(\sum_{t=1}^{S} \pi_{[t]}\right) = q(1) = 1$$

so that the decision weights sum to 1. The basic idea of the rank-dependent approach is that more weight may be placed on extreme outcomes than on intermediate outcomes. In particular, maximin arises when $q(\pi_{[1]}) = 1$*, so that all the weight is placed on the worst outcome. Other special cases of the rank-dependent model include expected utility, which arises when* q *is linear, and Yaari's (1987) dual model, which arises when* u *is linear. Yaari's model may be interpreted as expected-value maximization with respect to rank-dependent transformed probabilities.*

Many other decision criteria discussed in the literature on choice under uncertainty may be interpreted as specifications of a preference function $W: Y^S \rightarrow \Re$. These examples have been selected because they have been used fairly widely and because they exhibit a range of properties that prove useful in analysis of behavior. For example, the expected-utility function is smoothly differentiable whenever u is smooth, and is also additively separable across states. Rank-dependent expected-utility preferences are consistent with a wide range of observed behavior, but sufficiently tractable to permit the derivation of sharp comparative static results in the stochastic production-function framework. Mean-variance analysis has the convenient property that all individuals with mean-variance preference agree on a definition of increasing risk, namely, that risk increases with variance.

3.3 RISK ATTITUDES

3.3.1 Benefit and Distance Functions

So far, we have talked in general terms of an individual's preferences as being represented by a nondecreasing continuous function, W, of state-contingent returns. For the most part, analysis of decision making under uncertainty has been carried out directly in terms of such preference functions. However, an important lesson learned in modern producer and consumer theory is that alternative representations of preferences often have analytic advantages. For example, Shephard's (1953) production–cost duality was originally developed between a distance function for the production function and the cost function, and not between the cost function and the production function itself. It turns out that considering alternative representations of preferences allows us to easily deduce important information about an individual's attitudes toward uncertain choices.

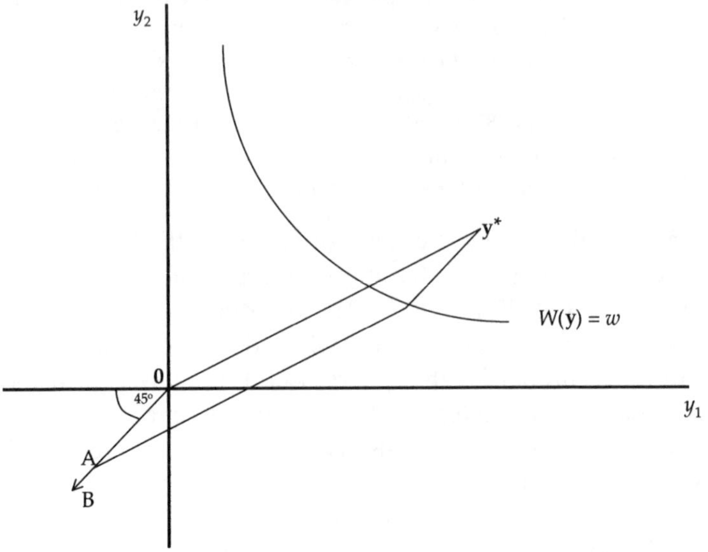

Figure 3.1 The benefit function.

Two alternative functional representations of preferences prove especially useful in our analysis. The first is a particular version of Luenberger's (1992) benefit function for the preference structure. For given $\mathbf{g} \in \Re^S_+$, the *benefit function*, $B: \Re \times Y^S \to \Re$, is defined by

$$B(w, \mathbf{y}) = \max\{\beta \in \Re : W(\mathbf{y} - \beta\mathbf{g}) \geq w\} \qquad \mathbf{g} \in \Re^S_+$$

if $W(\mathbf{y} - \beta\mathbf{g}) \geq w$ for some β, and $-\infty$ otherwise. The benefit function gives the largest translation of the state-contingent return vector $\mathbf{y}$ in the direction of the reference vector $-\mathbf{g}$ that is consistent with the translated vector yielding a preference level of at least w. It is illustrated in Figure 3.1 for the state-contingent income pair labeled $\mathbf{y}^*$ by the ratio OA/OB. There the reference vector is given by the equal-income vector, and, in what follows, because of the importance of translations parallel to the equal–income income ray in the analysis of risk attitudes, we shall always evaluate the benefit function for $\mathbf{g} = \mathbf{1}^S$. Blackorby and Donaldson (1978) refer to this version of the benefit function as the translation function.

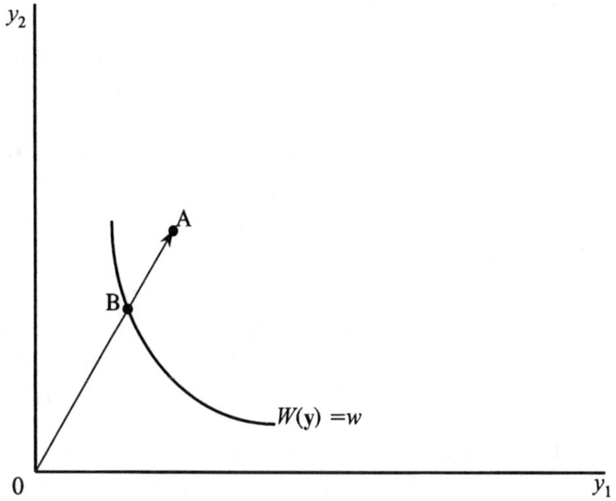

Figure 3.2 The distance function.

The second functional representation of preferences, which is relevant when $\mathbf{y}$ is restricted to be nonnegative,[2] is the Shephard (1953) – Malmquist (1953) distance function $D:\Re_+^S \times \Re \rightarrow \Re_+$ defined by

$$D(\mathbf{y}, w) = \sup\{\lambda > 0 : W(\mathbf{y}/\lambda) \geq w\} \qquad \mathbf{y} \in \Re_+^S.$$

Visually, the Shephard–Malmquist distance function for the preference structure is given by the largest radial contraction of the state-contingent return vector that is consistent with the radially contracted return vector still yielding a preference level of at least w. It is illustrated in Figure 3.2 by the ratio OA/OB for the point labeled A, and is the analog for preferences of the output-distance function considered in Chapter 2.

The properties of both of these functions are well-known (Blackorby and Donaldson 1978; Luenberger 1992; Chambers, Chung and Färe 1996; Färe 1988) and are summarized for later use in the following pair of lemmas:[3]

2. The reason for this requirement is that a radial expansion is assumed to be desirable, that is, $W(\lambda \mathbf{y}) \geq W(\mathbf{y})$ whenever $\lambda \geq 1$. The assumption of monotonicity implies that this is always true when $\mathbf{y} \in \Re_+^S$.
3. These lemmas presume that W is strictly increasing and continuous in all its arguments.

Lemma 3.1: $B(w, \mathbf{y})$ *satisfies:*

(a) $B(w, \mathbf{y})$ *is nonincreasing in* w *and nondecreasing in* $\mathbf{y}$
(b) $B(w, \mathbf{y} + \alpha 1^S) = B(w, \mathbf{y}) + \alpha$, $\alpha \in \Re$ *(the translation property)*
(c) $B(w, \mathbf{y}) \geq 0 \Leftrightarrow W(\mathbf{y}) \geq w$, *and* $B(w, \mathbf{y}) = 0 \Leftrightarrow W(\mathbf{y}) = w$; *and*
(d) $B(w, \mathbf{y})$ *is jointly continuous in* $\mathbf{y}$ *and* w *in the interior of the region* $\Re \times Y^S$, *where* $B(w, \mathbf{y})$ *is finite.*

Lemma 3.2: $D(\mathbf{y}, w)$ *satisfies:*

(a) $D(\mathbf{y}, w)$ *is nonincreasing in* w *and nondecreasing in* $\mathbf{y}$
(b) $D(\mu\mathbf{y}, w) = \mu D(\mathbf{y}, w)$, $\mu > 0$ *(positive linear homogeneity)*
(c) $D(\mathbf{y}, w) \geq 1 \Leftrightarrow W(\mathbf{y}) \geq w$, *and* $D(\mathbf{y}, w) = 1 \Leftrightarrow W(\mathbf{y}) = w$
(d) $D(\mathbf{y}, w)$ *is upper semicontinuous in* w *and* $\mathbf{y}$ *jointly.*

We wish like to highlight two properties that will prove particularly important in what follows. The first is that, by Lemma 3.1(c) and Lemma 3.2(c), both the benefit function and the distance function are alternative representations of the preference structure given by the function *W*. Hence, in considering preferences, we are free to use either the preference function itself, the benefit function, or the distance function. Our choice therefore, will be dictated by analytic convenience. The second is the *translation property* of the benefit function Lemma 3.1.b and the corresponding homogeneity property of the distance function. These properties make it easy to deduce the relationship between the certainty equivalent and the various risk premia that we shall soon consider. The following lemma will be useful in characterizing arbitrary functions satisfying the translation property:

Lemma 3.3: *A continuous function* $f: Y^S \rightarrow \Re$ *satisfies the translation property if and only if it can be expressed as*

$$f(\mathbf{y}) = g(\mathbf{y} - \min\{y_1, \ldots, y_S\}\mathbf{1}^S) + \min\{y_1, \ldots, y_S\}$$

with g *continuous.*

Proof: By the translation property, $f(\mathbf{y} + \alpha\mathbf{1}^S) = f(\mathbf{y}) + \alpha, \alpha \in \Re$. Take $\alpha = -\min\{y_1, \ldots, y_S\}$ to establish necessity. Sufficiency is obvious.

Notice, in particular, that a number of other normalizations could have been used in Lemma 3.3. The domain restriction associated with the min function was chosen to ensure that the translated income vector is always consistent with an arbitrary preference structure.

In expected-utility theory, it has long been recognized that maximizing the certainty equivalent leads to the same economic choices as maximization of an expected-utility function. The same is also true for our general preference function. For any $\mathbf{y}$ and W, therefore, we define the *certainty equivalent* as the smallest certain income that leaves the individual as well off as $\mathbf{y}$. More formally,

$$e(\mathbf{y}) = \inf\{c \in \Re : W(c\mathbf{1}^S) \geq W(\mathbf{y})\}.$$

Geometrically, the certainty equivalent is the point of intersection between the indifference curve for $W(\mathbf{y})$ and the equal-incomes vector (the bisector). From the previous definitions, it is now obvious that the certainty equivalent can be easily expressed in terms of the benefit and distance functions:

$$e(\mathbf{y}) = 1/D(\mathbf{1}^S, W(\mathbf{y})) = -B(W(\mathbf{y}), \mathbf{0}^S). \tag{3.1}$$

Expression (3.1) and Lemmas 3.1 and 3.2 show that the certainty equivalent is a continuous, monotonic transformation of the preference function. Consequently, like the benefit and distance functions, the certainty equivalent is a complete characterization of preferences. Moreover, it has the advantage of being a cardinal measure of preferences that is, in principle, both measurable and observable. Thus, in many instances, it will prove more convenient for us to work in terms of certainty equivalents instead of the preference function directly.[4]

3.3.2 Probabilities and Distribution Functions

Intuitively, aversion to risk is a preference for certainty over risk. Our basic definition of risk aversion is the same: a preference for certainty over risk, usually interpreted to mean that a random variable $\mathbf{y}$ is less preferred than the certainty of receiving the expected value $\bar{y} = \Sigma_{s\in\Omega}\pi_s y_s$. The most common approach to these issues is to derive probabilities from axioms such as those of Savage (1954) and to

4. The idea of representing preferences under uncertainty as mean values (that is, by certainty equivalents) has previously been used by Chew (1983), developing the work of Hardy, Littlewood, and Pólya (1952).

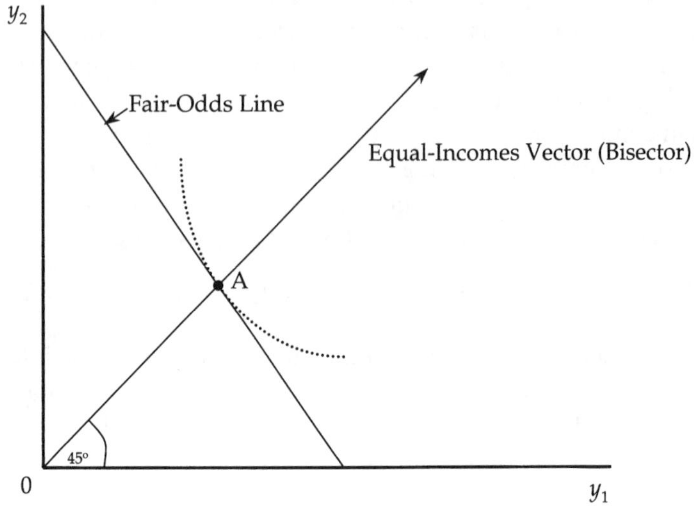

Figure 3.3 Probabilities and preferences.

define the expected value and risk aversion in terms of probabilities. In an alternative approach, adopted by Yaari (1969) and Quiggin and Chambers (1998a), the concepts of probability and risk aversion are defined simultaneously as follows:

> **Definition 3.1:** A decision maker is risk-averse with respect to the probability vector $\boldsymbol{\pi} \in \Pi$ if
>
> $$W(\bar{y}\boldsymbol{1}^S) \geq W(\boldsymbol{y}), \forall \boldsymbol{y},$$
>
> *where* $\bar{y}\boldsymbol{1}^S$ *is the state-contingent outcome vector with* $\bar{y} = \Sigma_{s\in\Omega}\pi_s y_s$ *occurring in every state of nature.*

If preferences are smoothly differentiable, the vector of probabilities is proportional to the marginal rate of substitution between state-contingent incomes (as given by the slope of the indifference curve) where the indifference curve intersects the equal-incomes vector. Figure 3.3 illustrates. There we have drawn a negatively-sloped line and labeled it the *fair-odds line*. The slope of this line is given by $-\pi_1/\pi_2$, which we take to be the probabilities derived from the individual's preference structure. Using these probabilities, all points on the fair-odds line have an equal expected value, and this

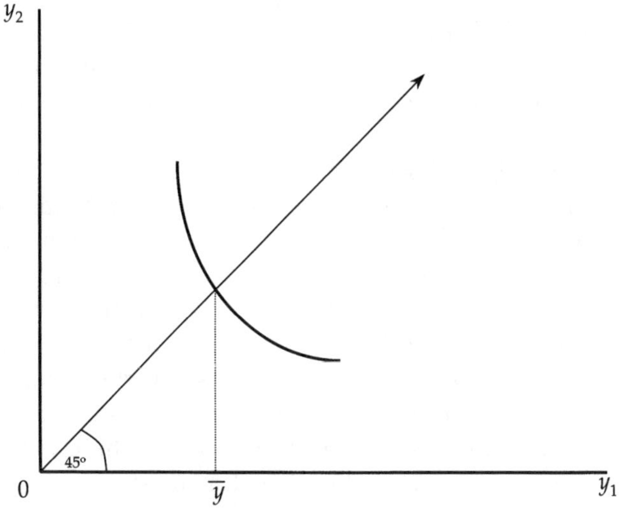

Figure 3.4 Probabilities and the marginal rate of substitution at the bisector.

expected value is given by projecting the point of intersection between the fair-odds line and the equal-incomes vector, which we have labeled as point A, onto either of the axes. If these probabilities are derived from a risk-averse individual's preference function, then the point on the equal-incomes vector (the bisector) must be at least weakly preferred to all other points on the fair-odds line. Each of these other points again has the same expected value as A, but are more dispersed than A. Unlike at A, the same income does not occur in both states of nature. Thus, quite intuitively, these points can be thought of as riskier than A. So if the individual is risk-averse, A should lie on a higher indifference curve than all other points on the fair-odds line. Given that the preference function is nondecreasing in each state-contingent income, indifference curves in a neighborhood of the bisector must be convex to the origin, as illustrated by the dotted curve.

Now to see why the indifference curve just *sits* on the fair-odds line at the bisector, consider Figure 3.4 where we have drawn a convex-to-the-origin indifference curve that intersects the equal-income vector. At the bisector, the value of the preference functional is

$W(\bar{y}, \bar{y})$. Now pass the fair-odds line (not drawn) through that point. Each point on the fair-odds line has an expected value equaling $\bar{y}$, but if the individual is (strictly) risk-averse, then any movement along it to the northwest or the southeast from $(\bar{y}, \bar{y})$ must result in a lower level of preference, whereas any movement to the northeast of $(\bar{y}, \bar{y})$ must result in a higher level of preference given that the preference function is increasing in all state-contingent outcomes. So, if the fair-odds line were to cut this indifference curve at the bisector, more dispersed state-contingent outcome vectors would be preferred to the certain outcome with the same expected value. This violates our notion of risk aversion. Hence, the tangency. At certainty outcomes (points along the equal-income vector), a risk averter's marginal rate of substitution between state-contingent incomes is the same as that of a risk-neutral individual. In a sense, because there is locally no uncertainty, the risk averter is locally risk-neutral.

If the preference structure is smoothly differentiable, our definition of risk aversion means that all indifference curves must have the same slope at the bisector, and that this slope must be equal to minus the ratio of probabilities. Hence, for smoothly differentiable preference structures, the probabilities in the definition can be calculated by

$$\pi_s = \frac{\partial W(\mathbf{1}^S)/\partial y_s}{\sum_s \partial W(\mathbf{1}^S)/\partial y_s} = \frac{\partial W(c\mathbf{1}^S)/\partial y_s}{\sum_s \partial W(c\mathbf{1}^S)/\partial y_s}, \qquad \forall c \in \Re.$$

Note that these probabilities obviously sum to 1 as required and are always nonnegative if the preference function is nondecreasing in state-contingent outcomes.

More generally, however, our probabilities need not be unique if the preference function is not smoothly differentiable in the neighborhood of the equal-incomes ray. Figure 3.5 illustrates just such a case in which the indifference curve maintains its convex-to-the-origin shape but is kinked at the bisector. As illustrated, both fair-odds line A and fair-odds line B (indeed, an infinity of such fair-odds lines) are consistent with our definition of risk aversion.

Example 3.6: *Consider the maximin preference structure introduced earlier in this chapter:*

$$W(\mathbf{y}) = min\{y_1, \ldots, y_S\}.$$

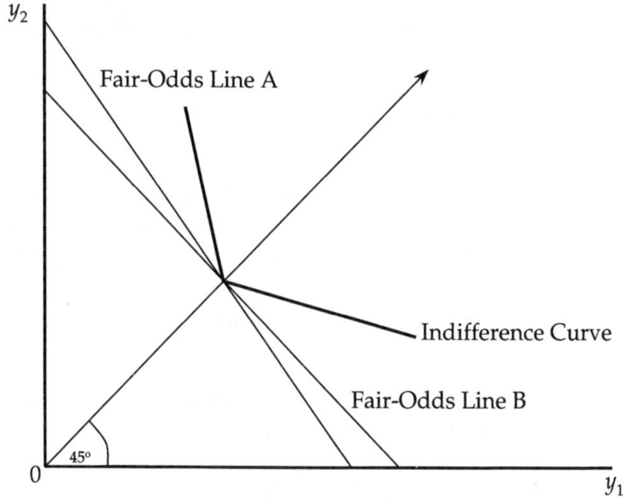

Figure 3.5 Risk aversion without unique probabilities.

This preference structure is nondecreasing, quasi-concave, and symmetric in the sense that interchanging the outcomes for any two states of nature has no effect on the individual's evaluation of the state-contingent income vector. We now show that an individual with maximin preferences is risk-averse for all possible probabilities in our sense. Notice that for any given vector $\pi \in \Re_+^S$ *satisfying* $\Sigma_{s\in\Omega}\,\pi_s = 1$ *that* $\Sigma_{s\in\Omega}\pi_s y_s \geq \min\,\{y_1, \ldots, y_S\}$, *whence*

$$\sum_{s\in\Omega} \pi_s y_s = W\left(\sum_{s\in\Omega} \pi_s y_s \mathbf{1}^S\right) \geq W(\boldsymbol{y}).$$

Accordingly, any individual with such preferences is risk-averse in our sense. His indifference curves are L-shaped indifference curves with the vertex at the point of intersection between the indifference curve and the bisector. Such an individual is infinitely risk-averse in the sense that he only cares what happens in the worst state of nature because his marginal rate of substitution is zero. He cannot be compensated for a unit fall in his lowest state-contingent income by even an infinitely large increase in a higher state-contingent income. Or perhaps more intuitively, individuals with these type of preferences pursue certainty at all cost.

Example 3.7: *The single most popular objective function used in the analysis of decision making under uncertainty is the expected-utility functional,*

$$W(\boldsymbol{y}) = \sum_{s\in\Omega} \pi_s u(y_s),$$

where $u:\Re \rightarrow \Re$ *is strictly increasing and strictly concave. A straightforward application of Jensen's inequality for the probabilities that define the expected-utility functional implies*

$$u\left(\sum_{s\in\Omega} \pi_s y_s\right) = W\left(\sum_{s\in\Omega} \pi_s y_s \boldsymbol{1}^S\right) \geq \sum_{s\in\Omega} \pi_s u(y_s),$$

where the inequality is strict if u *is strictly concave. Moreover, if* u *is also smoothly differentiable, it follows immediately that*

$$\frac{\partial W(\boldsymbol{1}^S)/\partial y_s}{\sum_s \partial W(\boldsymbol{1}^S)/\partial y_s} = \frac{\pi_s u'(\sum_{s\in\Omega} \pi_s y_s)}{\sum_s \pi_s u'(\sum_{s\in\Omega} \pi_s y_s)} = \pi_s,$$

so that the indifference curves for the expected-utility functional are just tangent to the fair-odds line at the bisector. Hence, the expected-utility function represents a special case of our definition of risk-averse preferences. Because risk neutrality is a special case of the expected-utility functional, it follows trivially that it too is a special case of our definition of risk aversion.

For a given probability vector $\boldsymbol{\pi}$, and a random variable $\mathbf{y}$, we define the *cumulative distribution function* $F(\bullet; \mathbf{y}, \boldsymbol{\pi}): \Re \rightarrow \Re_+$ by

$$F(t; \mathbf{y}, \boldsymbol{\pi}) = \sum_{\{s: y_s \leq t\}} \pi_s.$$

Thus, F is a step function, taking jumps of π_s at the values y_s for $s \in \Omega$, as illustrated in Figure 3.6.[5] F is monotonic and upper semicontinuous.

5. When Ω is a general-measure space, F may be continuous, or may be upper semicontinous with jumps at points of discrete probability mass. To deal with this case, sums of the form

$$\sum_{\{s: y_s \leq t\}} g(y_s)\pi_s$$

must be replaced by Lebesgue–Stieltjes integrals of the form

$$\int_{-\infty}^{t} g(\tau)\, dF(\tau; \mathbf{y}).$$

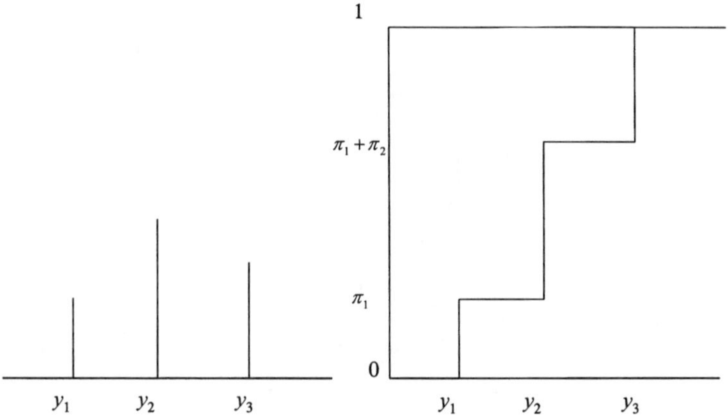

Figure 3.6 The probability distribution function and the cumulative distribution function.

A risk-averse decision maker with probability vector π is *probabilistically sophisticated* (Machina and Schmeidler 1992) if, for any $\mathbf{y}$, $\mathbf{y}'$ such that $F(t; \mathbf{y}, \boldsymbol{\pi}) = F(t; \mathbf{y}', \boldsymbol{\pi})$, $\forall t$, $W(\mathbf{y}) = W(\mathbf{y}')$. Intuitively, therefore, a probabilistically sophisticated decision maker regards equally probable states of nature as interchangeable. It's easy to see that individuals can be risk-averse but not probabilistically sophisticated. For example, individuals with state-dependent preferences display preferences that are not symmetric across states of nature (see Hirshleifer and Riley [1992]). Much of the analysis in this chapter, and in this book, applies to individuals who are risk-averse for some $\boldsymbol{\pi}$, but who need not be probabilistically sophisticated. However, concepts such as generalized Schur-concavity, which we introduce in Section 3.5 and which play an important role in much of our analysis, incorporate the symmetry properties of probabilistically sophisticated preferences.

3.3.3 Risk Premiums

Our definition of risk aversion implies that if a person is risk-averse, she must be willing to sacrifice some amount of sure income to ensure

5. (cont'd) Apart from the technical complications associated with sets of measure zero, the process of translation is straightforward. In the applications dealt with in this book, however, the added generality achieved in this way is usually not accompanied by added insight.

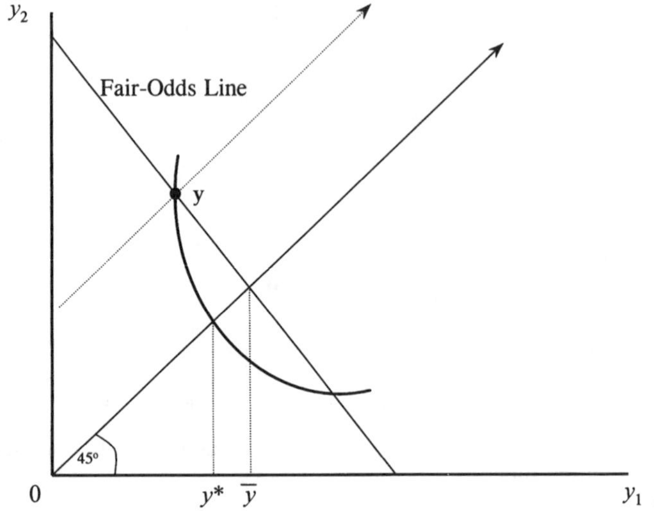

Figure 3.7 The absolute risk premium and constant absolute risk aversion.

receiving a nonstochastic income vector. Recall that our definition of risk aversion requires that she always be better off receiving the mean income with certainty than any other risky prospect with the same mean. In perhaps more familiar terms, she must possess a nonnegative *absolute risk premium*, $r(\mathbf{y})$:

$$\begin{aligned} r(\mathbf{y}) &= \max\{c : W((\bar{y} - c)\mathbf{1}^S) \geq W(\mathbf{y})\} \\ &= B(W(\mathbf{y}), \bar{y}\mathbf{1}^S). \end{aligned}$$

The absolute risk premium is illustrated in Figure 3.7 for the point labeled $\mathbf{y}$ as the income difference $\bar{y} - y^*$. By our definition of risk aversion, a risk averter must prefer receiving the mean income with certainty to receiving the corresponding state-contingent income vector. Risk aversion, therefore, is recognized as a preference for certainty. The absolute risk premium is the maximum amount that one can subtract from mean income and still have the resulting income, occurring with certainty, preferred to the original state-contingent income vector. Therefore, it measures her *willingness to pay for certainty*. If $r(\mathbf{y}) \geq 0$, Lemma 3.1(c) implies that the state-contingent income vector with mean income occurring in each state, that is, for which the mean income occurs with certainty, is always at least as desired as **y**.

Visually, it is apparent from Figure 3.7 that the absolute risk premium is the difference between the mean income and the certainty equivalent. We confirm this visual intuition formally by using the translation property of the benefit function (Lemma 3.1.b) to establish that

$$\begin{aligned} r(\mathbf{y}) &= B(W(\mathbf{y}), \bar{y}\mathbf{1}^S) \\ &= \bar{y} + B(W(\mathbf{y}), \mathbf{0}_S) \\ &= \bar{y} - e(\mathbf{y}), \end{aligned}$$

where the final equality follows by equation (3.1). Moreover, it follows immediately that

$$r(c\mathbf{1}^S) = 0 \text{ for all } c.$$

Example 3.8: *For the maximin preference structure*

$$W(\boldsymbol{y}) = \min\{y_1, \ldots, y_S\},$$

and the absolute risk premium is given by

$$\begin{aligned} r(\boldsymbol{y}) &= Max\{c : \min\{\bar{y} - c, \ldots, \bar{y} - c\} \geq \min\{y_1, \ldots, y_S\}\} \\ &= Max\{c : \bar{y} - c \geq \min\{y_1, \ldots, y_S\}\} \\ &= \bar{y} - \min\{y_1, \ldots, y_S\} \\ &= W(\bar{y}\boldsymbol{1}^S) - W(\boldsymbol{y}), \end{aligned}$$

and the certainty equivalent is simply min $\{y_1, \ldots, y_S\}$.

Example 3.9: *For expected utility, the absolute risk premium (assuming strictly monotonic preferences) is the difference between the mean and a generalized quasi-addition:*

$$\begin{aligned} r(\boldsymbol{y}) &= Max\left\{c : u(\bar{y} - c) \geq \sum_{s \in \Omega} \pi_s u(y_s)\right\} \\ &= Max\left\{c : \bar{y} - c \geq u^{-1}\left(\sum_{s \in \Omega} \pi_s u(y_s)\right)\right\} \\ &= \bar{y} - u^{-1}\left(\sum_{s \in \Omega} \pi_s u(y_s)\right), \end{aligned}$$

and the certainty equivalent is the generalized quasi-addition, $u^{-1}\left(\sum_{s \in \Omega} \pi_s u(y_s)\right)$.

Alternatively, when all state-contingent net returns are nonnegative,[6] the preference for certainty can be expressed as requiring the existence of a positive scalar $v(\mathbf{y}) \geq 1$, such that

$$W\left(\frac{\bar{y}\mathbf{1}^S}{v(\mathbf{y})}\right) = W(\mathbf{y}).$$

Following Arrow (1965) and Pratt (1964), we shall define the *relative risk premium* by

$$\begin{aligned} v(\mathbf{y}) &= \sup\left\{\lambda > 0 : W\left(\frac{\bar{y}\mathbf{1}^S}{\lambda}\right) \geq W(y)\right\} \\ &= D(\bar{y}\mathbf{1}^S, W(\mathbf{y})). \end{aligned}$$

From Equation (3.1) and Lemma 3.2.b, it follows immediately that

$$\begin{aligned} v(\mathbf{y}) &= \bar{y}D(\mathbf{1}^S, W(y)) \\ &= \frac{\bar{y}}{e(\mathbf{y})}. \end{aligned}$$

Example 3.10: *For expected utility, the relative risk premium is given by*

$$v(\boldsymbol{y}) = \frac{\bar{y}}{u^{-1}(\sum_{s \in \Omega} \pi_s u(y_s))},$$

and for maximin preferences, the relative-risk premium is given by

$$v(\boldsymbol{y}) = \frac{\bar{y}}{min\{y_1, \ldots, y_S\}}.$$

3.3.4 Constant Absolute and Relative Risk Aversion

The notions of constant absolute risk aversion and constant relative risk aversion play an important role in expected-utility theory and provide the basis for a number of well-known results. For the more

6. The requirement for nonnegativity arises because the distance function is defined only on $\Re^S_+$. For given W, the definition of $v(\mathbf{y})$ makes sense for all $\mathbf{y}$ such that $W(\lambda\mathbf{y}) \geq W(\mathbf{y})$ whenever $\lambda \geq 1$. As with the distance function, the assumption of monotonicity implies that this is always true when $\mathbf{y} \in \Re^S_+$.

general class of preferences that we employ in this book, these concepts are equally important. Expected-utility theorists typically define these notions in terms of ratios of partial derivatives of an ex post utility function. Besides being inherently unintuitive, such derivative-based definitions are needlessly cumbersome and limited. In fact, it's an easy matter to define equivalent concepts for general preferences directly in terms of the absolute and relative risk premiums. Deploying the benefit and distance functions will then yield particularly simple and intuitive characterizations of constant absolute and relative risk aversion for general preferences. We define the following:

Definition 3.2: W *displays constant absolute risk aversion (CARA) if, for any* $\mathbf{y}$, *for* $t \in \Re$,

$$r(\mathbf{y} + t\mathbf{1}^S) = r(\mathbf{y}).$$

Definition 3.3: W *displays constant relative risk aversion (CRRA) if, for any* $\mathbf{y}$, $t \in \Re_{++}$,

$$v(t\mathbf{y}) = v(\mathbf{y}).$$

Equivalently, CARA requires that

$$e(\mathbf{y} + t\mathbf{1}^S) = e(\mathbf{y}) + t \tag{3.2}$$

for all $t \in \Re$ and CRRA requires that for $t \in \Re_{++}$:

$$e(t\mathbf{y}) = te(\mathbf{y}).$$

Replacing the equalities in Definitions 3.2 and 3.3 with appropriate inequalities yields concepts of decreasing absolute risk aversion (DARA), increasing absolute risk aversion (IARA), decreasing relative risk aversion (DRRA), and increasing relative aversion (IRRA). More formally:

Definition 3.4: W *displays decreasing absolute risk aversion if, for any* $\mathbf{y}$, $t > 0$,

$$r(\mathbf{y} + t\mathbf{1}^S) \leq r(\mathbf{y}).$$

W *displays increasing absolute risk aversion if, for any* $\mathbf{y}$, $t > 0$,

$$r(\mathbf{y} + t\mathbf{1}^S) \geq r(\mathbf{y}).$$

Definition 3.5: W *displays decreasing absolute risk aversion if, for any* $\mathbf{y}$, $t > 1$,

$$v(t\mathbf{y}) \leq v(\mathbf{y}).$$

W *displays increasing absolute risk aversion if, for any* $\mathbf{y}$, $t > 1$,

$$v(t\mathbf{y}) \geq v(\mathbf{y}).$$

More general notions of decreasing and increasing risk aversion have been defined (Quiggin and Chambers 2000), but Definitions 3.4 and 3.5 are adequate for this book.

Example 3.11: *A famous result from the expected-utility literature is that wealth increases have no effect on one's allocation of wealth between a safe and a risky asset (for example, Hirshleifer and Riley 1992, Chapter 3) if the expected-utility function is consistent with CARA. We use this example to demonstrate that this result is characteristic of the more general class of CARA functions and not peculiar to the expected-utility model. Consider a two-asset world. The first asset, denoted by* A, *is the safe asset and yields a return of $1 in each state of nature. Normalize units so that its price equals 1. The second asset, denoted by* B, *will be called the risky asset because it yields a different return in each state of nature. Denote the vector of associated state-contingent returns by* $\mathbf{y}^B$ *and that asset's price by* p^B. *If the individual's wealth is given by* E, *then it will be allocated between purchasing units of* q^A *and* q^B *to maximize her preferences, as characterized by the certainty equivalent* $e(\mathbf{y})$, *where* $\mathbf{y} = q^A \mathbf{1}^S + q^B \mathbf{y}^B$ *subject to the budget constraint* $E = q^A + p^B q^B$. *Substituting the budget constraint into the definition of the state-contingent returns vector, therefore, reduces this problem to*

$$\max_{q^B}\{e((E - p^B q^B)\mathbf{1}^S + q^B \mathbf{y}^B)\}.$$

If preferences exhibit constant absolute risk aversion, then the fact that

$$e(\mathbf{y} + t\mathbf{1}^S) = e(\mathbf{y}) + t$$

for all t *allows us to further decompose this problem to*

$$\max_{q^B}\{(E - p^B q^B) + e(q^B \mathbf{y}^B)\} = E + \max_{q^B}\{e(q^B \mathbf{y}^B) - p^B q^B\}.$$

Accordingly, the optimal amount of the risky asset purchased is chosen to solve

$$\max_{q^B}\{e(q^B \mathbf{y}^B) - p^B q^B\}.$$

The solution to this final problem is independent of the individual's wealth. Hence, we conclude that for any general preference structure, W, *consistent with CARA, an individual's purchase of the risky asset is independent of her wealth.*

Constant absolute risk aversion can be visualized pictorially with the aid of Figure 3.7. It requires that sliding the return vector parallel to the equal-income vector (that is, either adding or subtracting the same amount from each state's returns) doesn't change the risk premium or the slope of the indifference curve. Pictorially, this means that as one moves away from **y** along the dotted vector parallel to the bisector, one cuts successive indifference curves at points of equal slope. Constant absolute risk aversion, therefore, implies that indifference curves are parallel in the direction of the bisector.

Constant relative risk aversion, on the other hand, says that radial expansions or contractions of the state-contingent return vector should not alter the individual's attitude toward risk. Pictorially, therefore, any ray from the origin should cut all indifference curves at points of equal slope. In a word, indifference curves are radial blowups of one another. Given this geometric intuition, it is not surprising therefore, that we can establish:

Result 3.1: W *displays CARA if and only if* W *is* translation homothetic,[7] *that is, a continuous nondecreasing transformation of a function satisfying the translation property in Lemma 3.1.b.* W *displays CRRA if and only if* W *is homothetic, that is, a monotonic transformation of a linearly homogeneous function.*

To prove necessity of the first part, suppose that the preference structure satisfies CARA, so that it satisfies the translation property, $e(\mathbf{y} + \alpha \mathbf{1}^S) = e(\mathbf{y}) + \alpha$. By (3.1) and the basic properties of the benefit function [in particular, Lemma 3.1(a) and 3.1(d)], it then follows that

7. Blackorby and Donaldson (1978) have referred to translation homothetic as unit translatable. Chambers and Färe (1998) define and discuss the more general notion of translation homotheticity.

the preference function must be a continuous monotonic transformation of a function satisfying the translation property. To go the other way, let $W(\mathbf{y}) = F(f(\mathbf{y}))$, where F is continuous and nondecreasing, and f is continuous, monotonic, and satisfies the translation property. Then by Lemma 3.3, f can be expressed as

$$f(\mathbf{y}) = \min\{y_1, \ldots, y_S\} + g(\mathbf{y} - \min\{y_1, \ldots, y_S\}\mathbf{1}^S).$$

By definition,

$$\begin{aligned} r(\mathbf{y}+\alpha\mathbf{1}^S) &= \max\{c: F(f((\bar{y}+\alpha-c)\mathbf{1}^S)) \geq F(f(\mathbf{y}+\alpha\mathbf{1}^S))\} \\ &= \max\{c: f((\bar{y}+\alpha-c)\mathbf{1}^S) \geq f(\mathbf{y}+\alpha\mathbf{1}^S)\} \\ &= \max\{c: f((\bar{y}-c)\mathbf{1}^S) \geq f(\mathbf{y})\} \\ &= r(\mathbf{y}). \end{aligned}$$

The proof of the second part follows similarly.

Example 3.12: *Consider the special case of mean-variance preferences, linear and additively separable in the mean and the standard deviation*

$$W(\boldsymbol{y}) = \bar{y} - k\sigma[\boldsymbol{y}].$$

The absolute risk premium is $k\sigma[\mathbf{y}]$, *the relative risk premium is* $k\sigma[\mathbf{y}]/\bar{y}$, *and the standard deviation is both linearly homogeneous and invariant to translations of the income vector in a direction parallel to the equal-income ray. Hence, this preference function displays both constant absolute and constant relative risk aversion.*

Example 3.13: *It is well known that the only class of expected-utility preferences consistent with CARA are additive transformations of the negative exponential, and the only expected-utility preferences consistent with CRRA are homogeneous preferences. Consider the case of the negative exponential expected-utility function*

$$W(\boldsymbol{y}) = 1 - \sum_{s\in\Omega} \pi_s exp(-ry_s).$$

Its certainty equivalent is

$$e(\boldsymbol{y}) = -r^{-1} ln\left(\sum_{s\in\Omega} \pi_s exp(-ry_s)\right).$$

Notice that

$$\begin{aligned} e(\boldsymbol{y} + t\boldsymbol{1}_s) &= -r^{-1} ln\left[\sum_{s\in\Omega} \pi_s exp(-r(y_s + t))\right] \\ &= -r^{-1} ln\left[exp(-rt)\sum_{s\in\Omega} \pi_s exp(-ry_s)\right] \\ &= -r^{-1} ln\left(\sum_{s\in\Omega} \pi_s exp(-ry_s)\right) + t. \end{aligned}$$

A similar calculation will establish that homogeneous expected-utility preferences satisfy our definition of CRRA.

Example 3.14: *Maximin preferences display both CRRA and CARA. For CARA,*

$$\begin{aligned} r(\boldsymbol{y} + t\boldsymbol{1}^s) &= \sum_{s\in\Omega} \pi_s(y_s + t) - min\{y_1 + t, \ldots, y_S + t\} \\ &= r(\boldsymbol{y}), \end{aligned}$$

whereas for CRRA,

$$\begin{aligned} v(t\boldsymbol{y}) &= \frac{t\bar{y}}{min\{ty_1, \ldots, ty_S\}} \\ &= v(\boldsymbol{y}). \end{aligned}$$

Both mean-standard deviation preferences and maximin preferences have indifference curves that are not smoothly convex to the origin. In mathematical terms, they are not strictly quasi-concave[8]. For example, maximin preferences are characterized by L-shaped Leontief-type indifference curves that permit no substitutability between state-contingent incomes. Any preference structure that has indifference curves that are smoothly convex to the origin (parabola-shaped indifference curves for which the marginal rate of substitution is smoothly diminishing) cannot exhibit both CARA and CRRA. Figure 3.8 illustrates why. By Result 3.1, any preference function exhibiting CARA must have indifference curves that have equal

8. A function $h: \Re^k \to \Re$ is quasi-concave if

$$h(\theta\mathbf{v} + (1-\theta)\mathbf{v}') \geq \min\{h(\mathbf{v}), h(\mathbf{v}')\},$$

$0 < \theta < 1$. The function is strictly quasi-concave if the weak inequality is replaced by a strong inequality.

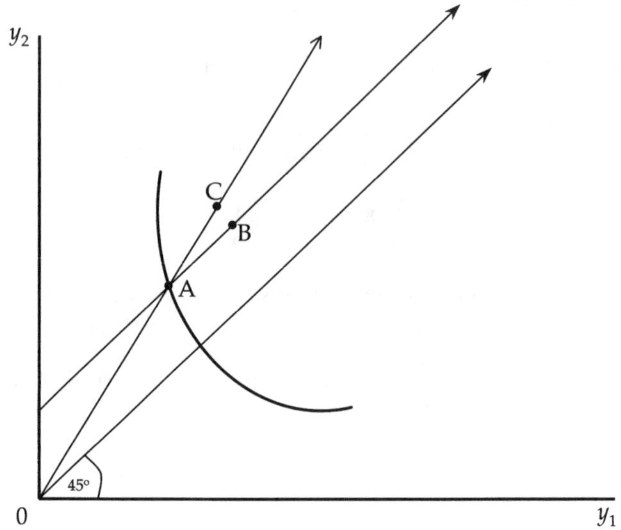

Figure 3.8 Constant absolute and constant relative risk aversion.

slope as one proceeds along rays parallel to the bisector. To see this geometric property intuitively, recall from (3.2) that

$$e(\mathbf{y} + \alpha \mathbf{1}^S) = e(\mathbf{y}) + \alpha.$$

Differentiating both sides of this expression with respect to y_s gives

$$e_s(\mathbf{y} + \alpha \mathbf{1}^S) = e_s(\mathbf{y}),$$

where subscripts denote partial derivatives. The slope of the associated indifference curves, therefore, satisfies

$$\frac{e_s(\mathbf{y} + \alpha \mathbf{1}^S)}{e_t(\mathbf{y} + \alpha \mathbf{1}^S)} = \frac{e_s(\mathbf{y})}{e_t(\mathbf{y})}, \qquad \alpha \in \Re.$$

Hence, as one proceeds out parallel to the bisector, one encounters successive indifference curves at points with equal slope.

Similarly, any preference function exhibiting CRRA must have indifference curves that are radial blowups of a reference indifference curve. Now consider point A in Figure 3.8, which is on a smoothly convex indifference surface. If the preference structure exhibits CARA, points like B must have the same marginal rate of substitution between state-contingent outcomes as A. If it is simultaneously to have CRRA, however, a point like C, which we take to be on the same indifference curve as B and which has the same relative state-contingent incomes as A, must have the same marginal rate of substitution as A and B. This can only happen if the slope at B and the slope at C are the same. Quasi-concavity, which implies a diminishing rate of marginal substitution between state-contingent incomes, ensures that B and C can have the same slope only if the segment of the indifference curve connecting them is linear. Thus, jointly CARA and CRRA preferences violate strict quasi-concavity. Moreover, preferences that can jointly exhibit CARA, CRRA, and strict risk aversion must have indifference curves that are kinked at the bisector and flat everywhere else. This is the genesis of the well-known result that the only expected-utility preferences that are consistent with CARA and CRRA are risk-neutral ones. As is well-known, under expected-utility preferences, CRRA implies DARA, and CARA implies IRRA. This result is true more generally for strictly quasi-concave preferences.

> **Result 3.2:** *Suppose* W *is strictly quasi-concave and displays CRRA. Then* W *displays DARA. Suppose* W *is strictly quasi-concave and displays CARA. Then* W *displays IRRA.*

To prove this result, assume that preferences are strictly quasi-concave. Strict quasi-concavity of W implies that the certainty equivalent must also be strictly quasi-concave. Hence,

$$e(\lambda \mathbf{y} + (1-\lambda)e(\mathbf{y})\mathbf{1}^S) > \min\{e(\mathbf{y}), e(e(\mathbf{y})\mathbf{1}^S)\} \\ = e(\mathbf{y}), \qquad 0 < \lambda < 1.$$

By (3.2), CARA requires that the left-hand side of this expression can be written

$$e(\lambda \mathbf{y}) + (1-\lambda)e(\mathbf{y}),$$

from which it follows immediately that

$$e(\lambda \mathbf{y}) > \lambda e(\mathbf{y}), \qquad 0 < \lambda < 1.$$

which is the definition of IRRA. Now observe that

$$\mathbf{y} + ke(\mathbf{y})\mathbf{1}^S = (1+k)\left(\frac{1}{1+k}\mathbf{y} + \frac{k}{1+k}e(\mathbf{y})\mathbf{1}^S\right), \qquad k > 0.$$

Hence, by CRRA,

$$\begin{aligned} e(\mathbf{y} + ke(\mathbf{y})\mathbf{1}^S) &= (1+k)e\left(\frac{1}{1+k}\mathbf{y} + \frac{k}{1+k}e(\mathbf{y})\mathbf{1}^S\right) \\ &> (1+k)e(\mathbf{y}) \\ &= e(\mathbf{y}) + ke(\mathbf{y}), \end{aligned}$$

where the inequality follows by the presumption of strict quasi-concavity. Hence, CRRA preferences must display DARA.

Any preference function displaying both CRRA and CARA, by Result 3.1, may be expressed as a monotonic transformation of a function of the form

$$f(\mathbf{y}) = g(\mathbf{y} - \min\{y_1, \ldots, y_S\}\mathbf{1}^S) + \min\{y_1, \ldots, y_S\},$$

where g is positively linearly homogeneous, nondecreasing, and continuous. Quiggin and Chambers (1998a) show that this condition is necessary and sufficient for preferences to be both CARA and CRRA. Except in the case of risk neutrality, differentiable preferences cannot display both CRRA and CARA. Quiggin and Chambers (1998a) also show that Result 3.2 holds if the requirement for strict quasi-concavity is replaced by a requirement that W be differentiable.

3.4 INCREASES IN RISK

The fundamental building block for a notion of risk aversion that goes deeper than a simple preference for certainty is a clear definition of what it means for one state-contingent income vector to be *riskier* than another. Our notion of risk aversion only implies a preference for the mean outcome with certainty over any stochastic outcome. Almost by definition, the mean outcome with certainty will be *less risky* than any stochastic outcome with the same mean. But to this point, we have said nothing about how to assess the riskiness of two stochastic outcomes. Once we can do this, then we can strengthen our notion of risk aversion to mean that an individual is risk averse in this extended sense if he always prefers a less risky state-contingent income vector to a more risky one.

Many different definitions of the statement "$\mathbf{y}'$ is riskier than $\mathbf{y}$" have been offered. No one definition is best for all purposes. In general, there is a trade-off between the desire to be able to compare as many pairs of state-contingent vectors as possible and the desire to maintain consistency with the idea that a person with risk-averse preferences should prefer a nonstochastic vector to a risky vector with the same mean.

The key issue is the difference between a (*total*) *ordering* and a *partial ordering* of state-contingent incomes. By an ordering, we mean a way of ranking different state-contingent outcomes. And when we talk about riskiness orderings in what follows, we always restrict ourselves to orderings that rank state-contingent vectors possessing the same mean. Ideally, this ranking system should satisfy some simple properties. Suppose we denote this riskiness ordering by the generic operator, L. The expression

$$\mathbf{y}L\mathbf{y}'$$

should then be read as $\mathbf{y}$ *is less risky than* $\mathbf{y}'$. We emphasize that it is maintained that $\Sigma_{s\in\Omega}\pi_s y_s = \Sigma_{s\in\Omega}\pi_s y'_s$. We will say L gives a *partial ordering* of state-contingent outcomes if it satisfies two properties. First, if $\mathbf{y}L\mathbf{y}'$ and $\mathbf{y}'L\mathbf{y}$, then $\mathbf{y}$ and $\mathbf{y}'$ are equally risky. And, second, L is transitive in the following sense: if $\mathbf{y}^o L\mathbf{y}'$ and $\mathbf{y}L\mathbf{y}^o$, then $\mathbf{y}L\mathbf{y}'$. If in addition, L can be used to rank *all* state-contingent income vectors with common means, we say that it provides a *total ordering* of state-contingent incomes.

To see why we may not want to rely exclusively on total orderings, consider the oldest, and still most popular, interpretation of the statement "$\mathbf{y}L\mathbf{y}'$," namely, "$\mathbf{y}'$ has a higher variance than $\mathbf{y}$." This provides a total ordering (It is clearly transitive and capable of comparing all possible state-contingent income vectors with common means). But it also has problems. For instance, it is consistent with preferences only if W is a member of the mean-variance class (Example 3.4). And more importantly, there exist many examples of pairs $(\mathbf{y}, \mathbf{y}')$, where $\mathbf{y}'$ has the higher variance but would nonetheless be preferred by reasonable risk-averse decision makers. The reader can visualize this by imagining two separate income distributions with common means but with the one for the riskier $\mathbf{y}'$ skewed to the right (toward the higher incomes) and **y** to the left (toward the lower incomes).

We have two goals in this section: first, to provide some partial orderings, L, of riskiness that can be systematically related with families of preference relations in the sense that whenever one finds $\mathbf{y}L\mathbf{y}'$, it is always true that, for any preference relation in the family, $W(\mathbf{y}) \geq W(\mathbf{y}')$. Second, we show how total orderings of riskiness can be induced from specific preference relations.

3.4.1 Multiplicative Spreads

If one considers how to make a particular income vector riskier, it seems natural to think in terms of taking the incomes in the "bad" states of nature and making them worse and taking the incomes in the good states of nature and making them even better. As long as the mean is held constant, this process clearly increases the dispersion of the state-contingent income vector. To make this *riskifying* process complete, one needs a natural demarcation between the good and bad states. If we take "bad" to mean below average and "good" to mean above average, then the mean is that marker. One of the most generally accepted notions of an increase in risk, the *multiplicative spread*, formalizes this intuition.

Consider two vectors $\mathbf{y}, \mathbf{y}'$, such that $\bar{y} = \bar{y}'$. We say that $\mathbf{y}'$ *is derived from* **y** *by a multiplicative spread*, if for some $k \geq 1$,

$$(y_s' - \bar{y}) = k(y_s - \bar{y}), \qquad \forall s.$$

Multiplicative spreads inherently depend on preferences because they are defined for a particular probability measure, which itself must be deduced from the preference structure.

Geometrically, a multiplicative spread of **y** is represented in Figure 3.9 by moving away from the bisector on the fair-odds line to a point like $\mathbf{y}'$. The multiplicative spread, thus, can define only a partial ordering because it only compares a given point with points farther away from the bisector on the fair-odds lines than it. The multiplicative spread will not relate points on opposite sides of the bisector. The only point on the fair-odds line that can be compared with all other points on the fair-odds line by using a multiplicative spread is the certainty point (where the fair-odds line intersects the bisector).

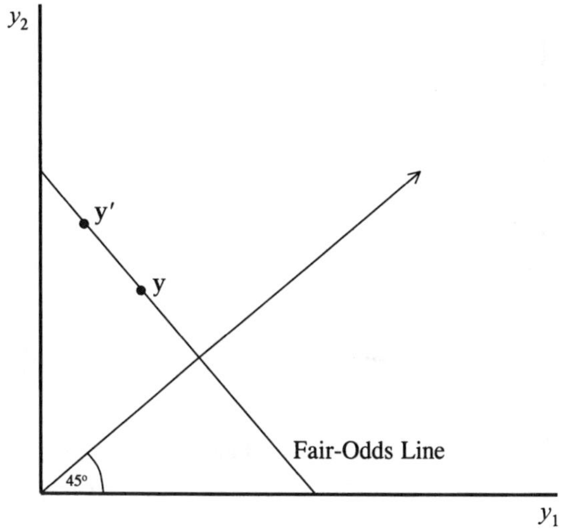

Figure 3.9 A multiplicative spread.

From Figure 3.9, one can certainly visualize that preference relations having indifference curves (not drawn) that are convex to the origin will always satisfy $W(\mathbf{y}) \geq W(\mathbf{y}')$ whenever $\mathbf{y}'$ has been derived from $\mathbf{y}$ by a multiplicative spread. More formally, it turns out that the statement that $\mathbf{y}'$ has been derived from $\mathbf{y}$ by a multiplicative spread implies that all risk-averse individuals with quasi-concave preferences will prefer $\mathbf{y}$ to $\mathbf{y}'$. Hence, for the class of quasi-concave preferences, the fact that $\mathbf{y}'$ has been derived from $\mathbf{y}$ by a multiplicative spread implies $W(\mathbf{y}) \geq W(\mathbf{y}')$.

This assertion is easily shown to be true. In vector notation, if $\mathbf{y}'$ has been derived from $\mathbf{y}$ by a multiplicative spread, then

$$\mathbf{y} = \left(1 - \frac{1}{k}\right)\bar{y}\mathbf{1}_S + \frac{1}{k}\mathbf{y}'. \tag{3.3}$$

So if the preference relation is quasi-concave and risk-averse,

$$\begin{aligned} W(\mathbf{y}) &= W\left(\left(1 - \frac{1}{k}\right)\bar{y}\mathbf{1}_S + \frac{1}{k}\mathbf{y}'\right) \\ &\geq \min\{W(\bar{y}\mathbf{1}_S), W(\mathbf{y}')\} \\ &= W(\mathbf{y}'), \end{aligned}$$

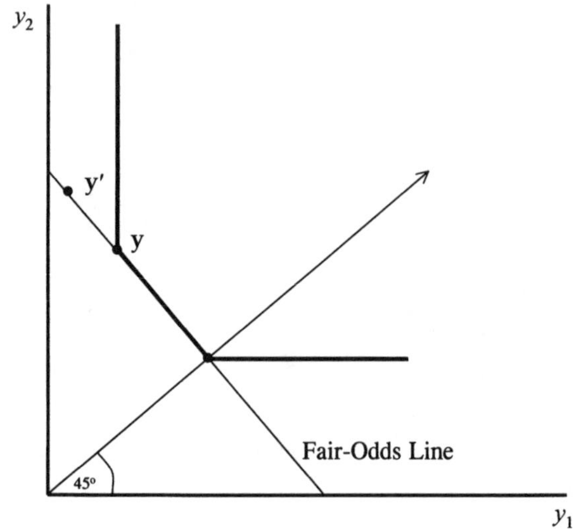

Figure 3.10 Multiplicative spreads and quasi-concave preferences.

where the last equality follows from the presumption that the individual is risk averse. The result is illustrated by Figure 3.10.

The fact that the risk ordering "$\mathbf{y}'$ has been derived from $\mathbf{y}$ by a multiplicative spread" implies that "$W(\mathbf{y}) \geq W(\mathbf{y}')$ for every risk-averse and quasi-concave W" is an example of a more general class of *stochastic dominance* relationships. The essential idea of stochastic dominance is the existence of a relation between a riskiness partial ordering, L, and a class, $\mathcal{W}$, of preference functions such that $\mathbf{y}L\mathbf{y}' \Rightarrow W(\mathbf{y}) \geq W(\mathbf{y}')$ for any W belonging to the class $\mathcal{W}$.

Comparing the partial ordering induced by the multiplicative spread relationship with the ordering induced by the variance, we see that the variance yields a total ordering of riskiness, but one that is only preserved by a limited class of preference functions. By contrast, the multiplicative spread ordering is a partial ordering, but is preserved by all quasi-concave preference functions. This is an example of a more general trade-off between partial orderings and total orderings. Total riskiness orderings can compare all state-contingent income vectors with the same means, but they generally are only consistent with a more limited class of preference functions than partial orderings. In the following section, we consider an intermediate case.

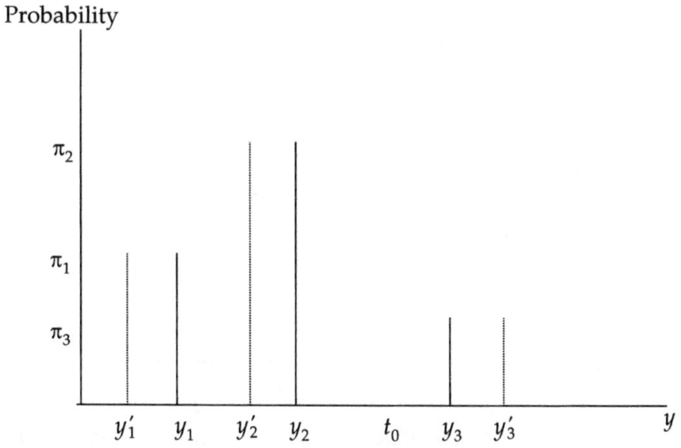

Figure 3.11 Simple mean-preserving spread.

3.4.2 Majorization and Rothschild–Stiglitz Increases in Risk

Multiplicative spreads have the property that good-state outcomes (those with $y_s > \bar{y}$) get better, whereas bad-state outcomes get worse. If $S = 2$, any mean-preserving change that increases the good-state outcome, and reduces the bad-state outcome, has this property. Hence, it is a multiplicative spread. But for $S > 2$, the equivalence breaks down. Thus, we consider *simple mean-preserving spreads*. $\mathbf{y}'$ is derived from $\mathbf{y}$ by a simple mean-preserving spread if, for some t_0,

$$(y_s - t_0)(y'_s - y_s) \geq 0, \qquad \forall s, \tag{3.4}$$

and $\Sigma_{s\in\Omega}\pi_s y_s = \Sigma_{s\in\Omega}\pi_s y'_s$. Figure 3.11 illustrates for the case $S = 3$.

A special case of a simple mean-preserving spread is *a pairwise spread*, where $\mathbf{y}'$ is obtained from $\mathbf{y}$ by replacing outcome y_s with $y_s + \delta$ and outcome $y_t \leq y_s$ with $y_t - (\pi_s/\pi_t)\delta$. Any simple mean-preserving spread can be constructed as a sequence of pairwise spreads. We illustrate with an example.

Example 3.15: *Suppose* $S = 3$, $\mathbf{y}'$ *is derived from* $\mathbf{y}$ *by a simple mean-preserving spread, and the states are ordered so that* $y_1 \leq y_2 \leq y_3$. *Then* $y'_1 \leq y_1$ *and* $y'_3 \geq y_3$. *Suppose for concreteness that* $y'_2 \leq y_2$. *The move from* $\mathbf{y}$ *to* $\mathbf{y}'$ *can be made in two steps, as follows.*

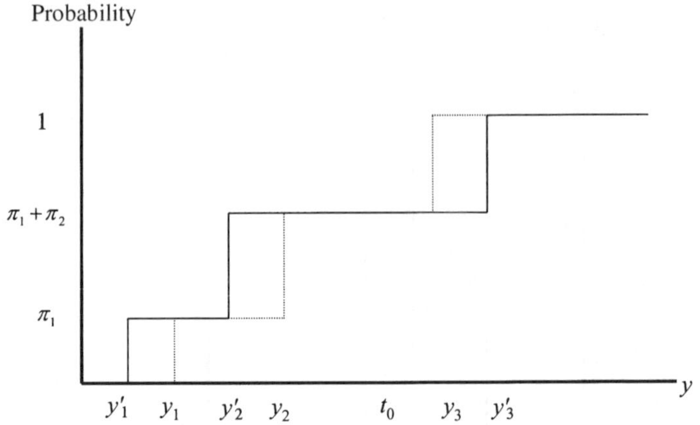

Figure 3.12 Cumulative distribution functions for a simple mean-preserving spread.

First, replace y_1 *by* y_1' *and* y_3 *by* $y_3^o = y_3 + (\pi_1/\pi_3)(y_1 - y_1')$. *Since* $\Sigma_{s\in\Omega}\pi_s y_s = \Sigma_{s\in\Omega}\pi_s y_s'$ *and* $y_2' \le y_2$, $y_3^o \le y_3'$. *Next, replace* y_3^o *by* y_3' *and* y_2 *by* $y_2' = y_2 + (\pi_1/\pi_3)(y_3' - y_3^o)$.

Another way to examine a simple mean-preserving spread is to determine what one does to the state-contingent income distribution. Consider Figure 3.12, which illustrates the cumulative distribution functions for **y** and **y**′ depicted in Figure 3.11. The cumulative distribution function for **y**′ (depicted by the unbroken-line segments) cuts that for **y** (depicted by broken-line segments) only once. The cumulative distribution function for **y**′ has more area under the region for very low outcomes than that for **y**. If **y**′ is derived from **y** by a simple mean-preserving spread, this is generally true. More formally, if **y**′ is derived from **y** by a simple mean-preserving spread, then

$$(F(t; \mathbf{y}, \boldsymbol{\pi}) - F(t; \mathbf{y}', \boldsymbol{\pi}))(t - t_0) \ge 0. \tag{3.5}$$

Expression (3.5) is our definition of a simple mean-preserving spread.

Simple mean-preserving spreads need not be transitive. Thus, to obtain a partial ordering, we use a property of simple mean-preserving spreads that is apparent from Figure 3.11. Notice that for the critical value t_0, $F(t_0; \mathbf{y}, \boldsymbol{\pi}) = F(t_0; \mathbf{y}', \boldsymbol{\pi})$. Furthermore, the partial mean for **y** up to t_0 is larger than the corresponding partial mean for **y**′, implying that

$$\sum_{y'_s \le t_0} \pi_s y'_s \le \sum_{y_s \le t_0} \pi_s y_s. \tag{3.6}$$

Suppose that $F(t_0; \mathbf{y}, \boldsymbol{\pi}) = F(t_0; \mathbf{y}', \boldsymbol{\pi}) < 1$ for at least one t_0, and that for each such t_0, (3.6) holds. Using the increasing rearrangement of $\mathbf{y}$, we can find an s, $1 \le s < S$, such that

$$y_{[s]} \le t_0 < y_{[s+1]}.$$

Denote this s by $s(t_0)$, and correspondingly, for the increasing rearrangement of $\mathbf{y}'$, choose $s'(t_0)$ such that

$$y'_{[s'(t_0)]} \le t_0 < y'_{[s'(t_0)+1]}.$$

Then, by the definition of the cumulative distribution function,

$$\begin{aligned} F(t_0; \mathbf{y}, \boldsymbol{\pi}) &= \pi_{[1]} + \pi_{[2]} + \ldots + \pi_{[s(t_0)]} \\ &= \pi'_{[1]} + \pi'_{[2]} + \ldots + \pi'_{[s'(t_0)]} \\ &= F(t_0; \mathbf{y}', \boldsymbol{\pi}). \end{aligned}$$

Now consider the integral of $F(\bullet; \mathbf{y}, \boldsymbol{\pi})$ for this discrete distribution over the range $[-\infty, t_0]$. It is given by

$$\begin{aligned} &(t_0 - y_{[s(t_0)]})F(t_0; \mathbf{y}, \boldsymbol{\pi}) + \sum_{s=2}^{s(t_0)} (y_{[s]} - y_{[s-1]})F(y_s; \mathbf{y}, \boldsymbol{\pi}) \\ &\quad = t_0 F(t_0; \mathbf{y}, \boldsymbol{\pi}) - \sum_{s=1}^{s(t_0)} \pi_{[s]} y_{[s]}. \end{aligned}$$

This fact when combined with (3.6) and the supposition that $F(t_0; \mathbf{y}, \boldsymbol{\pi}) = F(t_0; \mathbf{y}', \boldsymbol{\pi})$ implies that

$$\sum_{s=2}^{s'(t_0)} (y'_{[s]} - y'_{[s-1]})F(y'_{[s-1]}; \mathbf{y}', \boldsymbol{\pi}) \ge \sum_{s=2}^{s(t_0)} (y_{[s]} - y_{[s-1]})F(y_{[s-1]}; \mathbf{y}, \boldsymbol{\pi}) \tag{3.7}$$

for all t_0 such that $F(t_0; \mathbf{y}, \boldsymbol{\pi}) = F(t_0; \mathbf{y}', \boldsymbol{\pi})$. A similar argument shows that (3.7) must hold whenever $F(t_0; \mathbf{y}, \boldsymbol{\pi}) = F(t_0; \mathbf{y}', \boldsymbol{\pi}) = 1$. By the continuity of the integral, (3.7) must also hold at any point where $F(t_0; \mathbf{y}, \boldsymbol{\pi})$ and $F(t_0; \mathbf{y}', \boldsymbol{\pi})$ intersect. Further, since the cumulative distribution function is upper semicontinuous, if (3.7) holds whenever $F(t_0; \mathbf{y}, \boldsymbol{\pi})$ and $F(t_0; \mathbf{y}', \boldsymbol{\pi})$ intersect, it must hold for all t_0. For the general case when the cumulative distribution function may be continuous or a mixture of discrete jumps and continuous components, the same

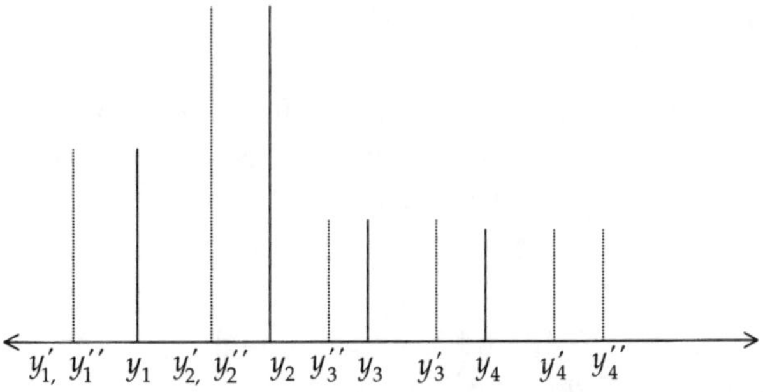

Figure 3.13 A Rothschild–Stiglitz spread derived from two simple mean-preserving spreads.

relationship may be expressed in terms of Lebesgue–Stieltjes integrals as

$$\int^{t0} F(t; \mathbf{y}', \boldsymbol{\pi})dt \geq \int^{t0} F(t; \mathbf{y}, \boldsymbol{\pi})dt.$$

Expression (3.7) defines a transitive ordering of state-contingent incomes. Hence, it can define a partial ordering. As long as $\Sigma_{s\in\Omega}\pi_s y_s = \Sigma_{s\in\Omega}\pi_s y'_s$, (3.7) holds if and only if **y**′ may be derived from **y** as the limit of a sequence of simple mean-preserving spreads (Rothschild and Stiglitz 1970).[9]

Rothschild and Stiglitz (1970) characterize (3.7) by saying that **y**′ has "more weight in the tails" than **y**. This idea is illustrated in Figure 3.13. There **y**′ is derived from **y** by a sequence of two simple mean-preserving spreads. (The intermediate distribution is denoted y''.)

When (3.7) is satisfied, we will write

$$\mathbf{y} \preceq_\pi \mathbf{y}',$$

and say that **y** *is less risky than* **y**′ *in the sense of Rothschild and Stiglitz*. The relation $\mathbf{y} \preceq_\pi \mathbf{y}'$ might also be read as **y**′ *π-majorizes* **y** by analogy with the notion of majorization introduced in Chapter 2

9. Note that, in the previous discussion, we have implicitly assumed probabilistic sophistication, that is, the requirement that two state-contingent vectors with the same F should be regarded as equally good. However, the definition: "**y**′ is riskier than **y** if and only if **y**′ may be derived from **y** as the limit of a sequence of simple mean-preserving spreads" applies to general preferences.

(Marshall and Olkin 1979). If all probabilities are equal, majorization and (3.7) are equivalent concepts. Having generalized the concept of majorization in this way, we will shortly introduce a corresponding generalization of the notion of Schur-concavity.

One of the main reasons for our interest in (3.7) is that $\mathbf{y} \preceq_\pi \mathbf{y}'$ if and only if for any risk-averse expected-utility preference function $W(\mathbf{y}) \geq W(\mathbf{y}')$ (Rothschild and Stiglitz 1970).[10,11] Because of this result, the ordering $\mathbf{y} \preceq_\pi \mathbf{y}'$ has been wrongly assumed by some writers to be the only correct interpretation of the statement "$\mathbf{y}'$ is riskier than $\mathbf{y}$." This interpretation presumes that expected-utility theory is the *only* basis for decision making under uncertainty. Expected-utility theory does not merit this primacy. For example, Landsberger and Meilijson (1990) have shown that one can produce examples of pairs such that $\mathbf{y} \preceq_\pi \mathbf{y}'$, but for which it could reasonably be asserted that $\mathbf{y}$ is riskier than $\mathbf{y}'$.

A large literature exists on the related concepts of a Rothschild–Stiglitz increase in risk and stochastic dominance. We have developed (3.7) in detail, rather than simply referring readers to the literature for three reasons. First, we want to stress the point that (3.7) holds if and only if $\mathbf{y}'$ may be derived from $\mathbf{y}$ as the limit of a sequence of pairwise spreads. Second, we want to emphasize that the risk-ordering $\mathbf{y} \preceq_\pi \mathbf{y}'$ is only one of a number of risk orderings one might reasonably consider. Finally, most discussion of stochastic dominance revolves around continuous probability distributions. We, therefore, felt it important to develop these ideas in some depth for the discrete case, which is the primary focus of this book.

> **Example 3.16:** *It is not true, for general risk-averse* W, *that* $\mathbf{y} \preceq_\pi \mathbf{y}' \Rightarrow W(\mathbf{y}) \geq W(\mathbf{y}')$. *Consider Yaari's dual model, the special case of the rank-dependent model discussed in Example 3.5 that arises when* u *is linear (for simplicity, assume* $u(y) = y$*). For this model,* W *is risk-averse if and only if* $q(p) \geq p, \forall p$. *To see that this is necessary, suppose* $q(p) < p$ *for some* p *and consider a*

10. Relaxing the requirement that the two vectors have equal means, $\mathbf{y}$ *is said to second-order stochastically dominate* $\mathbf{y}'$ if (3.7) holds and $\bar{y} \geq \bar{y}'$. Hadar and Russell (1969) and Hanoch and Levy (1969) independently showed that $\mathbf{y}$ second-order stochastically dominates $\mathbf{y}'$ if and only if for any risk-averse expected-utility preference function $W(\mathbf{y}) \geq W(\mathbf{y}')$. This is equivalent to the result of Rothschild and Stiglitz (1970).
11. Rothschild and Stiglitz (1970) give a third characterization of an increase in risk. They show that $\mathbf{y} \preceq_\pi \mathbf{y}'$ if and only if the distribution of $\mathbf{y}'$ can be derived from that of $\mathbf{y}$ by the addition of uncorrelated noise.

prospect $\mathbf{y}$ *yielding 0 with probability* p *and 1 with probability (1 – p). Then,*

$$W(\mathbf{y}) = 1 - q(p) > 1 - p = W(\bar{y}\mathbf{1}).$$

On the other hand, $\mathbf{y} \preceq_\pi \mathbf{y}' \Rightarrow W(\mathbf{y}) \geq W(\mathbf{y}')$ *if and only if* q *is concave.*

3.4.3. Total Orderings of Riskiness Induced by Preference Relations

We saw before that any mean-variance preference function W has the property that if $\bar{y} = \bar{y}'$, then $W(\mathbf{y}) \geq W(\mathbf{y}')$ if and only if $\mathbf{y}$ has a lower variance than $\mathbf{y}'$. Alternatively, we might choose some particular mean-variance preference function W, and define a risk ordering, $\preccurlyeq_W$, induced by the mean-variance preference function in the sense that $\mathbf{y} \preccurlyeq_W \mathbf{y}'$, if and only if $\bar{y} = \bar{y}'$ and $W(\mathbf{y}') \leq W(\mathbf{y})$. Clearly, then, $\mathbf{y} \preccurlyeq_W \mathbf{y}'$ if and only if $\mathbf{y}$ has a lower variance than $\mathbf{y}'$, and $\preccurlyeq_W$ is a total ordering. Furthermore, the same total ordering is obtained whichever mean-variance preference function W we choose.

In defining $\preccurlyeq_W$, however, there is really no need to presume that W is a mean-variance preference function. More generally, for *any arbitrary* W, we can define a total ordering of sets of the form $\{\mathbf{y}: \bar{y} = c\}$ by $\mathbf{y} \preccurlyeq_W \mathbf{y}'$ if and only if $\bar{y} = \bar{y}'$ and $W(\mathbf{y}) \geq W(\mathbf{y}')$.

For example, families of preferences may be represented in a simple two-parameter form for any W that displays CARA. Under CARA, the risk premium $r(\mathbf{y})$ is unaffected by changes in the mean arising from translations. Hence, it may be regarded as a measure of riskiness that is unaffected by the translations of the mean. Given preferences characterized by W with certainty equivalent,

$$e(\mathbf{y}) = \sum_{s \in \Omega} \pi_s y_s - r(\mathbf{y})$$

where $r(\mathbf{y})$ displays CARA. Then for any $k > 0$, the certainty equivalent

$$e(\mathbf{y}) = \sum_{s \in \Omega} \pi_s y_s - kr(\mathbf{y})$$

characterizes preference functions that give rise to the same total ordering of riskiness as does W and also display CARA. If $k > (<)1$, the resulting preferences are more (less) risk-averse than those characterized by W.

The approach put forward here enables us to construct a wide range of total orderings. The price of this tractability is a restrictive characterization of preferences. At the other extreme, we have seen that aversion to multiplicative spreads characterizes all quasi-concave preferences. Hence, choices that involve trade-offs between increases in the mean value and multiplicative spreads can be analyzed with very weak restrictions on preferences. Rothschild–Stiglitz increases in risk represent an intermediate case to which we now turn.

3.5 SCHUR-CONCAVITY AND GENERALIZED SCHUR-CONCAVITY

Preferences that are not consistent with expected utility may display aversion to Rothschild–Stiglitz increases in risk. Machina (1982) demonstrates this result using the concept of a local utility function, that is, an additively separable linear approximation to W in a neighborhood of some $\mathbf{y}$. From Machina's results, it follows that preferences will display aversion to Rothschild–Stiglitz increases in risk if and only if all the local utility functions are concave.

It is natural to consider whether there exists a maximal class of preference functions consistent with the partial ordering $\preceq_\pi$. In Chapter 2, we considered the partial ordering[12] $\preceq_m$ and discussed the concept of Schur-convexity. We now direct our attention to the case in which the elements of $\boldsymbol{\pi}$ are not necessarily equal, and, in so doing, generalize the notion of Schur-concavity to account for these unequal probabilities. We then relate this *generalized Schur-concavity* of W to corresponding properties of the risk premiums and the certainty equivalent.

For a given probability distribution $\boldsymbol{\pi}$:

> **Definition 3.6:** *A preference function* $W: \Re^S \to \Re$ *is generalized Schur-concave for* $\boldsymbol{\pi}$ *if* $\mathbf{y} \preceq_\pi \mathbf{y}' \Rightarrow W(\mathbf{y}) \geq W(\mathbf{y}')$.

12. In Chapter 2, we didn't refer to majorization as a partial ordering, but, in fact, it is. For the case of equal probabilities, majorization is equivalent to $\preccurlyeq_\pi$.

Some comments: first, the parallel notion of generalized Schur-convexity[13] is given by the requirement that $\mathbf{y} \preceq_{\pi} \mathbf{y}' \Rightarrow W(\mathbf{y}) \leq W(\mathbf{y}')$. Second, both generalized Schur-concavity and generalized Schur-convexity are conditional on the probability measure $\boldsymbol{\pi}$. If W is differentiable everywhere and, in particular, in a neighborhood of the ray $k\mathbf{1}^S$, then $\boldsymbol{\pi}$ is unique. If indifference curves are kinked at the bisector, however, W may be generalized Schur-concave with respect to more than one vector $\boldsymbol{\pi}$. Third, since whenever $F(t; \mathbf{y}', \boldsymbol{\pi}) = F(t; \mathbf{y}, \boldsymbol{\pi})$, $\mathbf{y}$ and $\mathbf{y}'$ are equivalent in the sense that $\mathbf{y} \preceq_{\pi} \mathbf{y}'$ and $\mathbf{y}' \preceq_{\pi} \mathbf{y}$, generalized Schur-concave or generalized Schur-convex preferences are probabilistically sophisticated.

Because of the prominence that we give to generalized Schur-concave preferences in later chapters, it provides a particularly convenient platform from which to explore the relationship between subjective probabilities and preferences. As a starting point, we consider Schur-concavity, the special case of generalized Schur-concavity that emerges when probabilities are equal. Our discussion is based on Figure 3.14.

Consider the point (y_1, y_2) in Figure 3.14. If probabilities are equal and the decision maker evaluates outcomes using a Schur-concave W, probabilistic sophistication implies that the decision maker is indifferent between point (y_2, y_1) and (y_1, y_2). (It's easy to demonstrate that the cumulative distribution functions for these two state-contingent vectors coincide.) Hence, (y_2, y_1) and (y_1, y_2) should lie on the same indifference curve. Moreover, all points lying between (y_2, y_1) and (y_1, y_2) on the equal probability fair-odds line (not drawn but it will have slope equaling minus 1) should be at least weakly preferred by a risk-averse decision maker to (y_2, y_1) and (y_1, y_2) because each of these points involves less dispersion between the high-income outcome and the low-income outcome. More formally, both (y_2, y_1) and (y_1, y_2) can be derived by taking a multiplicative spread of all points lying between them and the point on the bisector.

Risk aversion also implies that the point where the fair-odds line

13. As we will demonstrate in Chapters 4 and 6, the notion of generalized Schur-convexity is particularly important in the context of state-contingent technologies. Roughly put, it is the state-contingent analog of a nonstochastic technology because any risk-neutral person facing such a technology would always choose to produce in a nonstochastic fashion. However, it is not degenerately nonstochastic because producers could choose to produce a stochastic vector of state-contingent outputs.

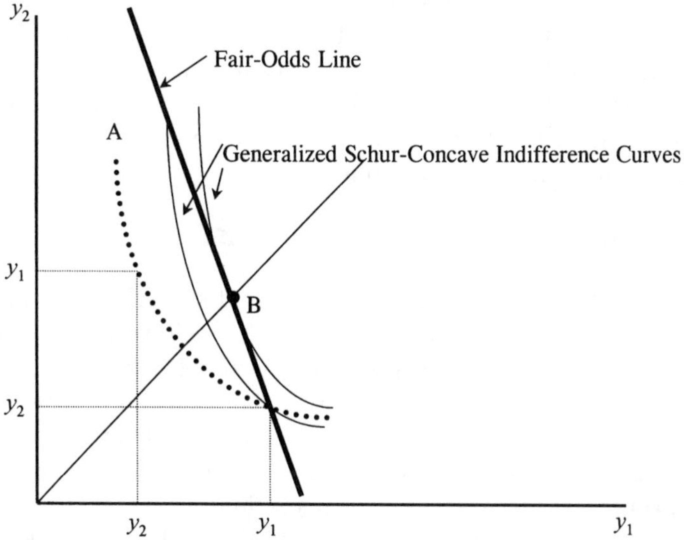

Figure 3.14 Generalized Schur-concave preferences.

intersects the bisector is at least weakly preferred to all points on the fair-odds line. A similar line of reasoning shows that (y_2, y_1) and (y_1, y_2) are at least weakly preferred to all points on the fair-odds line lying to the southeast of (y_1, y_2) and to the northwest of (y_2, y_1) because these latter points represent multiplicative spreads of (y_1, y_2) and (y_2, y_1), respectively. Together, these facts suggest that the indifference curve passing through (y_2, y_1) and (y_1, y_2) should be convex to the origin and symmetric around the bisector with the preference direction lying to the northeast. This is illustrated by the dotted curve labeled A. If the preference function is once differentiable, the decision maker's indifference curve must be just tangent to the fair-odds line at its intersection with the bisector. (Recall the fair-odds line now has slope equalling minus one.) Hence, we can conclude that Schur-concave preferences must have indifference curves symmetric around the bisector and tangent to the fair-odds line at the point of intersection between the fair-odds line and the bisector.

Now let's take up the case of generalized Schur-concave preferences, and consider the new fair-odds line passing through (y_1, y_2) for the case where $\pi_1 > \pi_2$. Again, under risk aversion, the point of intersection between the new fair-odds line and the bisector, which we have labeled B, at least weakly dominates all other points on the new fair-odds line. So moving away from B in either direction on the fair-odds line results in a drop in W. Movements along the fair-odds line must satisfy $dy_1 = (-\pi_2/\pi_1)dy_2$, so that the associated change in differentiable W from, say, $(\bar{y}, \bar{y})$ is given by

$$dW = \pi_2(W_2(\bar{\mathbf{y}})/\pi_2 - W_1(\bar{\mathbf{y}})/\pi_1)dy_2 \leq 0.$$

Because the weak inequality must hold regardless of whether the change in y_2 is positive or negative, it follows immediately that $W_2(\bar{\mathbf{y}})/\pi_2 = W_1(\bar{\mathbf{y}})/\pi_1$. So, again, we find that the decision maker's indifference curve must be tangent to the fair-odds line along the bisector. Of course, this just repeats the graphical manifestation of the fact that a risk-averse decision maker always prefers certainty to uncertainty. It also implies that increasing the subjective probability of the first state leads to a rotation of all the decision maker's indifference curves along the bisector. Hence, the shape of the decision maker's preference map hinges crucially on his or her subjective probabilities.

Now return to (y_1, y_2) in Figure 3.14. Notice that all points on the fair-odds line to its southeast represent multiplicative spreads of (y_1, y_2). They are riskier in this sense because the outcome in the low-income state, state 2, falls, whereas income in the high-income state, state 1, rises without changing the mean. Hence, movements in that direction should lower welfare for a risk-averse individual with generalized Schur-concave preferences, and conversely movements toward the bisector from (y_1, y_2) along the fair-odds line represent welfare improvements. ((y_1, y_2) can always be viewed as a multiplicative spread of any point on the fair-odds line between it and the bisector.) So at (y_1, y_2), the fair-odds line must cut the decision maker's indifference curve from above, implying that

$$W_2(y_1, y_2)/\pi_2 - W_1(y_1, y_2)/\pi_1 \geq 0.$$

At point (y_1, y_2), we have $y_1 > y_2$, and combining these two inequalities gives

$$(W_2(y_1, y_2)/\pi_2 - W_1(y_1, y_2)/\pi_1)(y_2 - y_1) \leq 0.$$

This last result, indicating that there is an inverse relationship between the partial derivatives of a generalized Schur-concave function normalized by the respective probabilities, and the size of its argument is general and represents an extension of Schur's famous characterization theorem for Schur-concave functions (Marshall and Olkin 1979, p. 56). Formally, we have:

Result 3.3: *If* $W: \mathfrak{R}^S \rightarrow \mathfrak{R}$ *is generalized Schur-concave and once continuously differentiable everywhere on its domain, then*

$$\left(\frac{W_s(\boldsymbol{y})}{\pi_s} - \frac{W_r(\boldsymbol{y})}{\pi_r}\right)(y_s - y_r) \leq 0,$$

for all s *and* r.

Proving this result is quite easy and illustrates how to constructively use a pairwise spread. First, pick y_s and y_r without loss of generality so that $y_r - y_s > 0$. Now consider the pairwise spread of $\mathbf{y}$ that arises by increasing y_r by the small positive amount δ, and decreasing y_s by the amount $(-\pi_r/\pi_s)\delta$. By generalized Schur-concavity, this pairwise spread of the original state-contingent income vector must lead to at least a weak decrease in welfare. Calculating out the welfare change establishes that

$$(W_s(\mathbf{y})/\pi_s - W_r(\mathbf{y})/\pi_r) \leq 0.$$

Combining this finding with $y_r - y_s > 0$ yields the result.

In later chapters, we will appeal to Result 3.3 and its obvious corollary:

Corollary 3.3.1: *If* $W: \mathfrak{R}^S \rightarrow \mathfrak{R}$ *is generalized Schur-convex and once continuously differentiable everywhere on its domain, then*

$$(W_s(\boldsymbol{y})/\pi_s - W_r(\boldsymbol{y})/\pi_r)(y_s - y_r) \geq 0,$$

for all s *and* r.

Therefore, if a differentiable preference function is generalized Schur-concave, there must exist a negative correlation between its partial derivatives normalized by their respective probabilities and the state-contingent incomes. Noting that the covariance between the vector with typical element $W_s(\mathbf{y})/\pi_s$ and the vector of state-contingent incomes can be written as

$$\sum_{s\in\Omega}\frac{W_s(\mathbf{y})}{\pi_s}\left(y_s-\sum_{s\in\Omega}\pi_s y_s\right)=\sum_{s\in\Omega}W_s(\mathbf{y})\left(y_s-\sum_{s\in\Omega}\pi_s y_s\right)$$

lets us establish upon using Result 3.3 that:

Corollary 3.3.2: *If* W: $\Re^S \to \Re$ *is generalized Schur-concave and once continuously differentiable everywhere on its domain, then*

$$\sum_{s\in\Omega}W_s(\boldsymbol{y})\left(y_s-\sum_{s\in\Omega}\pi_s y_s\right)\le 0.$$

Example 3.17: *Consider the expected-utility functional*

$$W(\boldsymbol{y})=\sum_{s\in\Omega}\pi_s u(y_s)$$

with u *strictly concave and once differentiable. Direct calculation establishes that*

$$(W_s(\boldsymbol{y})/\pi_s - W_r(\boldsymbol{y})/\pi_r) = u'(y_s)-u'(y_r)$$

and, given the strict concavity of u, *it follows immediately that*

$$(u'(y_s)-u'(y_r))(y_s-y_r)<0$$

in agreement with Result 3.3. Moreover, applying Corollary 3.3.2 establishes the well-known result

$$\sum_{s\in\Omega}\pi_s u'(y_s)\left(y_s-\sum_{s\in\Omega}\pi_s y_s\right)\le 0.$$

Generalized Schur-concave preference structures have the convenient property that the distance function and the benefit function inherit the preference function's generalized Schur-concavity (Blackorby and Donaldson 1980; Quiggin and Chambers 1998a). We have:

Result 3.4: *If* W *is generalized Schur concave, then*

(i) $\boldsymbol{y} \preceq_\pi \boldsymbol{y}' \Rightarrow D(\boldsymbol{y}, w) \ge D(\boldsymbol{y}', w), \forall w;$
(ii) $\boldsymbol{y} \preceq_\pi \boldsymbol{y}' \Rightarrow B(w, \boldsymbol{y}) \ge B(w, \boldsymbol{y}'), \forall w.$

To show (i), suppose that $\mathbf{y} \preceq_\pi \mathbf{y}'$. Because multiplication by a positive scalar preserves the partial order $\preceq_\pi$, it remains true that

$\mathbf{y}/D(\mathbf{y}', w) \preceq_{\pi} \mathbf{y}'/D(\mathbf{y}', w)$. The generalized Schur-concavity of W now implies

$$W(\mathbf{y}/D(\mathbf{y}',w)) \geq W(\mathbf{y}'/D(\mathbf{y}',w)),$$
$$= w$$

where the last equality follows by Lemma 3.2(c). Hence $D(\mathbf{y}, w) \geq D(\mathbf{y}', w)$, as claimed. Result 3.4(ii) is established by an exactly parallel argument.

An immediate consequence of the generalized Schur-concavity of the preference function is:

Corollary 3.4.1: *If* W *is generalized Schur-concave, the certainty equivalent is also generalized Schur-concave.*

Moreover, it follows immediately from the definition of the risk premium, Lemmas 3.1 and 3.2, and (3.1) that

Corollary 3.4.2: *If* W *is generalized Schur-concave, the absolute and relative risk premiums are generalized Schur-convex.*

Evaluating outcomes in terms of their certainty equivalents and risk premiums has a longstanding tradition in the analysis of decision making under uncertainty. From Corollaries 3.4.1 and 3.4.2, we conclude that, if a risk-averse individual with generalized Schur-concave preferences compares two state-contingent income vectors that satisfy $\mathbf{y} \preceq_{\pi} \mathbf{y}'$, the certainty equivalent for the less risky income vector is higher than the certainty equivalent for the more risky income vector, whereas the risk premium is higher for the riskier income vector. This is a particularly convenient property for generalized Schur-concave preferences to have because it implies that if one ranked income vectors according to the certainty equivalent and the risk premium, one would obtain identical rankings to those obtained directly from the preference function.

4 Indirect and Dual Representations of Stochastic Technologies

Chapter 2 developed the basic properties of the state-contingent technology, and Chapter 3 treated various objective functions. This chapter links the technology and producer preferences via an indirect technology, that is, a representation of the technology in terms of the optimized value of an objective function. Here the focus is on the minimum cost of achieving a given matrix of state-contingent outputs, and we refer to the resulting indirect objective function as the *effort-cost function.*

Before developing the effort-cost function and its properties, it's worthwhile to consider previous attempts at modeling technologies in terms of indirect objective functions. Because of the restrictive way that stochastic production was modeled in earlier studies, the task of specifying and interpreting well-defined cost functions has been a daunting one.[1] Moreover, the claim has even been made that *cost minimization is not consistent with standard preference structures such as the expected-utility model.* Although, as we show in Chambers and Quiggin (1998a) for the stochastic production-function model and in what follows for the state-contingent model, this claim is false, the confusion is understandable. The reader will probably best comprehend its source by recalling that nonstochastic cost functions are defined as the minimum cost of achieving a given level of output, be it a scalar or a vector. Consider, for example, the stochastic

1. To our knowledge, Chambers and Quiggin (1998a) contains the first general derivation of a cost function for the stochastic production function.

production-function model presented in Chapter 2. What is the natural objective for the decision maker in that model? Clearly, minimizing the cost of a given output is inappropriate because output is stochastic even after inputs are committed, and one cannot guarantee any level of ex post output. So what is the producer's goal? This confusion has led to the twin assertions that cost functions don't exist for stochastic technologies, and, more generally, that *duality theory doesn't apply to stochastic technologies.*

The primary goal of this chapter is to show unambiguously that both of these assertions are *false*. Well-defined cost functions, with all the usual properties, can be easily defined without making any unduly restrictive assumptions on the state-contingent production technology or on producer preferences. Moreover, in the linear pricing case, not only does a well-defined cost function exist, but by standard results in duality theory, it's dual to the production structure developed in Chapter 2. Knowledge of the indirect objective function is then a perfect substitute for knowledge of the state-contingent production technology. Duality theory applies for stochastic technologies just as it applies for nonstochastic technologies. The key is to recognize that the producer's goal is not to minimize the cost of producing a given ex post output, but *to minimize the cost of producing a given state-contingent output array*. This simple observation allows us to apply the existing theory of cost and production for nonstochastic technologies to the state-contingent technologies of Chapter 2.

4.1 DEFINING THE EFFORT-COST FUNCTION

Chapter 3 defined an effort-evaluation function, $g: \Re_+^N \rightarrow \Re_+$, which gives the producer's evaluation of what a particular input bundle, $\mathbf{x}$, is worth to her. The most familiar example is a producer purchasing inputs in a market where all inputs are in perfectly elastic supply. That is, a vector of strictly positive input prices, $\mathbf{w} \in \Re_{++}^N$, exists at which the producer can purchase as much of each input as desired. More generally, however, we want to allow for the case in which the producer's marginal evaluation of each input can respond nonlinearly to the amount of the inputs used. This generalization will prove particularly relevant in studying problems where $\mathbf{x}$ contains some nonpurchased, but still scarce and valuable, inputs. Examples here might include problems involving the allocation of family labor or personal time devoted to production.[2]

We typically assume that some subset of the following technical conditions is satisfied:

Properties of the Effort-Evaluation Function (G)

G.1. g is nondecreasing and continuous for all $\mathbf{x} \in \Re_+^N$
G.2. $g(\mu\mathbf{x}) = \mu g(\mathbf{x})$ for all $\mu > 0$, and $\mathbf{x} \in \Re_+^N$ (positive linear homogeneity)
G.3. $g(\mathbf{x} + \mathbf{x}^o) \leq g(\mathbf{x}) + g(\mathbf{x}^o)$ for all $\mathbf{x}, \mathbf{x}^o \in \Re_+^N$.

G.1 to G.3 are always satisfied under linear pricing. G.1 needs little interpretation other than to say that it requires that greater amounts of input cost more than lesser amounts and that input costs are, at least, reasonably smooth. G.2 is also straightforward – increasing any input vector proportionately along a ray from the origin or decreasing it along the same ray leads to a matching proportional increase or decrease in the value of g. The interpretation of G.3 is, perhaps, less obvious but still straightforward: G.3 tells us that if a producer evaluated two distinct input bundles separately, her evaluation would always exceed that obtained from evaluating the input bundles together. In a sense, therefore, the producer never loses by concentrating inputs in a single operation. We would thus expect to observe this phenomenon holding with a strict inequality, for example, when the producer perceives significant setup costs, monetary or psychic, associated with starting production operations at a new site. Under linear pricing, G.3 is satisfied as an equality. Together G.2 and G.3 imply a more familiar property:

G.3′ $g(\mu\mathbf{x} + (1-\mu)\mathbf{x}^o) \leq \mu g(\mathbf{x}) + (1-\mu)g(\mathbf{x}^o), 0 \leq \mu \leq 1$ (g is convex on $\Re_+^N$)

To understand why, first note that G.3 implies

$$g(\mu\mathbf{x} + (1-\mu)\mathbf{x}^o) \leq g(\mu\mathbf{x}) + g((1-\mu)\mathbf{x}^o).$$

Now apply G.2 to the right-hand side of this last expression to obtain the expression in G.3′ for arbitrary μ. Because it holds for arbi-

2. Effort evaluation functions of this type play a central role in the principal–agent analyses in Chapters 9 and 10.

trary μ, it also has to hold for μ restricted to lie between zero and one.

The *effort-cost function*, c: $\Re_{+}^{M\times S} \rightarrow \Re_{++}$, is defined by

$$c(\mathbf{z}) = \min_{\mathbf{x}}\{g(\mathbf{x}) : \mathbf{x} \in X(\mathbf{z})\}$$

if $X(\mathbf{z})$ is nonempty and $c(\mathbf{z}) = \infty$ if $X(\mathbf{z})$ is empty. $c(\mathbf{z})$ is the minimum cost of producing the state-contingent production array in an ex ante sense. The rest of this chapter will examine the properties of $c(\mathbf{z})$ under different assumptions on $X(\mathbf{z})$ and $g(\mathbf{x})$. We first treat the less general, but more generally familiar, case in which inputs are linearly priced.

4.2 LINEAR PRICING AND EFFORT COST

To distinguish the linear pricing case from the more general effort-evaluation model, we shall always write the effort-cost function, c: $\Re_{++}^{N} \times \Re_{+}^{M\times S} \rightarrow \Re_{++}$, in a slight abuse of notation, as

$$c(\mathbf{w}, \mathbf{z}) = \min_{\mathbf{x}}\{\mathbf{w}\cdot\mathbf{x} : \mathbf{x} \in X(\mathbf{z})\}, \qquad \mathbf{w} \in \Re_{++}^{N}.$$

Mathematically, $c(\mathbf{w}, \mathbf{z})$ is equivalent to the multiproduct cost function familiar from standard treatments of the theory of the firm (Chambers 1988; Färe 1988). Thus, there's little question about its existence under reasonable restrictions on $X(\mathbf{z})$. Moreover, the effort-cost function inherits all the properties usually associated with multiproduct cost functions. The key difference is that $\mathbf{z}$ does not represent an output combination that is actually achieved. Rather it retains its state-contingent interpretation, and $c(\mathbf{w}, \mathbf{z})$ represents the cost of arranging ex ante for this particular pattern of outputs.

4.2.1 Existence of the Effort-Cost Function

As long as we restrict attention to feasible state-contingent output configurations, that is, those with nonempty input sets, the minimum cost is well defined. Having set the problem up the way we have, the existence of the effort-cost function is obvious. However, given the debate about the existence of cost functions for stochastic production structures, it's apparently not trivial. So we'll take a moment to explain why. Consider the following argument. By restricting atten-

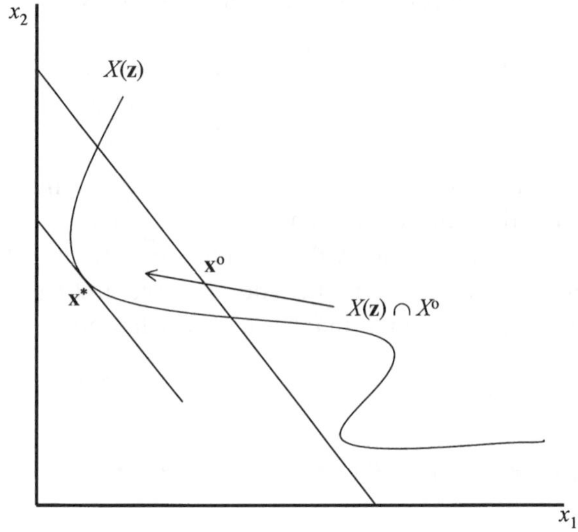

Figure 4.1 The existence of an effort-cost function.

tion to feasible state-contingent output matrices, we know that there's an input combination, call it $\mathbf{x}^o \in X(\mathbf{z})$, capable of producing the state-contingent output array. Now consider the auxiliary problem:

$$c(\mathbf{w}, \mathbf{z}) = \min_{\mathbf{x}} \{\mathbf{w} \cdot \mathbf{x} : \mathbf{x} \in X(\mathbf{z}) \cap X^o\},$$

where $X^o = \{\mathbf{x} : \mathbf{w} \cdot \mathbf{x} \leq \mathbf{w} \cdot \mathbf{x}^o\}$. If the input correspondence is closed, that is, property X.8 applies, then $X(\mathbf{z}) \cap X^o$ is a nonempty and compact set, and since the objective function is obviously continuous in $\mathbf{x}$, the Weierstrass theorem implies the existence of a minimum over this set. For all $\mathbf{x} \in X(\mathbf{z})$, but $\mathbf{x} \notin X^o$, $\mathbf{w} \cdot \mathbf{x} > \mathbf{w} \cdot \mathbf{x}^o$. This establishes that $c(\mathbf{w}, \mathbf{z}) \leq \mathbf{w} \cdot \mathbf{x}$ for all $\mathbf{x} \in X(\mathbf{z})$. When $X(\mathbf{z}) = \emptyset$, $c(\mathbf{w}, \mathbf{z}) = \infty$ by definition.[3]

Figure 4.1 illustrates this point. There the input set is nonconvex, but closed and nonempty. X^o pictorially consists of everything on or below the line segment passing through $\mathbf{x}^o$. Of course, the slope of the line segment is given by minus the ratio of the input prices. $X(\mathbf{z}) \cap X^o$ has minimal cost achieved at $\mathbf{x}^*$. The crucial property here,

3. This demonstration closely follows that for the nonstochastic case contained in Färe (1988).

besides nonemptiness, is the requirement that the lower boundary of $X(\mathbf{z})$ (its isoquant) actually be contained in $X(\mathbf{z})$. But, as we pointed out in Chapter 2, this is guaranteed by the assumption that the input correspondence is closed. We reiterate that closedness of the input correspondence is a property that cannot be contradicted by empirical observation.

Having established the existence of $c(\mathbf{w}, \mathbf{z})$, it's worth pointing out that, apart from the requirement that the producer would like to minimize cost, *its general properties are independent of the producer's attitudes toward risk*. As with all multiproduct cost functions, its properties derive from the minimization postulate and the characteristics of the technology. In fact, a little later we show that because the effort-cost function, in this case, is a "sufficient statistic" for the technology in the sense of McFadden (1978), the effort-cost function represents a convenient way of characterizing the technological uncertainties that producers face.

4.2.2 Properties of $c(\mathbf{w}, \mathbf{z})$

Like any multiproduct cost function for a nonstochastic technology, $c(\mathbf{w}, \mathbf{z})$ is nondecreasing, positively linearly homogeneous, concave, and continuous in the input prices. Furthermore, $c(\mathbf{w}, \mathbf{z})$ satisfies:

> **Shephard's Lemma:** *If an unique solution, $x(w, z) \in \Re^N_+$, exists to the minimization problem, the cost function is differentiable in* **w** *and*
>
> $$x(w, z) = \nabla_w c(w, z);$$
>
> *(where $\nabla_w c(\mathbf{w}, \mathbf{z})$ denotes the gradient of $c(w, z)$ in* **w***) and, if the cost function is differentiable in* **w***, there exists an unique solution to the cost minimization problem and*
>
> $$\nabla_w c(w, z) = x(w, z).$$

These properties are well-known consequences of the minimization postulate and need not be explained in detail here. Readers not familiar with multiproduct cost functions might wish to consult any of a number of texts on such matters (Chambers 1988; Färe 1988; Kreps 1990).

4.2.2.1 No Free Lunch and No Fixed Costs

The presumption that various combinations of X.1 to X.7 (from Chapter 2) apply imposes a number of properties on $c(\mathbf{w}, \mathbf{z})$. In what follows, we shall briefly examine each. First, consider X.1. By X.1, the effort-cost function for the null state-contingent output matrix is

$$c(\mathbf{w}, \mathbf{0}_{M\times S}) = \min_{\mathbf{x}} \{\mathbf{w}\cdot\mathbf{x} : \mathbf{x} \in \Re_{+}^{N}\} = 0.$$

In other words, because doing nothing is always possible there are *no fixed costs*. Also, by X.1, any nonzero state-contingent output configuration must cost a positive amount to produce. If the input set is empty, this is trivially true because the effort-cost function is then defined to equal infinity. But now suppose that the input set is nonempty; then because $\mathbf{w} \in \Re_{++}^{N}$, the second part of X.1 implies that $c(\mathbf{w}, \mathbf{z})$ is nonnegative. Therefore,

$$c(\mathbf{w}, \mathbf{z}) > 0 \text{ for } \mathbf{z} \geq \mathbf{0}_{M\times S}, \mathbf{z} \neq \mathbf{0}_{M\times S}.$$

In short, the aphorism – there is *no free lunch*.

4.2.2.2 Output Disposability and Marginal Cost

Let's now impose X.2, *free disposability of output* (in mathematical notation, $\mathbf{z}^o \geq \mathbf{z} \Rightarrow X(\mathbf{z}^o) \subseteq X(\mathbf{z})$). Recall that free disposability of outputs implies that it's always possible, by foregoing some ex ante output, to remove all production uncertainty. For a single-product, two-state technology, this means pictorially that one can produce on the bisector. We now show that the main economic consequence of free disposability is nonnegative marginal cost.

Because $X(\mathbf{z}^o) \subseteq X(\mathbf{z})$, any vector of inputs that can produce $\mathbf{z}^o$ must also be able to produce $\mathbf{z}$. And so, any solution (There may be more than one.) to the cost-minimizing problem for $\mathbf{z}^o$ has to be in $X(\mathbf{z})$. Denote any solution for $\mathbf{z}^o$ by $\mathbf{x}^o$. Because $\mathbf{x}^o \in X(\mathbf{z})$, the cheapest way of producing $\mathbf{z}$ can't be any more expensive than $\mathbf{x}^o$. Otherwise, the producer would choose to use $\mathbf{x}^o$ to produce $\mathbf{z}$. Consequently, $c(\mathbf{w}, \mathbf{z}) \leq c(\mathbf{w}, \mathbf{z}^o)$. Put in more familiar economic terms, the marginal cost of any state-contingent output is nonnegative.

Viewed in this light, free disposability of output doesn't seem all that presumptuous if the outputs are "goods" and not "bads." Here's why. "Good" outputs generally fetch positive marginal benefits. An optimizing firm, regardless of its risk preferences, chooses outputs so that their marginal benefits equal marginal costs. Hence, in equilibrium, with "good" outputs we'll only encounter situations where marginal cost is nonnegative so that the technology is at least locally consistent with free disposability of output. An example illustrates. Suppose there's a single output so that $M = 1$, and that that output is an agricultural commodity for which the presence of government price guarantees removes all price uncertainty. Also assume that the firm maximizes the expected value of the net return. Faced with this situation, an optimizer would choose state-contingent outputs, so that the marginal cost of each equals the guaranteed price times the probability of that state occurring. Each state-contingent marginal cost is, therefore, positive.

The foregoing doesn't imply that free disposability of output is universally acceptable or should be universally applied. Indeed, when the output in question is a "bad," we would strongly argue the opposite. But if one is not concerned, for example, about pollution, emissions, or agricultural runoff, then free disposability of state-contingent outputs is innocuous. (In Chapter 8, we will consider a problem where free disposability of outputs is not an innocuous assumption.) Even if the technology doesn't obey free disposability over all ranges of state-contingent outputs, it's observationally equivalent to one that does. And by that we mean that one cannot find a situation in which a rational producer would choose to produce at a point where free disposability doesn't apply.

Relaxing free disposability of output to weak output disposability, X.2.W, implies that $c(\mathbf{w}, \lambda\mathbf{z}) \leq c(\mathbf{w}, \mathbf{z})$ for $0 \leq \lambda \leq 1$. The logic is practically the same as that for output-free disposability implying nonnegative marginal costs. Therefore, we won't bother to repeat it. But two things should be noted. Weak output disposability doesn't imply that any state-contingent output's marginal cost is negative. It just doesn't rule that out. And, second, weak disposability of output still implies that state-contingent marginal cost is positive as long as one only considers movement outwards along a state-contingent output ray.

4.2.2.3 Input Disposability

Neither free input disposability nor weak input disposability impose any structure on $c(\mathbf{w}, \mathbf{z})$. Regardless of what type of input disposability is imposed on $X(\mathbf{z})$, the effort-cost function is always nondecreasing in input prices. Let $\mathbf{x}'$ be an element of the cost-minimizing solution when input prices are given by $\mathbf{w}'$. Now suppose that input prices fall from $\mathbf{w}'$ to $\mathbf{w}$. If she wants, the producer can still use $\mathbf{x}'$ to produce $\mathbf{z}$: all that's changed are prices, not the feasible input combinations. So the worst the producer can do is to decrease costs by $\mathbf{w}'\cdot\mathbf{x}' - \mathbf{w}\cdot\mathbf{x}' \geq 0$. In most cases, she can decrease costs even further by rearranging her input bundle in response to the price change. So costs can't rise as prices fall.

4.2.2.4 Producing an Infinitely Large State-Contingent Output Is Infinitely Costly

X.4, boundedness of state-contingent output, requires that no input bundle can produce any state-contingent output bundle having unboundedly large elements, that is, if $\|\text{vec } \mathbf{z}^k\| \to \infty$ as $k \to \infty$, then $\cap_{k\to\infty} X(\mathbf{z}^k) = \emptyset$. By our definition of the effort-cost function, the cost of producing any output configuration with unboundedly large elements then must also be unboundedly large, that is, if $\|\text{vec } \mathbf{z}^k\| \to \infty$ as $k \to \infty$, then $c(\mathbf{w}, \mathbf{z}^k) \to \infty$ as $k \to \infty$. It's prohibitively costly to produce an infinitely large output bundle.

4.2.2.5 Quasi-Concavity and Concavity of the Input Correspondence

X.5, which is expressed mathematically as $X(\mathbf{z}) \cap X(\mathbf{z}') \subseteq X(\lambda\mathbf{z} + (1 - \lambda)\mathbf{z}')$, $0 \leq \lambda \leq 1$, implies quasi-concavity of the input correspondence in outputs, or equivalently convex state-contingent output sets. Let's first examine

$$\min\{\mathbf{w}\cdot\mathbf{x} : \mathbf{x} \in (X(\mathbf{z}) \cap X(\mathbf{z}'))\}.$$

Call the solution to this particular problem, $\mathbf{x}^*$. Because $\mathbf{x}^*$ also belongs to $X(\lambda\mathbf{z} + (1 - \lambda)\mathbf{z}')$ under X.5, we now see that

$$\min\{\mathbf{w}\cdot\mathbf{x} : \mathbf{x} \in (X(\mathbf{z}) \cap X(\mathbf{z}^o))\} \geq c(\mathbf{w}, \lambda\mathbf{z} + (1-\lambda)\mathbf{z}').$$

Consequently, for any $\mathbf{x} \in X(\mathbf{z}) \cap X(\mathbf{z}^o)$, $\mathbf{w}\cdot\mathbf{x}$ is an upper bound on the cheapest way to produce any convex combination of $\mathbf{z}$ and $\mathbf{z}^o$, that is, $c(\mathbf{w}, \lambda\mathbf{z} + (1 - \lambda)\mathbf{z}^o) \leq \mathbf{w}\cdot\mathbf{x}$ for all $\mathbf{x} \in X(\mathbf{z}) \cap X(\mathbf{z}^o)$ and $0 \leq \lambda \leq 1$.

The next property of the technology that we investigate is concavity of the output correspondence, or in terms of input sets

$$\lambda X(\mathbf{z}) + (1-\lambda)X(\mathbf{z}') \subseteq X(\lambda\mathbf{z} + (1-\lambda)\mathbf{z}'), \qquad 0 \leq \lambda \leq 1$$

(X.7 and Z.7). (We intentionally skip over X.6, convexity of the input set, because it has no direct implication for the effort-cost function, and defer our discussion until we take up the duality between the cost function and the input correspondence.) In the case in which $M = 1$, X.7 corresponds to the requirement that the state-contingent production functions derived in the examples in Chapter 2 exhibit everywhere diminishing marginal productivity. Intuitively, it says that if one bundle of inputs can produce a given state-contingent output matrix, $\mathbf{z}$, and another bundle of inputs can produce another state-contingent output matrix, $\mathbf{z}^o$, any weighted average of these input bundles can produce the corresponding weighted average of the state-contingent output matrices. Economically, its implication is that the marginal cost of each state-contingent output is nondecreasing, that is, the effort-cost function is convex in state-contingent outputs:

$$c(\mathbf{w}, \lambda\mathbf{z} + (1-\lambda)\mathbf{z}') \leq \lambda c(\mathbf{w}, \mathbf{z}) + (1-\lambda)c(\mathbf{w}, \mathbf{z}'), \qquad 0 \leq \lambda \leq 1.$$

To establish this claim, notice that if $\mathbf{x}$ is the minimizing input bundle when the state-contingent output matrix is $\mathbf{z}$, and $\mathbf{x}'$ is the minimizing input bundle when the state-contingent output matrix is $\mathbf{z}'$, then by X.7 and Z.7, $\lambda\mathbf{x} + (1-\lambda)\mathbf{x}' \in X(\lambda\mathbf{z} + (1-\lambda)\mathbf{z}')$ for $0 \leq \lambda \leq 1$. Because $\lambda\mathbf{x} + (1 - \lambda)\mathbf{x}'$ can produce $\lambda\mathbf{z} + (1 - \lambda)\mathbf{z}'$, it must also be true that $\lambda\mathbf{wx} + (1-\lambda)\mathbf{wx}' \geq c(\mathbf{w}, \lambda\mathbf{z} + (1-\lambda)\mathbf{z}')$ by the definition of the effort-cost function. This establishes that effort cost is convex in state-contingent outputs on recognizing that $\lambda\mathbf{w}\cdot\mathbf{x} + (1 - \lambda)\mathbf{w}\cdot\mathbf{x}' = \lambda c(\mathbf{w}, \mathbf{z}) + (1 - \lambda)c(\mathbf{w}, \mathbf{z}')$.

4.2.2.6 List of Properties of the Effort-Cost Function

Summarizing, we have:

Properties of the effort-cost function under linear input pricing (CL)

If the technology satisfies X.8, then

CL.1. $c(\mathbf{w}, \mathbf{z})$ is positively linearly homogeneous, nondecreasing, concave, and continuous on $\Re^N_{++}$

CL.2. Shephard's Lemma

CL.3. If $X(\mathbf{z})$ satisfies X.1, $c(\mathbf{w}, \mathbf{z}) \geq 0$, $c(\mathbf{w}, \mathbf{0}_{M\times S}) = 0$, and $c(\mathbf{w}, \mathbf{z}) > 0$ for $\mathbf{z} \geq \mathbf{0}_{M\times S}$, $\mathbf{z} \neq 0_{M\times S}$

CL.4. If $X(\mathbf{z})$ satisfies X.2, $\mathbf{z}^o \geq \mathbf{z} \Rightarrow c(\mathbf{w}, \mathbf{z}^o) \geq c(\mathbf{w}, \mathbf{z})$

CL.4.W. If $X(\mathbf{z})$ satisfies X.2.W, $c(\mathbf{w}, \mathbf{z}) \geq c(\mathbf{w}, \lambda\mathbf{z})$ for $0 \leq \lambda \leq 1$

CL.5. If $X(\mathbf{z})$ satisfies X.4, $\|\text{vec } \mathbf{z}^k\| \to \infty$ as $k \to \infty \Rightarrow c(\mathbf{w}, \mathbf{z}^k) \to \infty$ as $k \to \infty$

CL.6. If $X(\mathbf{z})$ satisfies X.5, $c(\mathbf{w}, \lambda\mathbf{z} + (1 - \lambda)\mathbf{z}^o)) \leq \min\{\mathbf{w}\cdot\mathbf{x} : \mathbf{x} \in (X(\mathbf{z}) \cap X(\mathbf{z}^o))\}$, $0 \leq \lambda \leq 1$

CL.7. If $X(\mathbf{z})$ satisfies X.7, $c(\mathbf{w}, \mathbf{z})$ is convex over $\Re^{M\times S}_+$ and continuous over $\Re^{M\times S}_{++}$

4.2.3 Linear Pricing and the Duality between the Effort-Cost Function and the Input Correspondence

Under appropriate conditions, $c(\mathbf{w}, \mathbf{z})$ is also dual to $X(\mathbf{z})$ in the sense that:

$$X^*(\mathbf{z}) = \{\mathbf{x} : \mathbf{w}\cdot\mathbf{w} \geq c(\mathbf{w}, \mathbf{z}), \mathbf{w} \in \Re^N_{++}\}$$
$$= \cap_{w>0}\{\mathbf{x} : \mathbf{w}\cdot\mathbf{x} \geq c(\mathbf{w}, \mathbf{z})\} = X(\mathbf{z}).$$

In words, $X(\mathbf{z})$ can be recovered from $c(\mathbf{w}, \mathbf{z})$ by looking at the intersection of all the half spaces in input space, $\Re^N_+$, containing input bundles that are at least as costly as the cost-minimizing input choice for all positive input-price vectors. So in McFadden's (1978) terminology, $c(\mathbf{w}, \mathbf{z})$ is a "sufficient statistic" for $X(\mathbf{z})$.

Dual relations like this were once economic exotica, but in the last 20 years, they have become run of the mill. One can hardly read a paper on production or welfare economics without encountering some form of duality paraphernalia, be it Shephard's Lemma or concavity of the cost function. The state-contingent production approach allows direct application of these duality relationships, along with many of the associated advances in analytical techniques, to decision making under uncertainty. Hence, although the demonstration of the existence of a duality is just a direct application of existing duality

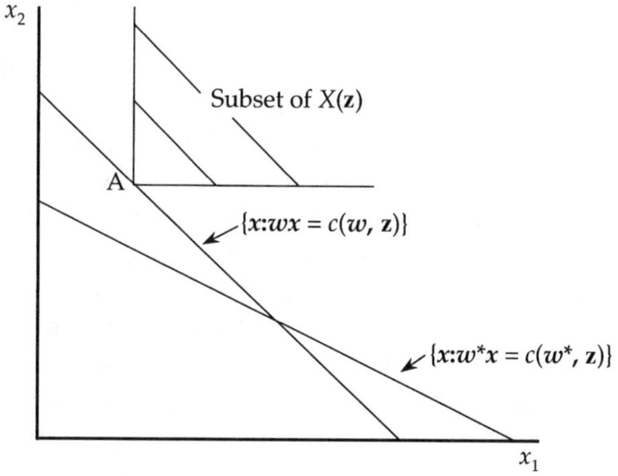

Figure 4.2 The duality between $X(z)$ and $c(w, z)$.

theorems (for example, Färe 1988, McFadden 1978), the realization that they can be applied in this manner is significant.

Let's now see why this dual relationship is sensible, at least visually. Suppose that input space can be represented as in Figure 4.2. Obviously, the set of points satisfying $\mathbf{w} \cdot \mathbf{x} = c(\mathbf{w}, \mathbf{z})$ is portrayed pictorially by a line segment with negative slope equal to minus the price ratio. Moreover, all cost-minimizing input combinations must lie somewhere on this line segment. For the sake of argument, let there be a unique cost minimizer and let it be point A. Because A can produce **z**, input-free disposability implies that all points to the northeast of A must also lie in $X(\mathbf{z})$.

Now imagine repeating this same process for all possible input-price vectors and taking the intersection of the resulting half spaces lying above each of these line segments. What emerges is an input set satisfying free disposability of inputs (X.3) and convexity (X.6). And, if $X(\mathbf{z})$ satisfies X.3 and X.6 (and several other properties), the resulting intersection of sets is exactly $X(\mathbf{z})$. But what happens if $X(\mathbf{z})$ doesn't satisfy these properties? A result that can be traced at least as far back as Samuelson (1947) tells us that it doesn't matter as long as producers minimize cost (See also, for example, Chambers 1988, Section 2.4.). The set that we do isolate by following this procedure is observationally equivalent to $X(\mathbf{z})$ in the sense that a cost minimizer facing $X^*(\mathbf{z})$ makes the same economic choices as a cost minimizer facing $X(\mathbf{z})$.

Conditions that will ensure this duality are that the input correspondence be closed (X.8), no free lunch ($\mathbf{0}_N \notin X(\mathbf{z})$ for $\mathbf{z} \geq \mathbf{0}_{M\times S}$ and $\mathbf{z} \neq \mathbf{0}_{M\times S}$) and no fixed costs ($X(\mathbf{0}_{M\times S}) = \Re_+^N$) (Together these represent X.1.), free disposability of inputs (X.3), and convexity of the input set (X.6 and, economically speaking, diminishing marginal rate of technical substitution). Notice, in particular, that the problematic property of free disposability of output (X.2) is not required to ensure either the existence of the effort-cost function or its dual relation with the input set. Moreover, in deriving $c(\mathbf{w}, \mathbf{z})$, it wasn't necessary to use either input free disposability (X.3) or convexity of the input set (X.6). However, $X^*(\mathbf{z})$ automatically satisfies these conditions and is observationally equivalent to $X(\mathbf{z})$ for a cost minimizer facing linear prices in that

$$c(\mathbf{w}, \mathbf{z}) = \min_{\mathbf{x}} \{\mathbf{w}\cdot\mathbf{x} : \mathbf{x} \in X^*(\mathbf{z})\}.$$

So, no true economic generality is lost by imposing (X.3) and (X.6) under linear pricing and cost minimization.

We don't present a proof of this duality in this book because many are already available. (McFadden 1978 and Färe 1988 are good references. For a more heuristic treatment, see Chambers 1988, Chapter 2.) However, if you're skeptical, you can convince yourself by showing that $X^*(\mathbf{z})$ actually satisfies these properties and that $X^*(\mathbf{z})$ must contain all (possible) cost-minimizing points.

Example 4.1: *Examples 2.1 and 2.2 discussed the finite-state analog of the stochastic production function, that is, the state-contingent production function when* M = *1. When the technology is output-cubical, the input set for the* S*-dimensional vector of state-contingent outputs is* $X(z) = \cap_s X_s(z_s)$, *where* $X_s(z_s) = \{x : z_s \leq f_s(x)\}$. *(Here,* $z \in \Re_{++}^S$ *and so* $z_s \in \Re_{++}$*.) Because, any candidate for the cost-minimizing input bundle must belong to each of the* S *scalar-output input sets,* X_s, s = *1, 2, . . . ,* S, *the minimum cost of producing the entire vector of state-contingent outputs has to satisfy*

$$c(w, z) \geq c_s(w, z_s), \qquad s = 1, 2, \ldots, S,$$

where

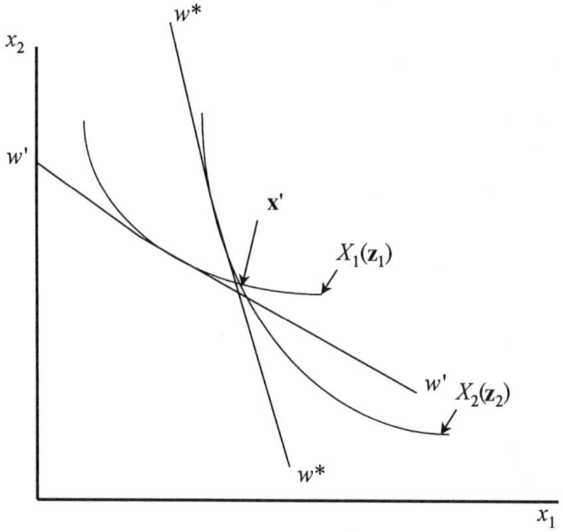

Figure 4.3 $c(w, z)$ for an output-cubical technology.

$$c_s(\mathbf{w}, z_s) = min\{\mathbf{w} \cdot \mathbf{x} : z_s \leq f_s(\mathbf{x})\}.$$

Thus, the smallest that $c(\mathbf{w}, z)$ *can be and still satisfy these* S *inequalities is the minimum cost of producing the most costly state-contingent output. Thus,*

$$c(\mathbf{w}, z) \geq max_{s=1,2,\ldots,S}\{c_s(\mathbf{w}, z_s)\}.$$

Here the notation on the right-hand side of the inequality denotes the maximum taken over the S *distinct ex post cost functions,* $c_s(\mathbf{w}, z_s)$. *The cost of producing the most costly state-contingent output provides a lower bound for the cost of producing the state-contingent output vector. Sometimes, this lower bound is achievable, but more generally it's not. Figure 4.3 illustrates the* S = 2, N = 2 *case. Remember that* $X(z)$ *is now the intersection of the two input sets* $X_1(z_1)$ *and* $X_2(z_2)$. *When relative input prices are given by the line segment* $\mathbf{w}^*\mathbf{w}^*$ *in the figure, the lower bound is achieved and* $c(\mathbf{w}^*, z) = c_2(\mathbf{w}^*, z_2) > c_1(\mathbf{w}^*, z_1)$. *However, when relative input prices are given by the line segment* $\mathbf{w}'\mathbf{w}'$, *the lower bound is not achieved and*

$$c(\mathbf{w}', z) = \mathbf{w}' \cdot \mathbf{x}' > c_1(\mathbf{w}', z_1) > c_2(\mathbf{w}', z_2).$$

Example 4.2: *Now consider the state-allocable input model from Chapter 2. Considering again the case of a single stochastic output, the input set is given by*

$$X(\boldsymbol{z}) = \sum_{s\in\Omega} X_s(z_s).$$

And so the effort-cost function is

$$\begin{aligned} c(\boldsymbol{w},\boldsymbol{z}) &= min\left\{\boldsymbol{w}\cdot\boldsymbol{x} : \boldsymbol{x} \in \sum_{s\in\Omega} X_s(z_s)\right\} \\ &= min\left\{\boldsymbol{w}\cdot\left(\sum_{s\in\Omega}\boldsymbol{x}^s\right) : \boldsymbol{x}^s \in X_s(z_s), \qquad s\in\Omega\right\} \\ &= \sum_{s\in\Omega} min\{\boldsymbol{w}\cdot\boldsymbol{x}^s : \boldsymbol{x}^s \in X_s(z_s)\} \\ &= \sum_{s\in\Omega} c_s(\boldsymbol{w}, z_s). \end{aligned}$$

Thus, for the state-allocable input technology, the cost-minimizing way of producing the state-contingent output vector equals the sum of the minimum costs of producing each component of the state-contingent output vector. This happens because input effort is allocable across states, and under linear pricing of inputs, so is the objective function: Costs can be broken down into costs allocated to each state. And because one input set is independent of the remaining input sets, the cheapest way to produce is to minimize cost in each state.

Example 4.3: *Suppose that the effort-cost function satisfies*

$$c(\boldsymbol{w}, \boldsymbol{z}) = \sum_{s\in\Omega} c_s(\boldsymbol{w}, z_s).$$

What happens if we try to apply the duality mapping to this technology? We have

$$\begin{aligned} X^*(\boldsymbol{z}) &= \cap_{\boldsymbol{w}>0}\{\boldsymbol{x} : \boldsymbol{w}\cdot\boldsymbol{x} \geq c(\boldsymbol{w},\boldsymbol{z})\} \\ &= \cap_{\boldsymbol{w}>0}\left\{\boldsymbol{x} : \boldsymbol{w}\cdot\boldsymbol{x} \geq \sum_{s\in\Omega} c_s(\boldsymbol{w},z_s)\right\} \\ &= \cap_{\boldsymbol{w}>0}\left\{\sum_{s\in\Omega}\boldsymbol{x}^s : \boldsymbol{w}\cdot\boldsymbol{x}^s \geq c_s(\boldsymbol{w},z_s)\right\} \\ &= \sum_{s\in\Omega}\cap_{\boldsymbol{w}>0}\{\boldsymbol{x}^s : \boldsymbol{w}\cdot\boldsymbol{x}^s \geq c_s(\boldsymbol{w},z_s)\} \\ &= \sum_{s\in\Omega} X_s^*(z_s), \end{aligned}$$

which is the input set for a technology with state-allocable inputs satisfying free disposability of inputs and convexity of the input set.

4.2.4 Input Use and Increases in Risk

In many empirical and theoretical applications, the role that inputs play in either mitigating or enhancing risk is of particular interest. Thus, at times, considerable attention has been devoted to the notions of *risk-reducing* and *risk-increasing inputs.* Intuitively, these notions seem clear: risk-reducing inputs reduce the riskiness of state-contingent outputs, and risk-increasing inputs increase the riskiness of state-contingent outputs. Standard examples are pesticides and chemical fertilizers, respectively, in crop production. Pesticides are not applied to increase yield in the absence of a pest outbreak so much as they are applied to control losses when outbreaks occur. Hence, pesticides dampen the dispersion of the state-contingent outputs, and thus are risk-reducing. Chemical fertilizers, on the other hand, can significantly increase yield if correct weather conditions prevail, but can also significantly decrease yield when these conditions don't prevail. Hence, they often amplify the dispersion of state-contingent outputs, and are risk-increasing. Having said this, the literature on production under uncertainty has struggled with formalizing a definition of risk-increasing and risk-reducing inputs that matches this simple intuition and that accords with general notions of increases and decreases in risk.[4]

The state-contingent approach advocated in this book leads to a rather different perspective. Rather than thinking of input choices, in combination with random variation, determining a stochastic output, we consider inputs and state-contingent outputs to be chosen jointly, in a preference-maximizing fashion. Hence, it is natural to think in terms of complementarity between input choices and more or less

4. Originally, an input was called risk-increasing if its effect on the producer's risk premium was positive and risk-reducing if it was negative. More commonly, an input is said to be risk-increasing if its application increases the variability of output in the single-output case. As pointed out in Chapter 3 and many other places, such effects cannot be recognized as pure changes in risk unless changes in mean returns are compensated for. Thus, the standard terminology is misleading at best, and we have chosen the current terminology to emphasize the distinction between our definitions and the less semantically correct one.

risky state-contingent output patterns rather than in terms of simple causal relationships between input choices and risk. This idea can be formalized in a natural way for the case of scalar output.

Suppose that $M = 1$ and that the effort-cost function is differentiable in input prices so that the cost-minimizing demand for the input n, by Shephard's Lemma, is

$$x_n(\mathbf{w}, \mathbf{z}) = \frac{\partial c(\mathbf{w}, \mathbf{z})}{\partial w_n}.$$

Now suppose, that we were comparing two distinct state-contingent output arrays, $\mathbf{z}^o$ and $\mathbf{z}'$, where $\mathbf{z}'$ is riskier than $\mathbf{z}^o$. Then, heuristically, $x_n(\mathbf{w}, \mathbf{z})$ would be a *risk complement* if $x_n(\mathbf{w}, \mathbf{z}') \geq x_n(\mathbf{w}, \mathbf{z}^o)$, and a *risk substitute* if $x_n(\mathbf{w}, \mathbf{z}') \leq x_n(\mathbf{w}, \mathbf{z}^o)$. That is, an input is a risk complement if more of it is used in producing riskier state-contingent output bundles than in producing less risky production arrays. Conversely, an input is a risk substitute if moving from a less risky situation to a more risky situation is associated with a decrease in that input's use.[5]

Once we have a definition of the concepts of "riskier" and "less risky," the definition accords exactly with our intuition. As we saw in Chapter 3, there are a number of alternatives available to us.

For example, we might rely on the concept of π – majorization, developed in Chapter 3, which is equivalent to the notion of riskiness in the sense of Rothschild and Stiglitz. π – majorization is particularly convenient because it offers a total riskiness ordering if preferences are generalized Schur-concave. On the other hand, as in Chapter 3, we may want to take advantage of a total riskiness ordering, $\preceq_W$, generated by an arbitrary preference function that is not generalized Schur-concave, but that satisfies $\mathbf{z}^o \preceq_W \mathbf{z}'$ whenever $\Sigma_{s\in\Omega}\pi_s z_s = \Sigma_{s\in\Omega}\pi_s z_s'$ and $W(\mathbf{z}^o) \geq W(\mathbf{z}')$. Normally, however, we confine our attention to generalized Schur-concave W, for which $\mathbf{z}^o \preccurlyeq_\pi \mathbf{z}' \Rightarrow \mathbf{z}^o \preccurlyeq_W \mathbf{z}'$. Whether we consider riskiness in terms of the Rothschild–Stiglitz notion or in terms of a general preference structure, we emphasize that we always confine ourselves to comparisons where means are held constant.

5. This idea was first put forward in Chambers and Quiggin (1996), where the terms "risk-increasing input" and "risk-reducing input" were used in place of "risk-complement" and "risk-substitute."

We are now ready to give a formal definition of risk complements and risk substitutes.

> **Definition 4.1:** *For an ordering of riskiness* $\preccurlyeq$, *input* n *is a risk complement (risk substitute) at* z^o *if* $z^o \preccurlyeq z' \Rightarrow x_n(w, z') \geq x_n(w, z^o)$ $(x_n(w, z') \leq x_n(w, z^o))$.

Several comments should be made about this definition. First, it's not a purely technological definition because it depends on both the technology and subjective probabilities, and because it's valid only under preferences giving rise to cost minimization. Second, it's a local notion as it's expressly given at a point in state-contingent output space. And, third, for the ordering $\preceq_\pi$, it immediately leads to an easy characterization of risk complements and risk substitutes in terms of the derivatives of $x_n(\mathbf{w}, \mathbf{z}^o)$ in the state-contingent outputs that is analogous to Result 3.3 in Chapter 3. Take any $\mathbf{z}^o$ and find two elements of it, say, z_r^o and z_s^o such that $z_r^o \geq z_s^o$. Now consider the following spread of state-contingent outputs pairwise from z^o to z':

$$z'_h = z_h^o, \qquad h \neq r, s$$

$$z'_r = z_r^o + \frac{\pi_s}{\pi_r}\delta$$

$$z'_s = z_s^o - \delta,$$

for $\delta > 0$, but differentiably small. Because the mean hasn't changed, but the dispersion between z_r and z_s has increased, $\mathbf{z}^o \preceq_\pi \mathbf{z}'$. Hence, for any generalized Schur-concave W, $\mathbf{z}^o \preceq_W \mathbf{z}'$. The associated change in the utilization of the input n is

$$\frac{\partial x_n(\mathbf{w}, \mathbf{z}^o)}{\partial z_r}\frac{\pi_s}{\pi_r}\delta - \frac{\partial x_n(\mathbf{w}, \mathbf{z}^o)}{\partial z_s}\delta,$$

which is positive if input n is a risk complement and negative if input n is a risk substitute. Hence, we conclude:

> **Lemma 4.1:** *Input* n *is a risk complement for a generalized Schur-concave preference structure at* z^o (M = *1) only if for all* r, s $\in \Omega$:

$$\left(\frac{\partial x_n(w, z^o)/\partial z_r}{\pi_r} - \frac{\partial x_n(w, z^o)/\partial z_s}{\pi_s}\right)(z_r^o - z_s^o) \geq 0.$$

Input n *is a risk substitute for a generalized Schur-concave preference structure at* z^o (M = *1) only if for all* r, s ∈ *Ω:*

$$\left(\frac{\partial x_n(w,z^o)/\partial z_r}{\pi_r} - \frac{\partial x_n(w,z^o)/\partial z_s}{\pi_s}\right)(z_r^o - z_s^o) \le 0.$$

4.3 NONLINEAR INPUT EVALUATION AND EFFORT COST

We now return to the more general effort-cost function:

$$c(\mathbf{z}) = \min_{\mathbf{x}}\{g(\mathbf{x}) : \mathbf{x} \in X(\mathbf{z})\},$$

with $c(\mathbf{z}) = \infty$ when $X(\mathbf{z}) = \emptyset$. The first order of business is to show that this minimum exists. If $\mathbf{z}$ is feasible, there has to be an $\mathbf{x}^o \in X(\mathbf{z})$. Now doing just as we did in the linear pricing case, we can consider the auxiliary problem:

$$\min_{\mathbf{x}}\{g(\mathbf{x}) : \mathbf{x} \in X(\mathbf{z}) \cap X'\},$$

where $X' = \{\mathbf{x} : g(\mathbf{x}) \le g(\mathbf{x}^o)\}$. By G.1, $g(\mathbf{x})$ is nondecreasing and continuous in $\mathbf{x}$, thus X' is a closed set. Therefore, as long as the input correspondence is closed (X.8), $X(\mathbf{z}) \cap X'$ is a nonempty and compact set. And since $g(\mathbf{x})$ is continuous in $\mathbf{x}$, the Weierstrass theorem implies that the minimum exists. By definition, for $\mathbf{x} \notin X'$ but $\mathbf{x} \in X(\mathbf{z})$, $g(\mathbf{x}) > g(\mathbf{x}^o)$. So, the effort-cost function is well-defined if the state-contingent output matrix is producible.

Having shown $c(\mathbf{z})$ exists, the next step is to determine its properties. Because these properties, in broad terms, are quite similar to properties CL, we first state them and then discuss them, without attempting any formal proof. A sketch of a proof is relegated to the appendix to this chapter.

Result 4.1: *If* X(*z*) *satisfies X.8 and* g(*x*) *satisfies G.1, then* c(*z*) *satisfies properties C.*

Properties of the Effort-Cost Function (C)

C.1. If $X(\mathbf{z})$ satisfies X.1, $c(\mathbf{0}_{M\times S}) = g(\mathbf{0}_N) \ge 0$ and $c(\mathbf{z}) \ge g(\mathbf{0}_N)$ for $\mathbf{z} \ge \mathbf{0}_{M\times S}$ and $\mathbf{z} \ne \mathbf{0}_{M\times S}$

C.2. If $X(\mathbf{z})$ satisfies X.2, $\mathbf{z}' \ge \mathbf{z} \Rightarrow c(\mathbf{z}') \ge c(\mathbf{z})$

C.2.W. If $X(\mathbf{z})$ satisfies X.2.W, $c(\lambda\mathbf{z}) \leq c(\mathbf{z})$ for $0 < \lambda < 1$

C.3. If $X(\mathbf{z})$ satisfies X.4, if $\|\text{vec } \mathbf{z}^k\| \to \infty$ as $k \to \infty$, $\lim_{k\to\infty} c(\mathbf{z}^k) = \infty$

C.4. If $X(\mathbf{z})$ satisfies X.5, $c(\lambda\mathbf{z} + (1 - \lambda)\mathbf{z}^o) \leq \min_{\mathbf{x}}\{g(X(\mathbf{z}) \cap X(\mathbf{z}^o))\}$;

C.5. If $g(\mathbf{x})$ satisfies G.3 and $X(\mathbf{z})$ satisfies X.7, $c(\lambda\mathbf{z} + (1 - \lambda)\mathbf{z}^o) \leq c(\lambda\mathbf{z}) + c((1 - \lambda)\mathbf{z}^o)$ for $0 < \lambda < 1$

C.6. If $g(\mathbf{x})$ satisfies G.3′ and $X(\mathbf{z})$ satisfies X.7, $c(\lambda\mathbf{z} + (1 - \lambda)\mathbf{z}^o) \leq \lambda c(\mathbf{z}) + (1 - \lambda)c(\mathbf{z}^o)$ for $0 < \lambda < 1$.

Property C.1 provides a lower bound for the effort-cost function. This lower bound might not be zero, because g may encompass some fixed costs. However, if there are no fixed costs in g, then $c(\mathbf{0}_{M\times S}) = 0$. Under linear pricing, free disposability of state-contingent outputs implies that effort cost is nondecreasing in each element of the state-contingent output matrix. And weak disposability of state-contingent outputs implies that effort cost is nondecreasing as one moves out along any ray in state-contingent output space. Both properties are preserved under nonlinear effort evaluation (C.2 and C.2.W). Property C.3 means that, even with nonlinear pricing, it's prohibitively costly to produce an unboundedly large state-contingent output.

Each of properties C.4 through C.6 says something different about the cost of producing convex combinations of state-contingent output configurations. Let's start with quasi-concavity of the input correspondence (X.5). By C.4, a consequence of the input correspondence being quasi–concave is an upper bound on the cost of producing any convex combination of state-contingent output configurations. This parallels property CL.6 under linear pricing. Unfortunately, in many instances, this upper bound won't be very informative. For example, let's suppose that $X(\mathbf{z}) \cap X(\mathbf{z}^o)$ is the empty set. Then, the upper bound is a noninformative infinity. By strengthening quasi-concavity of the input correspondence to concavity of the output correspondence (Z.7 and X.7), while also imposing subadditivity on the effort-evaluation function, we can show (C.5) that the cost of producing any convex combination of two state-contingent output configurations must be less than the cost of producing the components of the convex combination ($\lambda\mathbf{z}$) and ($(1 - \lambda)\mathbf{z}^o$) separately so that the effort-cost function inherits the subadditivity of the effort-evaluation function. As such, C.5 can be reinterpreted as a statement about marginal cost.

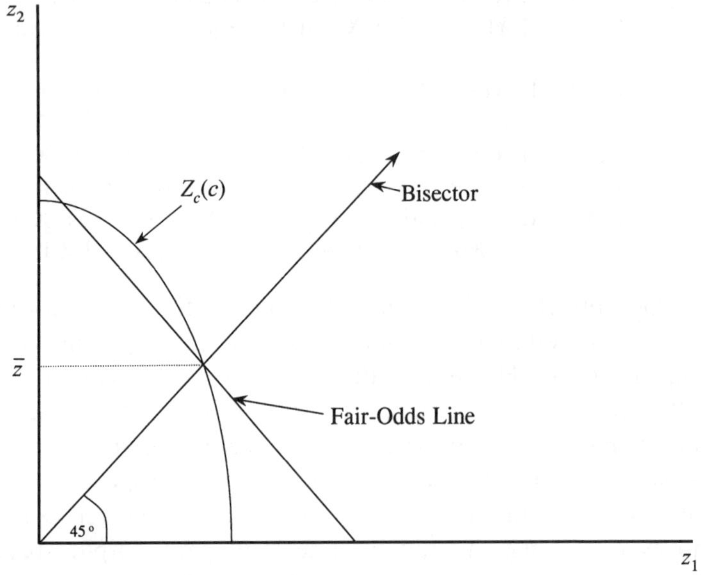

Figure 4.4 Effort-cost output set.

This can be seen a little more clearly by letting $\lambda\mathbf{z} = \mathbf{z}^*$ and $(1 - \lambda)\mathbf{z}^o = \mathbf{z}'$: Then

$$c(\mathbf{z}^* + \mathbf{z}') - c(\mathbf{z}') \leq c(\mathbf{z}^*).$$

The marginal cost of moving from $\mathbf{z}'$ to $\mathbf{z}^*$ is always less than the cost of producing $\mathbf{z}^*$ by itself. Hence, one is always better off producing $\mathbf{z}^* + \mathbf{z}'$ in a single operation or plant than in producing them in two separate operations.

Property C.6 implies two things. First, the effort-cost function is convex in state-contingent outputs. That means that the marginal cost of each state-contingent output is a nondecreasing function of the same state-contingent output. And second, the lower contour sets of the effort-cost function, that is, $Z_c(c) = \{\mathbf{z} : c(\mathbf{z}) \leq c\}$, are themselves convex. So when the marginal cost of each state-contingent output is positive, C.6 implies that one state-contingent output can be substituted for another only at increasing cost. Figure 4.4 illustrates in the $M = 1$, $S = 2$ case under the additional assumption that free disposability of state-contingent outputs also applies. Notice that C.6

implies the same properties for $Z_c(c)$ that convexity of the output set (Z.6 or X.6) implies for $Z(\mathbf{x})$. To emphasize the similarity between $Z(\mathbf{x})$ and $Z_c(c)$, we shall refer to the latter as the *effort-cost output set*. But in so doing, we remind the reader that X.6 is not generally sufficient to generate C.6.

Example 4.4: *An effort-cost function capable of satisfying properties C.1 through C.3 in the case of a single stochastic output (*M *= 1) is*

$$c(z) = \frac{1}{2}\sum_{r=1}^{S}\sum_{s=1}^{S}\beta_{rs}(z_r z_s)^{1/2},$$

with $\beta_{rs} = \beta_{sr}$. *A sufficient condition for this cost function to be globally convex (C.6) is that* $\beta_{rs} \leq 0$ *for all* $r \neq s$. *As long as all the* β_{rs} *are finite, this effort-cost function also satisfies C.3. And, finally, the reader should work out sufficient conditions for this effort-cost function to satisfy C.1, C.2, or C.2.W.*

4.4 THE REVENUE-COST FUNCTION

Generally, producers will not be directly interested in the matrix of state-contingent outputs that they produce. Instead, they will be interested in the vector of state-contingent returns that can be derived from this matrix of state-contingent outputs. For example, large-scale grain producers produce grain to sell and not to eat. Therefore, it's useful to have indirect representations of producer behavior in terms of state-contingent revenues rather than in terms of state-contingent outputs. We, therefore, define the *revenue-cost function*[6] $C: \Re_+^S \times \Re_{++}^{M\times S} \rightarrow \Re_+$ by

$$C(\mathbf{r},\mathbf{p}) = \min_{\mathbf{x},\mathbf{z}}\left\{g(\mathbf{x}) : \mathbf{x} \in X(\mathbf{z}), \sum_m p_{ms}z_{ms} \geq r_s, s \in \Omega\right\}$$

$$= \min_z\left\{c(\mathbf{z}) : \sum_m p_{ms}z_{ms} \geq r_s, s \in \Omega\right\}$$

if there exists a feasible state-contingent output matrix for which $\Sigma_m p_{ms}z_{ms} \geq r_s$, $s \in \Omega$ and ∞ otherwise. In words, the revenue-cost

6. Färe and Grosskopf (1994) have called the nonstochastic analog of the revenue-cost function the cost-indirect-revenue function. In what follows, for the sake of parsimony, we shall always use our more compact terminology.

function represents the cheapest way to produce a given vector of state-contingent revenues. Unlike the effort-cost function, which only involves choices over inputs, the revenue-cost function also involves choices over outputs; outputs and inputs are simultaneously adjusted to ensure attainment of a given vector of state-contingent revenues.

In view of our discussions of the effort-cost function under linear and nonlinear pricing, the properties of the revenue-cost function are self-evident. Therefore, we content ourselves with listing them and providing a brief intuitive discussion of each. A more formal derivation can be found in the Appendix to this chapter. We emphasize that these properties are similar to properties that we have already derived for the effort-cost function. With little loss of generality, the reader can refer back to earlier discussion to obtain a feel for the economic meaning of these results.

Properties of the Revenue-Cost Function (RC)

RC.1. If $c(\mathbf{z})$ satisfies C.1, $C(\mathbf{0}_S, \mathbf{p}) = g(\mathbf{0}_N) \geq 0$, $C(\mathbf{r}, \mathbf{p}) \geq g(\mathbf{0}_N)$ $\mathbf{r} \neq \mathbf{0}_S$

RC.2. If $c(\mathbf{z})$ satisfies C.2, $\mathbf{r}' \geq \mathbf{r} \Rightarrow C(\mathbf{r}', \mathbf{p}) \geq C(\mathbf{r}, \mathbf{p})$

RC.2.W. If $c(\mathbf{z})$ satisfies C.2.W, $C(\lambda\mathbf{r}, \mathbf{p}) \leq C(\mathbf{r}, \mathbf{p})$ for $0 \leq \lambda \leq 1$

RC.3. If $c(\mathbf{z})$ satisfies C.3, if $\|\mathbf{r}^k\| \to \infty$ as $k \to \infty$, $\lim_{k\to\infty} C(\mathbf{r}^k, \mathbf{p}) = \infty$

RC.4. If $c(\mathbf{z})$ satisfies C.6, C is convex in $\mathbf{r}$

RC.5. $\mathbf{p}' \geq \mathbf{p} \Rightarrow C(\mathbf{r}, \mathbf{p}') \leq C(\mathbf{r}, \mathbf{p})$

RC.6. $C(\mathbf{r}_{-s}, \theta r_s, \mathbf{p}_{-s}, \theta \mathbf{p}_s) = C(\mathbf{r}_{-s}, \theta r_s, \mathbf{p}_{-s}, \theta \mathbf{p}_s)$, $\theta > 0$

RC.7. $C(\mathbf{r}, \mathbf{p}) = C(\theta\mathbf{r}, \theta\mathbf{p})$, $\theta > 0$.

RC.1 places a lower bound on the revenue-cost function; it can't be negative. RC.2 and RC.2.W represent different monotonicity properties for the revenue-cost function reflecting different assumptions about the disposability of state-contingent outputs. In words, the former implies that the marginal cost of all state-contingent revenues is nonnegative, and the latter implies that radial expansions of state-contingent revenues carry with them positive marginal costs. RC.3 says that producing a state-contingent revenue vector with any infinitely large elements in it will be infinitely costly. RC.4 is a convexity result, which says that as long as the output correspondence is concave, the revenue-cost function will be convex in state-contingent revenues. Put another way, marginal cost of state-contingent revenues will be nondecreasing in revenue. RC.5 through RC.7 all reflect the same fact. The constraint set for the revenue-cost function is homogeneous of degree zero in state-contingent revenues and prices. Hence, rescaling them by the same positive factor has no effect on optimal revenue cost. On the other hand, rescaling only state-contingent output prices upward while keeping revenues constant makes it possible to attain a given vector of state-contingent revenues with state-contingent output matrices that, in an intuitive sense, are smaller. Hence, costs cannot rise from so rescaling state-contingent output prices.

4.5 MEASURING TECHNOLOGICAL RISK: THE CERTAINTY-EQUIVALENT REVENUE AND THE PRODUCTION-RISK PREMIUM

Just as risk averters pay a premium to ensure the certainty outcome, achieving the certainty outcome may prove costly. Heuristically, removing production uncertainty and producing the same nonstochastic output in each state should cost more than allowing stochastic production. The intuitive reason is clear: Most people appear averse to taking risk, but producers routinely use stochastic technologies. A plausible conjecture, therefore, is that removing risk is costly. If it were not, we'd expect to see, for example, farmers growing all their crops in greenhouses rather than in the open air subject to the vagaries of weather. So because uncertainty seems inherent in real-world situations, it proves advantageous to have cost-based measures of how hard it would be to achieve a nonstochastic production pattern.

For the revenue-cost function, $C(\mathbf{r}, \mathbf{p})$, and $\mathbf{r} \in \Re_{+}^{S}$, we define the (*cost*) *certainty equivalent revenue*, denoted by $e^c(\mathbf{r}, \mathbf{p}) \in \Re_{+}$, as the maximum nonstochastic revenue that can be produced at cost $C(\mathbf{r}, \mathbf{p})$, that is,

$$e^c(\mathbf{r}, \mathbf{p}) = \sup\{e : C(e\mathbf{1}_S, \mathbf{p}) \leq C(\mathbf{r}, \mathbf{p})\},$$

where $\mathbf{1}_S$ is the S-dimensional unit vector. Pictorially, therefore, the certainty equivalent revenue is given by the point where the bisector intersects the revenue isocost curve. Figure 4.5 illustrates under the

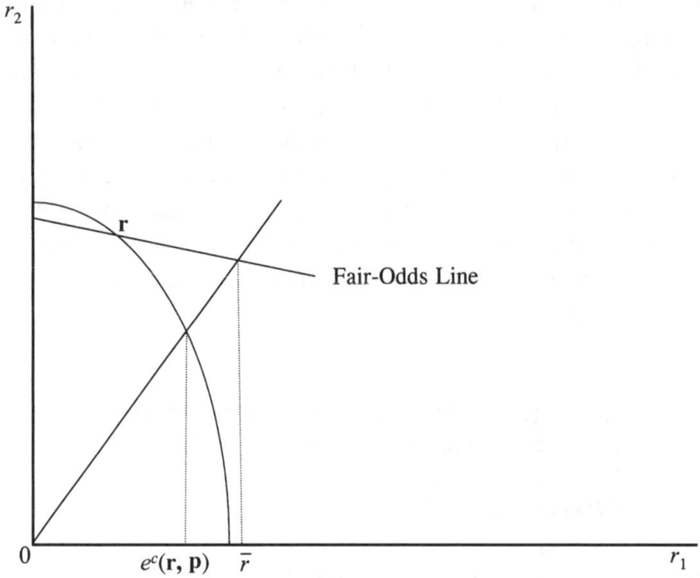

Figure 4.5 Certainty equivalent revenue and production risk premiums.

presumption that the revenue-cost function is nondecreasing and convex in state-contingent revenues so that its isocost curves are negatively sloped and concave to the origin.

By analogy with the absolute risk premium defined in Chapter 3, the *production-risk premium* is defined as the difference between mean revenue and the certainty equivalent revenue.[7] Notationally, letting $\bar{\mathbf{r}} \in \Re^s_+$ denote the vector with the mean of **r**,

$$\bar{r} = \sum_{s \in \Omega} \pi_s r_s,$$

occurring in each state, then the production-risk premium is defined by

$$p(\mathbf{r}, \mathbf{p}) = \bar{r} - e^c(\mathbf{r}, \mathbf{p})$$

and satisfies

7. The production-risk premium can always be expressed in terms of a benefit function for the effort-cost output set.

$$C(\mathbf{r}, \mathbf{p}) = C(\bar{\mathbf{r}} - p(\mathbf{r}, \mathbf{p})\mathbf{1}_S, \mathbf{p}) = C(e^c(\mathbf{r}, \mathbf{p})\mathbf{1}_S, \mathbf{p}). \tag{4.1}$$

The production-risk premium is illustrated in Figure 4.5 as the horizontal difference between the mean revenue, determined by the point where the fair-odds line through **r** intersects the bisector and the certainty-equivalent revenue.

The technology is said to be *inherently risky* at **r** if producing $\bar{\mathbf{r}}$ is more costly than producing **r** and *not inherently risky*[8] at **r** if producing $\bar{\mathbf{r}}$ is less costly than producing **r**. Under RC.2, the technology is inherently risky at **r** if and only if $p(\mathbf{r}, \mathbf{p})$ is positive, or, equivalently, if and only if the certainty equivalent revenue is no greater than the mean revenue. Both imply that producing $\bar{\mathbf{r}}$ is more costly than producing the stochastic **r**. There are costs to removing uncertainty. This seems the natural state of affairs. However, $p(\mathbf{r}, \mathbf{p})$ can be negative, implying that certainty is less costly than the stochastic output vector, and in this case, the technology is not inherently risky at **r**.[9] Notice, in particular, that in Figure 4.5 for the depicted fair odds, all points on the revenue-isocost curve below the bisector are not inherently risky.

This latter observation generally holds true. When the fair-odds line is not tangent to the revenue-isocost curve at the bisector,[10] there will exist points on the isocost curve where the technology is not inherently risky. However, a risk-averse or risk-neutral producer never produces in a region of the isocost curve where the technology is not inherently risky.

This implies that we can think in terms of a "good" state of nature and a "bad" state of nature. The good state, naturally, is the one in which the state-contingent revenue is chosen to be the highest. Given that the producer can produce at the bisector in Figure 4.6, this

8. Frequently, we will lapse into looser terminology and speak, for example, of a particular state-contingent revenue vector as being inherently risky. The reader should always understand this to mean that the technology is inherently risky at that state-contingent revenue vector.
9. In what follows, we define a class of technologies, the generalized Schur-convex, which are not inherently risky for any **r**. Chapter 6, which analyzes production in the presence of futures and forward markets, relies heavily on generalized Schur-convex technologies. Visually, these technologies have the fair-odds line tangent to the isocost curve at the bisector.
10. More generally when the gradient of the revenue-cost function at points on the equal-revenue vector is not proportional to the producer's subjective probabilities.

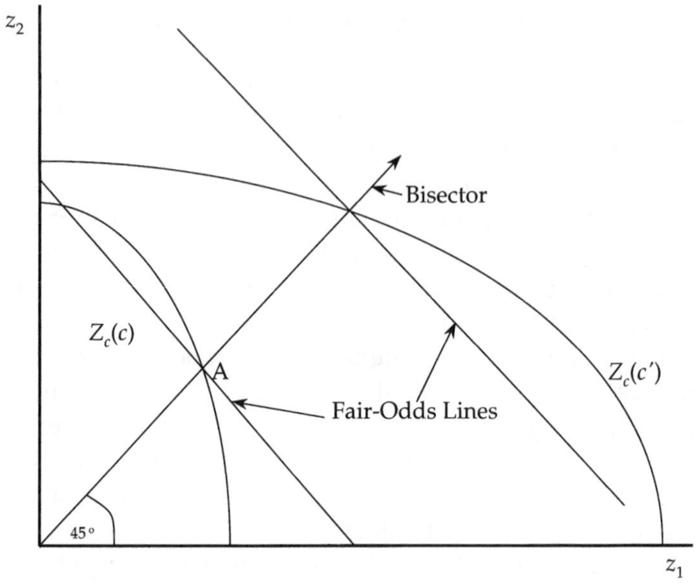

Figure 4.6 Good and bad states of nature.

literally implies that risk-averse producers typically will eschew a nonstochastic revenue pattern for a stochastic one. Risk-averse producers willingly choose to bear some production risk. Understanding why is easy.

Suppose a risk averter is initially at the point of intersection, A, between the isocost curve and the bisector in Figure 4.6. At that point, if the individual has differentiably smooth preferences, he will also be at a point where the fair-odds line is tangent to his indifference curve. (Recall the discussion in Chapter 3.) By moving away from the bisector along the isocost curve in a northwesterly direction, he obviously reaches a higher level of preference. However, movements along the isocost curve away from the bisector in a southeasterly direction bring him to a lower preference level. Hence, no risk-averse or risk-neutral individual whose subjective probabilities are given by the fair-odds line depicted in Figure 4.6 would ever locate below the bisector. State 2 would be the good state of nature in our terminology, and state 1 the bad state.

Notice, however, that for the general state-contingent technology, which state is the good state and which is the bad state is not determined solely by the technology. This can be visualized easily with the aid of Figure 4.6 by imagining a new fair-odds line (consistent with someone else's preferences) that would be tangent to the isocost curve below the bisector. For those subjective probabilities, state 1 would be the good state and state 2 the bad state. Figure 4.6 also illustrates that, even holding probabilities constant, good and bad states can change as costs change.

The split between good and bad, and indeed any finer ranking of states of nature, is thus inherently subjective for the general state-contingent production technology. This also accords with most people's view of the world. If it did not, it would be hard to explain why some individuals choose to engage in what many others would perceive as highly risky behavior. For example, one of the most common explanations of individuals engaging in the most severely punished criminal activities is also the simplest. They don't believe they'll be caught. Translated into our terms, this means that their subjective probability of being caught approaches zero. More generally, gradations such as good and bad are inherently subjective and very hard to quantify in purely objective terms. One of the greatest strengths of the state-contingent approach that we advocate is that it accommodates this reality. Perhaps the greatest intellectual weakness of the traditional output-cubical approach is that it does not,[11] as the following example illustrates.

Example 4.5: *Consider the isocost curve for a revenue-cost function of the form*

$$C(\boldsymbol{r}, \boldsymbol{p}) = \text{Max}_{1,2,\ldots,S}\{C^s(r_s, \boldsymbol{p})\},$$

which is a special case of a single-output-revenue cubical technology. Depicted in state-contingent revenue space, the isocost curve in the two-state case will be a rectangle. More generally, let's call the costliest state, state k. *Presuming that each* C^s *is strictly increasing and continuous, then for each state,* s, *the maximum revenue achievable at this level of revenue cost is*

$$r_s(C^k(r_k, \boldsymbol{p})) = \text{Max}\{\hat{r}_s : C^s(\hat{r}_s, \boldsymbol{p}) \le C^k(r_k, \boldsymbol{p})\}.$$

11. As we will show in Chapter 9, it is precisely this weakness of the output-cubical approach that inhibits its fruitful application in the area of principal–agent analysis.

The S-dimensional vector with $r_s(C^k(r_k, \boldsymbol{p}))$ *as its typical element defines the outermost vertex of the isocost frontier for this technology.*[12] *To see this, notice that by definition,*

$$C^s(r_s(C^k(r_k, \boldsymbol{p})), \boldsymbol{p}) = \text{Max}_{1,2,\ldots,S}\{C^s(r_s, \boldsymbol{p})\}.$$

However, increasing any state-contingent revenue beyond this point necessarily leads to a higher cost level. Now consider the certainty equivalent revenue for this technology. By definition,

$$C^s(e^c(\boldsymbol{r}, \boldsymbol{p}), \boldsymbol{p}) \le C^s(r_s(C^k(r_k, \boldsymbol{p})), \boldsymbol{p}), \qquad s \in \Omega.$$

Given the strict monotonicity of each ex post revenue cost function, it then follows immediately that

$$e^c(\boldsymbol{r}, \boldsymbol{p}) = \text{Min}_{1,2,\ldots,S}\{r_s(C^k(r_k, \boldsymbol{p}))\}.$$

Regardless of their attitudes toward risk, all individuals who are the residual claimants for their productive decisions would locate at the outermost vertex. The technology must be inherently risky at this point regardless of the preferences of the individual because

$$e^c(\boldsymbol{r}, \boldsymbol{p}) \le \sum_{s \in \Omega} \pi_s r_s(C^k(r_k, \boldsymbol{p}))$$

for all possible probability vectors.

By the definition of the certainty equivalent revenue and RC. 7, for $\lambda > 0$,

$$\begin{aligned} e^c(\lambda\mathbf{r}, \lambda\mathbf{p}) &= \sup\{e : C(e\mathbf{1}^S, \lambda\mathbf{p}) \le C(\lambda\mathbf{r}, \lambda\mathbf{p})\} \\ &= \sup\left\{e : C\left(\frac{e}{\lambda}\mathbf{1}^S, \mathbf{p}\right) \le C(\mathbf{r}, \mathbf{p})\right\} \\ &= \lambda \sup\left\{\frac{e}{\lambda} : C\left(\frac{e}{\lambda}\mathbf{1}^S, \mathbf{p}\right) \le C(\mathbf{r}, \mathbf{p})\right\} \\ &= \lambda e^c(\mathbf{r}, \mathbf{p}). \end{aligned}$$

12. By the outermost vertex, we mean the point on the isocost frontier that dominates all other points on the isocost frontier in a vector sense. Thus, if we specify all points on the frontier by the set I for isocost, then its vertex is given by the element $\mathbf{r}^{\max} \in I$ that satisfies

$$\mathbf{r}^{\max} \ge \tilde{r}$$

for all $\tilde{r} \in I$.

Thus, rescaling all state-contingent prices and revenues by the same factor just rescales the certainty equivalent revenue by the same factor. Since the certainty equivalent revenue is a cardinal measure of the individual's costs, this is a particularly advantageous property for it to have. Using this fact leads us to identify the following homogeneity properties for the certainty equivalent and the production-risk premium.

> **Lemma 4.2:** *The certainty equivalent revenue satisfies:* $e^c(\mu\mathbf{r}, \mu\mathbf{p}) = \mu e^c(\mathbf{r}, \mathbf{p})$, $\mu > 0$. *The production risk premium satisfies* $p(\mu\mathbf{r}, \mu\mathbf{p}) = \mu p(\mathbf{r}, \mathbf{p})$, $\mu > 0$.

Just as the certainty equivalent and the absolute risk premium are alternative characterizations of preferences, the certainty equivalent revenue and the production risk premium are alternative characterizations of the technology under RC.2.[13] Formally, this can be verified by examining (4.1) and noting that the certainty equivalent is a monotonic transformation of the revenue-cost function. Cost levels can be unambiguously ranked under RC.2 by comparing certainty-equivalent revenues.

In later chapters, it will prove useful to have classes of technologies that are easily characterized in terms of either the productionrisk premium or the certainty equivalent. We define a state-contingent technology as displaying *constant absolute riskiness* if for all $\mathbf{r}$, $t \in \Re$:

$$p(\mathbf{r} + t\mathbf{1}^S, \mathbf{p}) = p(\mathbf{r}, \mathbf{p}).$$

Following arguments made in Chapter 3 for CARA preferences, while using properties RC, (4.1), and Lemma 4.2, we find the following.

> **Result 4.2:** *If the revenue-cost function satisfies properties RC.1 to RC.7, the technology displays constant absolute riskiness if and only if the revenue-cost function can be expressed as*
>
> $$C(\mathbf{r}, \mathbf{p}) = \hat{C}(\mathbf{T}(\mathbf{r}, \mathbf{p}), \mathbf{p}),$$
>
> *where*

13. We can generalize this to RC.2.W by relying on the relative risk measures developed in what follows.

$$\mathrm{T}(\boldsymbol{r}+\delta \boldsymbol{1}^S, \boldsymbol{p}) = \mathrm{T}(\boldsymbol{r},\boldsymbol{p})+\delta, \qquad \delta \in \Re,$$
$$\mathrm{T}(\lambda \boldsymbol{r}, \lambda \boldsymbol{p}) = \lambda \mathrm{T}(\boldsymbol{r},\boldsymbol{p}), \qquad \lambda > 0,$$

and $\hat{C}(\boldsymbol{T}(\mathbf{r}, \mathbf{p}), \mathbf{p})$ *is homogeneous of degree zero in* $\mathrm{T}(\mathbf{r}, \mathbf{p})$ *and* $\mathbf{p}$*, nondecreasing in* $\mathrm{T}(\mathbf{r}, \mathbf{p})$*, and nonincreasing in* $\mathbf{p}$*.* $\mathrm{T}(\mathbf{r}, \mathbf{p})$ *can be chosen to be nondecreasing.*

Demonstrating this result is straightforward. Constant absolute riskiness implies

$$p(\mathbf{r}+t\mathbf{1}^S, \mathbf{p}) = p(\mathbf{r},\mathbf{p}),$$

which by the definition of the production-risk premium requires

$$\bar{r}+t-e^c(\mathbf{r}+t\mathbf{1}^S,\mathbf{p}) = \bar{r}-e^c(\mathbf{r},\mathbf{p})$$

whence

$$e^c(\mathbf{r}+t\mathbf{1}^S,\mathbf{p}) = e^c(\mathbf{r},\mathbf{p})+t.$$

Recalling from (4.1) that the revenue-cost function must be a monotonic transformation of the certainty-equivalent revenue then establishes that under constant absolute riskiness, the revenue-cost function must be a monotonic transformation of a certainty equivalent revenue having this last property. Letting $T(\mathbf{r}, \mathbf{p}) = e^c(\mathbf{r}, \mathbf{p})$ and using Lemma 4.2 establishes the homogeneity properties of T. The monotonicity properties follow from the properties of the revenue-cost function RC.

Geometrically, if a revenue-cost function displays constant absolute riskiness, rays parallel to the equal-revenue ray will cut successive isocost contours for the revenue-cost function at points of equal slope. For a differentiable technology displaying constant absolute riskiness, the marginal rate of transformation between state-contingent revenues is given by (subscripts denote partial derivatives)

$$\frac{T_s(\mathbf{r},\mathbf{p})}{T_k(\mathbf{r},\mathbf{p})}, \qquad k,s \in \Omega$$

and satisfies[14]

14. To obtain this result, differentiate both sides of

$$T(\mathbf{r}+\delta\mathbf{1}^S,\mathbf{p}) = T(\mathbf{r},\mathbf{p})+\delta, \qquad \delta \in \Re$$

with respect to r_s and r_k and take ratios.

$$\frac{T_s(\mathbf{r},\mathbf{p})}{T_k(\mathbf{r},\mathbf{p})} = \frac{T_s(\mathbf{r}+\delta\mathbf{1}^S,\mathbf{p})}{T_k(\mathbf{r}+\delta\mathbf{1}^S,\mathbf{p})}, \qquad \delta \in \Re, \forall k,\ s \in \Omega.$$

Hence, if the fair-odds line cuts a single isocost curve from above, say, at the bisector, it will cut all isocosts curves at the bisector from above. Therefore, technologies exhibiting constant absolute riskiness have the property that the good state of nature is unique across different revenue-cost levels.

The production-risk premium is an absolute measure of the inherent riskiness of the technology. A measure of the relative riskiness of the technology is given by the *relative production-risk premium*

$$r(\mathbf{r},\mathbf{p}) = \frac{\bar{r}}{e^c(\mathbf{r},\mathbf{p})}.$$

The relative production-risk premium and the production-risk premium are directly related. Slightly manipulating their respective definitions reveals that

$$r(\mathbf{r},\mathbf{p}) = \left(1 - \frac{p(\mathbf{r},\mathbf{p})}{\bar{r}}\right)^{-1},$$

from which we conclude a technology is inherently risky at $\mathbf{r}$ if and only if $r(\mathbf{r},\mathbf{p}) \geqslant 1$.

By analogy with the treatment of constant absolute riskiness, we say a technology displays *constant relative riskiness* if for all $\mathbf{r}$, $t \in \Re_{+}$,

$$r(t\mathbf{r},\mathbf{p}) = r(\mathbf{r},\mathbf{p}).$$

From this definition, properties RC, and Lemma 4.2, it follows almost immediately that:

> **Result 4.3:** *If the revenue-cost function satisfies properties RC.1 to RC.7, the technology displays constant relative riskiness if and only if the revenue-cost function can be expressed as*
>
> $$C(\boldsymbol{r},\boldsymbol{p}) = \bar{C}(\bar{\boldsymbol{T}}(\boldsymbol{r},\boldsymbol{p}),\boldsymbol{p}),$$
>
> *where*
>
> $$\bar{T}(\lambda\boldsymbol{r},\boldsymbol{p}) = \lambda\bar{T}(\boldsymbol{r},\boldsymbol{p}),$$
> $$\bar{T}(\boldsymbol{r},\lambda\boldsymbol{p}) = \bar{T}(\boldsymbol{r},\boldsymbol{p}), \qquad \lambda > 0,$$

and $\overline{\mathrm{C}}(\overline{\boldsymbol{T}}(\boldsymbol{r}, \boldsymbol{p}), \boldsymbol{p})$ is homogeneous of degree zero in $\overline{\mathrm{T}}(\boldsymbol{r}, \boldsymbol{p})$ and output prices, nondecreasing in $\overline{\mathrm{T}}(\boldsymbol{r}, \boldsymbol{p})$, and nonincreasing in output prices. $\overline{\mathrm{T}}(\boldsymbol{r}, \boldsymbol{p})$ can be chosen to be nondecreasing in the state-contingent revenues.

Therefore, technologies that have revenue-cost structures that are homothetic in revenues, that is, have isocost contours that are radial blowups of a reference isocost curve, exhibit constant relative riskiness. Technologies with constant relative riskiness also have unique good and bad states of nature across revenue-cost levels.

4.6 THE STRUCTURE OF EFFORT-COST FUNCTIONS

We have already seen that imposing structure on input sets imposes structure on the effort-cost function under linear pricing. Moreover, we have also determined that imposing structure on the production-risk premiums also imposes structure on the underlying revenue-cost function. We now investigate more generally how structural properties of input sets are reflected in the effort-cost functions derived from them.

4.6.1 Output-Cubical Technologies

When the technology is output-cubical, that is, there is no substitutability between state-contingent outputs, the input set can be written

$$X(\mathbf{z}) = \cap_s X_s(\mathbf{z}_s).$$

Denoting the cost minimizer by $\mathbf{x}(\mathbf{z})$, it must be true that $\mathbf{x}(\mathbf{z}) \in X_s(\mathbf{z}_s)$ for each s. Hence,

$$g(\mathbf{x}(\mathbf{z})) \geq \min\{g(\mathbf{x}) : \mathbf{x} \in X_s(\mathbf{z}_s)\} = c^s(\mathbf{z}_s),$$

for all s. This last expression implies that the effort-cost function must be an upper bound for the set of state-specific effort-cost functions, that is, $\{c^1(\mathbf{z}_1), \ldots, c^S(\mathbf{z}_S)\}$, and thus

$$c(\mathbf{z}) \geq \max\{c^1(\mathbf{z}_1), \ldots, c^S(\mathbf{z}_S)\}.$$

Pictorially, therefore, the isocost curves for the effort-cost function will inherit the cubical shape of output-cubical technologies.

4.6.2 State-Allocable Inputs

The input set for the state-allocable-input technology is

$$X(\mathbf{z}) = \sum_{s \in \Omega} X_s(\mathbf{z}_s).$$

Denoting $\mathbf{x}^s \in \operatorname{argmin}\{g(\mathbf{x}) : \mathbf{x} \in X_s(\mathbf{z}_s)\}$, under G.3, it must be true that

$$g\left(\sum_{s \in \Omega} \mathbf{x}^s\right) \leq \sum_{s \in \Omega} g(\mathbf{x}^s) = \sum_{s \in \Omega} c^s(\mathbf{z}_s).$$

Now since $\Sigma_{s \in \Omega} \mathbf{x}^s \in \Sigma_{s \in \Omega} X_s(\mathbf{z}_s)$, by the definition of the effort-cost function, it follows immediately that

$$c(\mathbf{z}) \leq g\left(\sum_{s \in \Omega} \mathbf{x}^s\right) \leq \sum_{s \in \Omega} c^s(\mathbf{z}_s)$$

as long as G.3 holds. In words, if the effort-evaluation function is subadditive, there must exist some positive externalities between production in different states of nature. Or put another way, preparing jointly for uncertainty is preferable to preparing independently for each state.

The subadditive structure, however, emerges from the presumption that the effort evaluation function is subadditive. Under linear pricing, these inequalities can be replaced by equalities so that

$$c(\mathbf{w}, \mathbf{z}) = \sum_{s \in \Omega} c^s(\mathbf{w}, \mathbf{z}_s).$$

4.6.3 Input-Homothetic Technologies

If the state-contingent technology is input-homothetic, its input sets can be written

$$X(\mathbf{z}) = h(\mathbf{z}) X',$$

where $h : \Re_+^{M \times S} \to \Re_{++}$, and $X' \subseteq \Re_+^N$ is a reference input set for some reference bundle of outputs. Assuming G.2, the positive linear homogeneity of $g(\mathbf{x})$, one obtains

$$\begin{aligned} c(\mathbf{z}) &= \min\{g(\mathbf{x}):\mathbf{x} \in h(\mathbf{z})X'\} \\ &= \min\{g(\mathbf{x}):\mathbf{x}/h(\mathbf{z}) \in X'\} \\ &= \min\{g(h(\mathbf{z})\,\mathbf{x}/h(\mathbf{z})):\mathbf{x}/h(\mathbf{z}) \in X'\} \\ &= h(\mathbf{z})\min\{g(\mathbf{x}^*):\mathbf{x}^* \in X'\} \\ &= h(\mathbf{z})c'(1), \end{aligned}$$

where $c'(1)$ represents the level of effort cost associated with achieving the reference input set X'. Consequently, under linear pricing,

$$c(\mathbf{w},\mathbf{z}) = h(\mathbf{z})c'(\mathbf{w},1).$$

4.6.4 Output-Homothetic Technologies

When the technology is output-homothetic, the effort-cost function under weak disposability of state-contingent outputs is defined by

$$\begin{aligned} c(\mathbf{z}) &= \min_{\mathbf{x}}\{g(\mathbf{x}):\mathbf{z} \in \mathbf{z}(\mathbf{x})Z'\} \\ &= \min_{\mathbf{x}}\{g(\mathbf{x}):O(\mathbf{z},\mathbf{x}) \leq 1\} \\ &= \min_{\mathbf{x}}\left\{g(\mathbf{x}):\frac{O'(\mathbf{z})}{z(\mathbf{x})} \leq 1\right\} \\ &= \min_{\mathbf{x}}\{g(\mathbf{x}):\mathbf{z}(\mathbf{x}) \geq O'(\mathbf{z})\} = c^{\mathbf{z}}(O'(\mathbf{z})), \end{aligned}$$

where $c^{\mathbf{z}}$ is the effort-cost function for the function $\mathbf{z}(\mathbf{x})$. The second equality follows by the fact that the output-distance function characterizes state-contingent output sets, and the third equality follows from results in Chapter 2 with $O'(\mathbf{z})$, the output-distance function for the reference set Z'. When the technology is homothetic, the effort-cost function is also homothetic in outputs, implying that isocost curves for the effort-cost function are radial expansions of the isocost curve for $c = 1$.

Result 4.4: *If* M = *1, and the technology satisfies weak disposability of state-contingent outputs, it exhibits constant relative riskiness in state-contingent outputs*[15] *if and only if it is output-homothetic.*

15. When there is only a single state-contingent output, the certainty equivalent output and the production risk premium in terms of state-contingent outputs, are defined exactly analogously to their analogs in terms of revenues.

Example 4.6: *The generalized Leontief technology*

$$c(z) = \frac{1}{2}\sum_{r=1}^{S}\sum_{s=1}^{S}\beta_{rs}(z_r z_s)^{1/2}$$

is output-homothetic as are all monotonic transformations of it. Technologies in this class have a common relative risk premium in outputs exhibiting constant relative riskiness given by

$$r(z) = \left\{ \frac{\sum_{r=1}^{S}\sum_{s=1}^{S}\beta_{rs}(z_r z_s)^{1/2}}{\bar{z}\sum_{r=1}^{S}\sum_{s=1}^{S}\beta_{rs}} \right\}^{-1}.$$

4.6.5 Schur-Convex Technologies

For $\mathbf{z} \in \Re_+^S$, the technology is Schur-convex if

$$\mathbf{z}' \preceq_m \mathbf{z} \Rightarrow X(\mathbf{z}) \subseteq X(\mathbf{z}').$$

We emphasize that this definition only applies when there exists only one state-contingent output. It does not generalize to the multiproduct case. For Schur-convex technologies,

$$\mathbf{z}' \preceq_m \mathbf{z} \Rightarrow c(\mathbf{z}') \leq c(\mathbf{z}).$$

The cost minimizer for $\mathbf{z}$ is always technically feasible for $\mathbf{z}'$. Hence, in minimizing cost for the latter, the producer can do no worse than he did in minimizing cost for the former. In other words, if one state-contingent output vector is majorized by another, the cost of producing that output vector is never any greater than the cost of producing the state-contingent output vector that majorizes it. Geometrically, Schur-convexity implies that isocost curves for the effort-cost function are symmetric about the bisector. Schur-convex technologies have the convenient property (due originally to Schur, and cited in Marshall and Olkin 1979, p. 57) that

$$\left(\frac{\partial c(\mathbf{z}')}{\partial z_r} - \frac{\partial c(\mathbf{z}')}{\partial z_n}\right)(z_r' - z_n') \geq 0.$$

Schur-convexity of the technology has several important implications for the production risk premium (now expressed in terms of state-contingent output) when all states are equally probable. First, when all states are equally probable, there is no inherent risk in the technology for any feasible state-contingent output. To see that this must be true, let $\bar{\mathbf{z}}$ denote the vector with the mean of $\mathbf{z}$ in each element. If all states are equally probable, $\bar{\mathbf{z}} \preceq_m \mathbf{z}$ and $c(\bar{\mathbf{z}}) \leq c(\mathbf{z})$. Accordingly, the certainty equivalent output must be greater than the mean output. This implies that the associated production risk premium is negative, or alternatively that the associated relative production risk premium is less than 1. In a word, it's always cheaper to be on the bisector than off it. Pictorially, generalized Schur-convex technologies are represented by isocost curves having slope equaling minus one at the bisector.

Second, it also turns out that the production risk premium is Schur-concave in state-contingent output. Put another way, with equal probabilities, the more risky the technology, the lower the production risk premium. This can be easily verified by comparing the risk premiums for two production vectors with the same mean, call them $\mathbf{z}$ and $\mathbf{z}'$, where $\mathbf{z}' \preceq_m \mathbf{z}$. Because the technology is not inherently risky, it follows easily from the definition of the production risk premium that $p(\mathbf{z}') \geq p(\mathbf{z})$.

4.6.6 Generalized Schur-Convex Technologies

When all states of nature are equally probable and outputs in all states of nature are equally valued, both a risk-neutral producer and a risk-averse producer facing a Schur-convex technology would choose to produce on the bisector, thus removing all production risk. Hence, as long as states are equally probable, a Schur-convex technology would be observationally equivalent to a nonstochastic technology in the absence of interstate differences in the valuation of output. Generally, however, because relative probabilities tell us something about individual's preferences regarding outcomes in different states of nature (see Chapter 3), there is no reason a priori to expect all states to be equally probable. One is naturally led to wonder whether there exists a technology that would be observationally equivalent to a nonstochastic technology when all states are not equally probable, but that is not trivially nonstochastic. The answer is yes, and for intuitive purposes, we shall refer to such technologies as generalized Schur-convex. A technology is generalized Schur-convex if the input correspondence satisfies

$$\mathbf{z}' \preceq_{\pi} \mathbf{z} \Rightarrow X(\mathbf{z}) \subseteq X(\mathbf{z}'),$$

where, as with Schur-convexity, we restrict attention to the case in which there is a single stochastic output, that is, $\mathbf{z} \in \mathfrak{R}_{+}^{S}$. Again, we emphasize that this definition does not generalize to the multiproduct case. If the technology is generalized Schur-convex, it must be true that

$$\mathbf{z}' \preceq_{\pi} \mathbf{z} \Rightarrow c(\mathbf{z}') \leq c(\mathbf{z}).$$

Generalized Schur-convexity corresponds to the case where one can produce the less risky state-contingent output vector at lower cost. That is, there are cost advantages to producing a nonstochastic production bundle. The reason that this happens, of course, is because if $\mathbf{z}' \preceq_{\pi} \mathbf{z}$, any input bundle that can produce $\mathbf{z}$ can also produce the less risky $\mathbf{z}'$. Hence, the cost-minimizing input combination for the less risky $\mathbf{z}'$ can never be more costly than that for $\mathbf{z}$.

From Corollary 3.3.1 in Chapter 3, if the effort-cost function is generalized Schur-convex, then for all s and r,

$$\left(\frac{\partial c(\mathbf{z}')/\partial z_r}{\pi_r} - \frac{\partial c(\mathbf{z}')/\partial z_s}{\pi_s}\right)(z_r' - z_s') \geq 0.$$

Our discussion of Schur-convex technologies should make it apparent that if the technology is generalized Schur-convex, then there is no inherent risk in the production process and that the production risk premium is always generalized Schur-concave, that is,

$$\mathbf{z}' \preceq_{\pi} \mathbf{z} \Rightarrow p(\mathbf{z}) - p(\mathbf{z}') \leq 0.$$

Because generalized Schur-convex technologies play an important role in several of the chapters that follow, we close this chapter with an example illustrating a generalized Schur-convex technology, its cost certainty equivalent, and its production risk premium (all expressed in terms of state-contingent output).

Example 4.7: *The effort-cost function*

$$c(z) = \sum_{s \in \Omega} \pi_s \exp(z_s)$$

is generalized Schur-convex. Generalized Schur-convexity can be verified by using the derivative property to obtain

$$(exp(z_s) - exp(z_r))(z_s - z_r) \geq 0.$$

Its production risk premium is

$$ln\left[exp\left(\sum_{s\in\Omega} \pi_s z_s\right) \Big/ \sum_{s\in\Omega} \pi_s exp(z_s)\right].$$

Because the exponential is convex, Jensen's inequality tells us that the term in square brackets is less than 1. This means that the production risk premium is negative, and that there's no inherent production risk with this technology for any state-contingent output. Here the cost certainty equivalent is

$$ln\left(\sum_{s\in\Omega} \pi_s exp(z_s)\right).$$

4.7 APPENDIX: DERIVATION OF PROPERTIES OF THE EFFORT-COST AND REVENUE-COST FUNCTIONS

4.7.1 Effort Cost

Deriving C.1 to C.6 is straightforward. Under X.1, $X(\mathbf{0}_{M\times S}) = \Re^N_+$, so that the effort-cost minimization problem corresponds to finding the cheapest point in $\Re^N_+$, whence $c(\mathbf{0}_{M\times S}) = \min\{g(\mathbf{x}) : \mathbf{x} \in \Re^N_+\}$. Now property G.1 implies that $g(\mathbf{0}_N) \leq g(\mathbf{x})$ for all $\mathbf{x} \in \Re^N_+$ and because $\mathbf{0}_N \in \Re^N_+$, the first part of C.1 follows immediately. Use this fact and X.1 to establish the second part of C.1.

If $\mathbf{x}'$ is the cost minimizer for $\mathbf{z}'$, free disposability implies $\mathbf{x}' \in X(\mathbf{z})$ for $\mathbf{z} \leq \mathbf{z}'$ and thus

$$c(\mathbf{z}) \leq c(\mathbf{z}'),$$

establishing C.2. C.2.W follows in an identical fashion under X.2.W. X.4 requires that if $\|\text{vec } \mathbf{z}^k\| \to \infty$ as $k \to \infty$, then $\cap_{k\to\infty} X(\mathbf{z}^k) = \emptyset$. Our definition of effort cost then yields C.3 for the limiting case.

Proving C.4 is also easy: quasi–concavity of the input correspondence, X.5, implies that

$$X(\mathbf{z}) \cap X(\mathbf{z}') \subseteq X(\lambda \mathbf{z} + (1-\lambda)\mathbf{z}').$$

Hence,

$$\begin{aligned}\min\{g(\mathbf{x}) : \mathbf{x} \in (X(\mathbf{z}) \cap X(\mathbf{z}'))\} &\geq \min\{g(\mathbf{x}) : \mathbf{x} \in X(\lambda \mathbf{z} + (1-\lambda)\mathbf{z}'))\} \\ &= c(\lambda \mathbf{z} + (1-\lambda)\mathbf{z}'),\end{aligned}$$

hence the result. Now turn to C.5: By X.7,

$$\lambda X(\mathbf{z}) + (1-\lambda)X(\mathbf{z}') \subseteq X(\lambda \mathbf{z} + (1-\lambda)\mathbf{z}'), \qquad 0 < \lambda < 1.$$

Thus, if $\mathbf{x}$ and $\mathbf{x}'$ represent solutions to the effort-cost problem for $\mathbf{z}$ and $\mathbf{z}'$, respectively, $\lambda\mathbf{x} + (1 - \lambda)\mathbf{x}'$ must be feasible for $\lambda\mathbf{z} + (1 - \lambda)\mathbf{z}'$, so that

$$\begin{aligned}c(\lambda \mathbf{z} + (1-\lambda)\mathbf{z}') &\leq g(\lambda \mathbf{x} + (1-\lambda)\mathbf{x}') \leq g(\lambda \mathbf{x}) + g((1-\lambda)\mathbf{x}') \\ &= c(\lambda \mathbf{z}) + c((1-\lambda)\mathbf{z}').\end{aligned}$$

The first inequality follows from feasibility, and the second follows from subadditivity of the effort-evaluation function (G. 3). Under X.7 and the stronger G.3′, a parallel argument establishes

$$c(\lambda \mathbf{z} + (1-\lambda)\mathbf{z}') \leq g(\lambda \mathbf{x} + (1-\lambda)\mathbf{x}') \leq \lambda g(\mathbf{x}) + (1-\lambda)g(\mathbf{x}'),$$

where the second inequality follows from convexity of the effort-evaluation function.

Having proved that convexity of $c(\mathbf{z})$ follows from G.3′ and X.7 (concavity of the state-contingent output correspondence), we now show that we can isolate conditions weaker than X.7 but stronger than X.6 (convexity of the output set), which will give a $c(\mathbf{z})$ with convex $Z_c(c)$. If $Z_c(c)$ is convex, then $c(\mathbf{z})$ is quasi-convex by definition, that is,

$$c(\lambda \mathbf{z} + (1-\lambda)\mathbf{z}') \leq \max\{c(\mathbf{z}), c(\mathbf{z}')\}.$$

Now reconsider our derivation of the convexity property of $c(\mathbf{z})$, and notice that if for each $\lambda \in (0, 1)$, there exists a corresponding $\theta \in (0, 1)$ such that $\theta X(\mathbf{z}) + (1 - \theta)X(\mathbf{z}') \subseteq X(\lambda z + (1 - \lambda)\mathbf{z}')$, we can then rewrite the chain of inequalities that proved C.6 to accommodate this property as

$$\begin{aligned}c(\lambda \mathbf{z} + (1-\lambda)\mathbf{z}') &\leq g((\theta \mathbf{x} + (1-\theta)\mathbf{x}') \leq g(\theta \mathbf{x}) + g((1-\theta)\mathbf{x}') \\ &= \theta g(\mathbf{x}) + (1-\theta)g(\mathbf{x}') = \theta c(\mathbf{z}) + (1-\theta)c(\mathbf{z}').\end{aligned}$$

Now since $c(\lambda\mathbf{z} + (1 - \lambda)\mathbf{z}')$ has been shown to be no greater than a convex combination of $c(\mathbf{z})$ and $c(\mathbf{z}')$, it must be true that $c(\lambda\mathbf{z} + (1 - \lambda)\mathbf{z}') \le \max\{c(\mathbf{z}), c(\mathbf{z}')\}$. We summarize this property as:

C.6a. If for each $\lambda \in (0, 1)$ there exists a $\theta \in (0, 1)$ such that $\theta X(\mathbf{z}) + (1 - \theta)X(\mathbf{z}') \subseteq X(\lambda z + (1 - \lambda)\mathbf{z}')$, and $g(\mathbf{x})$ satisfies G.3′, then

$$c(\lambda\mathbf{z} + (1 - \lambda)\mathbf{z}') \le \max\{c(\mathbf{z}), c(\mathbf{z}')\}, \qquad \lambda \in (0,1).$$

4.7.2 Revenue Cost

We now turn to a derivation of the properties of the revenue-cost function while relying on the properties of the effort-cost function derived earlier. Property RC.1 follows immediately from C.1 on noting first that the state-contingent revenue vector $\mathbf{0}_S$ can be produced by $\mathbf{0}_{M\times S}$. Accordingly, the cost of producing this revenue vector can be no greater than the cost of this state-contingent output matrix, and applying C.1 yields the first part of the result. The second part follows from C.1 after noting that producing a state-contingent revenue vector with at least one positive entry requires producing a state-contingent output matrix with at least one positive entry.

RC.2 and RC.2.W follow trivially from their counterparts, C.2 and C.2.W.

By the definition of the revenue-cost function, it has to be true that if $\|\mathbf{r}^k\| \to \infty$, then for finite output prices the only state-contingent output matrices capable of producing them must also have norms that grow unboundedly large. Now apply C.3.

Consider the convex combination of revenues given by $\lambda\mathbf{r} + (1 - \lambda)\mathbf{r}^o$. Let the optimal state-contingent output matrices derived in the revenue-cost problem for $\mathbf{r}$ and $\mathbf{r}^o$, respectively, be $\mathbf{z}$ and $\mathbf{z}^o$. Obviously, $\lambda\mathbf{z} + (1 - \lambda)\mathbf{z}^o$ is feasible for $\lambda\mathbf{r} + (1 - \lambda)\mathbf{r}^o$. So by C.6,

$$\begin{aligned} c(\lambda\mathbf{r} + (1 - \lambda)\mathbf{r}^o, \mathbf{p}) &\le c(\lambda\mathbf{z} + (1 - \lambda)\mathbf{z}^o) \\ &\le \lambda c(\mathbf{z}) + (1 - \lambda)c(\mathbf{z}^o) \\ &= \lambda C(\mathbf{r}, \mathbf{p}) + (1 - \lambda)C(\mathbf{r}^o, \mathbf{p}), \end{aligned}$$

which establishes RC.4.

To establish RC.5, consider two sets of state-contingent prices, $\mathbf{p}$ and $\mathbf{p}'$, where $\mathbf{p}' \geq \mathbf{p}$. Let the minimizer for $\mathbf{p}$ be $\mathbf{z}$. Obviously, since $\mathbf{p}' \geq \mathbf{p}$, $\mathbf{p}' \cdot \mathbf{z} \geq \mathbf{r}$, so that $C(\mathbf{r}, \mathbf{p}')$ can be no larger than $C(\mathbf{r}, \mathbf{p})$. RC.6 and RC.7 follow by the definition of the revenue-cost function.

5 The Theory of State-Contingent Production

In Chapters 3 and 4, we developed tools for the analysis of objective functions and cost functions, showing the symmetry between such concepts as risk aversion for preferences and inherent riskiness for state-contingent production. This symmetry is appealing in itself. More importantly, it forms the basis for a new analysis of the problem of production under uncertainty, that is, the choice of state-contingent output and revenue vectors that maximize the producer's objective function.

We do not assume expected-utility preferences. Beginning with Allais (1953), many criticisms of the expected-utility hypothesis have been raised.[1] By now, it is generally acknowledged that individuals systematically violate several of the key axioms underlying expected-utility preferences. Even in the face of its obvious weaknesses, however, many theorists concerned with modeling uncertainty persist in maintaining the expected-utility hypothesis. Perhaps the most defensible argument in support of this persistence is the claim that useful results can't be obtained for more general preference structures. Along with Chapter 3, this chapter and the two that follow show that, from this perspective, the expected-utility hypothesis is largely redundant with state-contingent models. Comparative static analysis may be conducted in terms of generalized behavioral properties of preferences, such as constant absolute risk aversion

1. Machina (1987) gives a summary of the evidence and some of the alternatives to, and generalizations of, expected utility theory proposed in response to this evidence.

and generalized Schur-concavity. The additive separability property that characterizes expected utility preferences need not play a crucial role.

The goal of this chapter is to provide a basic behavioral theory for individuals facing production and price uncertainty for a generalized version of the Sandmovian net returns model. Our strategy is to begin by studying in considerable depth the optimal production decisions for risk-neutral producers. We then consider, in turn, maximin preferences and generalized Schur-concave preferences.

5.1 RISK NEUTRALITY

Under risk neutrality with linear input pricing, the producer chooses state-contingent outputs to maximize her expected return from production. Her optimization problem can be written in terms of the effort-cost function developed in Chapter 4 as

$$\max_{\mathbf{z}}\left\{\sum_{s\in\Omega}\pi_s\sum_{m=1}^{M}p_{ms}z_{ms}-c(\mathbf{w},\mathbf{z})\right\},$$

which can be conveniently reduced to the following S-dimensional problem:

$$\max_{\mathbf{r}}\left\{\sum_{s\in\Omega}\pi_s r_s - C(\mathbf{w},\mathbf{r},\mathbf{p})\right\},$$

where

$$C(\mathbf{w},\mathbf{r},\mathbf{p}) = \min\left\{c(\mathbf{w},\mathbf{z}):\sum_{m=1}^{M}p_{ms}z_{ms}\geq r_s,\quad s\in\Omega\right\}$$

if there exists a state-contingent output array capable of producing $\mathbf{r}$, and ∞ otherwise. With a slight abuse of terminology and notation, we refer to $C(\mathbf{w}, \mathbf{r}, \mathbf{p})$ as the *revenue-cost function*. It's the revenue-cost function from Chapter 4 derived under linear input pricing. Our basic assumption is that $c(\mathbf{w}, \mathbf{z})$ satisfies properties CL.1 to CL.5 and CL.7 from Chapter 4. The properties of $C(\mathbf{w}, \mathbf{r}, \mathbf{p})$ that follow are listed as CR. (These amount to a rewriting of RC.1 to RC.7 for the linear pricing case with the addition of Shephard's Lemma.) Because these properties are so similar to properties RC in Chapter 4, no formal proof is offered.

Properties of the Revenue-Cost Function (CR)

CR. 1. $C(\mathbf{w}, \mathbf{r}, \mathbf{p})$ is positively linearly homogeneous, nondecreasing, concave, and continuous in $\mathbf{w} \in \Re^N_{++}$
CR. 2. Shephard's Lemma
CR. 3. $C(\mathbf{w}, \mathbf{r}, \mathbf{p}) \geq \mathbf{0}$, $C(\mathbf{w}, \mathbf{r}, \mathbf{p}) > 0$, $\mathrm{r} \geq 0$, $\mathrm{r} \neq 0$
CR. 4. $\mathbf{r}' \geq \mathbf{r} \Rightarrow C(\mathbf{w}, \mathbf{r}', \mathbf{p}) \geq C(\mathbf{w}, \mathbf{r}, \mathbf{p})$
CR. 5. $\mathbf{p}' \geq \mathbf{p} \Rightarrow C(\mathbf{w}, \mathbf{r}, \mathbf{p}') \leq C(\mathbf{w}, \mathbf{r}, \mathbf{p})$
CR. 6. $C(\mathbf{w}, \mathbf{r}_{-s}, \theta r_{s,}, \mathbf{p}_{-s}, \theta \mathbf{p}_s) = C(\mathbf{w}, \mathbf{r}, \mathbf{p})$, $\theta > 0$
CR. 7. $C(\mathbf{w}, \mathbf{r}, \mathbf{p}) = C(\mathbf{w}, \theta\mathbf{r}, \theta\mathbf{p})$, $\theta > 0$
CR. 8. $C(\mathbf{w}, \mathbf{r}, \mathbf{p})$ is convex in $\mathbf{r}$.

For simplicity, we assume that $C(\mathbf{w}, \mathbf{r}, \mathbf{p})$ is always smoothly differentiable in all state-contingent revenues. Thus we specifically rule out the approach that dominates the existing literature, in which a (stochastic or nonstochastic) production function determines a nondifferentiable state-contingent revenue-cost function (see Chapter 4, Example 4.1). The first-order conditions on $\mathbf{r}$ may be written in the notation of complementary slackness as

$$\pi_s - C_s(\mathbf{w}, \mathbf{r}, \mathbf{p}) \leq 0, \qquad r_s \geq 0, \qquad s \in \Omega,$$

where

$$C_s(\mathbf{w}, \mathbf{r}, \mathbf{p}) = \frac{\partial C(\mathbf{w}, \mathbf{r}, \mathbf{p})}{\partial r_s}.$$

That is, the marginal cost of increasing revenue in any state is at least equal to the subjective probability of that state. Pictorially, therefore, we represent the producer equilibrium by a hyperplane tangent to an isocost curve of the producer. Figure 5.1 illustrates. The slope of the hyperplane is determined by the ratio of the producer's subjective probabilities, the fair-odds line, and the isocost curve is determined by the equilibrium level of revenue cost. This is exactly analogous to the representation of production equilibrium in the nonstochastic multiproduct case. Instead of determining an optimal mix of outputs as in the nonstochastic multiproduct case, however, the producer equilibrium now determines the optimal mix of state-contingent

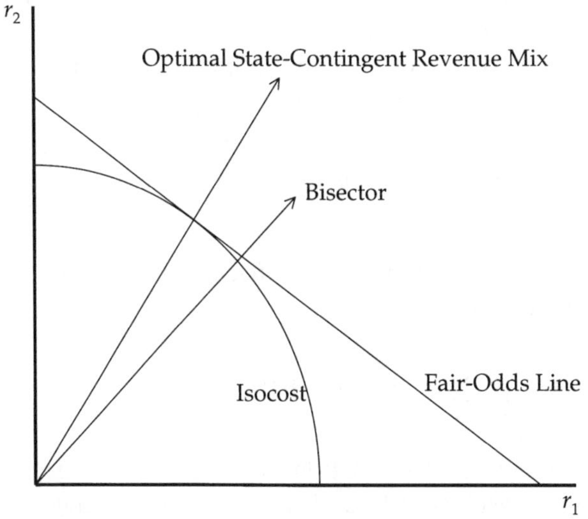

Figure 5.1 Risk-neutral production equilibrium.

revenues. This analogy naturally suggests interpreting the producer's subjective probabilities as the producer's subjective prices of the state-contingent revenues.

Summing the first-order conditions on **r** yields an *arbitrage condition*:

$$\sum_{s\in\Omega} C_s(\mathbf{w},\mathbf{r},\mathbf{p}) \geq \sum_{s\in\Omega} \pi_s = 1. \tag{5.1}$$

To see why we refer to (5.1) as an arbitrage condition, notice that the far left-hand side of the expression represents the derivative of the cost function in the direction of the equal-revenue ray (the bisector in Figure 5.1), that is,

$$\sum_{s\in\Omega} C_s(\mathbf{w},\mathbf{r},\mathbf{p}) = \left.\frac{\partial C(\mathbf{w},\mathbf{r}+\gamma\mathbf{1}^S,\mathbf{p})}{\partial\gamma}\right|_{\gamma=0}.$$

So, $\Sigma_{s\in\Omega}\ C_s(\mathbf{w},\ \mathbf{r},\ \mathbf{p})$ is the marginal cost of increasing all state-contingent revenues by the same small amount, and (5.1) requires that this cost be at least as large as the uniform increase in returns. If it were not, the decision maker could increase profit with certainty by increasing each state-contingent revenue. For an interior solution, (5.1) must hold as an equality.

We shall refer to the set of revenue vectors **r** satisfying (5.1) for given **w**, **p** as the *efficient set*, denoted $\Xi(\mathbf{w}, \mathbf{p})$,

$$\Xi(\mathbf{w}, \mathbf{p}) = \left\{ \mathbf{r} : \sum_{s \in \Omega} C_s(\mathbf{w}, \mathbf{r}, \mathbf{p}) \geq 1 \right\}.$$

We call the boundary of $\Xi(\mathbf{w}, \mathbf{p})$ the *efficient frontier* and note that its elements are given by

$$\overline{\Xi}(\mathbf{w}, \mathbf{p}) = \left\{ \mathbf{r} : \sum_{s \in \Omega} C_s(\mathbf{w}, \mathbf{r}, \mathbf{p}) = 1 \right\}.$$

Because the revenue-cost function is positively linearly homogeneous in input prices (CR.1) and homogeneous of degree zero in $(\mathbf{r}, \mathbf{p})$ (CR.7), it is linearly homogeneous in $(\mathbf{w}, \mathbf{r}, \mathbf{p})$. Therefore, differentiating both sides of

$$C(\theta \mathbf{w}, \theta \mathbf{r}, \theta \mathbf{p}) = \theta C(\mathbf{w}, \mathbf{r}, \mathbf{p}), \qquad \theta > 0$$

with respect to r_s gives

$$\theta C_s(\theta \mathbf{w}, \theta \mathbf{r}, \theta \mathbf{p}) = \theta C_s(\mathbf{w}, \mathbf{r}, \mathbf{p}),$$

which implies that marginal cost is homogeneous of degree zero in prices and revenue

$$C_s(\theta \mathbf{w}, \theta \mathbf{r}, \theta \mathbf{p}) = C_s(\mathbf{w}, \mathbf{r}, \mathbf{p}).$$

This homogeneity property of marginal cost allows us to establish the following property of the efficient set:

> **Lemma 5.1** *$\Xi(\theta \mathbf{w}, \theta \mathbf{p}) = \theta \Xi(\mathbf{w}, \mathbf{p})$ and $\overline{\Xi}(\theta \mathbf{w}, \theta \mathbf{p}) = \theta \overline{\Xi}(\mathbf{w}, \mathbf{p})$, $\theta > 0$. That is, the efficient set and the efficient frontier are positively linearly homogeneous in input and output prices.*

We establish this result for the efficient set, and leave the extension to the efficient frontier to the reader. By the definition of the efficient set,

$$\begin{aligned}\Xi(\theta\mathbf{w},\theta\mathbf{p}) &= \left\{\mathbf{r}:\sum_{s=1}^{S} C_s(\theta\mathbf{w},\mathbf{r},\theta\mathbf{p}) \geq 1\right\} \\ &= \left\{\mathbf{r}:\sum_{s=1}^{S} C_s\left(\mathbf{w},\frac{\mathbf{r}}{\theta},\mathbf{p}\right) \geq 1\right\} \\ &= \theta\left\{\frac{\mathbf{r}}{\theta}:\sum_{s=1}^{S} C_s\left(\mathbf{w},\frac{\mathbf{r}}{\theta},\mathbf{p}\right) \geq 1\right\} \\ &= \theta\Xi(\mathbf{w},\mathbf{p}).\end{aligned}$$

Here the second equality follows by the fact that $C_s(\mathbf{w}, \mathbf{r}, \mathbf{p})$ is homogeneous of degree zero in all prices and revenues. Expanding all state-contingent output prices and input prices radially, therefore, expands the efficient set by the same proportion. Consequently, expanding input and output prices proportionately leads a risk-neutral individual to an equiproportional increase in optimal state-contingent revenues.

Different risk-neutral decision makers may hold different subjective probabilities. However, a revenue vector $\mathbf{r}$ is potentially optimal for some risk-neutral decision maker only if (5.1) holds. If (5.1) holds for an arbitrary revenue vector, $\hat{\mathbf{r}}$ say, then that revenue vector is consistent with expected profit-maximizing behavior for an individual with the subjective probabilities $\hat{\pi}_s = C_s(\mathbf{w}, \hat{\mathbf{r}}, \mathbf{p})$.

5.1.1 Constant Absolute Riskiness

The efficient frontier is easily characterized under the presumption that the revenue cost function displays constant absolute riskiness. An analysis parallel to that used to establish Result 4.2 in Chapter 4 establishes the following:

Lemma 5.2 *The technology displays constant absolute riskiness if and only if the revenue-cost function can be represented as*

$$C(\boldsymbol{w},\boldsymbol{r},\boldsymbol{p}) = \hat{C}(\boldsymbol{w},\boldsymbol{T}(\boldsymbol{r},\boldsymbol{p},\boldsymbol{w}),\boldsymbol{p}),$$

where

$$\mathrm{T}(\boldsymbol{r}+\delta\boldsymbol{1}^S,\boldsymbol{p},\boldsymbol{w}) = \mathrm{T}(\boldsymbol{r},\boldsymbol{p},\boldsymbol{w})+\delta, \qquad \delta\in\Re,$$
$$\mathrm{T}(\lambda\boldsymbol{r},\lambda\boldsymbol{p},\lambda\boldsymbol{w}) = \lambda\mathrm{T}(\boldsymbol{r},\boldsymbol{p},\boldsymbol{w}),\ \mathrm{T}(\boldsymbol{r},\boldsymbol{p},\lambda\boldsymbol{w}) = \mathrm{T}(\boldsymbol{r},\boldsymbol{p},\boldsymbol{w}), \qquad \lambda>0,$$

and $\hat{C}(\mathbf{w}, \mathbf{T}(\mathbf{r}, \mathbf{p}, \mathbf{w}), \mathbf{p})$ *is positively linearly homogeneous in input prices, homogeneous of degree zero in* $T(\mathbf{r}, \mathbf{p}, \mathbf{w})$ *and* $\mathbf{p}$*, nondecreasing in* $T(\mathbf{r}, \mathbf{p}, \mathbf{w})$*, and nonincreasing in* $\mathbf{p}$. $T(\mathbf{r}, \mathbf{p}, \mathbf{w})$ *is nondecreasing and convex in the state-contingent revenues, and* $\hat{C}$ *is convex in* $T(\mathbf{r}, \mathbf{p}, \mathbf{w})$.

$T(\mathbf{r}, \mathbf{p}, \mathbf{w})$ can be interpreted intuitively as a *revenue aggregate*, which satisfies several convenient properties including

$$T(\mathbf{r}+\delta\mathbf{1}^S, \mathbf{p}, \mathbf{w}) = T(\mathbf{r}, \mathbf{p}, \mathbf{w}) + \delta.$$

Differentiating this last expression with respect to δ and evaluating the expression at $\delta = 0$ gives

$$\sum_{s\in\Omega} T_s(\mathbf{r}, \mathbf{p}, \mathbf{w}) = 1 \tag{5.2}$$

while differentiating with respect to r_s gives

$$T_s(\mathbf{r}+\delta\mathbf{1}^S, \mathbf{p}, \mathbf{w}) = T_s(\mathbf{r}, \mathbf{p}, \mathbf{w}), \qquad \forall\delta. \tag{5.3}$$

Substituting these results into the first-order conditions for an interior solution yields

$$\frac{\pi_s}{\pi_k} = \frac{T_s(\mathbf{r}, \mathbf{p}, \mathbf{w})}{T_k(\mathbf{r}, \mathbf{p}, \mathbf{w})} = \frac{T_s(\mathbf{r}+\delta\mathbf{1}^S, \mathbf{p}, \mathbf{w})}{T_k(\mathbf{r}+\delta\mathbf{1}^S, \mathbf{p}, \mathbf{w})}, \qquad \delta\in\Re, \forall k, s\in\Omega. \tag{5.4}$$

From (5.4) we conclude, by using the homogeneity properties of the revenue aggregate cited in Lemma 5.2, that the *expansion path in state-contingent revenue space*, that is, the set of revenues satisfying condition (5.4), is simultaneously homogeneous of degree zero in input prices and parallel to the equal-revenue vector. The latter result follows because (5.4) establishes that if a point $\mathbf{r}^*$ is on the expansion path, then so too must be $\mathbf{r}^* + \delta\mathbf{1}^S$. Pictorially, these latter points are represented by the points on the ray parallel to the bisector that passes through $\mathbf{r}^*$. Moreover, substituting (5.2) into the definition of the efficient set gives

$$\begin{aligned}\Xi(\mathbf{w}, \mathbf{p}) &= \left\{\mathbf{r}: \frac{\partial\hat{C}(\mathbf{w}, \mathbf{T}(\mathbf{r}, \mathbf{p}, \mathbf{w}), \mathbf{p})}{\partial T}\sum_{s\in\Omega} T_s(\mathbf{r}, \mathbf{p}, \mathbf{w}) \geq 1\right\} \\ &= \left\{\mathbf{r}: \frac{\partial\hat{C}(\mathbf{w}, \mathbf{T}(\mathbf{r}, \mathbf{p}, \mathbf{w}), \mathbf{p})}{\partial T} \geq 1\right\}.\end{aligned}$$

Hence, the efficient frontier uniquely determines the optimal level of **T** (**r**, **p**, **w**), and thereby the revenue-cost level. Because the efficient frontier uniquely determines the level of $C(\mathbf{w}, \mathbf{r}, \mathbf{p})$, we conclude that all elements of the efficient frontier must be equally costly. As later developments will show, this property of constant absolute riskiness has important comparative static implications. Summarizing:

> **Result 5.1:** *If the revenue-cost function exhibits constant absolute riskiness, the expansion path is homogeneous of degree zero in input prices and parallel to the equal-revenue vector. Further, all elements of the efficient frontier are equally costly.*

For interior solutions, all individuals possessing a technology satisfying constant absolute riskiness will incur the same level of cost regardless of their (risk-neutral) preferences toward state-contingent outcomes. Put another way, when the technology exhibits constant absolute riskiness, the optimal level of cost is independent of a risk-neutral decision maker's subjective probabilities. In turn, this means that the producer's scale of operation, as measured by her cost level, is independent of her subjective view of the uncertain world.

This result can be explained as follows. When the revenue-cost function satisfies constant absolute riskiness, it can be written in terms of a single revenue aggregate $T(\mathbf{r}, \mathbf{p}, \mathbf{w})$. This revenue aggregate is positively linearly homogeneous in revenues and state-contingent prices, homogeneous of degree zero in input prices, and has the property that when all revenues increase by the same amount the aggregate goes up by that same amount. Because the arbitrage condition requires that the marginal cost of increasing all revenues by the same amount should equal one, then for such a technology, the arbitrage condition reduces to requiring that the marginal cost of the aggregate should equal one. This requirement uniquely determines the optimal revenue aggregate and thus cost.

We now consider what constant absolute riskiness implies about the producer's optimal response to rescaling input prices. For an interior solution, on rescaling input prices, the arbitrage condition (5.1) becomes

$$\frac{\partial \hat{C}(\mu\mathbf{w}, \hat{T}(\mathbf{r}, \mathbf{p}, \mu\mathbf{w}), \mathbf{p})}{\partial T} = \frac{\partial \hat{C}(\mu\mathbf{w}, \hat{T}(\mathbf{r}, \mathbf{p}, \mathbf{w}), \mathbf{p})}{\partial T} = 1,$$

where μ z> 0 is the rescaling factor for input prices. The first equality follows because $T(\mathbf{r}, \mathbf{p}, \mathbf{w})$ is homogeneous of degree zero in input prices (Lemma 5.2). The fact that the revenue-cost function is positively linearly homogeneous in input prices implies that this condition can be rewritten

$$\frac{\partial \hat{C}(\mathbf{w}, \mathbf{T}(\mathbf{r}, \mathbf{p}, \mathbf{w}), \mathbf{p})}{\partial T} = \frac{1}{\mu}.$$

Therefore, we conclude that if $\mu < 1$, the convexity of $\hat{C}$ in $\mathbf{T}(\mathbf{r}, \mathbf{p}, \mathbf{w})$ implies that the optimal $\mathbf{T}(\mathbf{r}, \mathbf{p}, \mathbf{w})$ increases as a result of a rescaling of input prices. Conversely, when $\mu > 1$, a rescaling of input prices leads to a decline in the revenue aggregate. From (5.4), the expansion path is homogeneous of degree zero in $\mathbf{w}$ and parallels the equal-revenue ray. The fact that the revenue aggregate increases as input prices are proportionately decreased when combined with (5.4) now implies that all state-contingent revenues go up or down by the same amount in response to a rescaling of input prices.

Now consider what happens when output prices expand or contract radially. Even when the revenue-cost function exhibits constant absolute riskiness, a proportional change in output prices generally affects the expansion path. Hence, all state-contingent revenues need not expand equally in this case. However, it is true that effort must increase as a result of a radial expansion of output prices. When output prices are changed proportionately, the arbitrage condition (5.1) determining the optimal revenue aggregate can now be rewritten as

$$\frac{\partial \hat{C}(\mathbf{w}, T(\mathbf{r}, \mu\mathbf{p}, \mathbf{w}), \mu\mathbf{p})}{\partial T} = 1.$$

By using the homogeneity properties of $\hat{C}$ and T, this condition is equivalent to

$$\frac{\partial \hat{C}\left(\mathbf{w}, T\left(\frac{\mathbf{r}}{\mu}, \mathbf{p}, \mathbf{w}\right), \mathbf{p}\right)}{\partial T} = \mu.$$

Evaluating the left-hand side at the state-contingent revenues that were optimal before price rescaling reveals that it is smaller than the right-hand side if $\mu > 1$. Consequently, the optimal level of T (and thus revenue cost) must increase.

> **Result 5.2:** *If the revenue-cost function satisfies constant absolute riskiness, a proportional increase in input prices leads a risk-neutral producer to decrease all state-contingent revenues by the same amount. A proportional decrease in input prices leads to all state-contingent revenues increasing by the same amount. Increasing (decreasing) output prices proportionately leads to an increase (decrease) in the revenue aggregate and revenue cost.*

The second part of Result 5.2 can be strengthened when output price is nonstochastic, and there is only a single stochastic output (M = 1). Then, because there is a single state-contingent output, the revenue aggregate and the revenue-cost function can be written as, respectively,

$$T(\mathbf{r}, \mathbf{p}, \mathbf{w}) = T(p\mathbf{z}, p\mathbf{1}^S, \mathbf{w}) = pT(\mathbf{z}, \mathbf{1}^S, \mathbf{w})$$

and

$$\hat{C}(\mathbf{w}, pT(\mathbf{z}, \mathbf{1}^S, \mathbf{w}), p\mathbf{1}^S) = \hat{C}(\mathbf{w}, T(\mathbf{z}, \mathbf{1}^S, \mathbf{w}), \mathbf{1}^S)$$

by exploiting the homogeneity properties of the revenue aggregate and the revenue-cost function. A risk-neutral entrepreneur facing such a technology chooses the state-contingent output vector $\mathbf{z} \in \Re_+^S$ to

$$\max_{\mathbf{z}} \left\{ p \sum_{s \in \Omega} \pi_s z_s - \hat{C}(\mathbf{w}, T(\mathbf{z}, \mathbf{1}^S, \mathbf{w}), \mathbf{1}^S) \right\}.$$

The associated first-order conditions are

$$p\pi_s - \hat{C}_T(\mathbf{w}, T(\mathbf{z}, \mathbf{1}^S, \mathbf{w}), \mathbf{1}^S) T_s(\mathbf{z}, \mathbf{1}^S, \mathbf{w}) \leq 0, \qquad z_s \geq 0$$

in the notation of complementary slackness. Accordingly, the expansion path for an interior solution obeys

$$\frac{\pi_s}{\pi_k} = \frac{T_s(\mathbf{z}, \mathbf{1}^S, \mathbf{w})}{T_k(\mathbf{z}, \mathbf{1}^S, \mathbf{w})} = \frac{T_s(\mathbf{z} + \delta\mathbf{1}^S, \mathbf{1}^S, \mathbf{w})}{T_k(\mathbf{z} + \delta\mathbf{1}^S, \mathbf{1}^S, \mathbf{w})}$$

for all δ.

The expansion path is parallel to the equal-output vector and independent of the level of the nonstochastic output price. The risk-neutral individual's location on the expansion path is determined by summing these first-order conditions over all states while using (5.2) to obtain the first-order condition (the arbitrage condition) for the output aggregate:

$$p - \hat{C}_T(\mathbf{w}, T(\mathbf{z}, \mathbf{1}^S, \mathbf{w}), \mathbf{1}^S) \le 0.$$

Or, the output aggregate is set to equate its marginal cost to its price. Increasing the nonstochastic output price then naturally leads to an increase in T. This yields the conclusion that we were looking for. Increasing the nonstochastic output price leads to an expansion of the state-contingent output vector along a ray that parallels the equal-outcome vector.

Result 5.3: *If the revenue-cost function exhibits constant absolute riskiness and* $\boldsymbol{z} \in \Re^S_{++}$, $\boldsymbol{p} = \mathrm{p}\boldsymbol{1}^S$, *with* $p \in \Re_{++}$, *the state-contingent output vector for a risk-neutral producer expands parallel to* $\boldsymbol{1}^S$ *in response to an increase in* p.

5.1.2 Constant Relative Riskiness

A similar analysis may be undertaken for constant relative riskiness. In that case, we have the following straightforward analog to Result 4.3 from Chapter 4.

Lemma 5.3: *The technology displays constant relative riskiness if and only if the cost function can be represented as*

$$C(\boldsymbol{w}, \boldsymbol{r}, \boldsymbol{p}) = \overline{C}(\boldsymbol{w}, \overline{\boldsymbol{T}}(\boldsymbol{r}, \boldsymbol{p}, \boldsymbol{w}), \boldsymbol{p}),$$

where

$$\overline{T}(\lambda \boldsymbol{r}, \boldsymbol{p}, \boldsymbol{w}) = \lambda \overline{T}(\boldsymbol{r}, \boldsymbol{p}, \boldsymbol{w}), \qquad \overline{T}(\boldsymbol{r}, \boldsymbol{p}, \lambda \boldsymbol{w}) = \overline{T}(\boldsymbol{r}, \boldsymbol{p}, \boldsymbol{w})$$
$$\overline{T}(\boldsymbol{r}, \lambda \boldsymbol{p}, \boldsymbol{w}) = \overline{T}(\boldsymbol{r}, \boldsymbol{p}, \boldsymbol{w}), \qquad \lambda > 0,$$

and $\overline{C}(\boldsymbol{w}, \overline{\boldsymbol{T}}(\boldsymbol{r}, \boldsymbol{p}, \boldsymbol{w}), \boldsymbol{p})$ *is positively linearly homogeneous in input prices, homogeneous of degree zero in* $\overline{T}(\boldsymbol{r}, \boldsymbol{p}, \boldsymbol{w})$ *and output prices, nondecreasing in* $\overline{T}(\boldsymbol{r}, \boldsymbol{p}, \boldsymbol{w})$, *and nonincreasing in output prices.* $\overline{T}(\boldsymbol{r}, \boldsymbol{p}, \boldsymbol{w})$ *is nondecreasing and convex in the state-contingent revenues, and* $\overline{C}$ *is convex in* $\overline{T}(\boldsymbol{r}, \boldsymbol{p}, \boldsymbol{w})$.

By using Lemma 5.3, the risk-neutral individual's objective function is now

$$\max_{\mathbf{r}}\left\{\sum_{s}\pi_s r_s - \overline{C}(\mathbf{w}, \overline{\mathbf{T}}(\mathbf{r}, \mathbf{p}, \mathbf{w}), \mathbf{p})\right\},$$

and the associated first-order conditions for this problem are

$$\pi_s - \frac{\partial \overline{C}(\mathbf{w}, \overline{T}(\mathbf{r}, \mathbf{p}, \mathbf{w}), \mathbf{p})}{\partial \overline{T}}\overline{T}_s(\mathbf{r}, \mathbf{p}, \mathbf{w}) \leq 0, \qquad r_s \geq 0, \qquad s \in \Omega$$

in the notation of complementary slackness. For an interior solution,

$$\frac{\pi_s}{\pi_k} = \frac{\overline{T}_s(\mathbf{r}, \mathbf{p}, \mathbf{w})}{\overline{T}_k(\mathbf{r}, \mathbf{p}, \mathbf{w})}, \qquad \forall s, k.$$

By Lemma 5.3, the right-hand side of this expression is unaffected by proportional changes in either input prices or output prices and is also homogeneous of degree zero in state-contingent revenues. Hence, as long as input prices or output prices move proportionally, the optimal mixture of state-contingent revenues (that is, relative state-contingent revenues) is unchanged.

Now consider how a proportional reduction in input prices affects the optimal $\overline{T}(\mathbf{r}, \mathbf{p}, \mathbf{w})$. By complementary slackness and the positive linear homogeneity of $\overline{T}(\mathbf{r}, \mathbf{p}, \mathbf{w})$ in state-contingent revenues, the first-order conditions imply

$$\sum_{s}\pi_s r_s = \frac{\partial \overline{C}(\mathbf{w}, \overline{T}(\mathbf{r}, \mathbf{p}, \mathbf{w}), \mathbf{p})}{\partial \overline{T}}\overline{T}(\mathbf{r}, \mathbf{p}, \mathbf{w}). \tag{5.5}$$

Because $\overline{C}(\mathbf{w}, \overline{T}(\mathbf{r}, \mathbf{p}, \mathbf{w}), \mathbf{p})$ is convex in $\overline{T}(\mathbf{r}, \mathbf{p}, \mathbf{w})$, the right-hand side of (5.5) is an increasing function of $\overline{T}(\mathbf{r}, \mathbf{p}, \mathbf{w})$.

Factoring in a proportional reduction in input prices leads the right-hand side of (5.5) to fall, implying that if nothing else changes, $\overline{T}(\mathbf{r}, \mathbf{p}, \mathbf{w})$ must adjust upward to restore equilibrium. Thus:

> **Result 5.4:** *If the revenue-cost function displays constant relative riskiness, a proportional reduction (increase) in all input prices leads to a proportional increase (reduction) in all state-contingent revenues for a risk-neutral producer.*

In this case, the statement of the equivalent result in terms of output prices is straightforward. The revenue aggregate is now homogeneous of degree zero in output prices (Lemma 5.3) so that a proportional change in output prices changes (5.5) to

$$\sum_s \pi_s r_s = \frac{\partial \overline{C}(\mathbf{w}, \overline{T}(\mathbf{r}, \mathbf{p}, \mathbf{w}), \lambda\mathbf{p})}{\partial \overline{T}} \overline{T}(\mathbf{r}, \mathbf{p}, \mathbf{w}),$$

which, using the homogeneity properties of $\overline{C}$ and $\overline{T}$ from Lemma 5.3 can be rewritten successively as

$$\begin{aligned}\sum_s \pi_s r_s &= \frac{\partial \overline{C}(\mathbf{w}/\lambda, \overline{T}(\mathbf{r}, \mathbf{p}, \mathbf{w})/\lambda, \mathbf{p})}{\partial \overline{T}} \overline{T}(\mathbf{r}, \mathbf{p}, \mathbf{w}) \\ &= \frac{1/\lambda\, \partial \overline{C}(\mathbf{w}, \overline{T}(\mathbf{r}, \mathbf{p}, \mathbf{w})/\lambda, \mathbf{p})}{\partial \overline{T}} \overline{T}(\mathbf{r}, \mathbf{p}, \mathbf{w}) \\ &= \frac{\partial \overline{C}(\mathbf{w}, \overline{T}(\mathbf{r}/\lambda, \mathbf{p}, \mathbf{w}), \mathbf{p})}{\partial \overline{T}} \overline{T}(\mathbf{r}/\lambda, \mathbf{p}, \mathbf{w}).\end{aligned}$$

Evaluating this transformed expression at the original optimal revenues establishes that if $\lambda > 1$, the left-hand side must be smaller than the right-hand side. Hence, because the right-hand side is nondecreasing in the revenue aggregate, revenue must rise, leading us to conclude:

> **Corollary 5.4.1:** *If the revenue-cost function displays constant relative riskiness, a proportional increase (reduction) in all state-contingent output prices leads to a proportional increase (reduction) in all state-contingent revenues for a risk-neutral producer.*

5.2 MAXIMIN PREFERENCES

Risk neutrality is the polar case of net returns corresponding to the absence of aversion to risk. For purposes of comparison, we start our analysis of risk-averse decision making by considering the most extreme form of risk aversion as typified by the maximin objective function. Maximin preferences are particularly interesting for several reasons. They correspond to maximal risk aversion and thus offer a convenient polar case. They also simultaneously exhibit both constant absolute risk aversion and constant relative risk aver-

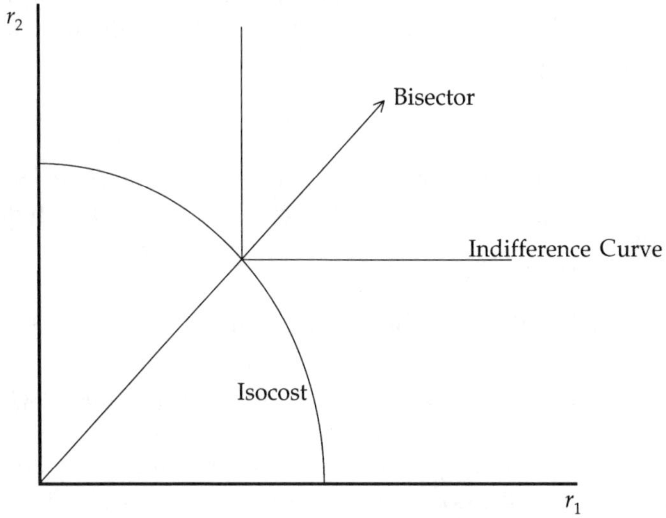

Figure 5.2 Maximin-production equilibrium.

sion (see Chapter 3, Example 3.14). Finally, maximin preferences are not consistent with the expected-utility hypothesis, except as a polar case.

The producer's problem is now

$$\max_{\mathbf{r}}\{\min\{r_1 - C(\mathbf{w}, \mathbf{r}, \mathbf{p}), \ldots, r_S - C(\mathbf{w}, \mathbf{r}, \mathbf{p})\}\}$$
$$= \max_{\mathbf{r}}\{\min\{r_1, \ldots, r_S\} - C(\mathbf{w}, \mathbf{r}, \mathbf{p})\}.$$

Because the objective function is not smoothly differentiable, the Kuhn–Tucker theorem cannot immediately guide identification of an optimum. Nevertheless, the producer should produce where her indifference curve just "sits" on one of her isocost curves. Because maximin preferences have indifference curves that are "L-shaped" around the equal-revenue ray, we therefore expect her to locate at a point on the equal-revenue ray. In other words, the producer chooses a nonstochastic production pattern. (Figure 5.2 illustrates.)

This is quite easy to show. Moreover, the producer chooses to produce where the efficient frontier, identified earlier, intersects the equal-revenue ray. Let $\mathbf{r}^*$ denote the producer's optimal state-contingent revenue vector. Now suppose, contrary to our assertion, that $\mathbf{r}^*$ does not lie on the equal-revenue vector, and consider perturbing any single element of $\mathbf{r}^*$, say r_s, by the small amount δr_s. The associated variation in the producer's objective function is

$$(\delta^{\min} - C_s(\mathbf{w}, \mathbf{r}, \mathbf{p}))\delta r_s,$$

where $\delta^{\min} = 1$ if $r_s \in \min\{r_1, \ldots, r_S\}$ and 0 otherwise. So if $r_s \notin \min\{r_1, \ldots, r_S\}$, the variation in the producer's objective function is

$$-C_s(\mathbf{w}, \mathbf{r}, \mathbf{p})\delta r_s,$$

which implies that the producer's welfare can be increased by decreasing this state-contingent revenue toward the equal-revenue vector. Hence, the optimal state-contingent revenue vector must involve no revenue uncertainty.

Because the optimal production pattern can involve no revenue uncertainty, the decision maker's problem reduces to

$$\max_r \{r - C(\mathbf{w}, r\mathbf{1}^S, \mathbf{p})\}$$

with the associated first-order condition

$$1 - \sum_{s \in \Omega} C_s(\mathbf{w}, r\mathbf{1}^S, \mathbf{p}), \qquad r \geq 0$$

in the notation of complementary slackness. This last condition implies that the revenue choice must satisify (5.1) and hence be on the efficient frontier if r is strictly positive. Putting these arguments together, and using Lemma 5.1, leads us to conclude that:

> **Result 5.5:** *A producer with maximin preferences completely stabilizes revenue and, for an interior solution, produces where the efficient frontier intersects the equal-revenue vector. A proportional increase in input and output prices leads to a proportional increase in the optimal nonstochastic revenue.*

Because the producer locates on the efficient frontier, the immediate implication is that there must exist a set of probabilities that would lead a risk-neutral producer to choose this same nonstochastic revenue pattern. Those probabilities are given by $C_s(\mathbf{w}, r\mathbf{1}^S, \mathbf{p}), s \in \Omega$. Hence, by appropriately choosing probabilities, we can always identify a risk-neutral producer who would exactly mimic the production choices of even the most risk-averse of producers.

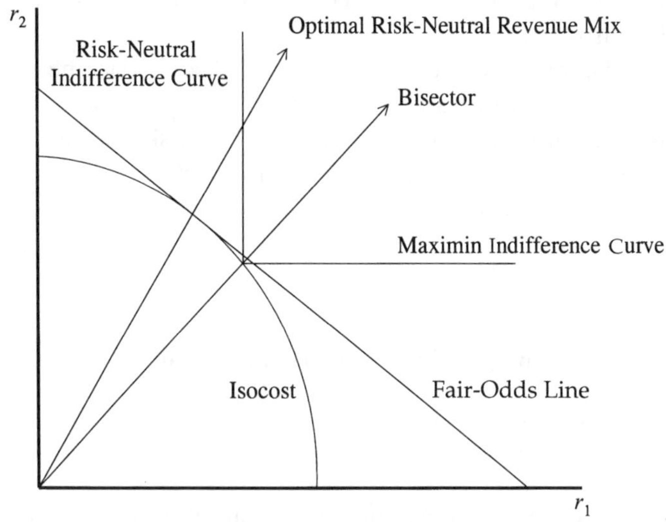

Figure 5.3 Risk-neutral and maximin-production equilibria with constant absolute riskiness.

Assuming that $C(\mathbf{w}, r\mathbf{1}^S, \mathbf{p})$ exhibits constant absolute riskiness and applying Result 5.1 gives:

> **Corollary 5.5.1:** *If the producer has maximin preferences and uses a technology exhibiting constant absolute riskiness, then, for an interior solution, the producer incurs the same level of cost as a risk-neutral producer.*

This latter case is illustrated in Figure 5.3. There we have drawn the isocost curve associated with the efficient frontier under the presumption of constant absolute riskiness. The risk-neutral producer, with fair odds as depicted, produces at the point of tangency between the fair-odds line and the isocost curve. The completely risk-averse producer facing the same technology produces on the same isocost curve but at the bisector.

Figure 5.3 illustrates the essential differences between the behavior of a risk-neutral individual and a risk averter that emerge when we consider more general risk-averse preferences. The risk averter sacrifices expected returns in order to self-insure by arranging (in her view) a less risky production pattern than would be chosen by a risk-neutral individual. Higher expected returns are sacrificed for more stable returns.

When the technology exhibits constant absolute riskiness, this producer's response to a radial contraction of input prices or a radial expansion of output prices parallels that of a risk-neutral individual. In the case of a radial change in input prices, the first-order condition for an interior solution requires

$$\frac{\partial \hat{C}(\mu \mathbf{w}, T(r\mathbf{1}^S, \mathbf{p}, \mu \mathbf{w}), \mathbf{p})}{\partial T} = 1,$$

which, by the homogeneity properties of Lemma 5.2, reduces to

$$\frac{\partial \hat{C}(\mathbf{w}, T(r\mathbf{1}^S, \mathbf{p}, \mathbf{w}), \mathbf{p})}{\partial T} = \frac{1}{\mu},$$

so that $T(r\mathbf{1}^S, \mathbf{p}, \mathbf{w})$ must increase if input prices decrease proportionately.[2] By Lemma 5.2, this also means that the maximin individual's optimal certain revenue must increase as a result of a proportional decrease in input prices. Similar arguments establish that a proportional change in output prices transforms the producer's first-order conditions to

$$\frac{\partial \hat{C}(\mathbf{w}, T(r/\mu \mathbf{1}^S, \mathbf{p}, \mathbf{w}), \mathbf{p})}{\partial T} = \mu,$$

implying that $T(r\mathbf{1}^S, \mathbf{p}, \mathbf{w})$ and r must increase as a result of a proportional increase in state-contingent output prices.

> **Corollary 5.5.2:** *If the producer has maximin preferences and uses a technology exhibiting constant absolute riskiness, a proportional increase (decrease) in state-contingent output prices or a proportional decrease (increase) in input prices leads to an*

2. Here the argument relies on the fact that $\hat{C}(\mathbf{w}, T(r\mathbf{1}^S, \mathbf{p}, \mathbf{w}), \mathbf{p})$ is positively linearly homogeneous in input prices, where

$$\hat{C}(\lambda \mathbf{w}, T(r\mathbf{1}^S, \mathbf{p}, \mathbf{w}), \mathbf{p}) = \lambda \hat{C}(\mathbf{w}, T(r\mathbf{1}^S, \mathbf{p}, \mathbf{w}), \mathbf{p}).$$

Differentiating both sides with respect to T gives

$$\frac{\partial \hat{C}(\lambda \mathbf{w}, T(r\mathbf{1}^S, \mathbf{p}, \mathbf{w}), \mathbf{p})}{\partial T} = \lambda \frac{\partial \hat{C}(\mathbf{w}, T(r\mathbf{1}^S, \mathbf{p}, \mathbf{w}), \mathbf{p})}{\partial T}.$$

Using this result along with the homogeneity properties of T leads to the desired result.

increase (decrease) in the optimal nonstochastic revenue chosen by the producer and an increase (decrease) in her revenue cost.

The intuition behind Corollary 5.5.2 is straightforward. An individual with maximin preferences acts to maximize "sure profit" instead of expected profit. When her technology exhibits constant absolute riskiness, the shape of her isocost is unchanging along the equal-revenue ray and all other rays parallel to it. Moreover, her revenue aggregate along that ray consists of

$$\begin{aligned} T(r\mathbf{1}^S, \mathbf{p}, \mathbf{w}) &= rT(\mathbf{1}^S, \mathbf{p}, \mathbf{w}) \\ &= r. \end{aligned}$$

The first equality follows from the positive linear homogeneity of the revenue aggregate. The second follows on noting that by Euler's theorem on homogeneous functions and (5.2),

$$T(\mathbf{1}^S, \mathbf{p}, \mathbf{w}) = \sum_{s\in\Omega} T_s(\mathbf{1}^S, \mathbf{p}, \mathbf{w}) = 1.$$

Accordingly, under constant absolute riskiness, the maximin individual's problem reduces to the simple one of maximizing the sure profit given by

$$r - \hat{C}(\mathbf{w}, r, \mathbf{p}).$$

Therefore, it's natural and intuitive to expect that, as output prices rise proportionately, revenue should expand, and similarly that as input prices fall proportionately, revenue should rise.

When a producer with maximin preferences uses a technology displaying constant relative riskiness, his level of revenue cost relative to that of a risk-neutral individual depends critically on the level of the certain revenue that he produces. In this case, the first-order conditions and complementary slackness require

$$r = \frac{\partial \overline{C}(\mathbf{w}, \overline{T}(r\mathbf{1}^S, \mathbf{p}, \mathbf{w}), \mathbf{p})}{\partial \overline{T}} \overline{T}(r\mathbf{1}^S, \mathbf{p}, \mathbf{w}).$$

The right-hand side of this expression, by Lemma 5.3, is a nondecreasing function of the revenue aggregate. Therefore, from (5.5), the revenue aggregate here can be higher than that used by a risk-neutral individual only if the nonstochastic revenue produced here exceeds mean revenue produced by the risk-neutral individual. Conversely, the revenue aggregate here will be lower than that for a risk-neutral individual only if the certain revenue is lower than the risk-neutral individual's mean revenue. And because $\overline{C}$ is nondecreasing in the revenue aggregate, we have:

> **Corollary 5.5.3:** *If the producer has maximin preferences and uses a technology exhibiting constant relative riskiness, then the producer incurs a greater level of revenue cost than a risk-neutral producer (who uses the same technology) if and only if her certain revenue exceeds the risk-neutral individual's mean revenue.*

Now consider how a rescaling of input prices affects the producer's optimal choice of the nonstochastic revenue. In that instance, Lemma 5.3 implies that the complementary slackness conditions become

$$r = \frac{\partial \overline{C}(\mu \mathbf{w}, \overline{T}(r\mathbf{1}^S, \mathbf{p}, \mathbf{w}), \mathbf{p})}{\partial \overline{T}} \overline{T}(r\mathbf{1}^S, \mathbf{p}, \mathbf{w}),$$

which can now be rewritten as

$$\frac{r}{\mu} = \frac{\partial \overline{C}(\mathbf{w}, \overline{T}(r\mathbf{1}^S, \mathbf{p}, \mathbf{w}), \mathbf{p})}{\partial \overline{T}} \overline{T}(r\mathbf{1}^S, \mathbf{p}, \mathbf{w}),$$

so that a radial decrease in input prices must lead to an increase in $\overline{T}(r\mathbf{1}^S, \mathbf{p}, \mathbf{w})$ and in the nonstochastic revenue as well.

Similarly, a radial expansion of the state-contingent output prices transforms the first-order condition to

$$r = \frac{\partial \overline{C}(\mathbf{w}, \overline{T}(r\mathbf{1}^S, \mu\mathbf{p}, \mathbf{w}), \mu\mathbf{p})}{\partial \overline{T}} \overline{T}(r\mathbf{1}^S, \mu\mathbf{p}, \mathbf{w}).$$

By the homogeneity properties of $\overline{C}$ and $\overline{T}$,[3] this expression can be rewritten as

$$\mu r = \frac{\partial \overline{C}(\mathbf{w}, \overline{T}(r\mathbf{1}^S, \mathbf{p}, \mathbf{w})/\mu, \mathbf{p})}{\partial \overline{T}} \overline{T}(r\mathbf{1}^S, \mathbf{p}, \mathbf{w}),$$

from which we conclude that $\overline{T}$, and thus r, must rise if $\mu > 1$.

3. Because $\overline{C}$ is homogeneous of degree zero in the revenue aggregate and output prices, the marginal cost of the revenue aggregate must be homogeneous of degree minus one in these same arguments.

Corollary 5.5.4: *If the producer has maximin preferences and uses a technology exhibiting constant relative riskiness, then a radial expansion (contraction) of output prices or a radial contraction (expansion) of input prices leads to an expansion (contraction) of both revenue cost and the optimal nonstochastic revenue.*

5.3 GENERALIZED SCHUR-CONCAVE PREFERENCES

We now turn to differentiable generalized Schur-concave preferences. The producer chooses state-contingent revenues to maximize

$$W(\mathbf{y}) = W(\mathbf{r} - C(\mathbf{w}, \mathbf{r}, \mathbf{p})\mathbf{1}_S).$$

The first-order condition on r_s is

$$W_s(\mathbf{y}) - C_s(\mathbf{w}, \mathbf{r}, \mathbf{p})\sum_{t\in\Omega} W_t(\mathbf{y}) \le 0, \qquad r_s \ge 0,$$

with complementary slackness. The arbitrage condition derived from summing these first-order conditions is

$$\sum_{s\in\Omega} C_s(\mathbf{w}, \mathbf{r}, \mathbf{p}) \ge 1 \tag{5.6}$$

just as in the case of expected profit maximization and maximin preferences. We conclude from (5.6) that a producer with generalized Schur-concave preferences chooses a revenue vector that is in the efficient set. Hence, there always exists a vector of probabilities that will lead a risk-neutral individual to choose the same production pattern as that chosen by one with generalized Schur-concave preferences.

Observe, as we have illustrated with the maximin case, that condition (5.6) holds with equality for an interior solution even in the absence of differentiability of W. Suppose that

$$\sum_{s\in\Omega} C_s(\mathbf{w}, \mathbf{r}, \mathbf{p}) > 1,$$

and that $\mathbf{r}$ is strictly positive. Then revenue can be reduced by one unit in every state of the world, generating a cost reduction of more than one unit, leading to an increase in profit with probability 1.

Pictorially, the production equilibrium is illustrated by a tangency between the producer's indifference curve and one of her isocost curves.

Arbitrage condition (5.6) can be reinterpreted in terms of a portfolio choice problem discussed in Example 3.11 in Chapter 3. There, we reconfirmed a well-known result from expected-utility theory that an individual with CARA preferences allocating wealth between a safe and a risky asset would have her optimal holding of the risky asset unaffected by changes in wealth. By choosing to produce, an individual effectively establishes a claim on a risky asset whose state-contingent returns are the associated state-contingent revenues. The producer's opportunity cost of purchasing this risky asset is the decrease in wealth, in every state of nature, that just equals cost. Put another way, the cost of the risky asset is a reduction in her holding of the safe asset, wealth. Hence, the producer's decision making under uncertainty is parallel to the portfolio choice problem of allocating a fixed amount of preexisting wealth between a safe asset and risky assets.

Now reconsider the arbitrage condition in this light. If the producer raises revenue in each state by one dollar, the market value of the risky asset goes up by exactly one dollar. However, the associated decrease in her holding of the safe asset is $\Sigma_{s\in\Omega}C_s(\mathbf{w}, \mathbf{r}, \mathbf{p})$. If this is less than a dollar, then the increase in the value of the risky asset exceeds the decrease in her holdings of the safe asset, and the producer always has an incentive to expand her holding of the risky asset.

When viewed in this light, the familiar result from Sandmovian theory that optimal production decisions are independent of changes in base wealth when preferences exhibit CARA is simply another manifestation of the basic result that individuals' holdings of risky assets are independent of their wealth levels if they have CARA preferences. Our next example shows that this is true for more general preference structures than expected utility.[4]

> **Example 5.1:** *To this point, we have ignored the presence of preexisting wealth in our analysis of production decisions. Suppose, however, that the producer has an initial wealth endowment of* w_o, *and that she is interested solely in the sum of this initial wealth*

4. It's obviously true in the case of maximin preferences.

endowment and her net revenue from producing. Then her objective function expressed in certainty equivalent terms is

$$e(w_o \boldsymbol{1}_S + \boldsymbol{y}) = e(w_o \boldsymbol{1}_S + \boldsymbol{r} - C(\boldsymbol{w}, \boldsymbol{r}, \boldsymbol{p})\boldsymbol{1}_S).$$

If preferences exhibit CARA, then it follows immediately from Chapter 3 that the producer's objective is

$$\max_r \{e(\boldsymbol{r}) + w_o - C(\boldsymbol{w}, \boldsymbol{r}, \boldsymbol{p})\} = w_o + \max_r \{e(\boldsymbol{r}) - C(\boldsymbol{w}, \boldsymbol{r}, \boldsymbol{p})\}.$$

Obviously, production decisions are independent of her initial wealth. This example also illustrates that, in the presence of CARA, the net-returns model is a special case of the separable effort model discussed in Chapter 3.

An immediate implication of (5.6) and Lemma 5.2 is that an individual with generalized Schur-concave preferences and a technology exhibiting constant absolute riskiness incurs the same level of costs as a risk-neutral producer (as well as one with completely risk-averse preferences). Hence:

Result 5.6: *If the producer has generalized Schur-concave preferences and uses a technology exhibiting constant absolute riskiness, the producer incurs the same level of cost as a risk-neutral producer and a producer with maximin preferences.*

The economic implication of this result is that an individual's choice of cost level is "separate" from her risk preferences if the technology exhibits constant absolute riskiness.[5] Regardless of her risk preferences, she will choose the unique cost level associated with the efficient frontier. Hence, when measured in terms of revenue cost, her optimal scale of operation is independent of her risk preferences. Her risk preferences serve to determine where on the isocost curve she operates:

Corollary 5.6.1: *If the producer has generalized Schur-concave preferences and uses a technology exhibiting constant absolute riskiness, her optimal cost level is independent of her risk preferences.*

Result 5.6 can be illustrated with the use of Figure 5.3. A person with generalized Schur-concave preferences and a technology with

5. We shall encounter more such separation results in Chapter 6.

constant absolute riskiness will produce on the isocost curve between the bisector and the point of risk-neutral production. In particular, since a risk-neutral producer maximizes expected profits at given $\boldsymbol{\pi}$, any other producer operating on the efficient set with the same level of cost must have lower expected profit and, therefore, lower expected revenue.

Therefore, under these conditions, the expected profit-maximizing vector of net returns must be riskier (that is, in terms of the risk ordering $\preccurlyeq w$) than the vector of net returns chosen by the risk-averse producer once differences in means have been corrected for. To confirm this statement, denote the optimal state-contingent revenue vector for the risk-neutral individual by $\mathbf{r}^N$ and the optimal state-contingent revenue vector for the risk-averse individuals by $\mathbf{r}^A$. A producer producing at $(\Sigma_s\pi_s r_s^A/\Sigma_s\pi_s r_s^N)\mathbf{r}^N$ must find herself beneath the equilibrium isocost curve. Notice that because the risk-neutral individual maximizes profit and because all producers (be they risk-averse or risk-neutral) operate at the same cost level, then

$$(\sum_s \pi_s r_s^A / \sum_s \pi_s r_s^N)\mathbf{r}^N \leq \mathbf{r}^N.$$

CR.2 then implies that this normalized revenue vector, which has the same mean as $\mathbf{r}^A$ but the same state-contingent revenue mix as the risk-neutral individual, must lie below the equilibrium isocost curve.

Now, $(\Sigma_s\pi_s r_s^A/\Sigma_s\pi_s r_s^N)\mathbf{r}^N$, being no more costly than $\mathbf{r}^A$, could have been adopted by the risk averter, but wasn't. Hence, a simple revealed preference argument implies that, in terms of the preference function W,

$$W(\mathbf{r}^A - C(\mathbf{w}, \mathbf{r}^A, \mathbf{p})) \geq W((\sum_s \pi_s r_s^A / \sum_s \pi_s r_s^N)\mathbf{r}^N - C(\mathbf{w}, \mathbf{r}^A, \mathbf{p})),$$

which establishes our claim.

> **Corollary 5.6.2:** *If the producer has generalized Schur-concave preferences and uses a technology exhibiting constant absolute riskiness, then* $\mathbf{r}^A \preceq_W (\Sigma_s\pi_s r_s^A/\Sigma_s\pi_s r_s^N)\mathbf{r}^N$.

An individual with generalized Schur-concave preferences using a technology exhibiting constant absolute riskiness always adopts a state-contingent revenue vector that is more risky, after correcting for mean differences, than that adopted by an individual with maximin preferences. (This follows trivially because an individual with maximin preferences tolerates no risk.) But this revenue choice is less risky than that of a risk-neutral individual.

Combining Result 3.3 from Chapter 3 with the first-order conditions for an interior solution shows that an optimally chosen state-contingent revenue vector must be *risk-aversely efficient* (in the sense of Peleg and Yaari 1975) with respect to π:

$$r_s \geq r_t \Leftrightarrow \frac{C_s(\mathbf{w}, \mathbf{r}, \mathbf{p})}{\pi_s} \leq \frac{C_t(\mathbf{w}, \mathbf{r}, \mathbf{p})}{\pi_t},$$

or

$$\left(\frac{C_s(\mathbf{w}, \mathbf{r}, \mathbf{p})}{\pi_s} - \frac{C_t(\mathbf{w}, \mathbf{r}, \mathbf{p})}{\pi_t}\right)(r_s - r_t) \leq 0. \tag{5.7}$$

Because the preference function is generalized Schur-concave, then, in the neighborhood of the equilibrium, the revenue-cost function must behave as though it, too, were generalized Schur-concave. Notice, in particular, that if the revenue-cost function is also generalized Schur-convex, then (5.7), along with Corollary 3.3.1 from Chapter 3, implies that the risk averter will always produce on the equal-revenue vector. The reasoning here is easy. Generalized Schur-convex revenue-cost structures are characterized by the fact that there's always a cost advantage to producing a nonstochastic revenue. Because a nonstochastic revenue is always cheaper to produce than any other state-contingent revenue vector with the same mean, the producer does not have to sacrifice any expected return to diminish risk. Consequently, he completely stabilizes his return.

The notion of risk-averse efficiency is due to Peleg and Yaari (1975) and can be heuristically identified with the notion that for any state-contingent revenue vector satisfying it, there will be some risk-averse individual who would optimally adopt that vector if she incurred the same level of revenue cost. Pictorially, it manifests the fact that the fair-odds line in Figure 5.3 cuts the optimal isocost curve at the optimal state-contingent revenue pair.

We define the *risk-aversely efficient set for* π as consisting of those elements of the efficient set satisfying (5.7).

By complementary slackness, as long as the preference function is differentiable,

$$\frac{\sum_{s\in\Omega} W_s(\mathbf{y})r_s}{\sum_{s\in\Omega} W_s(\mathbf{y})} = \sum_{s\in\Omega} C_s(\mathbf{w}, \mathbf{r}, \mathbf{p})r_s. \tag{5.8}$$

Corollary 3.3.2 in Chapter 3 implies

$$\sum_{s\in\Omega} W_s(\mathbf{y})\left(y_s - \sum_{s\in\Omega} \pi_s y_s\right) \leq 0.$$

Substituting $y_s = r_s - C(\mathbf{w}, \mathbf{r}, \mathbf{p})$, this last inequality implies

$$\sum_{s\in\Omega} \pi_s r_s \geq \frac{\sum_{s\in\Omega} W_s(\mathbf{y})r_s}{\sum_{s\in\Omega} W_s(\mathbf{y})}, \tag{5.9}$$

which when combined with (5.8) establishes that

$$\sum_{s\in\Omega} \pi_s r_s - \sum_{s\in\Omega} C_s(\mathbf{w}, \mathbf{r}, \mathbf{p})r_s \geq 0.$$

This last expression represents the marginal change in expected profit associated with a small radial expansion of the revenue vector. Because it is nonnegative, we have:

> **Result 5.7:** *If* $\mathbf{r}$ *is a risk-aversely efficient revenue vector, a small radial expansion in* $\mathbf{r}$ *leads to an increase in expected profits.*

An early analog of Result 5.7 was first proved by Sandmo (1971) for the expected-utility model with a nonstochastic technology and stochastic prices. We illustrate the meaning of Result 5.7 for his model with an example.

> **Example 5.2:** *Sandmo (1971) studied the case of a firm with expected-utility preferences using a nonstochastic technology to produce a single output that fetched a stochastic price. Let the cost function for the nonstochastic output,* $z \in \Re_+$, *be denoted by the strictly increasing and strictly convex* $c^c(\mathbf{w}, z)$, *where the superscript* c *reminds the reader that output is certain. Although one can operate directly in terms of this cost function to verify the analog of Result 5.7, it is of interest to derive the revenue-cost function associated with this technology. By definition,*

$$
\begin{aligned}
C(\boldsymbol{w},\boldsymbol{r},\boldsymbol{p}) &= \min\{c^c(\boldsymbol{w},z):z\boldsymbol{p}\geq \boldsymbol{r}\}\\
&= \min\{c^c(\boldsymbol{w},z):z\geq r_s/p_s, \qquad s\in\Omega\}\\
&= c^c\left(\boldsymbol{w}, \max_{1,2,\ldots,S}\{r_s/p_s\}\right).
\end{aligned}
$$

It's an easy matter, which we leave as an exercise for the reader, to verify properties CR for this cost structure. The producer's problem, under generalized Schur-concave preferences, is now to

$$\max_{\boldsymbol{r}}\left\{W\left(\boldsymbol{r}-c^c\left(\boldsymbol{w}, \max_{1,2,\ldots,S}\{r_s/p_s\}\right)\boldsymbol{1}_S\right)\right\}.$$

We first demonstrate the obvious result[6] *that in the optimum*

$$r_s = (p_s/p_1)r_1, \qquad s\in\Omega.$$

Suppose that this last equality did not hold and pick any r_k *such that*

$$r_k/p_k < \max_{1,2,\ldots,S}\{r_s/p_s\}.$$

If this inequality holds at the optimum, there must exist an arbitrarily small but positive perturbation in r_k that preserves the inequality. Let this perturbation be called δ, and notice that as a result of this perturbation, the producer's objective function changes by

$$W_k(\boldsymbol{y})\delta > 0$$

as long as preferences are strictly increasing in all incomes. Generally, therefore, the state-contingent revenue vector is proportional to the vector of state-contingent prices in the optimum. Making this substitution allows us to rewrite the Sandmovian problem in our context as

$$\max_{r_1}\{W(r_1 - c^c(\boldsymbol{w}, r_1/p_1),\ldots, r_1(p_S/p_1) - c^c(\boldsymbol{w}, r_1/p_1))\},$$

with the corresponding first-order condition.

$$\sum_{s\in\Omega} W_s(\boldsymbol{y})\frac{p_s}{p_1} - \frac{c_z^c(\boldsymbol{w}, r_1/p_1)}{p_1}\sum_{s\in\Omega} W_s(\boldsymbol{y}) \leq 0, \qquad r_1 \geq 0,$$

6. If we derived the optimum directly in terms of the nonstochastic output, this argument would not be needed.

or

$$\sum_{s\in\Omega} W_s(\boldsymbol{y})(p_s - c_z^c(\boldsymbol{w}, r_I/p_I)) \le 0, \qquad r_I \ge 0,$$

in the notation of complementary slackness. For the case of expected utility, we obtain

$$\sum_{s\in\Omega} \pi_s u'(y_s)(p_s - c_z^c(\boldsymbol{w}, r_I/p_I)) \le 0, \qquad r_I \ge 0,$$

which is the exact first-order condition obtained by Sandmo (1971).

For generalized Schur-concave preferences, identical arguments to those that lead up to Result 5.7 now establish the exact analog for this model to Result 5.7:

$$\left(\sum_{s\in\Omega} \pi_s p_s - c_z^c(\boldsymbol{w}, r_I/p_I)\right) z \ge 0.$$

So if $z > 0$*, the expected price is greater than marginal cost. Along with the presumption that costs are strictly convex in the nonstochastic output, this last inequality implies that an individual with generalized Schur-concave preferences will always produce less than a risk-neutral individual facing the same technology and the same subjective probabilities.*

The state-contingent analog to Result 5.7 for expected-utility preferences was established in Chambers and Quiggin (1997).

Now consider what happens when an individual uses a technology displaying constant relative riskiness. By the first-order conditions and complementary slackness,

$$\frac{\sum_{s\in\Omega} W_s(\mathbf{y}) r_s}{\sum_{s\in\Omega} W_s(\mathbf{y})} = \frac{\partial \bar{C}(\mathbf{w}, \bar{T}(\mathbf{r}, \mathbf{p}, \mathbf{w}), \mathbf{p})}{\partial \bar{T}} \bar{T}(\mathbf{r}, \mathbf{p}, \mathbf{w}). \tag{5.10}$$

Expression (5.5), on the other hand, indicated that a risk-neutral individual using the same technology would choose expected revenue so that

$$\frac{\partial \bar{C}(\mathbf{w}, \bar{T}(\mathbf{r}, \mathbf{p}, \mathbf{w}), \mathbf{p})}{\partial \bar{T}} \bar{T}(\mathbf{r}, \mathbf{p}, \mathbf{w}) = \sum_s \pi_s r_s. \tag{5.11}$$

Because $\overline{C}$ (**w**, $\overline{T}$(**r**, **p**, **w**), **p**) is convex in $\overline{T}$, a risk averter will incur more effort cost than a risk-neutral individual with the same technology if and only if their directional derivative of $\overline{C}$ in the direction of $\overline{T}$ (the right-hand side of [5.10]) is greater than the left-hand side of (5.11). When this fact is used in conjunction with (5.8), we obtain:

> **Result 5.8:** *If the producer has generalized Schur-concave preferences and uses a technology exhibiting constant relative riskiness in state-contingent revenues, the producer incurs a greater level of revenue cost than a risk-neutral producer only if her mean revenue exceeds the risk-neutral individual's mean revenue.*

Finally, we present a short example, which shows what happens when producer's risk preferences exhibit constant relative riskiness.

> **Example 5.3:** *If the producer's risk preferences are characterized by constant relative risk aversion, it is more convenient to work in terms of certainty equivalents than in terms of preferences. Recall from Result 3.1 in Chapter 3 that if an individual's preferences exhibit constant relative risk aversion, her certainty equivalent is positively linearly homogeneous in state-contingent returns. We want to examine what happens to her revenue choices when the input prices and the state-contingent output prices she faces are proportionately rescaled. Her objective function then becomes*

$$\begin{aligned}
&\max_{r}\{\mathrm{e}(\boldsymbol{r} - \mathrm{C}(\lambda \boldsymbol{w}, \boldsymbol{r}, \lambda \boldsymbol{p})\boldsymbol{1}_S)\} \\
&\quad = \max_{r}\{\mathrm{e}(\boldsymbol{r} - \lambda \mathrm{C}(\boldsymbol{w}, \boldsymbol{r}/\lambda, \boldsymbol{p})\boldsymbol{1}_S)\} \\
&\quad = \max_{r}\{\mathrm{e}(\lambda(\boldsymbol{r}/\lambda) - \lambda \mathrm{C}(\boldsymbol{w}, \boldsymbol{r}/\lambda, \boldsymbol{p})\boldsymbol{1}_S)\} \\
&\quad = \lambda \max_{r/\lambda}\{\mathrm{e}(\boldsymbol{r}/\lambda) - \mathrm{C}(\boldsymbol{w}, \boldsymbol{r}/\lambda, \boldsymbol{p})\boldsymbol{1}_S)\},
\end{aligned}$$

> *where the first equality follows by the homogeneity properties of the revenue-cost function and the last equality follows by the positive linear homogeneity of her certainty equivalent. From this chain of equalities, it follows that rescaling prices in this way leads the decision maker to rescale her optimal certainty equivalent and her optimal revenue by the same proportion.*

II Applications

6 Production with Futures and Forward Markets

Chapter 5 used the tools developed in the first four chapters to analyze the production decisions of risk-neutral and risk-averse producers whose only recourse in coping with uncertainty is to vary the commitment of inputs and the allocation of state-contingent outputs. In reality, many contingent-claim markets exist, and producers can use these markets to spread some of the production and price risk they face.

The state-contingent markets most directly relevant to producers are futures and production-insurance markets. The former are especially important in coping with price uncertainty, and the latter are especially important in coping with production uncertainty. A large literature exists on the effects of the existence of futures markets on risk-averse producer decision making (Anderson and Danthine 1983; Danthine 1978; Holthausen 1979; Feder, Just, and Schmitz 1980). Virtually all of it treats risk-averse producers using a nonstochastic technology in the presence of price uncertainty.

This chapter examines how futures and forward markets affect the optimal decisions of risk-averse producers facing *both* price and production uncertainty. (Chapter 7 examines the impact of production insurance on risk-averse producer decisions.) Naturally, the treatment here is in state-contingent terms. The producers that we consider allocate inputs to trade off increased output in one state of nature against reduced output in another. Producers determine endogenously how much production risk to bear. We sharpen our focus at times by assuming that the technology is not inherently risky.

We first present the basic theoretical model. Then, for purposes of comparison, we survey, using a state-contingent approach, the main results that have been obtained for producers facing only price risk in the presence of a forward market for the commodity produced. We show that this problem reduces to a simple one of picking the optimal size of a random variable whose inherent relative riskiness is predetermined. Then we analyze producer behavior with both price and production risk in the presence of a complete forward market for the commodity. After developing some preliminary results on the hedging and production equilibrium, we develop conditions for the optimal hedge to be positive (for the producer to go short) or negative (for the producer to go long). Next, we show that, under plausible conditions, with the ability to hedge price risk in an unbiased forward market, *a risk-averse producer will never willingly adopt a nonstochastic technology if given the alternative of adopting an uncertain production technology*. Producers having access to an unbiased forward market, therefore, always prefer to bear some production risk to none. The reason is straightforward. Producers are not inherently interested in either price or production risk but in the revenue risk that they engender. Hence, their optimal production decisions will involve balancing production risk (which they can affect) against price risk (which they can't affect) in an attempt to smooth the revenue risk that they care about.

A standard result from finance theory (Hirshleifer and Riley 1992; Luenberger 1995) is that the existence of a complete set of contingent markets that spans the state space will result in an equilibrium in which all agree on production decisions regardless of their risk preferences. In short, an individual producer's production decision is independent of his risk preferences. This finding has come to be known as a *separation result*. Townsend (1978) showed that if the rank of the matrix of spot prices equals the number of states, forward or futures contracts would also have this spanning or separating property. Our first separation result, derived in the case of two states, generalizes Townsend's result by showing that the ability to arbitrage across production states (in the terminology of Chapter 5, picking a production vector that is in the efficient subset) effectively relaxes the requirement that the spot price matrix have the same rank as the number of states. It does this by creating a hedging opportunity internal to the firm's production decisions that can be used to replace one of the external hedging opportunities. After demonstrating this separation result, we show that if the forward market is unbiased in the two-state case, a risk-averse producer facing both price and production risk will choose the same production equilibrium as a risk-neutral producer and then create an optimal hedge that completely smooths his income stream.

We next analyze a firm with an uncertain technology facing more than one contingent market in which to hedge. Where the second contingent market represents a futures market for a commodity related to, but distinct from, the commodity produced by the firm (for example, Soft Red Winter wheat futures for a Dark Spring wheat producer), participation in such a market is typically referred to as *cross hedging*. More generally, our analysis applies to participation in any derivative market, or to construction of "home-made" derivatives, such as "straddles" based on offsetting contracts in two or more markets. We close the chapter by establishing a general separation (spanning) result.

6.1 THE MODEL

The model is the same as in Chapter 5, with the simplifying assumption that $M = 1$, that is, in each state of nature, a single output is produced. We examine a producer with a strictly increasing and strictly generalized Schur-concave net-returns objective function $W(\mathbf{y})$, risk-averse for probabilities $\boldsymbol{\pi}$, producing state-contingent outputs $\mathbf{z} \in \Re^S_+$, and facing state-contingent output (spot) prices $\mathbf{p} \in \Re^S_{++}$. The producer faces price as well as production uncertainty. Typically, we shall presume that the objective function is smoothly differentiable in all arguments, but at certain points, it will prove advantageous to relax that assumption. Input quantities and prices are given by $\mathbf{x} \in \Re^N_+$, $\mathbf{w} \in \Re^N_{++}$. We denote by I^* the subset of $\Re^S_{++}$ consisting of vectors of the form $t\,\mathbf{1}^S$, $t > 0$, that is, vectors with every entry equal to t.

We examine two alternative forward-market structures: a single forward market and K futures markets. The forward market operates in the following fashion. At the time input decisions are made, the producer can execute costlessly a forward contract that entitles him to sell the amount h forward at the price q. (If the producer goes "short" then $h > 0$, and if the producer goes "long", then $h < 0$.) The

K futures markets operate as follows. There are K futures markets where the producer can take either a long or a short position. In each market at the current futures price q^k, the producer can execute either a long or a short contract denoted by $h^k \in \Re$ giving him or her the ability to sell or take delivery of h^k units of the commodity in question at some later date. These commodities need not be the commodity that the producer produces. For each futures contract, there exists a state-contingent price vector $\mathbf{f}^k \in \Re_{++}^S$ of the same basic structure as $\mathbf{p}$, that is, if Nature chooses s from Ω, then the ex post price of the kth commodity (or the futures contract) is f_s^k. (In the special case where one of the futures commodities is the same commodity as the individual produces, $f_s^k = p_s$.) Denote by $\mathbf{b}^k \in \Re^S$ the vector with typical element $b_s^k = f_s^k - q^k$. This is the vector of basis risk.

In the case of a single forward contract, net returns are given by

$$y_s = p_s z_s + h(q - p_s) - c(\mathbf{w}, \mathbf{z}).$$

In the multiple-futures case,

$$y_s = p_s z_s + \sum_k h_k b_s^k - c(\mathbf{w}, \mathbf{z}).$$

Much of our analysis is devoted to the case where choosing a relatively less risky production plan is less costly than choosing a more risky production plan. Under fairly weak conditions, it is possible for the producer to achieve a certain output (that is, $\mathbf{z} \in I^*$) at some cost. However, because there is no general reason to suppose that producers will equalize state-contingent outputs, the existence of this possibility does not provide a true analog of the nonstochastic production case. Thus, we focus on the case, developed in Chapter 4, in which production is not inherently risky, specifically where $c(\mathbf{w}, \mathbf{z})$ is generalized Schur-convex for the same probabilities for which the producer is risk-averse.

6.2 NONSTOCHASTIC PRODUCTION

Let us first consider the degenerate case in which the production technology is nonstochastic. Instead of a vector of state-contingent outputs, there is only one output that the producer chooses. That output occurs with probability 1. We denote the cost function for that nonstochastic output by $c^c(\mathbf{w}, z)$, where superscript c is meant to remind the reader that output is always certain. This cost function has the same properties in input prices as the effort-cost function. We shall also assume that it is strictly increasing and strictly convex in the nonstochastic output, $z \in \Re_+$.

The producer faces price risk and can hedge this price risk in a forward market. Therefore, her objective function is

$$W(z\mathbf{p} + h(q\mathbf{1}^S - \mathbf{p}) - c^c(\mathbf{w}, z)),$$

where, as usual, $\mathbf{1}^S$ denotes the S-dimensional unit vector.

The producer's first-order conditions are

$$\sum_{s \in \Omega} W_s(\mathbf{y})(p_s - c_z^c(\mathbf{w}, z)) \le 0, \qquad z \ge 0,$$
$$\sum_{s \in \Omega} W_s(\mathbf{y})(q - p_s) = 0$$

in the notation of complementary slackness. (Because the hedge can be either short or long, the second first-order condition must hold as an equality.) Using the first-order condition for the optimal hedge in the first expression shows that the producer chooses the nonstochastic output according to

$$q - c_z^c(\mathbf{w}, z) \le 0, \qquad z \ge 0.$$

The producer equates the marginal cost of output to the forward price. Therefore, any two producers facing the same production structure and the same forward market will produce the same level of output regardless of their risk preferences. This is the most commonly recognized separation result.

The explanation is simple. Because output is nonstochastic but price is stochastic, choosing the output level is equivalent to picking the "size" of the random-revenue vector (or cast in terms of portfolio choice, the size of the risky asset). Notice that changing output changes all state-contingent revenues proportionately. In terms of Figure 6.1, this means that the producer is choosing where to locate on the ray emanating from the origin and labelled **p** with slope equaling the ratio of relative prices. Because output is nonstochastic, the state-contingent revenue mix is constant and given by the relative

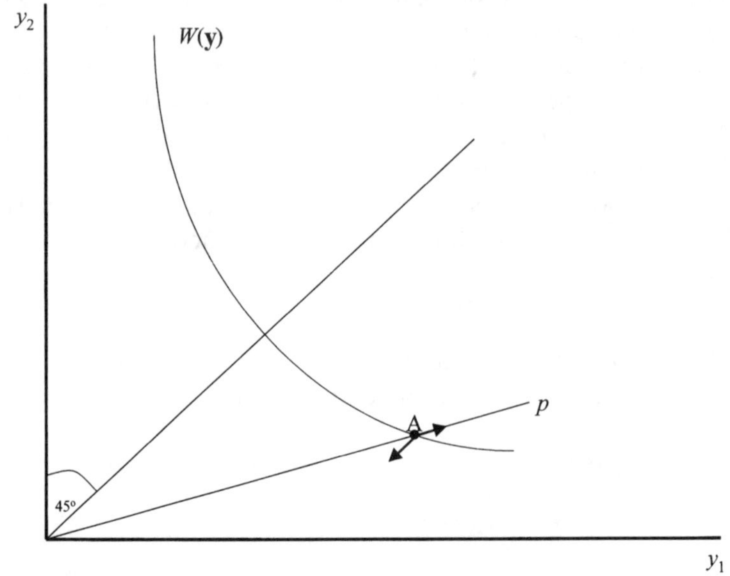

Figure 6.1 Determining the optimal nonstochastic output.

state-contingent prices. Therefore, if the producer is originally at, say, point A in Figure 6.1, increasing output expands revenues along the state-contingent price vector, **p**. The producer's associated welfare gain is given by the derivative of W in the direction of **p**, $\Sigma_{s\in\Omega} W_s(\mathbf{y}) p_s$. This is illustrated by the arrow emanating from A outward in the direction of **p**.

As the producer expands output, however, she also incurs a reduction of $c_z^c(\mathbf{w}, z)$ in each state-contingent net revenue. This reduces her state-contingent revenue vector in a direction parallel to the equal-income ray. The effect on her welfare is given by the derivative of W in the direction of the bisector, $c_z^c(\mathbf{w}, z)\, \Sigma_{s\in\Omega} W_s(\mathbf{y})$. This is illustrated by the arrow emanating from A downward in the direction of the bisector. In the absence of a hedging opportunity, the optimal point on the state-contingent price vector occurs where the positive welfare movement in the direction of the price vector is exactly balanced by the negative movement in the direction of the equal-income ray.

If a hedging opportunity exists, increasing the hedge does two things. First, it increases all state-contingent incomes risklessly by the amount of the change in the hedge times the forward price. This increases net returns parallel to the equal-income ray. Second, it slides state-contingent returns back along the state-contingent price vector by the amount of the hedge. This movement represents the welfare effect associated with the spot income lost as a result of the hedge. The optimal hedge requires that the marginal movement along the price vector just equal the outward movement in the direction of the equal-income ray. But from before, this marginal movement along the price vector, in equilibrium, must equal the opportunity cost of raising production by one unit. Hence, the hedging opportunity lets the producer arbitrage his production decisions against the position taken in the forward market. Because of the arbitrage opportunity, the riskless increase in state-contingent revenue associated with expanding the hedge just balances the opportunity cost of raising production by one unit.

We now examine the magnitude of the optimal hedge. Start with the simplest possible case in which the forward market is viewed by the producer as an unbiased predictor of the spot price in the sense that

$$q = \sum_{s \in \Omega} \pi_s p_s .$$

In this case, the producer's objective function is

$$W\left(p_1(z-h) + h\sum_{s \in \Omega} \pi_s p_s - c^c(\mathbf{w}, z), \cdots, p_s(z-h) + h\sum_{s \in \Omega} \pi_s p_s - c^c(\mathbf{w}, z) \right).$$

By setting the hedge equal to the level of production, the producer ensures that she receives expected profit with probability 1. Hence, she can choose z to maximize expected profit. Because she is risk-averse, she can do no better than this. Thus, she chooses to fully hedge while producing where marginal cost equals the expected price and selling the entire crop in the forward market.

Now consider the case in which the futures price is not an unbiased predictor of the spot price. There are two possibilities,

$$q > \sum_{s \in \Omega} \pi_s p_s$$

and the reverse. To analyze the magnitude of the hedge, recall that for a strictly generalized Schur-concave function, Corollary 3.3.2 in Chapter 3 implies

$$(z-h)\sum_{s\in\Omega} W_s(\mathbf{y})\left(p_s-\sum_{s\in\Omega}\pi_s p_s\right)<0.$$

Meanwhile the first-order condition for the optimal hedge requires

$$\sum_{s\in\Omega} W_s(\mathbf{y})(q-p_s)=0.$$

Using this optimal hedging condition in the former gives

$$(z-h)\left(q-\sum_{s\in\Omega}\pi_s p_s\right)\sum_{s\in\Omega} W_s(\mathbf{y})<0.$$

Hence, the magnitude of the hedge *is determined* by $(q - \Sigma_{s\in\Omega}\, \pi_s p_s)$. If this expression is positive, implying that the forward price is above the expected spot price, the producer's optimal hedge is positive and larger than the crop that he produces. If it's negative, the hedge is smaller than the level of the crop produced.

Example 6.1: *In this example, we consider a class of preferences for which there is no nontrivial production or hedging equilibrium when the technology is nonstochastic and exhibits constant returns to scale. Let the producer's preferences exhibit constant relative risk aversion. By Result 3.1 from Chapter 3, her preferences must be homothetic. Hence, the producer's objective function can now be expressed as*

$$\mathrm{H}(\mathrm{F}(\mathrm{z}\boldsymbol{p}+\mathrm{h}(\mathrm{q}\boldsymbol{1}^{\mathrm{S}}-\boldsymbol{p})-\mathrm{c}^{\mathrm{c}}(\boldsymbol{w},\mathrm{z}))),$$

where H *is increasing, and* F *is strictly increasing and positively linearly homogeneous. (*F *can be taken to be the certainty equivalent.) No generality is lost in taking the producer's objective function as*

$$\mathrm{F}(\mathrm{z}\boldsymbol{p}+\mathrm{h}(\mathrm{q}\boldsymbol{1}^{\mathrm{S}}-\boldsymbol{p})-\mathrm{c}^{\mathrm{c}}(\boldsymbol{w},\mathrm{z})).$$

Now suppose in addition that the cost function is consistent with constant returns to scale so that it, too, is positively linearly homogeneous, that is,

$$c^c(\boldsymbol{w}, z) = zc^c(\boldsymbol{w}, 1).$$

(Notice that constant returns to scale violates our previous assumption that the $c^c(\boldsymbol{w}, z)$ *is strictly convex.) Under these assumptions, the producer's problem can be rewritten as that of choosing the level of output and the percentage of output hedged,* $\hat{h} = h/z$, *to maximize*

$$zF(\boldsymbol{p} + \hat{h}(q\boldsymbol{I}^S - \boldsymbol{p}) - c^c(\boldsymbol{w}, 1)).$$

Because the objective function is linear in the level of output, the optimal output is set at either infinity or zero. And because the optimal output is set at either zero or infinity, the percentage of the hedge will not be well defined, being either trivially zero, or trivially plus or minus infinity.

In Figure 6.1, we saw that the production decisions in this model degenerate to picking the optimal "size" of the price vector. Hence, if "size doesn't matter" in the producer's risk preferences, as CRRA implies, her production decision will generally not be well defined. If she finds it desirable to produce any positive amount, she'll also find it desirable to produce an infinitely large amount. Constant relative riskiness of preferences implies that the size of the net revenue vector doesn't affect the producer's risk preferences, and constant returns to scale is sufficient to ensure that the size of the producer's output doesn't affect the producer's net returns as long as the hedge is chosen appropriately.

6.3 OPTIMAL BEHAVIOR IN THE ABSENCE OF FUTURES MARKETS

For a producer who faces both production and price uncertainty but does not have access to futures markets, the analysis of production decisions with the net-returns objective function presented in Chapter 5 is applicable. That analysis, however, was presented primarily in terms of the revenue-cost function $C(\mathbf{w}, \mathbf{r}, \mathbf{p})$. To develop the analysis of futures and forward contracts, it is useful to state results in terms of the effort-cost function $c(\mathbf{w}, \mathbf{z})$.

We begin by making some observations about the behavior of risk-neutral producers, not subject to price uncertainty, who choose $\mathbf{z}$ to solve the problem

$$\max_{\mathbf{z}}\left\{\sum_{s\in\Omega}\pi_s p_s z_s - c(\mathbf{w},\mathbf{z})\right\} \text{ for } \mathbf{p} = p\mathbf{1} \in I^*$$

or

$$\max_{\mathbf{z}}\left\{p\sum_{s\in\Omega}\pi_s z_s - c(\mathbf{w},\mathbf{z})\right\}.$$

The first-order conditions for an optimum are given by

$$p\pi_s - \frac{\partial c(\mathbf{z})}{\partial z_s} \le 0, \qquad z_s \ge 0,\ s \in \Omega,$$

in the notation of complementary slackness.

It is straightforward to derive analogs of the results in Chapter 5 for the cases when $c(\mathbf{w}, \mathbf{z})$ displays constant absolute riskiness and constant relative riskiness. This is left to the reader as an exercise. In this chapter, our attention will be focused on price uncertainty. We have already considered what happens when production is completely nonstochastic, and now we want to focus on the case when the effort-cost function is everywhere not inherently risky.

In the absence of price uncertainty, the revenue-cost function is nowhere inherently risky if and only if the effort-cost function is nowhere inherently risky in the sense defined in Chapter 4. Thus, cost structures where production is nowhere inherently risky have the unique property that in the absence of price uncertainty, a risk-neutral individual will always choose an output vector $\mathbf{z} \in I^*$. To see this, consider any $\mathbf{z} \notin I^*$. Let its mean $\Sigma_{s\in\Omega}\, \pi_s z_s$ be denoted $\bar{z}$ and the vector with the mean appearing in each element be $\bar{z}\mathbf{1}^S = \bar{\mathbf{z}}$. Now observe that, for any $\mathbf{p} = p\mathbf{1}^S \in I^*$, expected revenue for $\bar{\mathbf{z}}$ is the same as for $\mathbf{z}$, namely, $p\bar{z}$. Since $\bar{\mathbf{z}}$ is less risky than $\mathbf{z}$, $c(\mathbf{w}, \bar{\mathbf{z}}) \le c(\mathbf{w}, \mathbf{z})$. A similar argument may be applied to show that, in the absence of price uncertainty and inherent technological risk, the solution to any cost minimization problem will lie in I^*.

Result 6.1: *If production is nowhere inherently risky, then, for* $\mathbf{p} \in \mathrm{I}^*$, *the solution,* $\mathbf{z}$ $(\mathbf{p})$, *to the problem,*

$$\max_{z}\left\{\sum_{s\in\Omega}\pi_s p_s z_s - c(\boldsymbol{w},\boldsymbol{z})\right\}$$

satisfies $\mathbf{z}(\mathbf{p}) \in I^*$, *or there exists an equivalent solution that satisfies this latter property. If production is not inherently risky, then, for* $\mathbf{p} \in I^*$, *the solution,* $\mathbf{z}(\mathbf{p}, r)$, *to the problem*

$$\min_{z}\left\{c(\mathbf{w},\mathbf{z}) : \sum_{s\in\Omega} \pi_s p_s z_s \geq r\right\}$$

satisfies $\mathbf{z}(\mathbf{p}, r) \in I^*$ *or there exists an equivalent solution that satisfies this latter property.*

Now consider the case of general **p**. Under the assumption that production is generalized Schur-convex,

$$c(\mathbf{w},\mathbf{z}) \geq c(\mathbf{w},\bar{\mathbf{z}}),$$

so, for any **p**, the optimal $\mathbf{z}(\mathbf{p})$ must satisfy

$$\sum_{s\in\Omega} \pi_s p_s z_s \geq \sum_{s\in\Omega} \pi_s p_s \bar{z}.$$

Moreover, by Corollary 3.3.1 in Chapter 3, it follows that

$$\left(\frac{\partial c(\mathbf{w},\mathbf{z})/\partial z_s}{\pi_s} - \frac{\partial c(\mathbf{w},\mathbf{z})/\partial z_t}{\pi_t}\right)(z_s - z_t) \geq 0,$$

and an interior solution for the first-order conditions then implies

$$(p_s - p_t)(z_s - z_t) \geq 0.$$

We summarize this as follows:

Result 6.2: *If production is generalized Schur-convex, the solution,* $\mathbf{z}(\mathbf{p})$, *to the problem*

$$\mathit{mix}_{z}\left\{\sum_{s\in\Omega} \pi_s p_s z_s - c(\mathbf{w}, \mathbf{z})\right\}$$

satisfies

$$\sum_{s\in\Omega} \pi_s p_s [z_s(p) - \bar{z})] \geq 0$$

and

$$(p_s - p_t)(z_s - z_t) \geq 0.$$

That is, cost functions where production is generalized Schur-convex always yield a state-contingent output vector for a risk-neutral producer that is positively correlated with the state-contingent price vector. The fact that the supply correspondence is positively sloped is a well-understood property of multioutput supply correspondences under certainty. Typically, it is referred to as the *law of supply*. Generally speaking, the law of supply requires each output to be nondecreasing in its own price. Result 6.2 establishes a subtly different result: when production is generalized Schur-convex, the covariance between $\mathbf{p}$ and $\mathbf{z}$ $(\mathbf{p})$ is nonnegative. That is, each state-contingent supply is not shown to be increasing in its own price (this is trivial), rather it is shown that state-contingent outputs are higher for states that have higher state-contingent prices. Thus, Result 6.2 might be interpreted as a *probabilistic law of supply*.

The first-order conditions for an optimum are given by

$$W_s(\mathbf{y})p_s - c_s(\mathbf{w},\mathbf{z})\sum_{t\in\Omega} W_t(\mathbf{y}) \leq 0, \qquad z_s \geq 0 \tag{6.1}$$

$(s = 1, 2, \ldots, S)$ in the notation of complementary slackness. Expression (6.1) implies that the marginal cost of producing the sth state-contingent output is always greater than or equal to the marginal utility of increasing the sth state-contingent output divided by the marginal utility of a sure increase in income. Figure 6.2a illustrates this equilibrium in state-contingent output space by a tangency between the producer's indifference curve and her isocost curve.

Adding the first-order conditions yields another version of the arbitrage condition [equation (5.11), derived in Chapter 5].

Lemma 6.1: *Producer equilibrium must satisfy*

$$\sum_{s\in\Omega}(c_s(\boldsymbol{w},\boldsymbol{z})/p_s) \geq 1,$$

with the inequality replaced by an equality in the case of an interior equilibrium.

This lemma does not depend crucially on the presumed differentiability of preferences. If it didn't hold, the producer could profitably increase all state-contingent returns risklessly by expanding production in each state of nature. But the lemma does depend crucially on

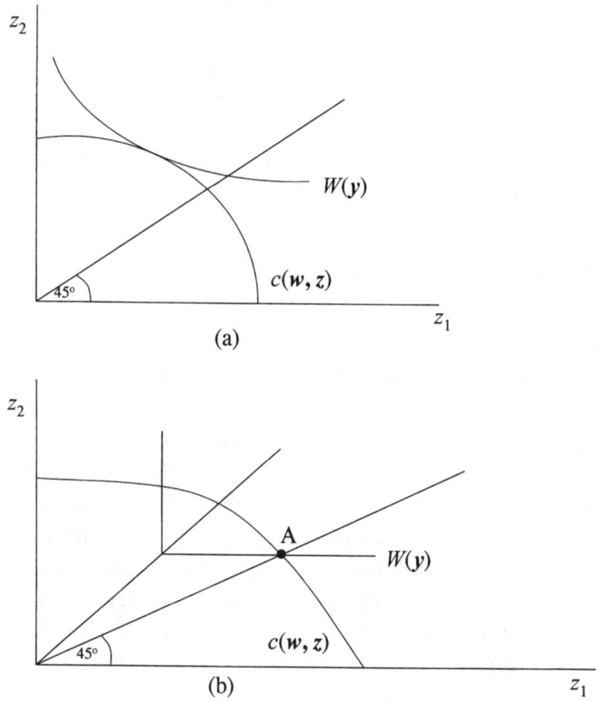

Figure 6.2 (a) Production equilibrium with no forward market. (b) Completely risk-averse preferences.

the assumption that the cost structure be smoothly differentiable. Example 6.2 illustrates.

Example 6.2: *Several times we have spoken of the output-cubical technology that forms the cornerstone of the modern theory of producer decision making under uncertainty and principal–agent analysis in rather pejorative terms. Economic choices for the output-cubical technology degenerate to the producer picking a single random variable with desirable risk characteristics. We use this example for two purposes: to explain our position, and to present a basis for comparison with the results for the truly state-contingent technology. Consider the effort-cost function for the output-cubical technology that satisfies*

$$c(\boldsymbol{w}, \boldsymbol{z}) = \max_{1,2,\cdots,S}\{c^s(\boldsymbol{w}, z_s)\}.$$

Generally, this cost function is not differentiable in the state-contingent outputs, and its effort-cost output set is cubical. Accordingly, standard maximization arguments cannot be used to determine what the producer's optimal state-contingent output choice looks like. Notice, however, that varying z_s *here results in the following variation in welfare if the producer's technology is output-cubical:*

$$\left[W_s(\boldsymbol{y})p_s - \delta^{max} c_z^s(\boldsymbol{w}, z_s) \sum_{t \in \Omega} W_t(\boldsymbol{y})\right] \delta z_s,$$

where $\delta^{max} = 1$ *if* $c^s(\boldsymbol{w}, z_s) \in max_{1,2,\ldots,S}\{c^s(\boldsymbol{w}, z_s)\}$ *and* 0 *otherwise. Hence, if* z_s *is not the costliest output to produce using the ex post technology, the producer always realizes a welfare gain by increasing production of* z_s. *Pictorially, one can envision the producer moving along one of the facets of the output cube until she reaches its vertex. Several observations merit consideration at this point. First, if the producer's cost is given, her choice of an optimal output mix is entirely independent of her risk preferences. Instead, her choice only depends on the monotonicity properties of her objective function. And, second, for a given level of cost, both a risk-neutral individual and a risk averter act in the same fashion, that is, they pick the point on the frontier of the effort-cost output set that corresponds to maximal expected revenue regardless of their subjective probabilities. Hence,* once the level of cost is determined, there is a complete separation between the production decision and the producer's risk preferences. All risk averters and all risk-neutral producers locate at the same point.

This observation also allows us to solve for $S - 1$ *of the state-contingent outputs in terms of a single state-contingent output, say, the first for convenience. The remaining* $S - 1$ *state-contingent outputs are defined by the implicit equations:*[1]

$$c^s(\boldsymbol{w}, z_s(\boldsymbol{w}, z_1)) = c^1(\boldsymbol{w}, z_1), \qquad s = 2, \cdots, S.$$

Choosing the first state-contingent output, therefore, is equivalent to picking the entire array of state-contingent outputs for the output-cubical technology. The reader can visualize this effect as the vertices of the effort-cost output cubes being connected by a "thread" defined by these implicit functions.

1. Formally, we need the ex post cost functions to be strictly increasing and differentiable for this approach to be fruitful.

The producer's objective function can now be expressed solely in terms of a single ex post cost function and the implicit functions as

$$max\{W(p_1 z_1 - c^1(\boldsymbol{w}, z_1), \cdots, p_S z_S(\boldsymbol{w}, z_1) - c^1(\boldsymbol{w}, z_1))\}.$$

The producer's optimal state-contingent output selection is governed by the single first-order condition:

$$W_1(\boldsymbol{y})p_1 + \sum_{s=2}^{S} W_s(\boldsymbol{y})p_s \frac{\partial z_s(\boldsymbol{w}, z_1)}{\partial z_1} - c_z^1(\boldsymbol{w}, z_1)\sum_{t\in\Omega} W_t(\boldsymbol{y}) \le 0, \qquad z_1 \ge 0.$$

Applying the implicit function theorem establishes that

$$\frac{\partial z_s(\boldsymbol{w}, z_1)}{\partial z_1} = \frac{c_z^1(\boldsymbol{w}, z_1)}{c_z^s(\boldsymbol{w}, z_s)},$$

so that the first-order condition becomes

$$c_z^1(\boldsymbol{w}, z_1)\sum_{s\in\Omega} W(\boldsymbol{y})\left(\frac{p_s}{c_z^s(\boldsymbol{w}, z_s)} - 1\right) \le 0, \qquad z_1 \ge 0.$$

Assuming that marginal cost is strictly positive, we may infer the following optimality condition. Using the "probabilities," $W_s(\boldsymbol{y}) / \sum_{t\in\Omega} W_t(\boldsymbol{y})$, *the producer chooses the first state-contingent output so that the expected value of the ratio of the spot-price to the ex post marginal-cost ratio never exceeds 1, or*

$$\sum_{s\in\Omega} \frac{W_s(\boldsymbol{y})}{\sum_{t\in\Omega} W_t(\boldsymbol{y})} \frac{p_s}{c_z^s(\boldsymbol{w}, \boldsymbol{z}_s)} \le 1 \tag{6.2}$$

with equality for an interior solution.

Expression (6.2) is analogous to the production arbitrage results contained in Lemma 6.1 and Chapter 5, but with some important differences. First, this single condition determines the entire optimal state-contingent output vector and not just its efficient set. So, the producer simply picks the point on the thread connecting the vertices of the effort-cost output cubes where the marginal gain from moving farther out along the thread is exactly matched by the marginal cost. Second, this condition depends inextricably on the producer's attitudes toward risk because the shadow probabilities are determined by those risk attitudes. Moreover, for an interior solution, it must be true that $p_s/c_z^s(w, z_s) \leq 1$*, implying that each state-contingent output must be less than what the producer would choose if she operated solely with the ex post technology.*

Following the terminology developed in Chapter 5, we might refer to output vectors satisfying Lemma 6.1 as belonging to the efficient set. Because both marginal costs and prices are nonnegative for an interior solution, Lemma 6.1 implies that $c_s(\mathbf{w}, \mathbf{z})/p_s \in (0,1)$ ($s = 1, 2, \ldots, S$). Hence, marginal cost for each state is always less than or equal to the corresponding state-contingent price. But this also implies that the ratios of marginal cost to state-contingent price can be interpreted as probabilities, or perhaps more accurately as *shadow probabilities*. In fact, these shadow probabilities are the probabilities that would convince a risk-neutral individual (facing the same $\mathbf{p}$ and the same technology) to produce the same state-contingent output vector as the risk-averse individual chooses. That is, $\mathbf{z}(\mathbf{p})$ is the solution to

$$\max_{\mathbf{z}}\left\{\sum_{s\in\Omega} c_s(\mathbf{w}, \mathbf{z}(\mathbf{p}))z_s - c(\mathbf{w}, \mathbf{z})\right\}.$$

Expression (6.1) suggests that as long as price uncertainty is present, risk-averse producers will not generally choose $\mathbf{z} \in I^*$ even if production is not inherently risky. That is, given price uncertainty, even strictly risk-averse producers will prefer a stochastic technology to a nonstochastic technology. By Result 6.1, certainty is a lower bound (cost wise) to any risky production choice with the same expected output. However, given the presence of price uncertainty, choosing a certain technology, even though it is cheap, exposes the producer to the whole range of price risk. This gives her no chance to self-insure by smoothing her income stream. Choosing uncertain production, on the other hand, allows the producer to use production risk to "self-insure' in the absence of a viable price-insurance alternative.

The producer can always choose an output vector that completely smooths net income. If the producer chooses $z_s = k/p_s$, returns are stabilized at $k - c(\mathbf{w}, \mathbf{z})$, and the producer has fully self-insured. An individual possessing completely risk-averse preferences will behave exactly in this manner, as we illustrate in Example 6.3. On the other hand, as we showed in Result 6.2, a risk-neutral producer with a generalized Schur-convex cost structure maximizes expected profit by producing higher outputs in higher-priced states. The extent to which the producer chooses to self-insure depends both on the relative costliness of providing self-insurance and on risk attitudes. Self-insurance is costly when production is not inherently risky because the producer always has to pay a premium for choosing a risky output vector (to balance the price risk) over a riskless one. Even then, however, a producer generally finds it optimal to expose herself to some production risk.

Example 6.3: *We saw in Chapter 5 that an individual with maximin preferences will produce where income is completely stabilized. A similar result applies here. Let's consider the intuitive argument first for the two-state case. There the producer's indifference curves are L-shaped with vertices located along the ray whose state-contingent output mix satisfies*

$$\frac{z_2}{z_1} = \frac{p_1}{p_2}.$$

Figure 6.2(b) illustrates for the case when $p_1 > p_2$. Suppose the producer stabilizes production completely. Then she locates somewhere on the production bisector, for example, point A. Because state 2 is the low-price state, production being nonstochastic implies that 2 is also the low-income state, and thus determines the producer's ultimate welfare level. This is portrayed visually by the vertex of the indifference curve that passes through A lying in the interior of the effort-cost output set for A. Hence, the producer is always better off by moving her production choice away from the bisector toward the output ray defining the vertices of the producer's indifference curve.

More formally, in this case, the producer's objective function is

$$min\{p_1 z_1, \cdots, p_s z_s\} - c(\boldsymbol{w}, \boldsymbol{z}).$$

The variation in the producer's objective function for an arbitrarily small variation in z_s is

$$(\delta^{min} p_s - c_s(\boldsymbol{w}, \boldsymbol{z}))\delta z_s,$$

where $\delta^{min} = 1$ *if* $r_s \in min\{r_1, \ldots, r_S\}$ *and 0 otherwise. So if* $r_s \notin min\{r_1, \ldots, r_S\}$, *the variation in the producer's objective function is*

$$-c_s(\boldsymbol{w},\boldsymbol{z})\delta z_s,$$

which implies that the producer's welfare can be increased by decreasing this state-contingent output until the state-contingent revenue hits the equal-revenue ray. This implies that the production pattern must satisfy

$$z_s = k/p_s$$

for all states. Hence, the producer's objective becomes one of

$$\max_k\{k - c(\boldsymbol{w},\boldsymbol{z}) : z_s = k/p_s, \quad s \in \Omega\},$$

with associated first-order conditions:

$$\sum_{s\in\Omega}(c_s(\boldsymbol{w}, k/\boldsymbol{p})/p_s) \geq 1, \qquad k \geq 0.$$

As long as marginal costs are strictly positive, the optimal choice is to pick the state-contingent output vector that belongs to the efficient set and that stabilizes state-contingent net incomes. This example demonstrates that there exist classes of risk-averse producers who voluntarily choose production uncertainty even in the presence of cost incentives to choose production certainty. The bottom line is simple: producers are concerned about revenue uncertainty and only worry about price or production uncertainty to the extent that it impinges on revenue uncertainty. Here producers are so risk-averse that regardless of the cost, they will balance price and production uncertainty exactly. As long as there is price risk, there will also be production risk.

6.4 OPTIMAL PRODUCER BEHAVIOR IN THE PRESENCE OF A SINGLE FORWARD MARKET

6.4.1 Some Basic Results

We now consider how the ability to hedge in a single forward market changes producer behavior. The Kuhn–Tucker conditions are

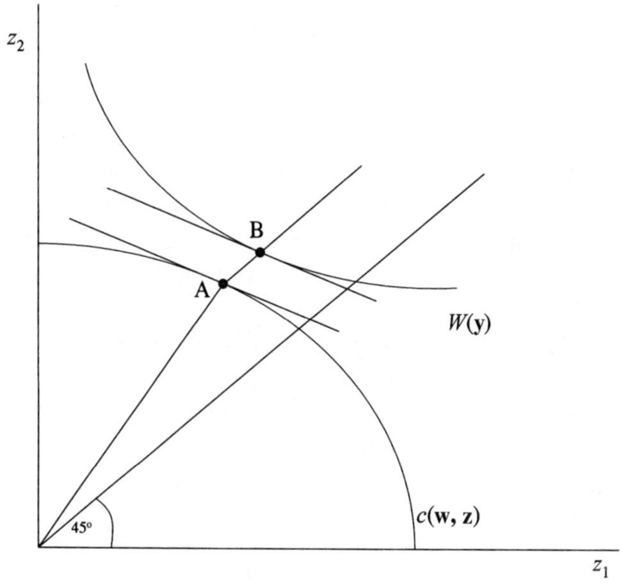

Figure 6.3 Hedging production equilibrium.

$$W_s(\mathbf{y})p_s - c_s(\mathbf{w},\mathbf{z})\sum_{t\in\Omega} W_t(\mathbf{y}) \le 0, \qquad z_s \ge 0 \tag{6.3}$$

$(s = 1, 2, \ldots, S)$, and

$$\sum_{t\in\Omega} W_s(\mathbf{y})(q - p_s) = 0.$$

The second condition holds as an equality because the optimal hedge can be either positive or negative.

This hedging-production equilibrium in state-contingent output space is illustrated in Figure 6.3. Suppose that the optimal state-contingent production allocation is given by point A. Hedging brings with it a nonstochastic increase in income in each state equal to q times the amount hedged, but also forces the producer to forego spot income of p_s on the amount hedged. The welfare change associated with a marginal change in the hedge is thus given by the derivative of $W(\mathbf{y})$ in the direction of the equal-output ray, $\sum_{t\in\Omega} W_s(\mathbf{y})(q - p_s)$. Hence, hedging allows the producer to move off the isocost curve in a direction parallel to the bisector in state-contingent output space to a point like B in Figure 6.3. But notice that, at B, the producer's marginal rate of substitution between state-contingent outputs must equal her marginal rate of transformation at A. If not, the producer could vary the state-contingent output choice in a fashion that would improve welfare while holding the hedge constant. So hedging, in effect, gives the producer the opportunity to choose a production equilibrium to ensure productive efficiency, but then to manipulate the dispersion of the state-contingent output vector in accordance with her risk attitudes.

An immediate implication of this graphical illustration and the discussion in Chapters 3 and 5 is that if the producer's preferences exhibit CARA, the optimal hedge level and the optimal production arrangement are independent of any pre-existing wealth.

Substituting the first expression in (6.3) into the second, and observing that Lemma 6.1 remains valid, yields the following:

Result 6.3: *At an interior equilibrium to (6.3),*

$$\sum_{s \in \Omega} c_s(\boldsymbol{w}, \boldsymbol{z}) = q,$$

and

$$\sum_{s \in \Omega} (c_s(\boldsymbol{w}, \boldsymbol{z})/p_s) = 1.$$

The first condition in Result 6.3 is an arbitrage condition between production and hedging behavior. The left-hand side is the cost of increasing output in every state of nature by one unit. Because this additional output could always be sold risklessly on the forward market for q, interior equilibrium requires that the marginal cost should always equal the forward price. If it didn't, there would exist unexploited opportunities for raising expected profit while holding risk constant. The first part of Result 6.3 is the stochastic generalization of the separation result obtained when production is nonstochastic. Here, however, it doesn't imply that the producer's production decision is independent of her risk preferences. What it does say is that *the scale of the producer's state-contingent output vector, as measured in the direction of the equal-output ray, is independent of risk preferences*. When production is nonstochastic, this scale degenerates trivially to the level of the nonstochastic output chosen. The second condition is simply a repetition of Lemma 6.1 and has similar implications.

The generalization of the nonstochastic separation result can be rewritten in a more informative fashion, after multiplying each $c_s(\mathbf{w}, \mathbf{z})$ by unity in the form of p_s/p_s, as

$$\sum_{s\in\Omega} p_s(c_s(\mathbf{w},\mathbf{z})/p_s) = q.$$

The second condition in Result 6.3 implies that the forward-market price should equal the expected value of the state-contingent output prices as evaluated in terms of the shadow probabilities $(c_s(\mathbf{w}, \mathbf{z})/p_s)$ if an interior equilibrium is to exist. Hence, the second condition in Result 6.3 implies that the producer optimizes by treating the forward-market price as a subjectively discounted (using the shadow probabilities) martingale of the state-contingent (spot) prices for the commodity. Because these shadow probabilities are the probabilities that would lead a risk-neutral individual to choose $\mathbf{z}$, this last condition implies that a risk-neutral individual facing these shadow probabilities should have no incentive to sell (or buy) any amount in the forward market. Therefore, this equilibrium condition can be recognized as a manifestation of standard arbitrage pricing results from finance theory (Milne 1995). An obvious consequence is:

> **Corollary 6.3.1:** *An interior equilibrium to (6.3) requires that* q *be a convex combination of the state-contingent prices.*

Corollary 6.3.1 establishes that an interior equilibrium is not consistent with the forward price either exceeding the largest state-contingent price or being smaller than the smallest state-contingent price. If these conditions were violated, the producer could make infinitely larger than expected profit by setting the hedge at plus infinity or minus infinity, respectively.

If the cost function is generalized Schur-convex, then by Corollaries 3.3.1 and 3.3.2 from Chapter 3,

$$\sum_{s\in\Omega} c_s(\mathbf{w},\mathbf{z})\left(z_s - \sum_{t\in\Omega}\pi_t z_t\right) \geq 0,$$

implying, of course, that marginal cost is positively correlated with the state-contingent outputs. Using this fact in conjunction with Result 6.3 establishes:

Corollary 6.3.2: *If the effort-cost function is generalized Schur-convex, then for any solution to (6.3),*

$$\sum_{s\in\Omega} c_s(\boldsymbol{w}, \boldsymbol{z})z_s \geq q\sum_{s\in\Omega} \pi_s z_s.$$

If the effort-cost function is generalized Schur-convex and $q \geq \Sigma_{s\in\Omega}\pi_s p_s$, *then for any solution to (6.3),*

$$\sum_{s\in\Omega} c_s(\boldsymbol{w}, \boldsymbol{z})z_s \geq \sum_{s\in\Omega} \pi_s p_s \sum_{s\in\Omega} \pi_s z_s.$$

The first equality in Result 6.3 has yet another interpretation. By that equality,

$$\sum_{s\in\Omega} \pi_s[c_s(\mathbf{w},\mathbf{z})/\pi_s] = q$$

the expected value of marginal costs, normalized by probabilities, equals the forward price. If the forward market is unbiased, Theorem 2.16 of Hardy, Littlewood and Pólya (1952, p. 26), applied to the harmonic and ordinary means,[2] implies

$$q\sum_{s\in\Omega} \pi_s p_s^{-1} > 1,$$

from which

$$\sum_{s\in\Omega} \pi_s(p_s - q)/p_s < 0$$

and

$$q\sum_{s\in\Omega} \pi_s(p_s - q)/p_s < 0,$$

$$\sum_{s\in\Omega} \pi_s(c_s(\mathbf{w},\mathbf{z})/\pi_s)(p_s - q)/p_s = \sum_{s\in\Omega} c_s(\mathbf{w},\mathbf{z}) - q\sum_{s\in\Omega}(c_s(\mathbf{w},\mathbf{z})/p_s)$$
$$= 0$$

2. This theorem implies that the mean is always larger than the harmonic mean, where the harmonic mean is, in this case, defined by

$$\left(\sum_s \frac{\pi_s}{p_s}\right)^{-1}.$$

using Result 6.3. Combining the last inequality with the equality yields:

Result 6.4: *If* $q = \sum_{s \in \Omega} \pi_s p_s$,

$$\sum_{s \in \Omega} \pi_s [c_s(\mathbf{w}, \mathbf{z})/\pi_s - q](p_s - q)/p_s > 0.$$

Because q is the expected value of $c_s(\mathbf{w}, \mathbf{z})/\pi_s$, Result 6.4 establishes that the covariance between $c_s(\mathbf{w}, \mathbf{z})/\pi_s$ and the percentage divergence of the state-contingent price from the forward price $(p_s - q)/p_s$ is positive. Hence, on average, one finds higher marginal costs associated with state-contingent prices higher than the forward price.

6.4.2 Hedging Results

When production is nonstochastic, the only way that the producer can affect her relative revenue mix[3] is by varying the hedge. But when production is stochastic, the producer has two tools to employ in trying to expand and smooth state-contingent revenues: the hedge and the state-contingent production mix. Determining the optimal combination of these two tools is more complicated than determining the optimal use of a single tool. Consequently, the literature that has relied on the output-cubical formulation of production under uncertainty has had relatively little to offer in this regard. Fortunately, however, the flexibility of the state-contingent production approach allows us to deduce a number of results.

In analyzing the optimal hedge, several points need to be kept firmly in mind. First, the essence of risk aversion is that marginal income gains in high-income states of nature bring small marginal welfare gains. Hence, we expect the producer's marginal utility of income to be inversely correlated with her state-contingent net revenues (Corollary 3.3.2 in Chapter 3). Second, although hedging brings with it the ability to increase the producer's certain income, it also creates a new form of risk, which can be thought of as hedging risk. The producer's marginal profit or loss on the hedge is the state-

3. Recall that with nonstochastic production in the absence of hedging, relative revenues are independent of output.

contingent variable $[q - p_s]$. This hedging risk can be manipulated along with the producer's production risk as the producer attempts to balance the price risk that she inherits from the spot market. Consequently, whether a state of nature is a high-returns or low-returns state depends on three things: the level of the spot price, the producer's output choice, and the producer's hedge.

As a consequence of the strict generalized Schur-concavity of $W(\mathbf{y})$ and Corollary 3.3.2 in Chapter 3,

$$\sum_{s\in\Omega} W_s(\mathbf{y})\left[y_s - \sum_{s\in\Omega}\pi_s y_s\right] < 0.$$

Expanding this expression term by term gives

$$\sum_{s\in\Omega} W_s(\mathbf{y})\Big[p_s z_s + h(q - p_s) - c(\mathbf{w},\mathbf{z}) - \sum_{t\in\Omega}\pi_t(p_t z_t + h(q-p_t) - c(\mathbf{w},\mathbf{z}))\Big] < 0.$$

Using the second expression in (6.3) reduces this expression to

$$\sum_{s\in\Omega} W_s(\mathbf{y})\left(p_s z_s - \sum_{t\in\Omega}\pi_t p_t z_t\right) < h\left(q - \sum_{s\in\Omega}\pi_s p_s\right)\sum_{s\in\Omega} W_s(\mathbf{y}). \tag{6.4}$$

Expression (6.3) and complementary slackness require

$$W_s(\mathbf{y})p_s z_s - c_s(\mathbf{w},\mathbf{z})z_s \sum_{s\in\Omega} W_s(\mathbf{y}) = 0, \qquad s\in\Omega.$$

Sum over s and subtract the result from (6.4) to get

$$\sum_{s\in\Omega} W_s(\mathbf{y})\left[\sum_{s\in\Omega} c_s(\mathbf{w},\mathbf{z})z_s - \sum_{s\in\Omega}\pi_s p_s z_s - h\left(q - \sum_{s\in\Omega}\pi_s p_s\right)\right] < 0.$$

The strict monotonicity of W when applied to this last expression now yields:

Result 6.5: *For any equilibrium for (6.3),*

$$\sum_{s\in\Omega}(\pi_s p_s - c_s)z_s + h\left(q - \sum_{s\in\Omega}\pi_s p_s\right) > 0.$$

The expression on the left-hand side in Result 6.5 is the marginal change in expected profit from a (small) radial expansion in all state-contingent outputs and h. Moreover, under the further assumption that $c(\mathbf{w}, \mathbf{z})$ is consistent with a constant returns-to-scale technology, it also equals expected profit. Hence:

Corollary 6.5.1: *At any equilibrium for (6.3), a (small) radial expansion of all state-contingent outputs will increase expected profit if* $q = \sum_{s \in \Omega} \pi_s p_s$. *If* $c(\mathbf{w}, \mu \mathbf{z}) = \mu c(\mathbf{w}, \mathbf{z})$ *for all* $\mu > 0$ *and* $q = \sum_{s \in \Omega} \pi_s p_s$, *expected profit must be positive.*

Result 6.5 and Corollary 6.5.1 show that a producer with strictly generalized Schur-concave preferences must forego some opportunities to raise expected profit, whether from her hedging operation or from her production decisions, to cope with the production and price risk. If a producer has exhausted all opportunities for raising expected profit by radial expansions of the state-contingent output vector, one can immediately determine the sign of the optimal hedge:

Corollary 6.5.2: *For any equilibrium for (6.3), if* $q < (>) \sum_{s \in \Omega} \pi_s p_s$, *the optimal hedge is negative (positive) if a differentiably small radial expansion in all state-contingent outputs decreases expected profit. If* $c(\mathbf{w}, \mu \mathbf{z}) = \mu c(\mathbf{w}, \mathbf{z})$ *for all* $\mu > 0$, *the optimal hedge is negative (positive) if expected profit from output is negative.*

Now using the first equality in Result 6.3 (the generalization of the nonstochastic separation result) gives:

Corollary 6.5.3: *For an interior equilibrium for (6.3),*

$$\sum_{s \in \Omega} (\pi_s p_s - c_s)(z_s - h) > 0.$$

Corollary 6.5.3 indicates that the states where the optimal hedge exceeds the state-contingent output will tend to be those where marginal expected profit from production sales, $(\pi_s p_s - c_s)$, is negative. In the states where this marginal profit is positive, the optimal hedge will tend to be less than the state-contingent output.

By applying Corollary 6.3.2 to Result 6.5, we obtain the following generalization of the rule determining the optimal hedge when production is nonstochastic:

Corollary 6.5.4: *If production is generalized Schur-convex, and* $\sum_{s\in\Omega}\pi_s p_s z_s = \bar{z}\sum_{s\in\Omega}\pi_s p_s$

$$\left(q-\sum_{s\in\Omega}\pi_s p_s\right)(h-\bar{z})\geq 0.$$

In the extreme case in which equilibrium output is not correlated with state-contingent price, the optimal hedge will be greater than expected output when the forward price is greater than the expected market price. (A special case of Corollary 6.5.4 occurs when production is nonstochastic, and the sign of the difference between the hedge and production is determined by the sign of the difference between q and the expected price, as we saw in our discussion of nonstochastic production.)

More generally by expression (6.4), the sign of the hedge depends critically on two factors: the expected gain made on each unit of the hedge $\left(q-\sum_{s\in\Omega}\pi_s p_s\right)$ and the covariance between state-contingent revenue and the marginal utility of that revenue as measured by $\sum_{s\in\Omega}W_s(\mathbf{y})\left(p_s z_s-\sum_{t\in\Omega}\pi_t p_t z_t\right)$. Generally, one expects this latter term to be negative because of the generalized Schur-concavity of the producer's objective function and her aversion to risk. However, one must recognize the role that the hedge plays in smoothing producer income across states of nature. A low state-contingent production-revenue state can also be a high state-contingent net-revenue state because of the ex post profit that the producer makes on the hedge. An example illustrates. Suppose that p_s is relatively low, and the producer chooses to produce a low output in state s. Then state s will be a low state-contingent production revenue state in the sense that one can expect $p_s z_s-\sum_{t\in\Omega}\pi_t p_t z_t\leq 0$. However, if the producer chooses to take a large short position, and $(q-p_s)>0$, her profit from the hedge in that state could easily counter her relatively low production income.

The hedge is not state-specific, and so whether the producer arranges production in this fashion depends on a critical interplay of her risk preferences, the state-contingent technology, and the forward price. For example, even though the spot price may be quite low in a particular state, the cost structure may so favor production in that state that the producer responds by allocating to it a high level of production. But even given these difficulties, the general intuition must hold on average. Given risk aversion, the producer's net income and marginal utility must covary negatively. So if production revenues and marginal utility covary positively, then, on average, the producer has to be making a loss in her high-revenue states and a gain in her low-revenue states.

Result 6.6 *If* $\sum_{s\in\Omega} W_s(\mathbf{y})(p_s z_s - \sum_{t\in\Omega} \pi_t p_t z_t) > 0$, *the optimal hedge is positive if* $(q - \sum_{s\in\Omega} \pi_s p_s) > 0$ *and negative if* $(q - \sum_{s\in\Omega} \pi_s p_s) < 0$.

We now consider more general conditions under which the optimal hedge is positive. Suppose that

$$(p_s - p_t)(p_s z_s - p_t z_t) \geq 0, \qquad s,t \in \Omega,$$

so that high-price states are also high-revenue states. Our approach to examining the optimal hedge in this instance is to assume that the hedge equals zero and then to calculate the variation in the producer's objective function for a small variation in the hedge to determine whether the producer should move toward a positive or a negative hedge. When this condition holds and the hedge equals zero,[4] by generalized Schur-concavity and Result 3.3 in Chapter 3,

$$(p_s - p_t)\left(\frac{W_s(\mathbf{y})}{\pi_s} - \frac{W_t(\mathbf{y})}{\pi_s}\right) \leq 0.$$

This inequality implies that the covariance between $W_s(\mathbf{y})/\pi_s$ and p_s is negative. Therefore,

$$\sum_{s\in\Omega} W_s(\mathbf{y})\left(p_s - \sum_{t\in\Omega} \pi_t p_t\right) \leq 0. \tag{6.5}$$

The variation in the producer's objective function for a small change in the hedge is

4. When the hedge equals zero, $y_s - y_t = p_s z_s - p_t y_t$.

$$\sum_{s\in\Omega} W_s(\mathbf{y})(q-p_s).$$

Using (6.5) implies that as long as $q \geq \sum_{s\in\Omega} \pi_s p_s$, this variation in the objective function is positive. This, in turn, implies that the producer should increase her hedge from zero to a positive number.[5] Hence, the optimal hedge will be positive.

> **Result 6.7:** *If* $(p_s - p_t)(p_s z_s - p_t z_t) \geq 0$ *for all* s *and* t, *the optimal hedge for (6.3) is positive if* $q - \sum_{s\in\Omega} \pi_s p_s$ *is positive.*

Results 6.6 and 6.7 establish what intuition would suggest: if the producer thinks that, on average, she can make a positive expected profit by doing so, she will sell the forward contract and take a short position ($h > 0$), as long as this does not interfere with her ability to smooth income variation arising from price uncertainty. If high-price states are also high-revenue states, hedging will reduce risk, as the name implies. Consider Result 6.6 in the context of the model with nonstochastic production. The risk characteristics in that case are determined by the state-contingent price vector and not by the production choice. If production revenues are positively correlated with marginal utility, then if the producer is risk-averse, her hedging profits must be negatively correlated with marginal utility. So, the unhedged amount is determined by the difference between the forward and the expected spot price.

Returning to the stochastic production case, now suppose that for some s and t, $p_s > p_t$ but $y_s < y_t$, so that, by the first-order conditions and Result 3.3 in Chapter 3,

$$\frac{\dfrac{\partial c(\mathbf{w},\mathbf{z})}{\partial z_s}\Big/\pi_s}{\dfrac{\partial c(\mathbf{w},\mathbf{z})}{\partial z_t}\Big/\pi_t} = \frac{p_s W_s(\mathbf{y})/\pi_s}{p_t W_t(\mathbf{y})/\pi_t} \geq \frac{p_s}{p_t} > 1.$$

If production is generalized Schur-convex, then Corollary 3.3.1 in Chapter 3 now implies $z_s > z_t$. Direct calculation establishes

5. Strictly speaking, we need to assume that the objective function is concave in the hedge to ensure a global optimum and hence this result.

$$\begin{aligned} y_s - y_t &= p_s z_s + h(q - p_s) - p_t z_t - h(q - p_t) \\ &= p_s z_s - p_t z_t + h(p_t - p_s), \end{aligned}$$

so, if $y_s < y_t$, $h > 0$ because $p_s z_s \geq p_t z_t$ and $p_t \leq p_s$.

> **Result 6.8:** *If production is generalized Schur-convex and if* $(p_s - p_t)(y_s - y_t) < 0$ *for any* s *and* t, $h > 0$.

Whence:

> **Corollary 6.8.1:** *If production is generalized Schur-convex,* $h < 0$ *only if* $(p_s - p_t)(y_s - y_t) \geq 0$ *for all* s *and* t.

Result 6.8 and Corollary 6.8.1 apply even when the forward price is less than the expected spot price. The basic idea behind these results is that producers will always choose a relatively high output in high-price, low-income states because both "substitution" and "income" effects push them in the same direction. When the producer goes long ($h < 0$), high-price, high-output states must be high-income states since both sales revenue and profits from futures trading are high. Taken together, this means that if the producer goes long, there can be no high-price, low-income states.

Corollary 6.8.1 is very important because it leads us to the stochastic generalization of the rule for determining the optimal hedge when production is nonstochastic. Put in words, if production is not inherently risky, a risk-averse producer always goes short in the forward market if the forward price is at least as large as her expected spot price. The intuitive argument is straightforward. Because production is not inherently risky, the producer always has a cost incentive to choose a nonstochastic output. And so, if she chooses a more costly stochastic output, it must be in an attempt to create production risk to balance price risk. Hence, her hedging decisions, on average, will be driven by the need to raise expected profits, and she will always sell forward if she expects to make a profit by doing so.

The formal argument is as follows. Suppose first that $h < 0$ and the technology is generalized Schur-convex, then, by Corollary 6.8.1, $(p_s - p_j)(y_s - y_j) \geq 0$. Using this fact and the generalized Schur-concavity of the producer's preferences establishes that (6.5) must hold. Now notice that the condition for the optimal hedge in (6.3) can always be written as

$$\left(q-\sum_{s\in\Omega}\pi_s p_s\right)\sum_{s\in\Omega}W_s(\mathbf{y})=\sum_{s\in\Omega}W_s(\mathbf{y})\left(p_s-\sum_{t\in\Omega}\pi_t p_t\right).$$

If $q-\sum_{s\in\Omega}\pi_s p_s>0$, (6.5) and this condition lead to a contradiction. Hence, we can conclude:

Result 6.9: *If* $q>\sum_{s\in\Omega}\pi_s p_s$ *and production is generalized Schur-convex, then* $h\geq 0$.

6.4.3 Production Uncertainty Is Preferable

Having generalized existing hedging results, we now establish a key result: given an unbiased forward market, a risk-averse producer with smooth preferences (a continuously differentiable *W*) never chooses *z* belonging to *I** even if there is a cost advantage to doing so. Given the discussion in Example 6.3, this result should be intuitively plausible. And as we show in our next example, the result definitely holds when preferences are completely risk-averse.

But to some, the result may seem paradoxical because it means that risk-averse producers prefer production uncertainty. However, the result, which appears to have been first recognized by Chambers and Quiggin (1997) for expected-utility maximizers, is at the same time simple and intuitive. Inherently, producers care nothing about either production or price uncertainty. Their preferences are over net returns. Therefore, the only reason they care about prices and output is because they affect the variability of their state-contingent returns. Moreover, by appropriately arranging their production plans, producers can balance price uncertainty against production uncertainty. So, to promote revenue smoothing, even the most risk-averse producers will want to expose themselves to some production uncertainty if there is price uncertainty.

Consider Figure 6.4, which is drawn under the assumption that costs are generalized Schur-convex and preferences are smooth. By the assumption on costs, the fair-odds line is tangent to the producer's isocost curve at the bisector (Corollary 3.3.1, Chapter 3). Suppose that the producer, contrary to our assertion, does completely stabilize production. Her production equilibrium can be represented by

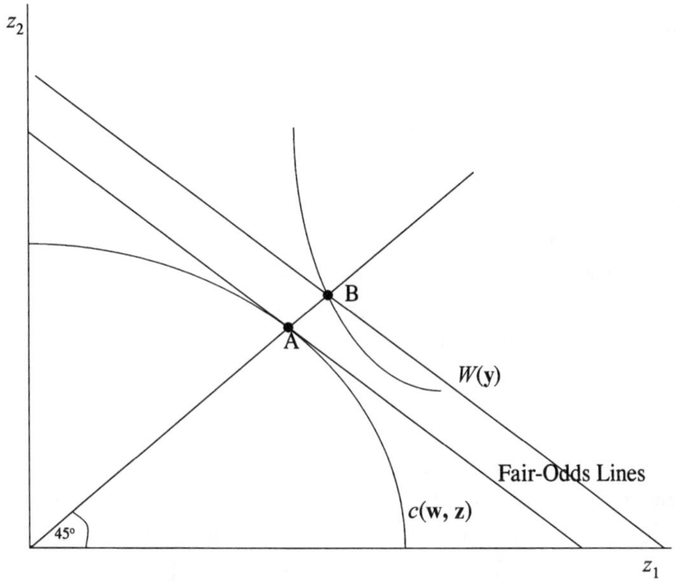

Figure 6.4 Producers prefer stochastic production.

point A in Figure 6.4. If she hedges, because production is nonstochastic and the forward market is assumed unbiased, her optimal hedge, given this production choice, is a complete hedge. So hedging moves her out from A along the bisector to a point like B, with a higher welfare level than she can attain at A. Notice, however, that we have drawn the fair-odds line as intersecting the producer's indifference curve at point B. This is because the producer's indifference curve, in state-contingent output space, has slope at the bisector equaling

$$\frac{W_1(\mathbf{y})p_1}{W_2(\mathbf{y})p_2} = \frac{\pi_1 p_1}{\pi_2 p_2},$$

where the equality follows from the producer's risk aversion and the fact that, by completely hedging, she has stabilized income. Hence, the fair-odds line cuts the producer's indifference curve.[6] Thus, a small

6. Notice that if the producer's indifference curve were drawn in net-return space, it would be tangent to the fair-odds line at the bisector. Here the illustration is in state-contingent output space.

adjustment in the production bundle along the fair-odds line in the direction of z_1 has no effect on effort cost because of the tangency between the isocost curve and the fair-odds line at the bisector, but it does lead to an increase in producer welfare because it lets the producer move from B slightly to the right along the fair-odds line. The producer, therefore, is always better off choosing a nonstochastic production bundle.

To demonstrate this intuition formally, suppose, to the contrary, that the producer chooses a nonstochastic state-contingent output vector, call it $z\mathbf{1}^S$, and that the technology exhibits generalized Schur-convexity. Her welfare level is

$$W((z-h)\mathbf{p}+(hq-c(\mathbf{w},z\mathbf{1}^s))\mathbf{1}^s).$$

Because $z\mathbf{1}^S$ represents her optimal output choice, setting the hedge is now equivalent to setting the hedge when production is nonstochastic. An argument identical to the one used in that case shows that with an unbiased forward market, the optimal hedge must be complete so that $z = h$. Hence, with the optimal hedge, her welfare is

$$W((qz-c(\mathbf{w},z\mathbf{1}^s))\mathbf{1}^s).$$

Now choose two states, say, s and t, such that $p_s < q < p_t$ (Such states must exist by the assumption that the forward market is unbiased.), and consider a small pairwise spread of the state-contingent output vector arrived at by reducing z_s and increasing z_t. Because the effort-cost structure is generalized Schur-convex, any pairwise spread of the output vector has no effect on cost in the immediate neighborhood of the equal-output ray. The change in income in state s, however, is

$$(p_s-q)dz_s>0,$$

and in state t is

$$(p_t-q)dz_t>0.$$

Income in all other states is unchanged. Hence, the producer is strictly better off. *Nonstochastic production is not optimal under these conditions.*

Thus, risk-averse producers generally do not prefer nonstochastic production to stochastic production when there is price uncertainty. Because producers have the flexibility to make production plans that prepare differentially for price risk, they will exploit this flexibility and price uncertainty optimally in developing a production plan that self-insures them against revenue risk.

> **Result 6.10:** *If production is generalized Schur-convex, preferences are smooth, there is price risk, and* $q = \sum_{s \in \Omega} \pi_s p_s$, *then any solution to (6.4) will not satisfy* $z \in I^*$.

We have already seen that risk-averse producers generally do not prefer nonstochastic production to stochastic production when there is price uncertainty. Result 6.10 shows that the existence of an unbiased futures market does not change this. Even though the producer could achieve certainty by producing $\mathbf{z} \in I^*$ and selling forward the entire output, this would forgo the chance of a guaranteed profit.

Result 6.10 demonstrates that smooth preferences are sufficient to ensure that producers do not completely stabilize production. In the following example, we demonstrate that producers with nonsmooth preferences may not stabilize production.

> **Example 6.4:** *Let's return again to the situation in which the producer is completely risk-averse so that her objective function is given by*
>
> $$min\{p_1(z_1 - h), \cdots, p_S(z_S - h)\} + qh - c(\boldsymbol{w}, \boldsymbol{z}).$$
>
> *The variation in the producer's objective function for an arbitrarily small perturbation in* z_s *is*
>
> $$(\delta^{min} p_s - c_s(\boldsymbol{w}, \boldsymbol{z}))\delta z_s,$$
>
> *where* $\delta^{min} = 1$ *if* $p_s(z_s - h) \in min\{p_1(z_1 - h), \ldots, p_s(z_s - h)\}$ *and 0 otherwise. So if* $r_s \notin min\{r_1, \ldots, r_s\}$, *the variation in the producer's objective function is*
>
> $$-c_s(\boldsymbol{w}, \boldsymbol{z})\delta z_s,$$
>
> *which implies that the producer's welfare can be increased by decreasing this particular state-contingent output until the unhedged revenue* $(z_s - h)$ *hits the equal-revenue ray. This implies that the production pattern must satisfy*

$$(z_s - h) = k/p_s$$

for all states. The only way production can be nonstochastic is if the state-contingent output price is also nonstochastic. Hence, the producer's objective becomes one of

$$max\left\{k + qh - c(\boldsymbol{w}, \boldsymbol{z}) : z_s = h + \frac{k}{p_s}, \qquad s \in \Omega\right\},$$

with associated first-order conditions

$$1 - \sum_{s \in \Omega} \frac{c_s(\boldsymbol{w}, \boldsymbol{z})}{p_s} \leq 0, \qquad k \geq 0$$

$$q = \sum_{s \in \Omega} c_s(\boldsymbol{w}, \boldsymbol{z}).$$

So, as we saw earlier and in Chapter 5, the completely risk-averse producer produces on the boundary of the output efficient set.

6.5 A SEPARATION THEOREM WITH STOCHASTIC PRODUCTION

When there are only two possible states of the world, hedging in a single forward market allows production decisions to be taken without reference to the producer's risk preferences. If $S = 2$, Result 6.3 implies

$$c_1(\mathbf{w}, \mathbf{z}) + c_2(\mathbf{w}, \mathbf{z}) = q,$$

and

$$c_1(\mathbf{w}, \mathbf{z})/p_1 + c_2(\mathbf{w}, \mathbf{z})/p_2 = 1.$$

Provided that there is price uncertainty ($p_1 \neq p_2$), this pair of equations may be solved to yield the following separation result.

Result 6.11: *If* S = 2 *and* p ∉ *I*, any interior production equilibrium for (6.4) satisfies:*

$$c_1(\boldsymbol{w}, \boldsymbol{z}) = p_1 \frac{q - p_2}{p_1 - p_2},$$

$$c_2(\boldsymbol{w}, \boldsymbol{z}) = p_2 \frac{p_1 - q}{p_1 - p_2}.$$

Result 6.11 is similar to previous separation results in the sense that risk preferences are absent from production plans, but it differs from previous separation results in two important ways. First, it is derived for a stochastic technology. Second, unlike previous separation results, production decisions depend on the distribution of spot prices as well as the forward price. Thus, this result, unlike previous separation results, applies when production is uncertain, but it also shows that producers must use knowledge about the entire spot-price distribution to make production decisions. And so, even though two individuals with different risk preferences and different subjective probabilities will make the same production decisions, the distribution of the spot price does matter in making this decision.

Example 6.5: *The separation result does not rely on any assumptions about the smoothness of the producer's preference function. From preceding examples, it should be clear that even a producer with completely risk-averse preferences will choose this same interior solution in the two-state case, as long as the effort-cost function is smoothly differentiable. However, if the effort-cost function is not smoothly differentiable, matters change drastically.*

To illustrate in the two-state case, notice first that a riskneutral producer with an output-cubical technology chooses z_1 *to satisfy*

$$\pi_1 p_1 + \pi_2 p_2 \frac{c_z^1(\boldsymbol{w}, z_1)}{c_z^2(\boldsymbol{w}, z_{2s})} = c_z^1(\boldsymbol{w}, z_1).$$

In words, the marginal cost of the reference output, here z_1, *is equated to the marginal cost from raising output in state 1 and the marginal gain from the increase in state 2 output that is elicited by the increase in the reference output. A risk averter, on the other hand, chooses* z_1 *to satisfy*

$$W_1(\boldsymbol{y})p_1 + W_2(\boldsymbol{y})p_2\left(\frac{c_z^1(\boldsymbol{w}, z_1)}{c_z^2(\boldsymbol{w}, z_2)}\right) = c_z^1(\boldsymbol{w}, z_1)[W_1(\boldsymbol{y}) + W_2(\boldsymbol{y})].$$

And when a forward market is available in which to hedge, the risk averter chooses the hedge according to

$$W_1(\boldsymbol{y})(q - p_1) + W_2(\boldsymbol{y})(q - p_2) = 0$$

which when combined with the production equilibrium for the risk averter yields

$$\frac{W_1(\boldsymbol{y})p_1}{W_1(\boldsymbol{y})p_1 + W_2(\boldsymbol{y})p_2} + \frac{W_2(\boldsymbol{y})p_2}{W_1(\boldsymbol{y})p_1 + W_2(\boldsymbol{y})p_2}\left(\frac{c_z^1(\boldsymbol{w}, z_1)}{c_z^2(\boldsymbol{w}, z_2)}\right)$$
$$= \frac{c_z^1(\boldsymbol{w}, z_1)}{q}.$$

Hence, even in the presence of a forward market, producers using an output-cubical technology make production decisions that depend on their risk preferences. The reason is simple. In the output-cubical model, because the producer cannot rearrange state-contingent outputs for a given cost level, there is no arbitrage opportunity between states of nature. The production choice is merely one of picking the size of the random production variable with its mix (dispersion) being predetermined by the fixed coefficient nature of the output set. Hence, by placing this artificial restriction on the production technology, previous analyses have precluded, by assumption, the type of separation result that we have just identified.

Result 6.11, which is generalized below, is best interpreted in terms of spanning arguments familiar from finance theory. To see the intuition, suppose that $S = 2$, but that there is no forward market. Then the best the producer can do is to make sure, at the margin, that there is no systematic loss in expected profitability, holding the riskiness of the production portfolio constant. As we said earlier, this arbitrage activity sets the scale of the producer's operation as measured in the direction of the bisector. This is the import of Lemma 6.1. Now if the producer is given access to a single forward market satisfying the conditions of Result 6.11, he can use that market to determine the optimal mix of state-contingent outputs, given his scale of operation. Hence, the producer's production arbitrage conditions combine with his hedging opportunities to span the states of nature thus effectively providing a complete set of contingent markets. Thus, in the case of $S = 2$, Townsend's criterion for forward markets to span the state space can be relaxed. Here the rank of the spot-price matrix is just one and not two as he requires. The producer's ability to cross-hedge over state-contingent outputs, which is a natural consequence of the net-returns objective function in the state-contingent approach, yields this result.

Earlier separation results require the producer to equate marginal cost of a nonstochastic output to the forward price, that is, to produce in the same fashion as a risk-neutral producer facing q. Here, however, the producer is producing in the same fashion as a risk-neutral producer (without access to a futures markets) who faces production and price uncertainty with the probabilities

$$\pi_1 = \frac{q - p_2}{p_1 - p_2},$$

$$\pi_2 = \frac{p_1 - q}{p_1 - p_2}.$$

Only when the forward market is unbiased will this production pattern correspond with that of a risk-neutral individual. In that special case, we have the condition determining the optimal hedge as

$$W_1(\mathbf{y})(q - p_1) + W_2(\mathbf{y})(q - p_2) = 0,$$

or

$$\frac{W_1(\mathbf{y})}{W_2(\mathbf{y})} = \frac{(q - p_2)}{(p_1 - q)} = \frac{\pi_1}{\pi_2}$$

where the final equality follows because the forward market is unbiased. The condition determining the optimal interstate production pattern is now given by

$$\frac{W_1(\mathbf{y})p_1}{W_2(\mathbf{y})p_2} = \frac{c_1(\mathbf{w}, \mathbf{z})}{c_2(\mathbf{w}, \mathbf{z})}$$

which, with the preceding equality, establishes that this is the same production pattern as for a risk-neutral individual. Notice, however, that the hedging equilibrium also implies

$$\frac{W_1(\mathbf{y})}{\pi_1} = \frac{W_2(\mathbf{y})}{\pi_2}$$

which, given strict risk aversion with respect to $\boldsymbol{\pi}$, requires that net revenue be totally stabilized, so that

$$p_1 z_1 + h(q - p_1) = p_2 z_2 + h(q - p_2)$$

which can be solved for h, the optimal hedge. This last equality, in combination with the first-order conditions (6.4) for $S = 2$, yields:

Result 6.12: *If* S = 2, $p \notin \boldsymbol{I}^*$, *and* $q = \pi_1 p_1 + \pi_2 p_2$, *a producer risk-averse with respect to* $\boldsymbol{\pi}$ *chooses the same production equilibrium as a risk-neutral producer:*

$$\pi_1 p_1 = c_1(\mathbf{w}, \mathbf{z})$$
$$\pi_2 p_2 = c_2(\mathbf{w}, \mathbf{z})$$

and completely smooths her income using the optimal hedge.

When facing an unbiased forward market, a risk-averse producer facing both production and price risk can completely smooth the income stream generated from expected profit maximization by appropriately setting his hedge. Result 6.6 can now be used to determine whether $h > 0$.

6.6 OPTIMAL PRODUCER BEHAVIOR IN THE PRESENCE OF MULTIPLE-FUTURES MARKETS

We now turn to an analysis of the producer's behavior when there exists an active set of K ($K > 1$) futures markets in which he or she can cross-hedge. These are most naturally thought of as futures markets closely related to the producer's own output, in which he or she can cross-hedge. However, the analysis applies more generally to participation in any derivative market, or to construction of "home-made" derivatives such as "straddles" based on offsetting contracts in two or more markets.

Again, the Kuhn–Tucker conditions are necessary for producer equilibrium. Therefore, the producer's optimal behavior is characterized by

$$W_s(\boldsymbol{y})p_s - c_s(\boldsymbol{w}, \boldsymbol{z})\sum_{t\in\Omega} W_t(\boldsymbol{y}) \geq 0, \qquad z_s \geq 0 \quad (s = 1, 2, \cdots, S),$$
$$\sum_{s\in\Omega} W_s(\boldsymbol{y})b_s^k = 0, \qquad (k = 1, 2, \cdots, K). \tag{6.6}$$

The first set of equations in (6.6) has exactly the same interpretation as the conditions given by (6.1) and (6.3). The second set of conditions in (6.6) represents a set of arbitrage conditions for the futures markets that requires the producer to realize zero expected marginal utility in each of her futures operations. These arbitrage relations and the first set of equations also yield an arbitrage relationship that connects the producer's production operation with her operations in the futures markets. Isolating $W_s(\mathbf{y})$ in the first S conditions and substituting into the K futures-market conditions yields:

> **Result 6.13:** *For an interior production equilibrium to (6.6), the producer's equilibrium must satisfy the arbitrage conditions:*
>
> $$\sum_{s\in\Omega}(c_s(\mathbf{w},\mathbf{z})/p_s)f_s^k = q^k \qquad (k=1,2,\cdots,K)$$
>
> *and*
>
> $$\sum_{s\in\Omega}(c_s(\mathbf{w},\mathbf{z})/p_s) = 1.$$

The second equality manifests Lemma 6.1. The first condition implies that the producer optimizes by treating the price for the kth futures contract as a subjectively discounted (using the shadow probabilities) martingale of the spot prices for the commodity specified in the futures contract.

Obvious analogs to Results 6.4 to 6.12 and their corollaries apply to Result 6.13 if there exists a k such that $b_s^k = (f - p_s)$, that is, if one of the futures markets is for the commodity that the producer actually produces. Therefore, we do not repeat them.

We now show that the separation result derived in the case of two states (Result 6.11) can be generalized in the sense that, if there are S states of the world, having $S - 1$ futures markets may suffice to hedge fully and to allow production decisions to be taken independently of risk preferences. To that end, we now introduce the following weaker version of Townsend's spanning condition:

Condition S: There exist $S - 1$ futures markets for which the matrix $F \in \Re^{S\times S}$ is invertible:

$$\mathbf{F} = [\mathbf{e}, \mathbf{f}^1, \cdots, \mathbf{f}^{s-1}],$$

where **e** denotes the S-dimensional unit vector.

> **Result 6.14:** *If condition S is satisfied, any interior solution to (6.6) will have the producer's production decisions independent of her risk preferences.*

Intuitively, when condition S is satisfied, the set of shadow probabilities consistent with each of the futures contracts being priced as a subjectively discounted martingale is uniquely determined by the matrix F and the vector of futures-contract prices. Hence, by standard arbitrage-pricing arguments, all individuals facing the same F and the same futures prices will choose the same shadow probabilities regardless of their risk preferences.

7 Production Insurance

Farming is risky. Subject to the vagaries of weather and the market, farmers routinely make decisions whose ultimate outcomes are highly uncertain. Early on, a number of market and nonmarket institutions evolved to cope with this uncertainty. For example, agricultural forward and option markets predate many other contingent-claim markets. Consequently, economic theorists interested in production decision making under uncertainty have focused much attention on agricultural markets. And, in some ways, the agricultural producer buffeted by multiple sources of uncertainty has become the primary theoretical metaphor for production decision making under uncertainty. When pressed, even pure economic theorists working in this area frequently resort to agricultural examples to illustrate their findings. Chapter 6, where we studied the impact of mechanisms designed to cope with stochastic prices (futures and forward markets), represented our initial analytic encounter with such problems. This chapter examines insurance mechanisms designed to help producers manage production risk. The explicit metaphor we adopt is crop insurance, but as with the results of Chapter 6, our analysis extends to any insurance or contingent claims market that can be accessed by producers facing stochastic production decisions of any type.

7.1 THE STATE-CONTINGENT TECHNOLOGY AND FARMER PREFERENCES

The state-contingent technology is the same that has been used in previous chapters. Uncertainty is modeled by "Nature" making a choice from a finite set of alternatives. Each of these alternatives is called a "state" and is indexed by a finite set of the form:

$$\Omega = \{1, 2, \cdots, S\},$$

where S denotes the number of states of nature. Production relations are governed by a state-contingent technology of the type discussed in Chapters 2 and 4.

The preferences of the representative producer (whom we often mnemonically refer to as the farmer) over returns and inputs are given by a generalized Schur-concave function (see Chapter 3) of net returns, $W: \Re^S \rightarrow \Re$:

$$W(\mathbf{r} - C(\mathbf{w}, \mathbf{r}, \mathbf{p})\mathbf{1}^s) = W(\mathbf{y}),$$

which is continuous and nondecreasing in all its arguments. Here $\mathbf{r} \in \Re^S_{+}$, as before, denotes a vector of state-contingent revenues, $\mathbf{y} \in \Re^S$ is a vector of state-contingent net returns, and $C(\mathbf{w}, \mathbf{r}, \mathbf{p})$ is the revenue-cost function used in Chapter 5.[1]

Insurers are risk-neutral and competitive. To start, we presume that insurers offer state-contingent contracts, that is, contracts that specify a net indemnity for each state of nature. The presumption is that the state of nature is observable to both the insurer and the farmer and hence *contractible*. By contractible, we mean that the state of nature can be used as the basis for a contract between the farmer and the insurer. Denote the insurance company's net indemnity in state $s \in \Omega$ by I_s.[2] We consider two separate cases. In the first, the provision of insurance by the insurer is costless, so that the insurer's net loss in a

1. Crop insurance is generally specified in terms of physical quantities instead of values. We work in terms of state-contingent revenues to preserve generality. Converting our results to physical quantities is straightforward.
2. The net indemnity can always be decomposed into two parts: a state-invariant premium and a state-contingent indemnity. If the state-contingent indemnity exceeds the premium, the net indemnity is positive. If the state-contingent indemnity is less than the premium, the net indemnity is negative.

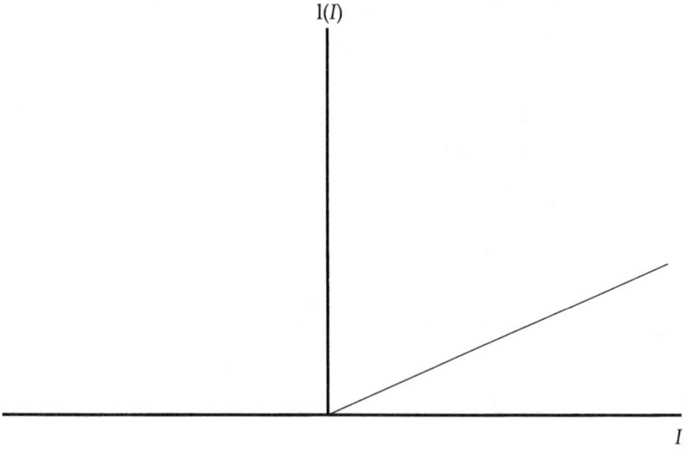

Figure 7.1 Angle loading factor.

state is given by that state's net indemnity. In the second, the provision of insurance is costly, and the insurer's cost of paying the net indemnity is represented by a continuous, nondecreasing, and convex function of the indemnity, $l(I)$, which we refer to as the insurer's *loading factor*.

One potentially plausible pattern for loadings is a linear loading for positive values of I (payouts) with no loading for negative values (premiums). It is represented in Figure 7.1 as a linear function emerging from the origin in the nonnegative orthant and following the axis for all negative values of the indemnity. The resulting loading function is weakly convex. This kind of function, called an *angle function*, is not differentiable at zero. The presumption is that insurers incur no variable cost in collecting premiums, but they do incur a constant marginal cost of making payments (indemnities) to farmers.

An important analytic advantage of this type of loading function is that, in a neighborhood of an indemnity vector **I** with no zero entries, its first derivatives are constant. The vector of first derivatives, and hence the "odds" at which the insurer is willing to offer insurance, will depend only on which states of nature involve payouts.

7.2 FARMER BEHAVIOR IN THE ABSENCE OF INSURANCE

As a point of reference, we recapitulate some results from Chapter 5 on optimal farmer behavior in the absence of crop insurance. The farmer's objective is

$$W^o = \max_{\mathbf{r}}\{W(\mathbf{r} - C(\mathbf{w}, \mathbf{r}, \mathbf{p})\mathbf{1}^s)\}.$$

Because the farmer's objective function is generalized Schur-concave, any interior solution belongs to the risk-aversely efficient subset. For an interior solution,

$$\sum_s \frac{\partial C(\mathbf{w}, \mathbf{r}, \mathbf{p})}{\partial r_s} = 1,$$
$$\left(\frac{\partial C(\mathbf{w}, \mathbf{r}, \mathbf{p})/\partial r_s}{\pi_s} - \frac{\partial C(\mathbf{w}, \mathbf{r}, \mathbf{p})/\partial r_t}{\pi_t}\right)(r_s - r_t) \leq 0, \qquad s,t \in \Omega.$$

Farmer cost, therefore, locally behaves as though it were generalized Schur-concave. Accordingly, any suitably small multiplicative spread[3] of the state-contingent revenue vector should lead to a fall in cost, and, thereby, to an increase in expected profit. Such a move is surely technically feasible, and the reason the farmer does not adopt it is because it leads to an increase in his or her risk exposure. An immediate implication is that if a risk-averse farmer and a risk-neutral farmer both spent the same amount on inputs, the risk-averse farmer would always optimally choose to produce a lower expected revenue than the risk-neutral farmer. We illustrate in Figure 7.2. The farmer's equilibrium is depicted as a tangency between the farmer's indifference curve and his isocost curve. Because preferences are generalized Schur-concave, the fair-odds line cuts the indifference curve and the isocost curve from below, as illustrated. A multiplicative spread of the equilibrium production vector is graphically portrayed as a small movement along the fair-odds line to the northwest, which, as illustrated, leads to a lower level of effort cost, and hence higher expected profits.

3. Here, we mean differentiably small.

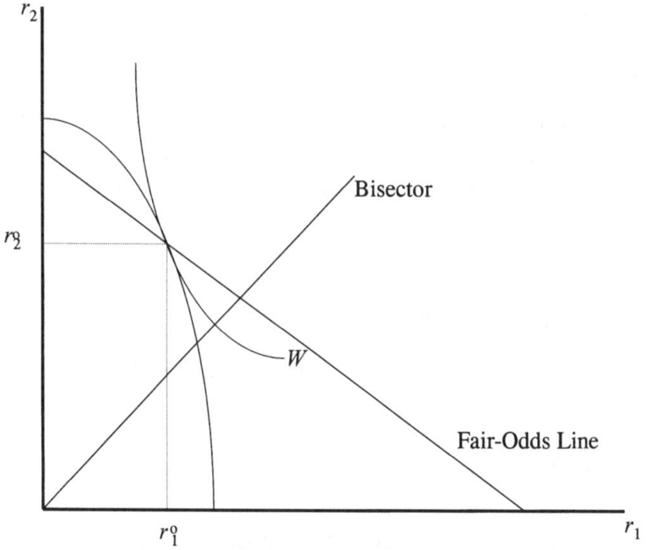

Figure 7.2 Production equilibrium without insurance.

7.3 FARMER BEHAVIOR IN THE PRESENCE OF ACTUARIALLY FAIR INSURANCE WITH NO LOADING FACTORS

Our first order of business is to determine whether the agricultural market is characterized by insurable risks. Following Chambers (1989b), we call the market *insurable* if there exists a set of net indemnities that at least break even for the insurer and that make the farmer better off than in the absence of crop insurance. To make this definition operational, it is necessary to specify a probability vector π. In line with the subjective approach to probability, which we have advocated in Chapter 3 and pursued in Chapter 5, this probability vector must be derived from the preferences of the insurer and the farmer. We require that there exists at least one common probability vector, π, with respect to which the insurer is risk-neutral and the farmer is risk-averse. Hence, in the absence of loading factors, an actuary employed by the insurer would regard as fair any contract for which

$$\sum_s \pi_s I_s = 0,$$

where $\mathbf{I} \in \Re^S$ denotes the vector of insurer's net indemnities. By the assumption that insurers are risk-neutral and competitive, in the absence of insurance loading costs, any equilibrium insurance contract offered by an insurance company must be *actuarially fair* in this sense.

Let

$$\mathbf{r}^o \in \arg\ \max\{W(\mathbf{r} - C(\mathbf{w}, \mathbf{r}, \mathbf{p})\mathbf{1}^s)\}$$

denote a solution to the farmer's no-insurance optimization problem, and

$$\bar{r}^o = \sum_s \pi_s r_s^o$$

denote the farmer's expected revenue in the absence of crop insurance. Now consider the following set of net indemnities:

$$I_s = \bar{r}^o - r_s^o, \qquad s \in \Omega.$$

When faced with this contract, if the farmer chooses to produce $\mathbf{r}^o$ (she need not), her utility is

$$W((\bar{r}^o - C(\mathbf{w}, \mathbf{r}^o, \mathbf{p}))\mathbf{1}_S) \geq W^o$$

with a strict inequality if the farmer has a strictly generalized Schur-concave objective function, that is, is strictly risk-averse. Similarly, for this choice of state-contingent revenues, it's easy to verify that the insurer's expected profit is zero. Therefore, we conclude that *in the absence of a loading factor, the market is insurable*. Opportunities exist for the insurance company and the farmer to make trades that leave both no worse off than in the absence of insurance, and that strictly improve a risk-averse farmer's situation.

Insurability is also illustrated in Figure 7.2. In the absence of crop insurance, the farmer locates his state-contingent production at a point of tangency between one of his indifference curves and one of his isocost curves. Because he has a generalized Schur-concave objective function, this point will be in the risk-aversely efficient set. As Figure 7.2 is drawn, the farmer is strictly risk-averse, so that the fair-odds line cuts his indifference curve from above. Expected revenue is given by the point where the fair-odds line through the state-contingent production point intersects the bisector. Because the farmer is strictly risk-averse, this expected revenue lies strictly above the farmer's indifference curve. Now if the farmer produces at $\mathbf{r}^o$, he incurs the same effort cost as before. Provided the insurance company offers him this type of indemnity structure, he can trade along the fair-odds line through $\mathbf{r}^o$ to the point where it intersects the bisector. The insurance company makes zero expected profit from this trade with the farmer, but the farmer is strictly better off. Hence, the production risk is insurable.

Having established that an opportunity for insurance exists, let's now consider how the farmer would optimally exploit the presence of crop insurance.[4] Given the freedom to choose any actuarially fair contract, the representative farmer's optimal production–insurance scheme solves

$$\max_{\mathbf{I},\mathbf{r}}\left\{W(\mathbf{r}+\mathbf{I}-C(\mathbf{w},\mathbf{r},\mathbf{p})\mathbf{1}^s):\sum_s \pi_s I_s = 0\right\}. \tag{7.1}$$

Recalling that

$$y_s = r_s + I_s - C(\mathbf{w},\mathbf{r},\mathbf{p})$$

shows that (7.1) can be rewritten after a simple change of variables as

$$\max_{\mathbf{y},\mathbf{r}}\left\{W(\mathbf{y}):\sum_s \pi_s y_s = \sum_s \pi_s r_s - C(\mathbf{w},\mathbf{r},\mathbf{p})\right\}.$$

The farmer, therefore, chooses her state-contingent revenue vector to

$$\max_{\mathbf{r}}\left\{\sum_s \pi_s r_s - C(\mathbf{w},\mathbf{r},\mathbf{p})\right\}.$$

To do otherwise would mean that she sacrifices expected profit that could be allocated to make *all* state-contingent net incomes higher. Since her objective function is nondecreasing in these state-

4. Here we view the farmer as choosing a net indemnity scheme to suit his or her peculiar needs. As long as the indemnity scheme offers a nonnegative profit, there will be a competitive insurer who will be willing to write that contract with the farmer.

contingent net incomes, she'll choose her production vector to maximize expected profit.

Presuming she does choose the expected profit-maximizing state-contingent revenue vector, then by her risk aversion,[5] the indemnity schedule (evaluated at the expected profit-maximizing state-contingent revenue)

$$I_s = \sum_t \pi_t r_t - r_s, \qquad s \in \Omega$$

dominates all others because it guarantees her a certain income of

$$\max_{\mathbf{r}} \left\{ \sum_s \pi_s r_s - C(\mathbf{w}, \mathbf{r}, \mathbf{p}) \right\},$$

which is the best that she could possibly hope for. You can't do better than make the maximum expected income in all states. Even a risk-neutral individual would at least weakly prefer this contract to all others. Moreover, this indemnity schedule breaks even for the insurer.

We've established that *risk-averse farmers who face an actuarially fair insurance contract will produce in the same fashion as a risk-neutral farmer*. Hence, in the presence of an actuarially fair insurance market, a risk-averse farmer's production pattern is independent of her risk preferences. An immediate implication is that a farmer's optimal revenue choice in the presence of an actuarially fair crop insurance contract belongs to the efficient set (see Chapter 5, Section 5.1). Because a farmer acts to maximize expected profit in the presence of full insurance, we have:[6]

> **Result 7.1:** *Expected profit from farming under actuarially fair crop insurance is never less than expected profit from farming in the absence of crop insurance.*

Moreover, the previous discussion establishes:

> **Result 7.2:** *A risk-averse farmer facing an actuarially fair insurance market will choose a production pattern that is independent*

5. Notice risk aversion with respect to $\boldsymbol{\pi}$ is sufficient here. We need not invoke generalized Schur-concavity of W.
6. Result 7.2 was derived in the single-output expected-utility case by Nelson and Loehman (1987).

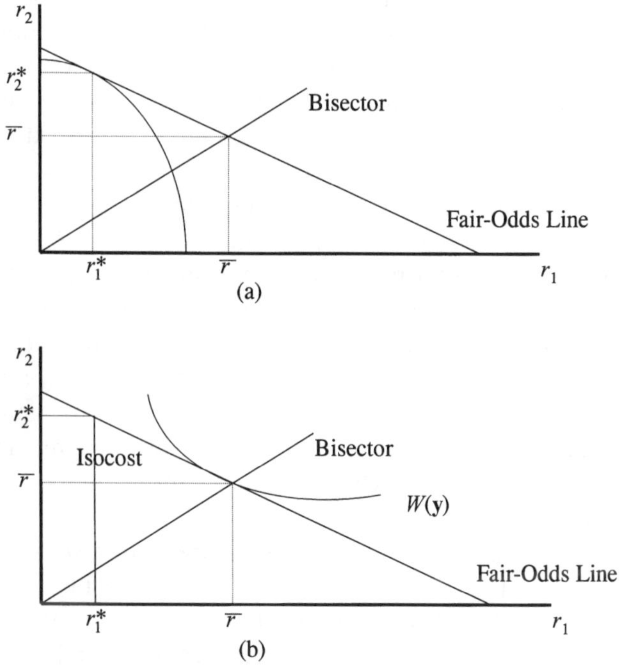

Figure 7.3 (a) Equilibrium with fair insurance. (b) Equilibrium with fair insurance and revenue-cubical technology.

of her risk preferences and is the same as that for a risk-neutral farmer facing the same probabilities. The farmer will always completely insure, so that $(I_s - I_t) = (r_t - r_s)$.

Figure 7.3(a) illustrates for the case of smooth preferences. The isocost curve in that figure represents the level curve of $C(\mathbf{w}, \mathbf{r}, \mathbf{p})$ as evaluated at the optimal level of state-contingent production. It is drawn as tangent to the fair-odds line at the optimal state-contingent production point (r_1^*, r_2^*) reflecting the fact that the farmer picks her revenue vector to maximize expected net income. As we found in Chapter 5, this is the production pattern that a risk-neutral producer facing the same probabilities would choose. The farmer will now trade with the insurance company along the fair-odds line until her marginal rate of substitution between state-contingent incomes is the same as the insurer's.

Because the farmer's preference structure is risk-averse, our discussion in Chapter 3 implies that it's tangent to the fair-odds line at the bisector. Therefore, the farmer trades with the insurance company along the fair-odds line tangent to her isocost curve to the point where that fair-odds line intersects the bisector, as illustrated by the point $(\bar{r}, \bar{r})$. The net indemnity in each state can then be measured from the horizontal and vertical axes, respectively, as the difference between $\bar{r}$ and the state-contingent revenues, $\bar{r} - r_i^*$. Much as the opening of trade allows a nation to move off its domestic transformation curve to improve its welfare, the possibility of insurance allows the farmer to trade off her isocost curve to improve her welfare. When cast in this context, the issue of insurability addressed earlier is analogous to determining whether there are gains from trade. The formal analogy is made complete by recognizing that a risk-neutral individual's "prices" for state-contingent revenues are given by the probabilities.

Because the farmer chooses to fully insure, if one were to depict the indemnity as a function of revenue, it would be illustrated by a line with slope equaling minus one reflecting that shortfalls in revenue from $\bar{r}$ are exactly matched by increases in the indemnity.

When the farmer's revenue-cost function exhibits constant absolute riskiness, a straightforward consequence of these results and Chapter 5 (Result 5.6, Corollary 5.6.2) is:

> **Corollary 7.2.1:** *If the farmer's revenue-cost function is characterized by constant absolute riskiness, then in the presence of actuarially fair insurance, she will incur the same level of revenue-cost and produce the same revenue aggregate as when she receives no insurance. With insurance, she will choose a riskier (in terms of the risk ordering $\preccurlyeq_W$) state-contingent revenue vector than in the absence of insurance (as evaluated at the no-insurance outcome).*

When W is differentiable, the representative farmer's first-order conditions for problem (7.1) are

$$\frac{\partial W(\mathbf{y})}{\partial y_s} - \lambda \pi_s = 0, \qquad s \in \Omega,$$

$$\frac{\partial W(\mathbf{y})}{\partial y_s} - \frac{\partial C(\mathbf{w}, \mathbf{r}, \mathbf{p})}{\partial r_s} \sum_{s \in \Omega} \frac{\partial W(\mathbf{y})}{\partial y_s} \le 0, \qquad r_s \ge 0, \quad s \in \Omega, \tag{7.2}$$

in the notation of complementary slackness. Here, λ is the nonnegative Lagrangian multiplier associated with the zero profit constraint for the insurance company. Because W is increasing in all state-contingent net revenues, $\lambda > 0$. This Lagrangian multiplier is interpretable in several ways. Most familiarly, it is the shadow value of the zero-profit constraint in the farmer's maximization problem. However, an alternative interpretation is also possible. Sum the first set of S conditions in (7.2) to obtain

$$\lambda = \sum_{s \in \Omega} \frac{\partial W(\mathbf{y})}{\partial y_s}, \qquad (7.3)$$

so that the Lagrangian multiplier can be interpreted as the derivative of the farmer's preference function in the direction of the equal income ray (the bisector). As we saw in Chapter 5, this directional derivative is economically interpretable as the marginal utility associated with raising all state-contingent incomes by one (small) unit. Expression (7.3), therefore, says that the insurer's opportunity cost of an extra dollar spent on indemnities must equal the farmer's marginal gain from receiving such a payment with certainty.

Before leaving our discussion of actuarially fair insurance, we note that it can also be interpreted as a parable about the superfluity of crop insurance. As discussed in Chapter 6, what's really important here is the ability of the farmer to design a production and indemnity scheme that spans the state space. Once this is done, the farmer can always design a production–indemnity scheme that removes all risk. But notice that we have only chosen to call the provider of the indemnity an *insurer*, mainly for mnemonic purposes. *If there exists an actuarially fair and complete contingent market of any kind, the farmer can always exploit that market to perfectly insure herself.* Hence, the contingent claim market need have nothing to do with farming or production in particular. We close this section with an example:

> **Example 7.1:** *We've been assuming that the revenue-cost function is smoothly differentiable. The availability of a differentiable cost function is an analytic advantage to working with our approach. However, as we saw in Chapter 5, if the technology is revenue-cubical (the value analog to the state-contingent production function technology), the revenue-cost function will not generally be*

differentiable. Consider the special case of this technology given by

$$C(\boldsymbol{w}, \boldsymbol{r}, \boldsymbol{p}) = max\{C^1(\boldsymbol{w}, r_1, \boldsymbol{p}_1), \cdots, C^S(\boldsymbol{w}, r_S, \boldsymbol{p}_S)\},$$

where $C^s(\boldsymbol{w}, r_s, \boldsymbol{p}_s)$ *is the ex post revenue-cost function associated with the* s*th state-contingent revenue function. When presented with an actuarially fair insurance contract, the farmer maximizes expected net returns from farming. The production equilibrium will thus be depicted as in Figure 7.3(b), where the farmer locates herself at the kink of a cubically shaped isocost frontier, and then trades from that point along the fair-odds line to the bisector.*

7.4 FARMER BEHAVIOR IN THE PRESENCE OF CONVEX LOADING FACTORS

If insurers behave competitively, any equilibrium insurance contract must make zero expected profit (loss). Therefore, in the presence of a convex loading factor, we have

$$\sum_s \pi_s (I_s + l(I_s)) = 0.$$

We define as *actuarially unfair* an insurance contract in which the expected value of net indemnities, $\Sigma_s \pi_s I_s$, evaluated at the probability vector $\boldsymbol{\pi}$ for which the insurer is risk-neutral, is negative. In a competitive insurance market, the expected value of the net indemnities will just cover the expected value of the loading factors. When this happens, the farmer's premium (pay-in) exceeds the expected value of her state-contingent indemnities (pay-outs). We continue to assume that the farmer is risk-averse for $\boldsymbol{\pi}$.

7.4.1 Production in the Presence of Actuarially Unfair Insurance

The farmer facing an actuarially unfair insurance market chooses her indemnity portfolio and her production pattern according to

$$\max_{\mathbf{I}\,\mathbf{r}} \left\{ W(\mathbf{r} + \mathbf{I} - C(\mathbf{w}, \mathbf{r}, \mathbf{p})) : \sum_{s \in \Omega} \pi_s (I_s + l(I_s)) = 0 \right\} \tag{7.4}$$

which, after recalling that

$$I_s = y_s - (r_s - C(\mathbf{w}, \mathbf{r}, \mathbf{p})),$$

can be rewritten as picking state-contingent net incomes and revenues to satisfy

$$\max_{\mathbf{yr}} \left\{ W(\mathbf{y}) : \sum_{s \in \Omega} \pi_s y_s = \sum_{s \in \Omega} \pi_s (r_s - l(I_s)) - C(\mathbf{w}, \mathbf{r}, \mathbf{p}) \right\}. \tag{7.5}$$

It's particularly enlightening to consider the solution to (7.4) under the strong assumption that payout states are determined a priori[7] and that l is the piecewise linear angle function illustrated in Figure 7.1. Then $l(I_s)$ is equal to lI_s, for some constant loading factor l, in payout states (i.e., states in which the net indemnity is strictly positive) and 0 in other states.[8] Define the subset of states in which a payout is made by the set $\Omega^p \subset \Omega$ and then note that (7.5) can be rewritten as

$$\max_{\mathbf{yr}} \left\{ W(\mathbf{y}) : \sum_{s \in \Omega} \pi_s^* y_s = \sum_{s \in \Omega} \pi_s^* r_s - C(\mathbf{w}, \mathbf{r}, \mathbf{p}) \right\},$$

where

$$\pi_s^* = \begin{cases} \dfrac{\pi_s (1+l)}{\sum_{t \in \Omega^p} \pi_t (1+l) + \sum_{t \notin \Omega^p} \pi_t}, & s \in \Omega^p \\[2ex] \dfrac{\pi_s}{\sum_{t \in \Omega^p} \pi_t (1+l) + \sum_{t \notin \Omega^p} \pi_t}, & s \in \Omega^p. \end{cases} \tag{7.6}$$

We refer to $\boldsymbol{\pi}^*$ as the vector of *loaded probabilities* and to the corresponding odds ratios as *loaded odds*. We emphasize, in general, that because the farmer chooses which states in which to receive payouts, $\boldsymbol{\pi}^*$ is endogenous.

Following arguments made in the case of actuarially fair insurance, the optimal choice of state-contingent revenues contingent on the choice of payout states must satisfy

7. For example, an insurance company might offer to make payouts only in the obviously bad states of nature, for example, hailstorms or flooding.
8. The choice of payout states is obviously endogenous in (7.4). We look at the problem in this recursive fashion to highlight the role that actuarially unfair contracts play in determining the producer's ultimate choice of state-contingent revenues.

$$\tilde{\mathbf{r}} \in \arg\max\left\{\sum_s \pi_s^* r_s - C(\mathbf{w}, \mathbf{r}, \mathbf{p})\right\}.$$

Suppose that the farmer chose any vector of state-contingent revenues other than $\tilde{\mathbf{r}}$. Then her state-contingent net incomes would satisfy

$$\sum_s \pi_s^* y_s \le \max_{\mathbf{r}}\left\{\sum_s \pi_s^* r_s - C(\mathbf{w}, \mathbf{r}, \mathbf{p})\right\}.$$

But if she chose to produce $\tilde{\mathbf{r}}$ instead, she would have the difference

$$\max_{\mathbf{r}}\left\{\sum_s \pi_s^* r_s - C(\mathbf{w}, \mathbf{r}, \mathbf{p})\right\} - \left(\sum_s \pi_s^* r_s - C(\mathbf{w}, \mathbf{r}, \mathbf{p})\right) \ge 0$$

that she could allocate either to a single state or spread smoothly over all states thereby increasing her welfare. She'll choose $\tilde{\mathbf{r}}$.

Thus, the separation between production and consumption choices observed in the case of actuarially fair insurance is present to a limited extent even when insurance is not actuarially fair. The limit arises, in this case, because a fixed loaded probabilities vector $\boldsymbol{\pi}^*$ is applicable only for indemnity vectors with an a priori specified set of payout states. Normally, the choice of payout states is made endogenously by the farmer in conjunction with his production decision. For example, the farmer always has the option of self-insurance, setting $\mathbf{I} = \mathbf{0}^S$ and producing the optimal output in the absence of insurance.

We illustrate using Figure 7.4. Figure 7.4(a) shows the set of indemnity vectors for which the insurer receives zero net profit. Note the kink at the origin. The combination of production and insurance may be illustrated by translating the origin to the farmer's revenue vector.[9] In Figure 7.4(b), this combination is illustrated for the optimal revenue vector, denoted A. The possibility of producing at A, and selecting an indemnity vector with a positive payout in state 1 augments the consumption possibility set by adding all points below the line segment AC. Observe that the choice of any other production point, along with an indemnity vector having a payout in state 1, would yield a strictly dominated consumption vector.

9. In this diagram, effort is implicitly held constant. For simplicity, assume that the technology displays constant absolute riskiness, so that all points on the efficient frontier have the same effort cost.

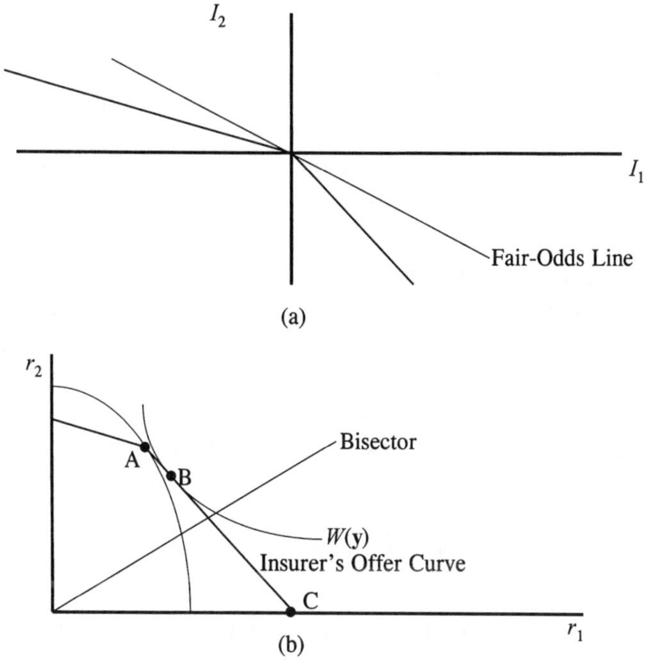

Figure 7.4 (a) The insurer's offer curve with linear loading factors. (b) Equilibrium with unfair insurance.

Now return to (7.5) in the case of a general loading factor $l(I)$, which, for simplicity, we shall take as smoothly differentiable. The producer's "budget constraint" in allocating state-contingent net incomes then assumes the form

$$\sum_{s\in\Omega}\pi_s y_s = \sum_{s\in\Omega}\pi_s r_s - \sum_{s\in\Omega}\pi_s l(y_s - (r_s - C(\mathbf{w},\mathbf{r},\mathbf{p}))) - C(\mathbf{w},\mathbf{r},\mathbf{p}).$$

Unlike the case of actuarially fair insurance, the producer's state-contingent net incomes enter this budget constraint nonlinearly. Changing one state's net income affects both sides of this budget constraint. Moreover, since the loading factor is convex, the right-hand side is a concave function of the producer's state-contingent net incomes. This happens because the insurer's losses (profits) are convex (concave) in the state-contingent indemnities. Therefore, he, too, now cares about the dispersion of his returns across different states of nature. This leads him to act in what might be called a "pseudo-risk-averse" manner. In choosing her state-contingent revenues and net incomes, the producer must now cope with the insurer's pseudo-risk-aversion. And when two "risk-averse" individuals contract with one another, they will contract to share the total risks both incur. This contracting process leads them to trade state-contingent incomes with one another until they equate their marginal rates of substitution over state-contingent net incomes. Using terminology borrowed from Hirshleifer and Riley (1992), they "mutually insure."[10] In the contracting process, the farmer's preferences toward risk (along with the insurer's) are inevitably mixed into her choice of state-contingent incomes and thus into her final production decision. Consequently, we generally cannot separate her production decisions from her attitudes toward risk.

Notice, however, that if we linearize the right-hand side of this "budget constraint," we get

$$\sum_{s\in\Omega}(\pi_s+\pi_s l'(I_s))r_s-\sum_{s\in\Omega}\pi_s l'(I_s)y_s-\sum_{s\in\Omega}(\pi_s+\pi_s l'(I_s))C(\mathbf{w},\mathbf{r},\mathbf{p}),$$

so that a linearized version of the budget constraint in (7.5) is

$$\sum_{s\in\Omega}\pi_s^* y_s=\sum_{s\in\Omega}\pi_s^* r_s-C(\mathbf{w},\mathbf{r},\mathbf{p}),$$

where these new loaded probabilities are defined as

$$\pi_s^*=\frac{\pi_s(1+l'(I_s))}{\sum_{s\in\Omega}\pi_s(1+l'(I_s))}. \tag{7.7}$$

Consequently, in the neighborhood of any solution to (7.5), one must have

$$\pi_s^*=\frac{\partial C(\mathbf{w},\mathbf{r},\mathbf{p})}{\partial r_s}\leq 0, \qquad s\in\Omega$$

with complementary slackness. Hence, the optimal production vector must maximize

10. Even when the insurer presents actuarially fair contracts, the farmer and the insurer can be viewed as mutually insuring. In this instance, because the insurer doesn't care about risk, it's optimal for him to bear it all as long as his expected return isn't diminished.

$$\max_{\mathbf{y}\mathbf{r}}\left\{W(\mathbf{y}):\sum_{s\in\Omega}\pi_s^* y_s=\sum_{s\in\Omega}\pi_s^* r_s-C(\mathbf{w},\mathbf{r},\mathbf{p})\right\},$$

where $\boldsymbol{\pi}^*$ is defined as in (7.7). However, the value of $\boldsymbol{\pi}^*$ will depend on the choice of indemnity vector **I**, which, in turn, depends on the farmer's risk preferences. Thus, for general loading factors, there is no separation between production and risk preferences. But once the loaded odds are given, the farmer's productive choice is identical to that of a risk-neutral individual with these loaded odds.

Summing these first-order conditions on **r** yields

$$\sum_{s\in\Omega}\frac{\partial C(\mathbf{w},\mathbf{r},\mathbf{p})}{\partial r_s}\geq\sum_{s\in\Omega}\pi_s^*=1 \tag{7.8}$$

again in the notation of complementary slackness. Thus, the farmer's production pattern will belong to the efficient set. But in the absence of constant marginal load factors, farmers do not produce at the point that maximizes the expected profit from farming.

Result 7.3: *Expected profit from farming under actuarially unfair crop insurance is never greater than expected profit from farming under actuarially fair crop insurance. Farmers facing actuarially unfair crop insurance will choose a state-contingent revenue vector that is in the efficient set and maximizes the expectation of profit calculated using the loaded probabilities* $\boldsymbol{\pi}^*$.

7.4.2 Net Income Under Actuarially Unfair Insurance

The nature of the net-income solution to this problem depends crucially on whether W is smoothly differentiable in a neighborhood of the equal-income vector. If W is smoothly differentiable, as we saw in Chapter 3, $\boldsymbol{\pi}$ is the unique probability vector for which the farmer is risk-averse. By contrast, when W is not smoothly differentiable, the farmer may be risk-averse for many different probability vectors, possibly including the odds implied by an actuarially unfair insurance contract.

7.4.2.1 The Differentiable Case

The farmer's first-order conditions for this problem are

$$\frac{\partial W(\mathbf{y})}{\partial y_s} - \lambda\pi_s(1 + l'(I_s)) = 0, \qquad s \in \Omega,$$

$$\frac{\partial W(\mathbf{y})}{\partial y_s} - \frac{\partial C(\mathbf{w}, \mathbf{r}, \mathbf{p})}{\partial r_s}\sum_{s\in\Omega}\frac{\partial W(\mathbf{y})}{\partial y_s} \leq 0, \qquad r_s \geq 0, \quad s \in \Omega, \tag{7.9}$$

in the notation of complementary slackness. Here λ is the strictly positive Lagrangian multiplier associated with the insurer's break-even constraint. (Note that its optimal value will not generally correspond to that of the Lagrangian multiplier in the previous section.) The first S of these conditions correspond to the first-order conditions for the indemnity in each of the S states of nature. The second S conditions correspond to the first-order conditions for the optimal choice of state-contingent revenues.

The first S conditions in (7.9) are a manifestation of Borch's (1962) well-known rule for optimal risk sharing. (Borch's rule requires that the marginal rates of substitution for state-contingent incomes for the insurer and the insuree are equalized.) Rewriting

$$\begin{aligned}\frac{\partial W(\mathbf{y})/\partial y_s}{\partial W(\mathbf{y})/\partial y_t} &= \frac{\pi_s(1 + l'(I_s))}{\pi_t(1 + l'(I_t))} \\ &= \frac{\pi_s^*}{\pi_t^*}, \qquad s,t \in \Omega.\end{aligned} \tag{7.10}$$

The farmer's equilibrium corresponds to a point of tangency between the indifference curve and the loaded-odds line and not to a tangency with the fair-odds line. Therefore, for a differentiable generalized Schur-concave preference structure, the farmer generally will not be fully insured. An exception occurs when the marginal loading factor is constant. Then the farmer completely stabilizes his or her income.[11]

As we've noted, with a strictly convex loading structure, a risk-

11. Notice, however, that if the marginal loading factor is a constant, the break-even constraint for the insurer becomes

$$(1 + l)\sum_s \pi_s I_s = 0,$$

from which

$$\sum_s \pi_s I_s = 0,$$

so that the same analysis as in the previous section applies.

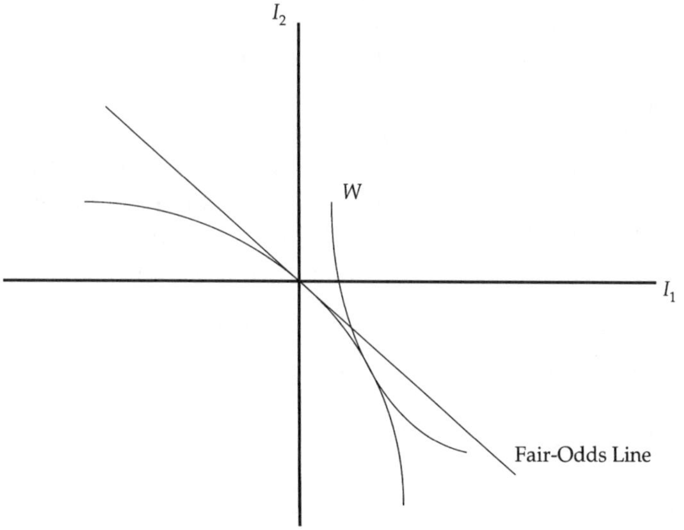

Figure 7.5 Equilibrium in the insurance market.

neutral insurer will appear to be risk-averse because his expected returns are a concave function of the state-contingent indemnities. Consequently, the insurer as well as the farmer cares about the dispersion of returns across the different states of nature.

These results are illustrated in Figure 7.5. There the net indemnity in state 2 is measured along the vertical axis and the net indemnity in state 1 is measured along the horizontal axis. The slope of the insurer's indifference curve in this space is given by $dI_2/dI_1 = -\pi_1^*/\pi_2^* \leq 0$, or minus the ratio of the loaded probabilities. Because the loaded probabilities change as the indemnity changes, the indifference curve is not a straight line. At the origin, however, the slope of the indifference curve equals the slope of the fair-odds line. Hence, the indifference curve passing through the origin is tangent to the fair-odds line at the origin and lies everywhere below that fair-odds line elsewhere. As depicted in Chapter 3, the indifference curves for the farmer's smoothly differentiable generalized Schur-concave objective function exhibit a diminishing marginal rate of substitution between state-contingent indemnities. Along the bisector in the northeast quadrant, the farmer's indifference curve is tangent to the fair-odds line. The equilibrium in the insurance market is there illustrated as a tangency between the farmer's and the insurer's indifference curves in the southeast quadrant. Thus, state 2 is the good state of nature, when the farmer's net indemnity is negative, and state 1 is the bad state of nature when the farmer's net indemnity is positive.

Even more can be said about the shape of the indemnity schedule that the farmer chooses under actuarially unfair insurance. By Result 3.3 in Chapter 3, the generalized Schur-concavity of the farmer's preference function implies that at an interior solution to (7.10)

$$[\lambda(1+l'(I_s)) - \lambda(1+l'(I_t))](y_s - y_t) \leq 0$$
$$\Rightarrow (l'(I_s) - l'(I_t))(y_s - y_t) \leq 0. \qquad (7.11)$$

On the other hand, the convexity of the loading factor implies

$$(l'(I_s) - l'(I_t))(I_s - I_t) \geq 0.$$

Combining this result with (7.11) shows that

$$(l'(I_s) - l'(I_t))(r_s - r_t) \leq 0,$$

and, consequently,

$$(I_s - I_t)(r_s - r_t) \leq 0. \qquad (7.12)$$

The farmer chooses her indemnity structure to balance high-revenue states with low-indemnity states and low-revenue states with high-indemnity states. This is the essence of insurance. However, in contrast with the actuarially fair case, the farmer does not fully insure against all revenue risk. We show this formally. Choose any two levels of state-contingent revenue such that $y_s - y_t \geq 0$. By (7.11) and the convexity of the loading factor in state-contingent indemnities, it follows that $(I_s - I_t) \leq 0$. Together, these two facts imply

$$r_s - r_t \geq -(I_s - I_t),$$

or

$$\frac{I_s - I_t}{r_s - r_t} \geq -1.$$

The net indemnity schedule, when graphed as a function of state-contingent revenues, must have a slope that lies between zero and minus one. So although farmers tend to balance low-revenue states against high-indemnity states, they never fully insure against downside risk by the purchase of insurance. Farmers *self-insure* in the sense that they adjust their production pattern to accommodate some of the remaining risk. This happens because, in the presence of convex loading factors, insurers care about the dispersion of state-contingent indemnities, and they act as though they were risk-averse. Insurers, like farmers, want to avoid low return states because they imply high indemnities for them. There is, thus, room for "mutual insurance" between farmers and insurers with both bearing some of the risk.

This can be seen by combining (7.9) and (7.8) to obtain

$$\left[\frac{\partial C(\mathbf{w},\mathbf{r},\mathbf{p})/\partial r_s}{\pi_s} - \frac{\partial C(\mathbf{w},\mathbf{r},\mathbf{p})/\partial r_t}{\pi_t}\right](r_s - r_t) \leq 0$$

so that a farmer facing actuarially unfair insurance will produce a risk-aversely efficient state-contingent revenue vector. Summarizing results we obtain:

Result 7.4: *In the presence of actuarially unfair insurance, a farmer with differentiable preferences produces in the risk-aversely-efficient set and chooses her indemnity schedule so that*

$$0 \geq \frac{(\mathrm{I}_s - \mathrm{I}_t)}{\mathrm{r}_s - \mathrm{r}_t} \geq -1, \qquad s,t \in \Omega.$$

The equilibrium in Result 7.4 is illustrated by Figure 7.6, where we have drawn an isocost curve and an indifference curve for the farmer. The presence of the insurance market allows the farmer to trade off her isocost curve along the insurer's zero-profit-offer curve toward the bisector by sacrificing production in the good state for an enhanced payment in the bad state. (The insurer's zero-profit offer curve is simply his zero-profit indifference curve, depicted in Figure 7.5, drawn taking the farmer's production point as the origin.) Because the net indemnity in the bad state is positive whereas the net indemnity in the good state is negative, it's easy to show that

$$-\frac{\pi_1(1+\mathrm{l}'(\mathrm{I}_1))}{\pi_2(1+\mathrm{l}'(\mathrm{I}_2))} = -\frac{\pi_1^*}{\pi_2^*} \leq -\frac{\pi_1}{\pi_2}.$$

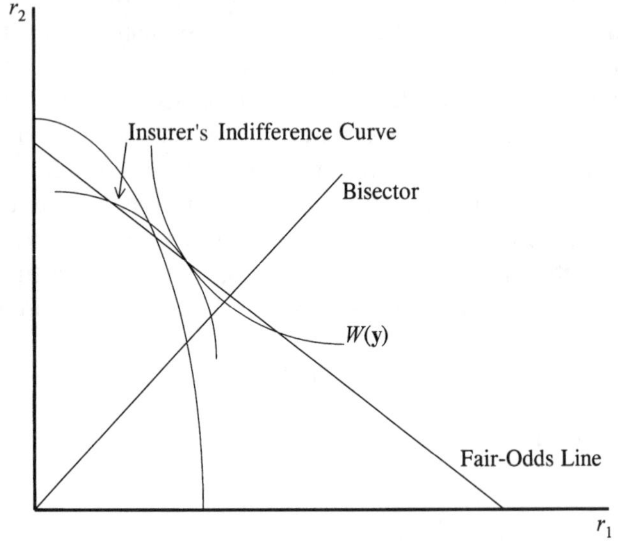

Figure 7.6 Equilibrium with unfair insurance.

Using the results of the last section, we find that the state-contingent production point lies to the southeast of the point on the isocost curve where a risk-neutral individual would produce while the equilibrium point on the farmer's indifference curve lies to the northwest of the bisector. The former reflects the risk-averse efficiency of the production choice, whereas the latter reflects the mutual insurance aspect of the insurance contract when there are strictly convex loading factors.

When the farmer's revenue-cost function is characterized by constant absolute riskiness, the fact that her choice of revenues is in the efficient set implies that she employs the same level of the revenue aggregate, $T(\mathbf{r}, \mathbf{p}, \mathbf{w})$, as she would if she were fully insured with actuarially fair insurance. The fact that the revenue vector she produces with actuarially unfair insurance is risk-aversely efficient, however, implies that it will also be less risky than the revenue vector that she would adopt in the presence of actuarially fair insurance. Using Result 5.6 and Corollary 5.6.2 from Chapter 5 gives:

Corollary 7.4.1: *If the farmer faces a revenue-cost function that exhibits constant absolute riskiness, then in the presence of actuarially unfair insurance, she will incur the same level of revenue-cost and produce the same revenue aggregate,* $T(\boldsymbol{r}, \boldsymbol{p}, \boldsymbol{w})$*, as when she receives actuarially fair insurance. With actuarially fair insurance, she will choose a riskier state-contingent revenue vector than for actuarially unfair insurance (as evaluated at the actuarially unfair insurance outcome).*

7.4.2.2 The Nondifferentiable Case

Most of the time, whether we assume W differentiable or not is a matter of convenience, trading off simplicity in the derivation and statement of results against the extra generality that comes from relaxing the assumption of differentiability. Usually, this trade-off is not very favorable. Little generality is gained at the expense of a loss of a fair amount of simplicity. In the analysis of insurance, however, the assumption of differentiability is crucial in deriving the result that a farmer faced with an actuarially unfair contract will never choose full insurance. We start by presenting an example of a class of farmers who will always fully insure regardless of whether they are offered an actuarially fair contract or not.

Example 7.2: *Take an individual with maximin preferences. In Chapter 5, we showed that, in the absence of insurance, she would produce where the efficient set intersects the equal-revenue vector. Denote that certain revenue as* r^o *and let the solution to the expected profit maximization problem be*

$$\hat{\boldsymbol{r}} \in \arg\max\left\{\sum_{s\in\Omega} \pi_s r_s - C(\boldsymbol{w}, \boldsymbol{r}, \boldsymbol{p})\right\}.$$

Any full-insurance indemnity structure of the form

$$I_s = \left(\sum_{s\in\Omega} \hat{\pi}_s \hat{r}_s\right) - \hat{r}_s, \qquad s \in \Omega,$$

$\Sigma_{s\in\Omega}\hat{\pi}_t = 1$*, that offers the farmer a certain return exceeding* $r^o - \boldsymbol{C}(\boldsymbol{w}, r^o \boldsymbol{1}^S, \boldsymbol{p})$*, leads the farmer to produce at the expected profit-maximizing outcome and then to trade with the insurance company to move to the equal-revenue vector regardless of whether it is actuarially fair at the insurer's true probabilities.*

Example 7.3: *This point may be also illustrated for the expected-utility case to show that it does not require the presence of total aversion to risk. Suppose* u *is concave, but has a kink at* y^o *so that there exist* u_1, u_2 *such that for any* $y' > y^o > y''$,

$$u'(y') > u_1 > u_2 > u'(y'').$$

Now suppose that in the absence of insurance, $r_1 < r_0 < r_2$, *and consider an insurance contract such that with full insurance,* $r_i + I_i = r_0$, $i = 1, 2$, *and*

$$\frac{\pi_2(1+l'(I_2))}{\pi_1(1+l'(I_1))} = \frac{\pi_2^*}{\pi_1^*} < \frac{u_1}{u_2}.$$

Then, full insurance will be optimal.

More generally, suppose that the optimal state-contingent revenue with convex loading factors is given by **r***. As we've just seen, in the smoothly differentiable case, **r*** can't be associated with full insurance. This is a consequence of Borch's rule (7.10), for optimal risk sharing between two individuals with smoothly differentiable preferences, and the assumption that the insurer and the farmer share common subjective probabilities. However, Borch's rule doesn't apply when the farmer's preference structure is not smoothly differentiable because the farmer may have many probabilities for which she is risk-averse.

In particular, the farmer may be risk-averse for the loaded probability vector $\boldsymbol{\pi}^*$ as well as for $\boldsymbol{\pi}$. If the farmer is risk-averse for $\boldsymbol{\pi}^*$, then for any **r**, the farmer would always prefer a full-insurance contract offering the outcome $\sum_{s=1}^{S} \pi_s^* r_s$ with certainty. And, consequently, the farmer would adopt full insurance if it were offered.

The convexity of l ensures that, provided fixed costs are small, a contract at least this favorable is available. Convexity of l implies, for any **I**, that

$$l(0) + \sum_{s \in \Omega} \pi_s l'(I_s) I_s \geq \sum_{s \in \Omega} \pi_s l(I_s),$$

where $l(0)$ is a *fixed loading factor* (the fixed cost associated with insurance). If it's small enough, then for $\mathbf{I} = \sum_{s=1}^{S} \pi_s^* r_s \mathbf{1}^S - \mathbf{r}$,

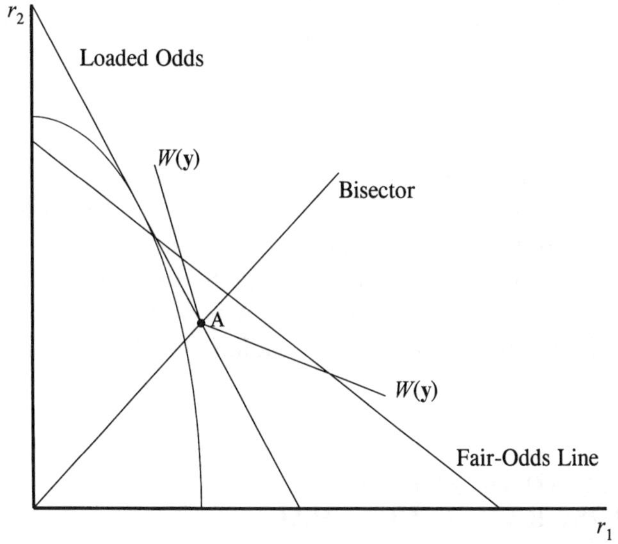

Figure 7.7 Full insurance with unfair odds.

$$\begin{aligned}\sum_{s\in\Omega}\pi_s(1+l(I_s)) &\leq \sum_{s\in\Omega}\pi_s(1+l'(I_s))I_s \\ &= \sum_{s\in\Omega}\left(\pi_s(1+l'(I_s))\left(\sum_{s\in\Omega}\pi_s^* r_s - r_s\right)'\right) \\ &= 0.\end{aligned}$$

So, the full-insurance contract offering indemnity $\mathbf{I} = \Sigma_{s\in\Omega}\pi_s^* r_s \mathbf{1}^S - \mathbf{r}$ will yield nonnegative expected profits to the insurer. This leads us to conclude that

> **Result 7.5:** *Suppose that for a zero-profit full-insurance contract **I**, the farmer is risk-averse for the loaded-probability vector $\boldsymbol{\pi}^*$. Then, with a sufficiently small fixed loading factor, the farmer will fully insure.*

This argument is illustrated by Figure 7.7, where we assume that the indifference curves are for an individual who exhibits both constant absolute risk aversion and constant relative risk aversion so that the indifference curves are kinked at the bisector, and are negatively sloped lines everywhere else. The production equilibrium is illustrated by a tangency between the line segment, whose slope is given by the ratio of the loaded probabilities:

$$-\frac{\pi_1^*}{\pi_2^*},$$

and the producer's isocost curve. As drawn, this line segment intersects the bisector at point A, which corresponds to a kink in the farmer's indifference curve. The farmer and the insurer trade along this line segment toward the bisector. Notice, in particular, that using these loaded probabilities, point A is preferred by the farmer to all other points she can get by trading along the insurer's offer curve.

7.5 NONSTATE-CONTINGENT INSURANCE CONTRACTS

In the two preceding sections, we have presumed that the insurance company can write contracts that are state-contingent. For the insurer to be able to do so, he must be able to observe which state of nature occurs. In turn, this means that the insurer can ascertain the exact conditions under which production takes place. This takes us back to our discussion of states of nature in Chapter 1. As we said there, just how one interprets the notion of a state depends critically on the problem at hand. The state includes all stochastic factors that impinge importantly on a producer's decisions.

To illustrate, suppose that the farmer is a citrus producer and that the only important source of uncertainty is the stochastic presence or absence of an early frost. That is, the stochastic presence or absence of early frost defines the state of nature. It seems reasonable that an insurer could observe the presence or absence of an early frost. If so, the insurer can fruitfully write state-contingent contracts, and the analysis of the preceding sections applies directly. However, this stylized situation is characterized by the source of uncertainty being both very specific and relatively easy to observe.

Unfortunately, in many instances, production risk is considerably more complicated and cannot be reasonably reduced to a relatively few factors. More typically, there are a variety of stochastic risks (rainfall, temperature, frost, and pest outbreaks) that producers face, and many of these are hard to observe precisely without prohibitively costly monitoring of the farmer's operation. Therefore, for many situations, it's implausible to assume that the insurance company can observe the state of nature. And if the insurance company cannot observe the state of nature, on what does it base its net indemnities? The most common situation is for the net indemnity to be based in some way on the farmer's observed output and other observables. Examples include: the difference between historic yields and current yield; the difference between the farmer's yield and some trigger level; and the difference between farmer's yield and average yield of farmers in apparently similar risk pools.

A complete analysis of all these differing options is worthy of a text in itself. Here we restrict attention to the case in which there are no loading costs and net indemnities assume the form[12]

$$I(r) = m - ir.$$

Such net indemnities involve producers receiving a fixed payment in each state that is adjusted in accordance with the amount of revenue realized. Here m can be interpreted as a state-invariant indemnity.

We first argue that no competitive insurance contract can offer net indemnities of this type with $i \geq 1$ in equilibrium. For a competitive insurance contract to be feasible, it must be true that

$$i \sum_s \pi_s r_s \geq m$$

where the vector of state-contingent revenues is chosen to solve

$$\max_r \{W((1-i)\mathbf{r} + (m - C(\mathbf{w}, \mathbf{r}, \mathbf{p}))\mathbf{1}^s)\}.$$

Now suppose that $i \geq 1$. Then, as long as the preference function is increasing in all state-contingent revenues, the farmer's optimal choice is to commit no effort and produce $\mathbf{r} = \mathbf{0}^S$. Consequently, the only contracts that the insurer can offer that make a nonnegative expected profit are trivial contracts with zero or negative state-invariant indemnity. Suppose the insurance company tries to offer an

12. In this section, the linear payment structure is imposed as an exogenous constraint. Such a payment structure does not normally arise as the optimal solution to moral hazard problems. For a treatment of nonlinear net indemnities in the expected-utility, stochastic production-function model, see Chambers (1989).

insurance contract with $m < 0$. The farmer is always better off refusing the insurance contract and either not farming or farming without crop insurance.[13]

An immediate implication is that *the farmer is hurt by the insurer's inability to discern which state of nature occurs*. If the insurer could ascertain the state, as we have already seen, the competitive insurance indemnity is

$$I_s = \sum_{t \in \Omega} \pi_t r_t - r_s,$$

which, in equilibrium, is a special case of this contract with $m = \Sigma_{t\in\Omega} \pi_t r_t$ and $i = 1$. From this observation, the insurer cannot offer the competitive insurance contract, which requires the producer to maximize expected profit while completely stabilizing her returns. Because this is the best that the farmer could possibly hope for, the farmer loses as compared to the case when the insurer can observe the state of nature. *As long as the insurance market is competitive, the farmer, and not the insurer, bears the brunt of adjusting to nonstate-contingent insurance contracts.*

More generally, contracts of the form $i = 1$ are contracts that provide complete revenue insurance for the farmer. Contracts providing complete revenue insurance can never be competitively offered if the state of nature is not observable, and the insurer must base his net indemnities on observed revenue. By completely insuring the farmer, the insurer creates a situation of *moral hazard* in which the farmer has no incentive to exert any effort if she accepts the contract. Facing this situation, an insurer who offers a complete insurance contract is doomed to losses. Complete insurance is not sustainable.

The reader will recall that previously we showed that, when the insurer faces a convex loading factor, and is thus forced to offer actuarially unfair state-contingent insurance contracts, these contracts do not offer full insurance. There the reason is the insurer's concerns about the distribution of indemnities as a result of the convex loading factors. Here a similar result emerges, but for a different reason. If the insurer fully insures the farmer, the farmer's net return in any

13. This argument applies for the entire class of differentiable indemnity contracts $I(r)$, which vary inversely with the level of realized state-contingent revenue.

state is not affected by any action she takes. The insurer, not the farmer, becomes the complete residual claimant for any variation in revenues. Consequently, the farmer, with nothing to gain, finds it optimal to take no action. In Chapter 9, we shall return to the problem of moral hazard when we study the optimal design of contracts in the presence of such adverse incentives.

Result 7.6: *No competitive insurance contract can be of the form*

$$I(r) = m - ir$$

with i $\geq$ *1. If the insurance company cannot observe the state of nature, it cannot implement an insurance contract that provides complete revenue insurance.*

Having established that insurance contracts of this form cannot provide complete insurance, we now investigate the farmer's optimal response to contracts of this form under the presumption that the farmer takes both (m, i) as given. As long as the farmer's preference function is smoothly differentiable[14] and generalized Schur-concave, any solution must be consistent with the following first-order conditions:

$$(1-i)\frac{\partial W(\mathbf{y})}{\partial y_s} - \frac{\partial C(\mathbf{w},\mathbf{r},\mathbf{p})}{\partial r_s}\sum_{s\in\Omega}\frac{\partial W(\mathbf{y})}{\partial y_s} \leq 0, \qquad r_s \geq 0, \quad s \in \Omega,$$

in the notation of complementary slackness. Summing these conditions yields an arbitrage condition:

$$\sum_s \frac{\partial C(\mathbf{w},\mathbf{r},\mathbf{p})}{\partial r_s} \geq 1 - i, \tag{7.13}$$

with an equality for an interior solution. Moreover, the generalized Schur-concavity of W shows that the solution must be risk-aversely efficient because optimality requires

$$\left(\frac{\partial C(\mathbf{w},\mathbf{r},\mathbf{p})/\partial r_s}{\pi_s} - \frac{\partial C(\mathbf{w},\mathbf{r},\mathbf{p})/\partial r_t}{\pi_t}\right)(r_s - r_t) \leq 0, \qquad s,t \in \Omega.$$

Expression (7.13) is a state-arbitrage condition for producers facing a crop-insurance contract of this form. Risklessly expanding all state-

14. The case of nondifferentiable preferences can be analyzed in the same fashion as in the preceding section.

contingent revenues by one unit must increase cost by $(1 - i)$ units.[15] For crop-insurance contracts of this type, expanding revenue by one dollar in each state only brings the farmer an extra state-contingent return of $(1 - i)$ dollars. Hence, if at the margin she could spend less than this amount to raise revenues in this fashion, she would always do so. The optimal scale of operation (in the direction of the equal-revenue vector) is reached when the farmer receives a zero marginal return from expanding all state-contingent revenues equally.

We conclude, therefore, that a producer facing an insurance contract of this type will not choose a state-contingent revenue vector that is on the efficient frontier. Farmers facing a nonstate-contingent insurance contract will farm on a smaller scale than farmers facing state-contingent revenue insurance or farmers not having access to insurance. When the technology exhibits constant absolute riskiness, a sharper result is available.

Result 7.7: *If the farmer's revenue-cost function is characterized by constant absolute riskiness and she faces a nonstate-contingent crop insurance contract, she incurs a lower level of cost than she would in the absence of crop insurance or in the presence of state-contingent crop insurance.*

If the farmer's revenue-cost function is characterized by constant absolute riskiness, it can always be expressed in the form (Lemma 5.2):

$$C(\mathbf{w}, \mathbf{r}, \mathbf{p}) = \hat{C}(\mathbf{w}, \mathbf{T}(\mathbf{r}, \mathbf{p}, \mathbf{w}), \mathbf{p}),$$

where the revenue aggregate, $T(\mathbf{r}, \mathbf{p}, \mathbf{w})$, satisfies the translation property. Applying (7.13) for an interior solution now requires

$$\frac{\partial \hat{C}(\mathbf{w}, \mathbf{T}(\mathbf{r}, \mathbf{p}, \mathbf{w}), \mathbf{p})}{\partial T} = 1 - i.$$

The fact that marginal cost is nondecreasing in the revenue aggregate then implies that the farmer chooses a lower revenue aggregate, and thus lower revenue cost, than a farmer who farms on the efficient frontier. As we have shown before, farmers facing state-contingent insurance or no insurance at all, farm on the efficient frontier.

15. Equation (7.13) applies for all differentiable indemnity structures of the type in footnote 13.

The farmer's preferences also play an important role in her production and insurance decisions. We illustrate by an example.

Example 7.4: *Suppose that the farmer's preferences are characterized by constant absolute risk aversion. We studied this case at length in Chapter 3, and there demonstrated (Result 3.1) that a preference function displays constant absolute risk aversion if and only if it's expressible as a monotonic transformation of a function displaying the translation property. As we saw in Example 5.1 of Chapter 5, the assumption of constant absolute risk aversion allows us to decompose the net-returns model into a special case of the separable-effort model. To recall why, it's easiest to work in terms of certainty equivalents. The farmer's problem is to*

$$\max_{\boldsymbol{r}}\{\mathrm{e}((1-\mathrm{i})\boldsymbol{r}+(\mathrm{m}-\mathrm{C}(\boldsymbol{w},\boldsymbol{r},\boldsymbol{p}))\mathbf{1}^{s})\}$$
$$=\mathrm{m}+\max_{\boldsymbol{r}}\{\mathrm{e}((1-\mathrm{i})\boldsymbol{r})-\mathrm{C}(\boldsymbol{w},\boldsymbol{r},\boldsymbol{p})\}$$

where the equality follows by CARA. Hence, changes in the unconditional payment, m, *have no effect on the optimal state-contingent revenue vector produced under this type of crop insurance. This finding generalizes an earlier result of Hölmstrom and Milgrom (1987) to nonexpected utility models. It's yet another manifestation of the basic result obtained in Chapter 3. For general preferences exhibiting CARA, an individual's allocation of wealth to a risky asset is unaffected by changes in the wealth level. Because* m *is nonstochastic, it can be viewed as a fixed increment to wealth, hence the result.*

Example 7.5: *Still assuming that preferences exhibit CARA, let's now examine what happens when the farmer's technology is of the revenue-cubical form*

$$\mathrm{C}(\boldsymbol{w},\boldsymbol{r},\boldsymbol{p})=\max\{\mathrm{C}^{1}(\boldsymbol{w},\mathrm{r}_1,\boldsymbol{p}_1),\cdots,\mathrm{C}^{S}(\boldsymbol{w},\mathrm{r}_S,\boldsymbol{p}_S)\}.$$

If each state-contingent production function exhibits constant returns to scale (a common assumption), the ex post cost functions all satisfy

$$\mathrm{C}^{s}(\boldsymbol{w},\mathrm{r}_s,\boldsymbol{p}_s)=\mathrm{r}_s\mathrm{C}^{s}(\boldsymbol{w},1,\boldsymbol{p}_s).$$

By arguments similar to those made in Chapter 6 for the output-cubical technology, producers facing this technology always choose their state-contingent revenues so that

$$r_s = r_1 \frac{C^1(\boldsymbol{w}, 1, \boldsymbol{p}_1)}{C^s(\boldsymbol{w}, 1, \boldsymbol{p}_s)}, \qquad s \in \Omega.$$

Thus, we conclude, somewhat paradoxically, that when faced with such a technology, the presence of a nonstate-contingent insurance contract does nothing to alter the inherent riskiness of the revenue vector chosen by the farmer. (It's worth noting that this conclusion remains true whether or not preferences exhibit CARA.) This happens because the optimal state-contingent revenue mix in this particular revenue-cubical technology is completely determined by the ratio of the now constant marginal costs regardless of whether or not insurance is purchased. All the presence of insurance does is to affect where on this state-contingent revenue ray the producer locates. Expressed in certainty equivalent terms, the producer's objective function can be rewritten as

$$m + Max_{r_1}\left\{e\left((1-i)r_1 \frac{C^1(\boldsymbol{w}, 1, \boldsymbol{p}_1)}{C^1(\boldsymbol{w}, 1, \boldsymbol{p}_s)}, \cdots, (1-i)r_1 \frac{C^1(\boldsymbol{w}, 1, \boldsymbol{p}_1)}{C^S(\boldsymbol{w}, 1, \boldsymbol{p}_s)}\right)\right.$$

$$\left. - r_1 C^1(\boldsymbol{w}, 1, \boldsymbol{p}_1)\right\}$$

$$= m + Max_{r_1}\left\{e\left(\frac{\nu}{C^1(\boldsymbol{w}, 1, \boldsymbol{p}_s)}, \cdots, \frac{\nu}{C^S(\boldsymbol{w}, 1, \boldsymbol{p}_s)}\right) - \frac{\nu}{1-i}\right\}$$

$$= m + \hat{E}\left(\frac{1}{1-i}\right),$$

where $\nu = (1-i)\, r_1 C^1(\boldsymbol{w}, 1, \boldsymbol{p}_1) \geq 0$, *and* $\hat{E}(1/(1-i))$, *by standard duality arguments (see Chambers 1988, Chapter 5) is a normalized profit function that is nonincreasing and convex in its argument,* $(1/(1-i))$. *Moreover, as long as there exists a unique solution to the maximization problem,* $\nu(1/(1-i))$, *then by Hotelling's Lemma,*

$$\hat{E}'\left(\frac{1}{1-i}\right) = -\nu\left(\frac{1}{1-i}\right)$$

$$= -(1-i)r_1\left(\frac{1}{1-i}\right)C^1(\boldsymbol{w}, 1, \boldsymbol{p}_1).$$

Generally, one will not be able to determine whether producers respond to an increase in the premium rate by moving out or back along the state-contingent revenue ray. As we have seen earlier, they are unaffected by changes in the fixed indemnity. Thus, raising the indemnity from zero to a positive number, as would happen with the introduction of insurance, has no effect on state-contingent revenues. Increasing i *does two things: it lowers the expected return from the existing point on the state-contingent revenue ray, and it affects the producer's perception of the riskiness of that point on the state-contingent revenue ray. Because the producer cannot alter the inherent riskiness of the optimal state-contingent revenue ray in response to this change in his perception of the risk, he can only respond to it in a blunt way by moving out or back along the optimal state-contingent revenue ray. When insurance is introduced, either all state-contingent revenues increase or they all decrease, depending on her perception of risk. One thing is certain, however. As the premium rate increases, by the convexity of* $\hat{E}(1/(1-i))$ *and Hotelling's Lemma, net insurance revenue from producing, that is, revenue less the state-contingent indemnity,* $i\mathbf{r}$*, must decline.*

7.5.1 The Equilibrium Nonstate-Contingent Insurance Contract

The discussion so far has dealt with the response of farmers to an insurance contract with exogenously given parameters m, i. We now focus on the restrictions on m and i imposed by the requirement that the expected profit for the insurer is equal to zero. In a competitive market, insurers will seek to offer the most attractive possible contract. Hence, the equilibrium position will be the constrained-optimal choice of m, i, namely, that which maximizes the welfare of farmers, subject to the requirement that insurers make zero profits.

Before discussing the derivation of the equilibrium contract, one point should be emphasized: we are considering a constrained-optimal solution. Our analysis has already shown that welfare could be increased if, instead of choosing the vector of state-contingent revenues that maximizes her welfare for the given (m, i), the farmer could contract with insurers to guarantee the choice of the profit-maximizing vector of state-contingent revenues in return for a contract offering complete insurance.

Any feasible contract may be characterized by a choice of $i \in [0, 1]$ and the value of $m \geq 0$ for which the farmer's welfare is maximized and the insurer's expected profit equals zero. Denote

$$\mathbf{r}(m,i) \in \arg\max\{W(\mathbf{r}(1-i)+(m-C(\mathbf{w},\mathbf{r},\mathbf{p}))\mathbf{1}^S)\}$$

and

$$V(m,i)=\arg\max\{W(\mathbf{r}(1-i)+(m-C(\mathbf{w},\mathbf{r},\mathbf{p}))\mathbf{1}^S)\}. \tag{7.14}$$

Therefore, the equilibrium insurance contract can be determined by solving the mathematical program that chooses (m, i) to maximize the farmer's utility subject to the zero-profit constraint for the insurer. More formally, it is

$$\max_{m,i}\left\{V(m,i):i\sum_{s\in\Omega}\pi_s r_s(m,i)=m\right\}.$$

Applying the envelope theorem to (7.14) gives

$$V_m(m,i)=\sum_{s\in\Omega}W_s(y_s(m,i)), \tag{7.15}$$

and

$$V_i(m,i)=-\sum_{s\in\Omega}W_s(y_s(m,i))r_s(m,i), \tag{7.16}$$

where $y_s(m, i) = r_s(m, i)\ (1 - i) + m - C(\mathbf{w}, \mathbf{r}(m, i), \mathbf{p})$. From expressions (7.15) and (7.16), we conclude that the slope of the farmer's indifference curve is given by

$$\frac{dm}{di}=\frac{\sum_{s\in\Omega}W_s(y(m,i))r_s(m,i)}{\sum_{s\in\Omega}W_s(y(m,i))}$$

which is nonnegative. Increasing the unconditional payment m is equivalent to risklessly raising all state-contingent incomes by the same amount. The corresponding welfare effect is given by the derivative of the welfare function in the direction of the equal-revenue vector, $\Sigma_{s\in\Omega} W_s(\mathbf{y}(m, i))$. On the other hand, raising the revenue premium, i, lowers the return the farmer realizes from a given vector of state-contingent revenues and thus lowers welfare. The welfare effect is given by $-\Sigma_{s\in\Omega} W_s(\mathbf{y}(m,i))r_s(m,i)$. Any increase in the unconditional payment must be balanced by an increase in the revenue premium to maintain indifference.

The slope of the insurer's indifference curve is given by

$$\frac{dm}{di} = \frac{\sum_{s\in\Omega} \pi_s r_s(m,i)\left(1+\frac{i}{r_s(m,i)}\frac{\partial r_s(m,i)}{\partial i}\right)}{1-i\sum_{s\in\Omega}\pi_s \frac{\partial r_s(m,i)}{\partial m}}.$$

We will simplify by assuming that preferences display constant absolute risk aversion, so that (see Example 7.4)

$$\frac{\partial r_s(m,i)}{\partial m} = 0.$$

Observing that when $i = 0$,

$$1+\frac{i}{r_s(m,i)}\frac{\partial r_s(m,i)}{\partial i} = 1,$$

whereas, as we have shown before, as i approaches unity, $r_s(m, i)$ goes to zero, and therefore

$$\left[1+\frac{i}{r_s(m,i)}\frac{\partial r_s(m,i)}{\partial i}\right] \to -\infty.$$

We may conclude that, provided $\partial r_s(m, i)/\partial i$ is suitably stable, dm/di will be monotonically decreasing and have a single zero. Hence, there will exist a unique tangency between the insurer's indifference curve, corresponding to zero expected profit, and the farmer's indifference curve.

This result may be explained as follows. An increase in the unconditional payment m, with a corresponding increase in i, has two effects. The first is the change in payments by the insurer $m - ir$. Since this change is positively correlated with net income $(1 - i)r + m$, and the expected value of $m - ir$ is unchanged, this effect is beneficial. The second effect arises from the reduction in r induced by the higher value of i. For values of i close to zero, the welfare effect of reduced output will also be close to zero, and the insurance effect will dominate. For larger values of i, the welfare effect of reduced output will grow while, since net income is less risky, the marginal insurance benefit will decline. Hence, there will exist a unique optimal $i \in [0, 1]$.

7.6 DISCUSSION

Some of this analysis has previously been developed for the case of expected-utility preferences and a technology based on stochastic production functions (Chambers 1989b; Nelson and Loehman 1987). The presumption of expected-utility maximization is particularly limiting because, as has been previously observed by Segal and Spivak (1990), the smoothness property of expected utility is crucial in deriving the result that less than full insurance will be chosen when the contract is actuarially unfair. We have shown (Result 7.5) that a producer with suitably kinked indifference maps can demand full insurance even if the odds are actuarially unfair from the insurer's perspective. The earlier restriction of the technology to the stochastic production function technology is unnecessary and limiting. Indeed, because the arbitrage condition (7.8) does not apply when the cost function is not differentiable, the stochastic production function is an intractable special case with implausible consequences (see examples 7.1 and 7.5). This limitation is particularly noticeable in the consideration of nonstate-contingent insurance contracts, where, for general differentiable cost functions, the effect of insurance in reducing the optimal scale of output is nicely characterized by (7.13).

The main purpose of the analysis has been to show how the state-contingent approach permits a complete theory of production insurance. However, many obvious extensions of our results suggest themselves. One is to drop the restriction to linear nonstate-contingent insurance contracts and allow for arbitrary payment schedules. This issue may be addressed using the methods developed in Chapters 8 to 10.

A second line of development is the analysis of more richly specified state spaces. Consider, for example, the case of rainfall insurance. If rainfall is the only state variable relevant to the determination of yields, and prices are certain, the preceding analysis shows that a rainfall insurance scheme will result in perfect insurance and the choice by all farmers of the output vector that maximizes expected profit. In reality, however, other factors such as pest infestations will affect yields, and farmers will also be affected by price uncertainty. To analyze a problem of this kind, the state space (see Chapter 1) may be considered as the Cartesian product of a set of possible rainfall levels and a set of other possible conditions affecting yields. Demand shocks may be taken into account by taking an additional Cartesian product.

Finally, it is a straightforward extension of the approaches in this chapter and Chapter 6 to analyze the properties of pure yield-based insurance contracts or yield-based futures contracts.

8 Production and Nonpoint-Source Pollution Regulation

Chapters 6 and 7 demonstrated that providing insurance mechanisms for risk-averse decision makers fundamentally changes their economic decisions. This chapter examines a slightly more complicated, and more realistic, version of the crop-insurance problem of Chapter 7. Now, instead of producing only crop and livestock outputs, the farmer also produces a "bad" output that we can think of intuitively as harmful chemical runoff from the farmer's land. Because runoff is a by-product of a lucrative activity for farmers, chemical runoff has a positive shadow value to farmers. Runoff, however, pollutes water and other ecosystems. Therefore, although farmers have private incentives to emit runoff, society at large wants to control runoff. If runoff were easily detected, the solution would be obvious and easy: make farmers bear the marginal social cost of their pollution. But runoff, by its very nature, is hard to detect. Even constant monitoring may not permit determination of the true extent of runoff because some runoff results from chemicals and other agents percolating through the soil into underground water supplies.

Government, therefore, lacks the capacity to implement a complete monitoring–taxation solution to the problem. To emphasize this aspect of the problem, we assume that runoff is only detectable and measurable (if at all) *after* it has entered the ecosystem. By then, identifying its original source (that is, the emitting farmer) is impossible. Chemical runoff is a *nonpoint-source pollutant*. Its effects can be felt, but its source cannot be identified. And since private insurers generally have no incentive to prevent farmers from polluting, runoff emission involves an externality between the farmer and rest of society. Government intervention seems needed.

Although pollution control is socially desirable, as our discussion of insurability showed in Chapter 7, it's also socially desirable to spread the production risk farmers face across the rest of society. Therein lies the rub, because mechanisms, such as futures markets or crop-insurance contracts, that mitigate the farmer's risk can also affect pollution incentives. For example, as we pointed out in Chapter 4, nitrogen fertilizer is usually thought of as a risk-increasing input, or, in our terminology, as a risk complement. If this is true, then insuring farmers, and thus making them marginally less risk-averse, should increase fertilizer use and, thereby, nitrogen runoff. The insurance objective and the runoff-control objective conflict.

In designing schemes to cope jointly with the social need for insurance and the associated pollution externality, one should recognize that monitoring all the actions that farmers take in organizing production is not feasible. In particular, "effort" to promote crops and livestock growth and to control runoff cannot be disentangled from one another and are unobservable. Moreover, because the farmer is the residual claimant and first handler of the crops and livestock produced, she can always divert them to her own consumption. This is particularly important when one pollution-producing output, for example, corn, is used by the farmer as an intermediate input in producing another pollution-producing output, for example, hogs. Hence, contrary to our assumptions in Chapter 7, ex post output may be observable only with constant (and prohibitively costly) monitoring. As a result, output-contingent insurance schemes of the type discussed in Chapter 7 could lead farmers to misrepresent their output if it were to their advantage. To emphasize this aspect of the problem, in this chapter we will assume that output is not observable, but that the state of nature is. In Chapter 9, we will turn the problem on its head and consider what happens when output is observable but the state of nature is not.

In the following sections, we first introduce the model. After we discuss the "first-best problem," we formulate the more realistic production-pollution problem and show it to be equivalent to an unconstrained nonlinear programming problem. The remaining sections discuss the properties of the optimal incentive scheme. Among other results, we establish that the optimal mechanism obeys a generalized version of the "inverse-elasticity" rule, and that pollution control generally requires leaving the farmer with a higher return in those states where the ability to emit pollution lowers the marginal cost of production, and a lower return in those states where pollution increases the marginal cost of production.

8.1 THE MODEL

Assume that there are three individuals: a corn farmer who produces both runoff and corn under conditions of uncertainty; an aggregate individual "Society"; and a planner. Only the farmer engages in productive activity. Uncertainty is modeled by "Nature" making a choice from among a finite set of alternatives. As usual, each of these alternatives is called a "state" and is indexed by a finite set of the form $\Omega = \{1, 2, 3, \ldots, S\}$. Once the index is given, all possible factors determining production and contracting conditions (weather, etc.) are known.

8.1.1 Preferences and Technology

Society is presumed to be risk-neutral over different wealth levels, while each farmer's preference structure does not depend on pollution directly. Rather, the farmer only cares about the single crop that she produces, which for mnemonic purposes we call corn, and the effort vector **x** that she uses to produce corn. We normalize the price of corn at one and assume that the farmer's preferences over returns and effort are given by a separable effort objective function of the form:

$$V(\mathbf{y}, \mathbf{x}) = W(\mathbf{y}) - g(\mathbf{x}).$$

Where $\mathbf{y} \in \Re^s$ denotes the farmer's vector of state-contingent consumption levels, $W(\mathbf{y})$ is generalized Schur-concave, and $g(\mathbf{x})$ is convex and nondecreasing in elements of the effort vector. We shall assume that $W(\mathbf{y})$ is smoothly differentiable unless otherwise noted.

Let **n** be a vector of state-contingent pollution levels and **z** a vector of state-contingent outputs. Production relations are governed by the state-contingent input correspondence X: $\Re_+^{2\times S} \to \Re_+^n$

$$X(\mathbf{n}, \mathbf{z}) = \{\mathbf{x} : \mathbf{x} \text{ can produce } (\mathbf{n}, \mathbf{z})\}.$$

It is assumed that **x** contains any inputs that are used solely for "abatement activities." We recognize that abatement actually involves a complex interaction between a number of inputs that cannot be separated from other production activities. This contrasts with previous principal–agent analyses of the relationship between production and pollution that unrealistically assume that abatement activities can be captured by a single scalar, or even discrete, variable. Consider, for example, the problem of nitrogen runoff. Nitrogen runoff depends not only on the farmer's direct abatement activities, such as building catchments to prevent runoff, but also on the amount of nitrogen applied, the care with which it is applied, the application of irrigation, and a host of other activities. Each of the latter have an abatement component, which cannot be trivially separated from their other roles in the production process.

Our general representation allows both pollution and corn output levels to be subject to uncertainty. However, for notational simplicity, we shall always treat $n \in \Re_+$ (one pollution level occurs in all states). Ex post, pollution in the amount n imposes a burden on society of $m(n)$, where $m: \Re_+ \to \Re_+$ is strictly increasing, strictly convex, and differentiable.[1]

8.1.2 Two Cost Functions

Two indirect representations of $X(n, \mathbf{z})$ are useful. The first is the *effort-cost function* defined by

$$c(n, \mathbf{z}) = \min_{\mathbf{x}} \{g(\mathbf{x}) : \mathbf{x} \in X(n, \mathbf{z})\}.$$

This is the effort-cost function defined in Chapter 4, with the output vector separated into its components n and $\mathbf{z}$. If X is a convex correspondence and exhibits free disposability of $\mathbf{z}$, $c(n, \mathbf{z})$ is nondecreasing in $\mathbf{z}$, and convex and continuous for both n and $\mathbf{z}$ restricted to the strictly positive orthant. We strengthen these technical requirements to permit the use of the calculus, by assuming that c is strictly convex in $\mathbf{z}$ and n, increasing in $\mathbf{z}$, and twice differentiable.

1. Results for nonscalar n, of course, are somewhat less clear-cut, but the same basic principles apply. The main difference that would emerge in our analysis would be that $n(z)$ and n defined in what follows would be vectors, and the discussions of *marginal-cost-reducing pollution* and risk-complementary and risk-substitute pollution would need to be modified to take account of that fact.

We define the farmer's *private-cost function* by

$$C(\mathbf{z}) = \min_n c(n, \mathbf{z}).$$

We call this the private-cost function to emphasize that the farmer privately chooses her optimal level of pollution, which is unobservable to the planner. For simplicity, we assume that a minimum exists for all relevant state-contingent output vectors. The strict convexity of $c(n, \mathbf{z})$ then guarantees that the farmer's optimal pollution choice for that vector of state-contingent corn production, denoted

$$n(\mathbf{z}) = \arg\min c(n, \mathbf{z}),$$

is unique, and that $C(\mathbf{z})$ is convex. To verify that $C(\mathbf{z})$ is convex, notice that the convexity of $c(n, \mathbf{z})$ ensures that

$$c(\lambda n(\mathbf{z}^o) + (1-\lambda)n(\mathbf{z}'), \lambda\mathbf{z}^o + (1-\lambda)\mathbf{z}')$$
$$\leq \lambda c(n(\mathbf{z}^o), \mathbf{z}^o) + (1-\lambda)c(n(\mathbf{z}'), \mathbf{z}').$$

Now because $\lambda n(\mathbf{z}^o) + (1 - \lambda)n(\mathbf{z}')$ is a potentially optimal level of nitrogen pollution for the state-contingent corn vector $\lambda\mathbf{z}^o + (1 - \lambda)\mathbf{z}'$, it follows that

$$c(n(\lambda\mathbf{z}^o + (1-\lambda)\mathbf{z}'), \lambda\mathbf{z}^o + (1-\lambda)\mathbf{z}')$$
$$\leq c(\lambda n(\mathbf{z}^o) + (1-\lambda)n(\mathbf{z}'), \lambda\mathbf{z}^o + (1-\lambda)\mathbf{z}'),$$

which establishes the desired convexity property. We assume that $C(\mathbf{z})$ is at least twice-differentiable and that $C_s(\mathbf{z})$ denotes the partial derivative of $C(\mathbf{z})$ with respect to z_s.

The first-order condition of the private-cost minimization problem requires the farmer's private marginal benefit from pollution to equal zero for an interior solution:

$$-c_n(n(\mathbf{z}), \mathbf{z}) = 0.$$

Given the convexity of $c(n, \mathbf{z})$ in n, differentiating this equilibrium condition implicitly shows that the way in which $n(\mathbf{z})$ reacts to changes in $\mathbf{z}$ is determined by the vector of second-partial derivatives with typical element $c_{ns}(n, \mathbf{z})$, $s \in \Omega$. In particular,

$$n_s(\mathbf{z}) \equiv \frac{\partial n(\mathbf{z})}{\partial z_s} = \frac{-c_{ns}(n(\mathbf{z}), \mathbf{z})}{c_{nn}(n(\mathbf{z}), \mathbf{z})},$$

which by the convexity of effort cost in pollution has the same sign as $-c_{ns}(n(\mathbf{z}), \mathbf{z})$. Accordingly, if a small increase in z_s increases the farmer's marginal benefit from pollution, that is, $c_{ns}(n, \mathbf{z}) < 0$, it will be associated with an increase in $n(\mathbf{z})$. Alternatively, by Young's Theorem,

$$n_s(\mathbf{z}) = \frac{-c_{sn}(n(\mathbf{z}), \mathbf{z})}{c_{nn}(n(\mathbf{z}), \mathbf{z})} \tag{8.1}$$

is positive (negative) if and only if an increase in n decreases (increases) the marginal cost of producing z_s.

To avoid technical difficulties associated with corner solutions, we also presume that the following *Inada conditions* are in force:

$$\lim_{z_s \to 0} C_s(\mathbf{z}) = 0$$

($s = 1, \ldots, S$), and

$$\lim_{y_s \to 0} W_s'(\mathbf{y}) = \infty.$$

8.1.3 The Planner

The planner is assumed to be a governmental entity that has sufficient legal authority to enforce contracts and that can commit to a corn-insurance scheme. The planner's task is to design a scheme that appropriately shares with society the production risk faced by farmers, and that provides farmers with the appropriate incentive for pollution control. The planner is assumed to know X, W, g, and m, and to observe ex post the state of nature.[2] Only the farmer knows effort and pollution. Therefore, although the planner, ex post, knows the technology and observes the physical state of nature (amount of rainfall, temperature-degree days, and so on), the planner does not observe the exact conditions under which production takes place. In short, *hidden action* exists in the sense that the farmer takes actions with consequences for all, but which remain hidden from the planner and others in society. We assume that pollution is either unobservable or noncontractible. Because the state of nature is jointly observable by the farmer and the planner, it can form the basis of a contract, and it is contractible in the sense that we used in Chapter 7. The insurance–pollution-control mechanism that the planner presents

2. See Chapters 1 and 7 for a discussion of the implications of this assumption.

to the farmer is represented by the vector of state-contingent net premiums $P \in \Re^S$ that we shall count in corn units.[3] (P_s can be either positive or negative [$s = 1, \dots, S$].)

8.2 THE FIRST BEST

For later comparison, a representation of the first best is convenient. Here the term "first best" is reserved for the situation where the planner can observe output, effort, and runoff pollution. The first best solves

$$\max_{n,\mathbf{z},P}\left\{\sum_{s\in\Omega}\pi_s P_s + W(\mathbf{z}-\mathbf{P}) - c(n,\mathbf{z}) - m(n)\right\},$$

where n, $\mathbf{z}$, and $P \in \Re^S$ are, respectively, the pollution level, state-contingent corn vector, and the state-contingent, net-insurance-premium vector.[4] Here $\boldsymbol{\pi} \in \Pi$ denotes a common vector of probabilities for which Society is risk-neutral and the farmer is risk-averse (see Chapter 3).

Optimizing with respect to the pollution level n gives

$$m'(n) + \frac{\partial c(n,\mathbf{z})}{\partial n} = 0$$

for an interior solution. The socially optimal level of pollution is determined by equating the marginal private benefit to the farmer of increasing pollution to its marginal social damage. Because the farmer benefits from pollution by reducing her cost of corn production, the socially optimal level of pollution will not generally be zero. Although pollution harms some individuals, it also has a positive economic rôle to play in reducing the farmer's costs.

Optimizing with respect to P_s gives, for an interior solution (ensured by the Inada conditions),

3. Notice, here, that in contrast with Chapter 7, where we worked in terms of net indemnities, we now find it convenient to work in terms of net premiums.
4. Strictly speaking, we should represent the planner's objective function in terms of the producer's certainty equivalent to ensure that we are always summing entities that can be enumerated in monetary units. However, as we showed in Chapter 3, the certainty equivalent is just a monotonic transformation of the preference structure, so little true generality is lost by proceeding in this manner.

$$\pi_s - W_s(\mathbf{z} - \mathbf{P}) = 0, \qquad s \in \Omega. \tag{8.2}$$

Expression (8.2) is yet another manifestation of Borch's (1962) rule for optimal risk sharing between risk-averse and risk-neutral individuals. Risk-neutral Society absorbs all the risk and provides the risk-averse farmers with full insurance. (In fact, the assumption that preferences are smoothly differentiable is not needed for this result. As we showed in Chapter 3 and Chapter 7, risk aversion ensures that the farmer's ex post return must be the same in every state of nature.) The following definition is convenient.

> **Definition 8.1:** *The first-best ex post return for the farmer is denoted* y^* *and is defined as the solution to the following implicit equation:*
>
> $$\pi_s - W_s(y^* \mathbf{1}s) = 0, \qquad s \in \Omega.$$

Substituting y^* into the societal objective function and choosing the state-contingent outputs optimally then gives

$$\frac{\partial c(n, \mathbf{z})}{\partial z_s} = \pi_s, \qquad s \in \Omega.$$

The marginal cost of each state-contingent output equals its expected benefit. Hence, as we saw in Chapter 7, the first-best scheme involves a separation between the farmer's production decisions and her risk preferences. She equates the marginal cost of pollution to its social cost and chooses the expected profit-maximizing state-contingent corn vector, which implies, of course, that she produces on the efficient frontier, as defined in Chapter 5. In return, Society provides her with full insurance.

To implement the first-best outcome, the planner can proceed almost exactly as in Chapter 7 after accounting for the effect that pollution has on Society. He specifies a vector of net premiums for the farmer such that

$$\hat{\mathbf{P}} = \hat{\mathbf{z}} - y^* \mathbf{1}^S,$$

and a marginal pollution tax of $m'(\hat{n}) = -c_n(\hat{n}, \hat{\mathbf{z}})$ on departures from the first-best pollution level, where circumflexes (ˆ) over variables denote their first-best values.

A farmer facing this two-part, state-contingent payment chooses $\mathbf{z}$ and n to

$$\max W(\mathbf{z}-\hat{\mathbf{z}}+(y^*+m'(\hat{n})(n-\hat{n}))\mathbf{1}^S)-c(n,\mathbf{z}).$$

The first-order conditions for an interior solution are

$$W_s(\mathbf{z}-\hat{\mathbf{z}}+(y^*+m'(\hat{n})(n-\hat{n}))\mathbf{1}^S)-c_s(n,\mathbf{z})=0,$$

$$\sum_s W_s(\mathbf{z}-\hat{\mathbf{z}}+(y^*+m'(\hat{n})(n-\hat{n}))\mathbf{1}^S)m'(\hat{n})+c_n(n,\mathbf{z})=0.$$

$\hat{\mathbf{z}}$ and $\hat{n}$ solve these equations. For this two-part scheme, Society's welfare is $\Sigma_s(\hat{z}_s - y^*) - m(\hat{n})$. Hence, we have shown that the farmer chooses the first best.

This insurance scheme only requires the ability to enforce a state-contingent net premium structure and a pollution tax. Therefore, it only requires that the state of nature and the level of pollution be observable. The farmer's ex post output need not be observable. (All the planner needs to determine the socially optimal level of state-contingent output, and thereby the optimal net premium in this framework, is knowledge of the farmer's production structure, which we assume he has.) This leads us to state our first result:

> **Result 8.1:** *If the planner observes pollution and* s, *the first best can be achieved even in the absence of ex post observations on output.*

This result extends to our framework a result originally due to Harris and Raviv (1979). The intuition behind it is easily explained. As long as the state of nature and pollution are observable and verifiable, the government can design a two-part payment scheme that transforms farmers into the social-residual claimants for all their production decisions. Because farmers now receive all the direct benefits from corn production and bear all the indirect costs imposed on Society through pollution, the government can rely on the farmer to selfishly choose the optimal vector of state-contingent outputs. Therefore, information on output is superfluous as long as the planner can observe her runoff.

8.3 AN ALGORITHM FOR THE HIDDEN-ACTION CORN-POLLUTION PROBLEM

The planner's task is to design a state-contingent reward scheme that balances the farmer's legitimate need for crop insurance against the adverse incentives that crop insurance may create for pollution control. In doing so, the planner faces several limitations. First, he cannot observe with any degree of accuracy the amount that the farmer pollutes or the amount that she produces. Hence, direct taxes on pollution and indirect taxes on corn production are ruled out. Second, although the planner knows the farmer's technology and preferences, the planner cannot observe the farmer's production practices. Consequently, the planner cannot rely on a command-and-control approach to solving the problem. In a word, production or pollution standards are not an option. And, finally, the planner also has to recognize that any scheme he tries to implement may cause the farmer to change her optimal behavior if his scheme changes the farmer's incentives. If the farmer is economically rational, once the scheme is announced, she will alter her production practices in reaction. This change in production practices, if not anticipated by the planner, can prevent the planner's scheme from having its intended effect.

That leaves the planner in the situation of having to induce the farmer to selfishly take actions that achieve the planner's goals. Given the informational setting we have assumed, the only tool that the planner has to achieve these goals is the vector of state-contingent premiums for the farmers. If the state of nature were not observable by the planner, ex post, the planner's problem would be characterized by both hidden action and hidden information. Because nothing is observable, nothing is contractible. Hence, only a fixed payment (i.e., the same charge in each state of nature) would be feasible. If output, but not the state of nature, is observable ex post, the current model becomes a moral hazard problem of the form discussed in Chapter 9.

We will say that a pollution-output allocation is *implementable* if the producer voluntarily adopts it in reaction to the vector of net premiums. The most basic restriction that must be placed on any implementable ex post pollution-output allocation is that it must be consistent with the self-interested maximizing behavior of the farmer.

Given the output allocation, an implementable pollution level must solve the private-cost-minimization problem. Thus, for the vector of state-contingent premiums, $\boldsymbol{P} \in \Re^S$ the state-contingent output vector must satisfy

$$\mathbf{z} \in \max_{\mathbf{z}}\{W(\mathbf{z}-\mathbf{P})-C(\mathbf{z})\}.$$

The planner's problem is, therefore:

Problem I. *Choose* $\mathbf{P} \in \Re^S$, $z \in \Re^S_+$ *(= 1, 2, . . . ,* N*) to*

$$\max\left\{\sum_{s\in\Omega}\pi_s P_s + W(z-\boldsymbol{P}) - c(n, z) - m(n(z)) : z \in \arg\max\{W(z-\boldsymbol{P}) - C(z)\}\right\}.$$

Intuition suggests that the solution to Problem I corresponds to the first-best solution only if it is in the farmer's private interest not to pollute when the first-best output is produced, that is, only if $n(\hat{\mathbf{z}}) = 0$. In this case, a state-contingent contract specifying $\boldsymbol{P} = \hat{\mathbf{z}} - y^*\mathbf{1}^S$ would lead to the farmer solving

$$\max\{W(\mathbf{z}-\mathbf{P})-C(\mathbf{z})\}$$

to choose $\hat{\mathbf{z}}$.

The converse is also true. First-best optimality requires

$$m' + c_n(\hat{n}, \hat{\mathbf{z}}) \geq 0$$

with equality for an interior optimum. By assumption, $m' > 0$, so an interior optimum cannot arise with $n = \hat{n}$ for any farmer solving the private-cost-minimization problem. Hence, any time that the first best requires polluting a positive amount, it cannot be implemented by the planner.

Result 8.2: *The solution to Problem I yields the first-best outcome if and only if*

$$n(\hat{z}) = 0.$$

Because the first best cannot be achieved if the farmer privately chooses to pollute a positive amount at $\hat{\mathbf{z}}$, the inability of the planner to observe the farmer's pollution carries a social cost that cannot be circumvented. Accordingly,

Corollary 8.2.1: *For any solution to Problem I, unless* $\mathrm{n}(\hat{z}) = 0$*, a social gain would exist if the farmer reduced pollution by a small amount, provided incentive effects are ignored.*

To understand the corollary, notice that the social gain from reducing pollution by a small amount ($\varepsilon > 0$) is (ignoring incentive effects)

$$(m'(n) + c_n(n, \mathbf{z}))\varepsilon,$$

which, by the farmer's private-cost minimization, reduces to

$$m'(n)\varepsilon > 0.$$

Hence, at the solution to Problem I, the planner should always want to reduce pollution further. However, the presence of the incentive constraints makes this further reduction in pollution suboptimal.

We are now ready to consider Problem I directly. Our next result, reminiscent of results in the literature on nonlinear pricing under asymmetric information (Chambers 1989a; Grossman and Hart 1983; Guesnerie and Laffont 1984; Weymark 1986) exploits this fact to establish that solutions to Problem I can be obtained through solving an alternative unconstrained optimization problem.

However, unlike the results of Chambers (1989a), Guesnerie and Laffont (1984), and Weymark (1986), our result is novel in that if we reformulate our model in terms of an expected-utility representation of farmer preferences, it will allow us to use a "first-order approach" to the agent's problem to concentrate the objective function. The approach is based on the recognition that the order of optimization in Problem I is irrelevant. Therefore, it is always possible first to fix **z** in Problem I and to choose the premium vector ***P*** conditional on **z**, which we denote as ***P***(**z**). Once the conditional optimization problem is solved, the **z** can be chosen optimally. Thus:

Result 8.3: *If z solves Problem I, then z also maximizes the following concentrated objective function:*

$$\max_{z}\{\mathrm{R}(z) - \mathrm{C}(z) - \mathrm{m}(\mathrm{n}(z))\},$$

where

$$\mathrm{R}(z) = \max_{\mathrm{P}}\left\{\sum_{s \in \Omega} \pi_s \mathrm{P}_s + \mathrm{W}(z - \boldsymbol{P}) : z \in \arg\max\{\mathrm{W}(z - \boldsymbol{P}) - \mathrm{C}(z)\}\right\}.$$

$R(\mathbf{z})$ is the maximum social return obtainable from the state-contingent vector $\mathbf{z}$ given the farmer's ability to privately choose her pollution level. The elements of its optimal solution,

$$P(\mathbf{z}) \in \arg\max\left\{\sum_{s\in\Omega} \pi_s P_s + W(\mathbf{z}-\mathbf{P}) : \mathbf{z} \right.$$
$$\left. \in \arg\max\{W(\mathbf{z}-\mathbf{P}) - C(\mathbf{z})\}\right\},$$

give the state-contingent net premiums that will simultaneously make it individually rational for the farmer to choose to produce the state-contingent vector $\mathbf{z}$ and make $\Sigma_{s\in\Omega}\pi_s P_s + W(\mathbf{z} - \boldsymbol{P})$ as large as possible subject to the constraint that the farmer's optimal reaction, once presented with $\boldsymbol{P}(\mathbf{z})$, is to choose $\mathbf{z}$.

If the farmer's preferences can be represented by a strictly concave expected-utility function satisfying the Inada condition $\lim_{y\to 0} u'(\mathbf{y}) = \infty$, then given the convexity of the farmer's private-cost function, the first-order conditions for $\mathbf{z}$ in the farmer's optimization problem are necessary and sufficient conditions for an unique optimum. Hence, $\boldsymbol{P}(\mathbf{z})$ can be obtained by inverting the farmer's first-order conditions

$$\pi_s u'(z_s - P_s(\mathbf{z})) = C_s(\mathbf{z}), \qquad s \in \Omega$$

to obtain

$$P_s(\mathbf{z}) = z_s - h\left(\frac{C_s(\mathbf{z})}{\pi_s}\right),$$

where $h(\cdot)$ is the inverse of $u'(\cdot)$. (This inverse must exist by the strict concavity of the expected-utility function.)

> **Corollary 8.3.1:** *If* W *is a strictly concave, smoothly differentiable, expected-utility function satisfying the Inada condition, then*
>
> $$\frac{\partial P_i(z)}{\partial z_i} = 1 - \frac{C_{ii}(z)/\pi_i}{u''(z_i - P_i)} \geq 1,$$
> $$\frac{\partial P_i(z)}{\partial z_j} = -\frac{C_{ij}(z)/\pi_i}{u''(z_i - P_i)}.$$

One cost structure that yields especially sharp results on $\boldsymbol{P}(\mathbf{z})$ in this context is that of state-allocable inputs (Chapters 2 and 4) when the effort-cost function assumes the general form

$$c(n, \mathbf{z}) = \left\{ \sum_{s \in \Omega} c_s(n_s, z_s) : n = \sum_{s \in \Omega} n_s \right\}.$$

This corresponds to the case where pollution plays a state-specific role in affecting the cost of producing state-contingent outputs. Pollution, in essence, is allocable across states of nature. It follows immediately that for this case

$$\begin{aligned} C(\mathbf{z}) &= \min \left\{ \sum_{s \in \Omega} c_s(n_s, z_s) : n = \sum_{s \in \Omega} n_s \right\} \\ &= \sum_{s \in \Omega} \min\{c_s(n_s, z_s)\} \\ &= \sum_{s \in \Omega} \chi_s(z_s), \end{aligned}$$

where $X_s(z_s)$ $(s \in \Omega)$ will always be assumed to be increasing, convex, and twice differentiable. We shall refer to this case as *pollution being allocable across states of nature*.

Several points should be noticed about Result 8.3 and its corollary. First, a simple closed-form solution to the farmer's optimization problem always exists under the expected-utility hypothesis. This follows from the Inada conditions, and contrasts strongly with other principal–agent problems (Grossman and Hart 1983; Holmstrom 1979). However, if the Inada conditions are relaxed, but the expected-utility hypothesis is maintained, a set of expressions based on the Kuhn–Tucker conditions replaces those in Result 8.3 and Corollary 8.3.1. *The decomposition of the problem always applies*. Second, the responsiveness of $\boldsymbol{P}(\mathbf{z})$ to changes in $\mathbf{z}$ has two key determinants: the farmer's attitudes toward corn risk and the effort-cost interdependencies (as measured by the second partial derivatives of the private-cost function between state-contingent outputs, C_{st}) between different states of nature. These effort-cost interdependencies measure the cost of self-insuring, and hence the responsiveness of $\boldsymbol{P}(\mathbf{z})$ is determined by the farmer's desire for insurance versus the cost of self-insurance.

The net premiums, $P_s(\mathbf{z})$, are the ones that would rationalize a privately optimizing farmer choosing the vector of state-contingent outputs, $\mathbf{z}$. These net premiums have the characteristic that, all else constant, the more risk-averse the farmer, the closer they will come to fully insuring the farmer by providing her with a fixed return in each state, that is, $\partial P_s(z)/\partial z_s = 1$, $\partial P_s(z)/\partial z_t = 0, s \neq t$. This is as it should be: a first-best crop-insurance contract fully insures the farmer. But fully insuring a risk-averse farmer does not give the appropriate incentives to control nonobservable pollution runoff, especially if pollution is associated with the use of a risk-complementary input. Hence, the ability to pollute without being observed means that the incentive contract must balance gains in controlling pollution obtained from manipulating the incentive scheme against losses in risk sharing that emerge from not fully insuring the farmer.

An optimal incentive contract in the presence of this form of hidden action requires the farmer to self-insure in the sense described in Chapter 7. The farmer has to bear some of the production risk. However, the more risk-averse the farmer, the larger will be the social losses that arise from not fully insuring the farmer. The larger these losses become, the more they tend to outweigh any efficiency gains obtained by making the farmer self-insure. We close this section with an example that illustrates both this point and the role that the differentiability assumptions play in determining unique solutions.

Example 8.1: *Suppose that the farmer's preferences are maximin:*

$$W(\boldsymbol{y}) = \min\{y_1, \ldots y_S\}.$$

Suppose also that the planner specifies the state-contingent premium vector $\tilde{\boldsymbol{P}}$. *As we saw in Chapters 5 and 7, when presented with this set of state-contingent premiums, the farmer stabilizes income across the states of nature. She chooses the corn-production vector*

$$\tilde{P}_s + \tilde{y} = z_s, \qquad s \in \Omega,$$

where

$$\tilde{y} \in \arg\max_{y}\{y - C(y\boldsymbol{1}^S + \tilde{\boldsymbol{P}})\},$$

if such an income level exists. In words, this means that the farmer increases all state-contingent outputs equally until she encounters the efficient frontier. From that point, she uses the state-contingent premium vector to move to her maximal point on the equal-revenue vector. One can visualize this decision process with the aid of Figure 8.1. As we have drawn it, the farmer pays

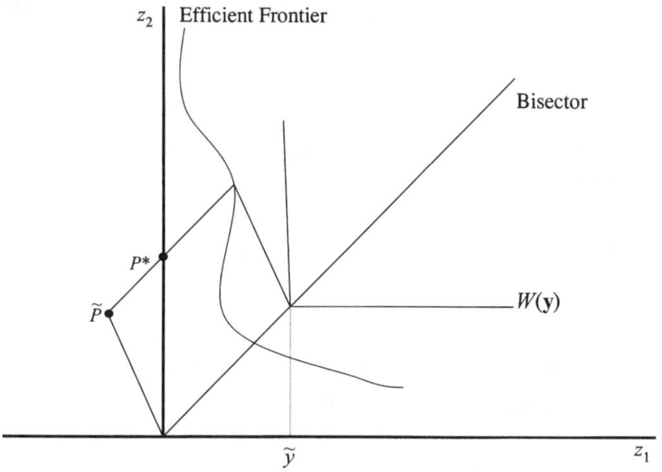

Figure 8.1 Maximin preferences and implementability.

a positive net premium (makes a net payment) in state 2 and pays a negative net premium (the indemnity exceeds the premium so the farmer receives a positive payment) in state 1. To determine her optimal production mix, she moves from $\tilde{\boldsymbol{P}}$ *parallel to the bisector until she encounters the efficient frontier, and then she trades from that production point to the point on the bisector* $\tilde{y}\boldsymbol{I}^S$

In contrast to the situation depicted for the differentiable expected-utility model, the farmer chooses her production vector to ensure that she is fully insured against production risk. Full insurance is optimal here precisely because the farmer is infinitely risk-averse. (Intuitively, it is the extreme limit of the earlier expected-utility model.) Going the other way, we see, therefore, that the only state-contingent crop vectors that can be implemented are ones that lie in the efficient set. And, moreover, we can immediately conclude that many different premium vectors can implement the same production point when preferences are maximin, as long as the production point is in the efficient set. Notice, that if $\tilde{\boldsymbol{P}}$ *implements* $\mathbf{z}$*, any positive translation of* $\tilde{\boldsymbol{P}}$ *parallel to the equal-revenue ray also implements* $\mathbf{z}$*. In Figure 8.1, this can be illustrated, for example, by noting that the point* $\boldsymbol{P}^*$ *implements the same point on the efficient frontier as* $\tilde{\boldsymbol{P}}$*.*

8.4 THE OPTIMAL INCENTIVE SCHEME AND PUBLIC PRICING

Using Result 8.3, for an interior optimum, that is, $z_s > 0$ ($s = 1, 2, \ldots, S$) the first-order necessary conditions for the planner's problem after using the farmer's first-order conditions require

$$\sum_{t\in\Omega}(\pi_t - W_t(\mathbf{z}-\mathbf{P}))\frac{\partial P_t}{\partial z_s} = m'(n)n_s(\mathbf{z}), \qquad s\in\Omega. \tag{8.3}$$

The right-hand side of (8.3) is the marginal pollution damage (benefit) caused by altering state-s contingent production. Because the private marginal cost of z_s can be increasing or decreasing in pollution depending on the role that pollution plays in the production process, $n_s(\mathbf{z})$ can be either negative or positive. The expression on the left-hand side is the inner product of the vector of differences between Society's marginal utility of corn and the farmer's ex post marginal utility of corn and the vector $\{\partial P_t(\mathbf{z})/\partial z_s\}$.

Because social efficiency in the absence of hidden action requires the farmer to be fully insured, that is,

$$\pi_t = W_t(\mathbf{z}-\mathbf{P}))$$

for every t, the expression $\pi_t - W_t(\mathbf{z} - \boldsymbol{P})$ can be rewritten as $(W_t(y^*\mathbf{1}) - W_t(\mathbf{z} - \boldsymbol{P}))$. This latter term measures the departure from complete risk sharing as required by the first best. Hence, expression (8.3) generalizes the well-known "inverse-elasticity" rule familiar from the public-pricing literature by requiring that divergences from perfect risk sharing should be inversely related to the $\partial P_t(\mathbf{z})/\partial z_s$.

Some interesting results follow from this observation. If, contrary to our assumptions, there's no pollution externality, that is, $m'(\cdot) = 0$ for all n, these divergences from complete risk sharing must be orthogonal to $\{\partial P_t(\mathbf{z})/\partial z_s\}$ for all s. Because the origin is orthogonal to all vectors, complete risk sharing is then consistent with the first-order conditions for optimality. This is as it should be. Results 1 and 2 together demonstrate that in the absence of the pollution externality, the first best can always be achieved by the choice of an appropriate state-contingent contract that provides full insurance to farmers. Because the farmer is the residual claimant for her production decision, when there's no pollution externality, she's the only one affected by these decisions, and Society's sole role in our model is to act as an insurer. As we saw in Chapter 7, the social optimum then requires farmers' ex post income to be the same in each state of nature, and that farmers choose n to minimize the cost of the associated ex post output vector.

When farmers' preferences are of the expected-utility form, (8.3) implies

$$\sum_t (\pi_t - \pi_t u'(z_t - P_t)) \frac{\partial P_t}{\partial z_s} = m'(n) n_s(\mathbf{z}).$$

If all state-contingent outputs are gross substitutes for one another in the private-cost-minimization problem (that is, $C_{st}(\mathbf{z}) \geq 0$, $\forall s, t$), then Corollary 8.3.1 implies $\partial P_t / \partial z_s \geq 0$ for all s and t. Moreover by (8.1), if pollution increases the marginal cost of state s's contingent output, the right-hand side of this expression is negative. Thus, at least one expression under the summation on the left-hand side must also be negative, so that for at least one t, $\pi_t - \pi_t u'(z_t - P_t) < 0$. The strict concavity of u, as required by strict risk aversion, then implies $z_t - P_t < y^*$. This leads us to the following result:

> **Result 8.4:** *If farmers' preferences are of the expected utility form, all state-contingent outputs are gross substitutes in the private-cost-minimization problem, and at least one state-contingent output's private marginal cost is increasing in pollution, at an interior optimum, there must exist a (at least one) state* t *for which* $y^* > z_t - P_t$. *If all state-contingent outputs are gross substitutes in the private-cost-minimization problem and at least one state-contingent output's private marginal cost is decreasing in pollution, at an interior optimum there must exist a (at least one) state* t *for which* $y^* < z_t - P_t$.

If pollution increases some marginal costs but not others, and the private-cost problem is characterized by gross substitutability among state-contingent outputs, it will be optimal for the planner to design a state-contingent insurance scheme that ensures that the farmer receives a smaller ex post return in some states (and a higher in others) than in the first best. Typically, therefore, the planner's optimal response to his inability to observe the farmer's pollution choices is to make the farmer self-insure by designing the state-contingent premium scheme so that her optimal response to it leaves her exposed to some upside and some downside risk. This jiggling of the state-contingent premiums is particularly evident when there are only two states of nature.

When $S = 2$, expression (8.3) implies for the expected-utility case that

$$(\pi_1 - \pi_1 u'(z_1 - P_1))\frac{\partial P_1}{\partial z_s} + (\pi_2 - \pi_2 u'(z_2 - P_2))\frac{\partial P_2}{\partial z_s} = m'(n)n_s(\mathbf{z}),$$

$s = 1, 2$. Solving yields

$$(\pi_1 - \pi_1 u'(z_1 - P_1)) = D^{-1}m'(n)\left[n_1(\mathbf{z})\frac{\partial P_2}{\partial z_2} - n_2(\mathbf{z})\frac{\partial P_2}{\partial z_1}\right],$$

$$(\pi_2 - \pi_2 u'(z_2 - P_2)) = D^{-1}m'(n)\left[n_2(\mathbf{z})\frac{\partial P_1}{\partial z_1} - n_1(\mathbf{z})\frac{\partial P_1}{\partial z_2}\right],$$

where $D > 0$ by the strict concavity of u and the convexity of C. Applying Corollary 8.3.1 gives:

> **Result 8.5:** *Suppose that* S = 2, *that the farmer has expected-utility preferences, that all state-contingent outputs are gross substitutes, and that pollution decreases the marginal cost of* z_1 *but increases the marginal cost of* z_2, *then at an interior optimum* $z_1 - P_1 > y^* > z_2 - P_2$.

Result 8.5 shows that the farmer's ex post return is highest for the state in which pollution decreases marginal cost and lowest in the state in which pollution increases marginal cost. When pollution decreases a state-contingent output's marginal cost, increases in that state-contingent output will lead the farmer to increase her pollution level in the solution to the private-cost-minimization problem. Hence, providing marginal incentives for producing more of that output also encourages pollution because it raises the farmer's shadow return from polluting. In designing the insurance–pollution-control scheme, the planner wants to blunt and not enhance the farmer's pollution incentives. Hence, he will try to avoid encouraging the production of state-contingent outputs whose marginal cost is decreasing in the pollution activity.

As we saw before, the incentive problems associated with fully insuring farmers arise because insurance typically gives the farmer inappropriate incentives for pollution control. Thus, some of the benefits from optimal risk sharing must be traded for marginal gains in pollution control. It is this latter fact that will lead the planner to tilt the premium schedule away from perfect insurance toward having the farmer bear some of the risk. Because the farmer is risk-averse and the residual claimant for her production, this tilting entails allowing the farmer a larger ex post return in those states where output raises the shadow return from polluting, thus blunting the marginal incentive to increase that state-contingent output (and hence pollution). Conversely, providing the farmer with a smaller ex post return for states in which pollution tends to increase marginal cost provides a greater marginal incentive for increasing that state-contingent output (thereby diminishing pollution).

The connection between the inverse-elasticity rule and the optimal mechanism is most apparent in the presence of state-allocable pollution, when the private-cost function can be written as

$$C(\mathbf{z}) = \sum_{s\in\Omega} \chi_s(z_s).$$

Applying Corollary 8.3.1 now gives

$$\frac{\partial P_t(\mathbf{z})}{\partial z_s} = 0, \qquad s \neq t.$$

Expression (8.3) for P_s ($s \in \Omega$) now reduces to

$$\{[\pi_s - \pi_s u'(z_s - P_s)][\partial P_s / \partial z_s]\} = m'(n)n_s(\mathbf{z}).$$

Result 8.6: *If the farmer's preferences are of the expected-utility form, and pollution is allocable across states, an interior optimal mechanism satisfies*

$$\frac{\partial P_s(z)}{\partial z_s}(1 - u'(z_s - P_s)) = \frac{m'(n)n_s(z)}{\pi_s}, \qquad s \in \Omega.$$

A trade-off exists between the risk sharing and pollution abatement that any state-contingent premium schedule must accommodate. The presence of state-allocable pollution crystallizes this trade-off. Now, the level of pollution allocated to each state depends only on the level of output in that state. Hence, it's intuitively appealing that the divergence from optimal risk sharing and the marginal externality associated with z_s have the same sign. Moreover, the marginal pollution externality is always at least as large as the divergence from optimal risk sharing (in absolute value). (Recall from Corollary 8.3.1 that $\partial P_s(\mathbf{z})/\partial z_s \geq 1$.)

It also follows from Result 8.6 that the more responsive $P_s(\mathbf{z})$ is to changes in z_s, the smaller will be the departure from optimal risk sharing required to accommodate a given marginal pollution externality. The intuition is apparent. With state-allocable inputs, $\partial P_s(\mathbf{z})/\partial z_s$ is the reciprocal of the change in z_s that a risk-averse farmer makes to respond to small changes in P_s. Moreover, $\partial P_s(\mathbf{z})/\partial z_s$ varies inversely with the farmer's risk aversion. Hence, when $\partial P_s(z_s)/\partial z_s$ is large, the farmer is not very risk-averse, and because she isn't very risk-averse, changes in the P schedule are relatively ineffective in changing production (and hence pollution) behavior because such changes have relatively little effect on the farmer's marginal utility. So no matter how much P is tilted in the s state, the farmer's optimal choice of the state-contingent output remains relatively stable. And, consequently, tilting P doesn't affect the amount of pollution that is allocated to that state of nature. Marginal departures from optimal risk sharing in those states, therefore, bring little if any gain in pollution control precisely because they do not cause any changes in the farmer's production of state-contingent outputs. Realizing this, a rational planner will recognize that only in states where tilting the incentive scheme affects production behavior significantly can one expect to have a significant effect on the farmer's pattern of pollution.

> **Corollary 8.6.1:** *Under the conditions of Result 8.6,* $y^* < z_s - P_s$ *if pollution decreases the private marginal cost of* z_s*; and* $y^* > z_s - P_s$ *if pollution increases the private marginal cost of* z_s*. If pollution is invariant to changes in* z*, then* $y^* = z_s - P_s$.

Corollary 8.6.1 extends Result 8.5 to cover the case of state-allocable pollution. If increasing a state's ex post output increases pollution, then with state-allocable pollution, the best policy is to leave the farmer with a higher return for that state than in the first best. With state-allocable inputs, the farmer effectively prepares for each state of nature independently. So, tilting the incentive scheme in any state affects only that state's contingent output. Thus, if Society decides to charge a low premium in state s, the strictly risk-averse farmer responds by expanding z_s alone. If z_s is complementary with pollution, the result is an added pollution incentive to the farmer.

8.5 RISK-SUBSTITUTING POLLUTION AND THE OPTIMAL RETURN

The preceding section showed that how pollution interacts with the ex post outputs in the private-cost-minimization problem is a crucial determinant of the optimal mechanism. This section takes up a related issue: how the ability to pollute affects the riskiness of the ex post output trajectory. Different production inputs affect the riskiness of output (to the farmer) in different ways. For example, chemical pesticides are usually seen as reducing the riskiness of output because they preserve output even in the worst states (severe pest infestations). Chemical fertilizers, on the other hand, are often seen as increasing the riskiness of output because they can actually decrease production in the event of severe moisture shortfalls. Because chemicals are the original source of much of the runoff pollution, reason then suggests that the degree of pollution will be related to the risk characteristics of the ex post output profile.

As in Chapter 4, we define pollution as a risk-complement (risk-substitute) if the cost-minimizing pollution level is increased with a shift to a riskier (less risky) output vector. For convenience, we restate Lemma 4.1 from that chapter in terms of the private-cost-minimizing pollution level (recall W is generalized Schur-concave):

Lemma 8.1: *Pollution is a risk complement at* z^o *only if for all* s,t $\in \Omega$:

$$\left(\frac{\partial n(z^o)/\partial z_t}{\pi_t} - \frac{\partial n(z^o)/\partial z_s}{\pi_s}\right)(z_t^o - z_s^o) \geq 0.$$

Pollution is a risk substitute at z *only if for all* s,t $\in \Omega$:

$$\left(\frac{\partial n(z^o)/\partial z_t}{\pi_t} - \frac{\partial n(z^o)/\partial z_s}{\pi_s}\right)(z_t^o - z_s^o) \leq 0.$$

Whether pollution is a risk complement or a risk substitute can have important implications for both the optimal incentive scheme and the pattern of the farmer's returns as the following demonstrate. (Recall from Chapter 2 that $\mathbf{z}_{[]}$ denotes the increasing rearrangement of $\mathbf{z}$. In what follows, we shall denote $n_{[s]}(\mathbf{z}) \equiv \partial n(\mathbf{z})/\partial z_{[s]}$.) Let $\mathbf{z}^*$ denote the optimal ex post output trajectory. Then Lemma 8.1 immediately implies:

Result 8.7: *Suppose that pollution is a risk substitute at the optimal state-contingent output. If pollution also decreases the private marginal cost of* $z_{[1]}$ ($n_{[1]}(\mathbf{z}^*) \geq 0$), *then pollution must decrease the private marginal cost of all other* $z_{[s]}$ ($s = 2, \ldots, S$). *Moreover,*

$$0 \leq \frac{n_{[1]}(z^*)}{\pi_{[1]}} \leq \frac{n_{[2]}(z^*)}{\pi_{[2]}} \leq \ldots \leq \frac{n_{[S]}(z^*)}{\pi_{[S]}}.$$

Corollary 8.7.1: *Suppose the farmer's preferences are of the expected-utility form. If there is state-allocable pollution, pollution decreases the private marginal cost of* $z_{[1]}$, *and pollution is a risk substitute; the farmer's optimal return is always greater than the first-best return.*

If pollution decreases the private marginal cost of the lowest state-contingent output, an expansion of that lowest state-contingent output will lead to an increase in pollution activity. If it is also a risk substitute, that is, reductions in the riskiness of the output distribution are associated with higher levels of pollution, then the largest state-contingent outputs will have larger probability-adjusted effects on pollution than the smallest state-contingent outputs. Consequently, pollution must vary positively with all state-contingent outputs. One can think here in terms of a risk substitute that partially generates the pollution runoff, but that also enhances crop growth in all states of nature. (Pesticides are sometimes claimed to have this characteristic of both enhancing output and limiting damage.) If pollution varies directly with all state-contingent outputs, in equilibrium, one expects the farmer's incentives to further expand output to be blunted when compared to the first best. The planner achieves this blunting effect by leaving the risk-averse farmer with higher ex post returns than in the first best.

8.6 SUMMARY

Previous chapters have shown that providing insurance mechanisms for risk-averse decision makers fundamentally changes their economic decisions. This chapter demonstrates that sometimes these changes can have adverse consequences for society that must be taken into account when designing or regulating insurance industries providing insurance to risk-averse farmers. In a world where there are imperfect markets, this is obvious. For example, an insurer who can only imperfectly observe a farmer's actions might insist on the farmer adopting observable risk-reducing practices as a precondition for obtaining insurance. If neither the farmer nor the insurer has an incentive to control the environmental damage associated with these practices, then it's likely that they will not be deployed at a socially optimal level. (An example here might be a commercial insurer insisting on widespread and observable application of chemical pesticides.) This chapter has tried to address this issue. Along the way, we have developed a general method for dealing with these double-headed (more formally, multitask) problems that we hope will prove applicable in a number of other areas. Among other things, our results show that the optimal design of such policies involves balancing the gains from proper provision of insurance against environmental losses. This in turn means that proper design requires an understanding of the role that polluting activities play in production practices and in affecting the farmer's attitudes toward risk.

In the next chapter, we turn the informational structure of this chapter on its head and assume that the state of nature is not observable but that output is. This change leads us directly to the moral-hazard problem briefly discussed in Chapter 7.

9 The Moral-Hazard Problem

In Chapter 7, when we discussed production insurance, and again in Chapter 8, we examined instances where actions taken by one individual stochastically and unobservably affect the welfare of another. When such relationships are subject to contracting or regulation (which can be recognized as a general form of contracting), they lead naturally to the type of problems that have been generically referred to as *principal–agent* or *moral-hazard models*. The moral-hazard problem illustrates the advantages of the state-contingent approach advocated in this book and the weaknesses of its competitors, including the stochastic-production function approach, the parametrized distribution formulation, and the outcome-state formulation. Historically, each of these other approaches has been tried in turn, and found to lead either to implausible corner solutions or to analytically intractable problems.

This chapter shows how the state-contingent production model presented in Chapters 2 and 4 allows us to resolve many of the difficulties encountered in earlier studies. Hence, in contrast to the existing folk wisdom, a state-space formulation of the moral-hazard problem leads to interesting and informative results. An important finding is that, once the first-stage of the moral-hazard problem is resolved, the final solution to the principal's problem can be computed by solving a simple nonlinear programming problem. Thus, standard optimization arguments allow us to develop a number of comparative-static results in an easy and intuitive manner.

Before we turn to the state-contingent moral-hazard model, we present a brief overview of the existing moral-hazard literature.

9.1 HISTORICAL DEVELOPMENT

The analysis of principal–agent problems was pioneered by Spence and Zeckhauser (1971) and Ross (1973) using a stochastic production-function approach. The problem was set up as follows. Output is determined by a stochastic production function $z(\theta) = f(x, \theta)$, where x is the effort (a scalar) committed by the agent, and θ is the state of nature. The principal's problem is to design a payment schedule, y(z), based on the stochastic output that maximizes $E[z - y]$ subject to the requirement that the agent attains an expected-utility level $E[u(y, x)]$ equal to some reservation level $\underline{u}$. The agent's preference structure is increasing in y and decreasing in x, and the agent maximizes expected utility.

There are two things to note here. The agent is specifically assumed not to care about the level of z except as it affects his returns. He has no direct preferences over the stochastic output. And, in theory, $y(z)$ can be increasing, decreasing, or constant in the amount of output produced.

If agents can rationally choose inefficient production arrangements, this formulation, however, leads to an important logical problem. Virtually all specifications of moral-hazard models assume that the agent chooses effort to

$$\max_{x}\{E[u(y(f(x,\theta)),x)]\}. \tag{9.1}$$

If the agent can choose to be productively inefficient, he has two choices to make, once he is presented with an award schedule, y(z). The first is to choose his effort, and the second is to choose the stochastic output that will occur when θ occurs. Hence, the agent's true problem is

$$\max_{x,z}\{E[u(y(z(\theta)), x)] : z(\theta) \le f(x,\theta)\}.$$

If u is nondecreasing in y, this can be rewritten as

$$\max_{x}\left\{E\left[u\left(\max_{z(\theta)}\{y(z(\theta)) : z(\theta) \le f(x,\theta)\}, x\right)\right]\right\}.$$

For this problem to be equivalent to (9.1), $y(z)$ must be increasing in z. If $y(z)$ is decreasing, the agent always rationally chooses $z(\theta) = 0$.[1]

The crucial point is that (9.1) does not recognize the very essence of the agency problem. To induce a rational agent to produce efficiently, the principal must provide the proper incentives. Formulation (9.1), on the other hand, assumes that unsupervised individuals always produce efficiently, even if it is not to their advantage. Unfortunately, this seemingly minor misspecification has caused even larger, and practically insurmountable, difficulties.

Mirrlees (1974) discovered that if uncertainty is represented by a stochastic production function not exhibiting weak disposability of output, and the number of states of nature is finite, the principal can achieve the first-best outcome by specifying an arbitrarily large penalty if output falls below $f(x^*, \theta_1)$, where θ_1 is the least favorable state of nature, and offering the fixed payment from the first-best contract otherwise. The only way the agent can avoid the penalty is to commit at least effort x^*. Because there is no payoff for any higher effort level, the agent will choose exactly x^*. In short, as long as one relies on a stochastic production-function formulation, there is no moral-hazard problem to resolve.[2]

This problem arises directly from the use of the stochastic production-function approach without allowing for inefficiency. Under this approach, output in every state is degenerately determined by the effort level. (See our discussion in Chapter 6.) Hence, once output in one state is known, output in every other state is known. (This seems implausible for most situations in which incentive schemes are offered.) If the agent is told that he will be severely punished for falling below some minimum target, but will receive no reward for performance above the target level, he will devote all his efforts to meeting the minimum target. In the general state-contingent production framework, this requires reallocating resources toward the least favorable state of nature and away from all of the others.

1. More generally, suppose that for $z^o < f(x, \theta)$, $y(f(x, \theta)) < y(z^o)$. Then the agent will always prefer a production plan with $z(\theta) = z^o$ to one with $z(\theta) = f(x, \theta)$.
2. Unfortunately, some have taken Mirrlees finding at face value rather than as an indication of problem misspecification. In particular, the literature on the economics of crime has relied on similar results to recommend, apparently seriously, that the best way to deter even petty crime is Draconian punishment. However, as subsequent developments in this chapter will make apparent, this "public execution of parking violators" finding disappears with a reasonable state-contingent production specification.

Thus, in our view, the appropriate response to the problem observed by Mirrlees is to abandon the apparent simplicity of the stochastic production-function approach in favor of the truer simplicity of the general representation of state-contingent production technology.

Unfortunately, this was "the road not taken." The problem was thought to lie not in the assumption of a stochastic production function, but in the use of a state-space representation. Hart and Holmstrom (1987) summarize the existing conventional wisdom when they say:

> Its [the state-space approach] main advantage is that the technology is presented in what appears to be the most natural terms. Economically, however, it does not lead to a very informative solution.

Mirrlees proposed a truly ingenious reformulation of the problem, replacing the stochastic production function with the parametrized distribution formulation. In this formulation, the scalar effort variable indexed a family of cumulative distribution functions over some given output space. As we have argued in Chapter 1 (and as Mirrlees and many others recognize), use of the parametrized distribution formulation leads to a fundamental identification problem. But, Mirrlees' reformulation also leads to a nontrivial moral-hazard problem.

The shift to a parametrized distribution formulation avoided the problem of a minimum output by permitting analysis to be undertaken in terms of distributions with fixed support. However, the basic problem was not resolved. Given reliable information about a single point on the cumulative distribution function of output, the entire distribution is immediately known. This point rapidly became apparent for what would otherwise appear to be the most natural case of a class of output distributions with fixed support, that arising when output is distributed continuously over the real line.

The difficulty with this case is that for points at the bottom tail of the distribution, the density is very small and declines rapidly as effort increases. It follows that a penalty imposed on outcomes in the bottom tail will be incurred with very low probability if the optimal effort is committed, but with rapidly increasing probability if effort is suboptimal. In effect, the occurrence of such an outcome is a very reliable signal that the effort level has been below the optimal level. Hence, the entire cumulative distribution function of output is below that generated by the optimal effort. By considering a sequence of penalty schemes operating at successively lower points in the bottom tail of the distribution, it is possible for the principal to obtain the first-best-effort level with an arbitrarily small probability of imposing the penalty and an expected payment arbitrarily close to the first-best level.

Even after the transition was made to the parametrized distribution formulation, numerous technical difficulties awaited the theoretical pioneers in this area (Grossman and Hart 1983; Harris and Raviv 1979; Holmstrom 1979; Shavell 1979). Grossman and Hart, in particular, surmounted numerous difficulties. First, even though, as we have shown earlier, the original formulation of the moral-hazard model implicitly assumes monotonicity of the payment schedule, this fact wasn't recognized. Consequently, theorists, recognizing that there is no general reason to expect monotonicity in the payment schedule, set out to deduce sufficient conditions for monotonicity given the stochastic production approach. Their tendency was to focus on conditions on the output distribution to ensure monotonicity instead of recognizing, as we show in what follows, that monotonicity was a necessary consequence of the freedom of agents to choose to produce inefficiently.

9.2 CHAPTER OVERVIEW

More than any other chapter, except Chapter 2, this chapter requires close reading in a somewhat consecutive fashion. So, to assist the reader through what may otherwise appear as a maze of rather technical arguments, we have included an overview of the developments that follow.

The remainder of the chapter is composed of four parts: a discussion and specification of the moral-hazard model in terms of a truly state-contingent technology; following Grossman and Hart (1983), an analysis of a first-stage cost-minimization problem by the principal; a depiction of the principal's solution of the moral-hazard problem as the solution of a simple nonlinear program that is only subject to nonnegativity constraints on the choice variable; and a concluding section that discusses possible extensions and applications of the moral-hazard model developed here.

In the first of these sections, we lay out the moral-hazard model in terms of the state-contingent technology developed in Chapters 2 and 4. After specifying the agent's technology, the preferences of the principal and the agent, and the moral-hazard problem itself, we develop several preliminary results that facilitate later analysis. Chief among them is the recognition that the payment scheme offered by the principal to the agent must be monotonic in the sense that (strictly) higher output realizations are always rewarded with (strictly) higher payments and that the optimal output configuration must be inherently risky in the sense of Chapter 4.

Next, we recognize that the principal's problem can be decomposed into two stages. In the first stage, the principal chooses the minimum expected payment to the agent that will resolve the incentive problems caused by the presence of moral hazard for a fixed set of state-contingent outputs. In the second stage, the principal picks the state-contingent outputs optimally. This section analyzes in detail the solution to the first-stage problem, which we refer to as the *agency-cost function*. In particular, we examine its equilibrium properties and obtain a number of comparative-static results. Among other things, we also demonstrate, following Weymark (1986), that under appropriate restrictions on the preferences and the technology, a closed-form solution exists for the first-stage problem. Moreover, this closed-form solution can be obtained by solving a simple linear program.

In the third section, we use the agency-cost function to formulate the principal's problem as a simple nonlinear program that is subject only to simple nonnegativity constraints on the choice variables. Because the moral-hazard problem is reducible to such a simple formulation, well-known arguments from optimization and duality theory can be applied to the problem's solution to obtain comparative-static results. Among the results established in this section are that the solution to the moral-hazard problem in terms of outputs must be marginally efficient in terms of the good-state output and risk-aversely efficient in the sense of Peleg and Yaari (1975) (discussed in Chapter 5).

The last section offers some observations on possible extensions of the model and a brief précis of an application of the moral-hazard model developed in this chapter to the economic analysis of criminal behavior.

9.3 STATE-CONTINGENT TECHNOLOGY AND THE AGENCY PROBLEM

9.3.1 Production and Preferences

The contracting problem is: A principal and an agent are contracting over the agent's production practices. The principal is the residual claimant, that is, the legal owner of any output produced by the agent, and the principal has the right to specify the contract provisions. The agent, on the other hand, is free to take the contract or leave it. But once the agent agrees to the contract, it is assumed to be enforceable. The information setting is as follows. The principal knows the agent's preferences and the production technology and can observe the level of output that the agent produces. However, the principal cannot observe either the state of nature that occurs, or the agent's effort level.

To simplify, we deal with the case in which there are only two states of nature, and an agent undertakes state-contingent production of a single good. Thus, the output set satisfies $Z(\mathbf{x}) \subseteq \Re_+^2$. We assume that the production technology satisfies the requirements for the existence of a strictly convex, strictly increasing, and twice-differentiable effort-cost function $C:\Re_+^2 \rightarrow \Re$. By assuming a differentiable effort-cost function, we rule out the output-cubical technology that provides the foundation of the standard moral-hazard model.

The agent's ex post preferences, $w:\Re \times \Re_+^n \rightarrow \Re$, are additively separable in effort and returns:

$$w(y, \mathbf{x}) = u(y) - g(\mathbf{x}).$$

We assume expected utility with known probabilities. The agent's reservation utility is given by $\underline{u} > -\infty$. She will only accept a contract that guarantees her at least the reservation expected utility. The agent is strictly risk-averse over state-contingent returns so that $u(y)$ is strictly increasing and strictly concave. The principal is risk-neutral. His preferences only depend on his return and not on the agent's effort.

Most of these simplifying assumptions can be modified quite easily. The crucial elements are the assumptions that, taking endowments of assets as given, the principal is less risk-averse than the agent, and that the agent possesses private information about her own actions and the state of nature.

9.3.2 The Agency Problem

Because the principal is risk-neutral and only concerned with his return from the contract, his problem is to design a contract that the agent willingly signs. The principal's *first-best problem* is to pick a state-contingent contract structure that maximizes his return, while offering the agent at least her reservation expected utility:

$$\max_{(\mathbf{y},\mathbf{z})} W^p = \pi_1(z_1 - y_1) + \pi_2(z_2 - y_2)$$

subject to:

$$\pi_1 u(y_1) + \pi_2 u(y_2) - C(z_1, z_2) \geq \underline{u}.$$

The contract structure in the first-best problem should be interpreted in the following way. The principal offers a state-contingent contract specifying the agent's payment and production level in each state of nature that offers the agent at least her reservation expected utility. The ability to specify such a state-contingent contract structure that is also enforceable requires that the principal be able to observe ex post which state of nature occurs.

The moral-hazard or second-best problem arises when it is assumed that the principal cannot observe, ex post, which element of Ω that "Nature" picks. Therefore, specifying such a state-contingent payoff–production contract incurs an incentive problem for the principal who cannot observe ex post which state of nature occurs. Only the agent has this information.

What the principal can observe (and base an enforceable contract on) is realized output. Let Ψ be the class of all functions $y: \Re_+ \to \Re$. Ψ, therefore, represents the possible payment schedules to the agent that the principal can choose from in designing a payment scheme that only depends on output observed ex post. In picking such a payment scheme, the principal has to ensure that it offers the agent at least her reservation expected utility and that it is *individually rational* in the sense that

$$(z_1, z_2) \in \arg\max\{\pi_1 u(y(z_1)) + \pi_2 u(y(z_2)) - C(z_1, z_2)\}$$

for $\mathbf{z}$ it is technically feasible. This constraint ensures that it is always to the agent's advantage to privately choose the state-contingent production vector that the principal wants to implement. We can, therefore, formally define the principal's *second-best problem* (the principal's problem subject to the informational constraints of the model) as choosing $y \in \Psi$ to maximize

$$W^P = \pi_1(z_1 - y(z_1)) + \pi_2(z_2 - y(z_2))$$

subject to

$$\pi_1 u(y(z_1)) + \pi_2 u(y(z_2)) - C(z_1, z_2) \geq \underline{u},$$

$$(z_1, z_2) \in \arg\max\{\pi_1 u(y(z_1)) + \pi_2 u(y(z_2)) - C(z_1, z_2)\},$$

for **z** it is technically feasible.

The only contracts that are feasible are ones that have $y(z)$ monotone increasing in the observed output. To see why, notice that the optimal pattern of state-contingent production, for the moment let's call it $\hat{\mathbf{z}}$, must satisfy

$$\pi_1 u(y(\hat{z}_1)) + \pi_2 u(y(\hat{z}_2)) - C(\hat{z}_1, \hat{z}_2) \geq \pi_1 u(y(z_1)) + \pi_2 u(y(z_2)) - C(z_1, z_2)$$

for all feasible **z**. Now suppose without loss of generality that

$$\hat{z}_2 > \hat{z}_1.$$

Hence, by free disposability of output and the previous inequality

$$\begin{aligned}\pi_1 u(y(\hat{z}_1)) + \pi_2 u(y(\hat{z}_2)) - C(\hat{z}_1, \hat{z}_2) &\geq \pi_1 u(y(\hat{z}_1)) + \pi_2 u(y(\hat{z}_1)) - C(\hat{z}_1, \hat{z}_1) \\ &= u(y(\hat{z}_1)) - C(\hat{z}_1, \hat{z}_1),\end{aligned}$$

which can be rewritten as

$$\pi_2(u(y(\hat{z}_2)) - u(y(\hat{z}_1))) \geq C(\hat{z}_1, \hat{z}_2) - C(\hat{z}_1, \hat{z}_1) > 0,$$

where the last inequality follows by the assumption that costs are strictly increasing in state-contingent outputs. Then, given that u is strictly increasing, $y(z)$ must be as well.[3]

Therefore, we could analyze the moral-hazard problem by considering the principal's choice over the class of strongly monotonic payment schedules. However, under relatively weak assumptions, the

3. Grossman and Hart (1983) recognized that, if the producer could destroy output after it was produced, contracts would be weakly monotonic. This represents a different informational structure than the current model where ex post output is assumed to be observable and contractible. See the further discussion in what follows.

principal's second-best problem is equivalent to one of designing a state-contingent contract structure, similar to those developed in Chapters 7 and 8, subject to a set of constraints that make it individually rational for the agent to pick the state-contingent production structure that corresponds to the solution to the principal's second-best problem.[4] The payment scheme associated with this alternative representation operates in the following fashion. When the agent realizes an ex post output of, say, z, she receives a payment of y_1 if $z = z_1$, a payment of y_2 if $z = z_2$, and an arbitrarily large negative payment otherwise.

In practice, arbitrarily large negative payments are normally not feasible, and, to be more realistic, the problem specification should include a minimum-payment constraint. If the minimum-payment constraint is binding, the participation constraint requiring a minimum level of expected utility for the agent in general, will be nonbinding (compare Lemma 9.1, which follows). The problem of determining an optimal contract in the presence of a binding minimum-payment constraint is one of determining an efficiency wage. In this chapter, it will be assumed that the minimum payment is nonbinding.

Formally, then, the equivalent problem is for the principal to choose y and $\mathbf{z}$ to maximize:

$$W^p = \pi_1(z_1 - y_1) + \pi_2(z_2 - y_2)$$

subject to

$$\text{(T.1)}\quad \pi_1 u(y_1) + \pi_2 u(y_2) - C(z_1, z_2) \geq \underline{u}$$

$$\text{(T.2)}\quad \pi_1 u(y_1) + \pi_2 u(y_2) - C(z_1, z_2) \geq u(y_1) - C(z_1, z_1)$$

$$\text{(T.3)}\quad \pi_1 u(y_1) + \pi_2 u(y_2) - C(z_1, z_2) \geq u(y_2) - C(z_2, z_2)$$

$$\text{(T.4)}\quad \pi_1 u(y_1) + \pi_2 u(y_2) - C(z_1, z_2) \geq \pi_1 u(y_2) + \pi_2 u(y_1) - C(z_2, z_1).$$

T.1 repeats the agent's voluntary participation constraint, saying that the contract offered by the principal must yield the agent her reservation expected utility. T.2 through T.4 are the constraints arising from the incentive problem that the principal faces. In words, they ensure that the agent finds it rational to pick the state-contingent

4. We are indebted to John Weymark for demonstrating the equivalence between the two approaches.

production structure (z_1, z_2) in return for the state-contingent reward structure (y_1, y_2).

To show that this problem is equivalent to the principal's second-best problem, we show that the set of allocations satisfying the constraints for the second-best problem and this problem are the same. The payment scheme for the second-best problem, $y(z)$, is state-independent and only depends on observed output. Hence, any allocation emerging from it, which is individually rational for the agent while guaranteeing the reservation expected utility, must satisfy constraints T.1 to T.4. If it did not, the agent would find it profitable to adopt (z_1, z_1), (z_2, z_2), or (z_2, z_1) in place of the second best (z_1, z_2).

To go the other way, consider an allocation $(\mathbf{y}^*, \mathbf{z}^*)$ that satisfies T.1 to T.4. The agent's reservation expected utility is guaranteed by T.1. All that remains is to show that the allocation is individually rational for the agent. Here the formal payment scheme is $y(\mathbf{z}) = y_i^*$ if either z_1^* or z_2^* is reported, and $y(\mathbf{z}) = -\kappa$, where $\kappa > 0$ and arbitrarily large. Since C is increasing on $\Re_+^2$ and y is constant except at z_1^* and z_2^*, a rational agent will never have $z_i > 0$ unless z_i is equal to z_1^* or z_2^*. It remains to rule out corner solutions in which the agent produces a zero output in one or both states of nature. The strict concavity of u implies that as the penalty $\kappa \to \infty$, $u(-\kappa) \to -\infty$. Hence, if κ is made large enough, it will never be rational for the agent to report anything other than z_1^* or z_2^*.

Given that the practical feasible set for the agent is now $\mathbf{z}^*$, and that constraints T.2 to T.4 rule out (z_1^*, z_1^*), (z_2^*, z_2^*), and (z_2^*, z_1^*), $\mathbf{z}^*$ will always be chosen by the agent. Thus, we have shown that the two problems are equivalent, and in the remainder of this chapter, we will deal exclusively with the solution to the second version of the second-best problem because it can be handled using nonlinear programming methods.

Following Grossman and Hart (1983), we observe that, given the additively separable agent's objective function assumed, the participation constraint (T.1) always binds regardless of whether we are considering the principal's first-best or second-best problem. Otherwise, the principal could reduce the payments in both states while keeping $u(y_2) - u(y_1)$ constant, thereby leaving constraints T.2 to T.4 unaffected. We state this fact as a lemma for future reference.

Lemma 9.1: *In any solution to the first-best problem or the second-best problem, the agent's participation constraint (T.1) must hold with equality.*

9.3.3 "Good" and "Bad" States of Nature

An immediate consequence of our earlier discussion and T.2 and T.3 is a monotonicity result on the optimal contract structure: T.2 and T.3 reduce to, respectively,

$$\text{(T.2')} \qquad \pi_2[u(y_2)-u(y_1)] \geq C(z_1, z_2)-C(z_1, z_1),$$

and

$$\text{(T.3')} \qquad \pi_1[u(y_1)-u(y_2)] \geq C(z_1, z_2)-C(z_2, z_2).$$

Suppose that $z_2 > z_1$. The fact that $C(z_1, z_2)$ is strictly increasing in both its arguments ensures that the right-hand side of T.2′ is positive. Therefore, the left-hand side must be positive as well, establishing that $y_2 > y_1$. If $z_1 > z_2$, T.3′ similarly implies $y_1 > y_2$. Now suppose that $z_1 = z_2$. T.2′ and T.3′ can only be satisfied if $y_1 = y_2$. This yields:

Lemma 9.2: *Any solution to the second-best problem in the presence of T.2 to T.4 must satisfy*

$$(y_1 - y_2)(z_1 - z_2) \geq 0$$

with equality only when both terms on the left-hand side are zero.

Despite its simplicity, Lemma 9.2 is significant because, in the parametrized distribution formulation of the moral-hazard problem, strong assumptions on either the agent's behavior or the outcome distribution (and hence on the agent's beliefs and preferences, because probabilities are inherently subjective) are required to ensure that the payment scheme will be monotonic. One is the monotone likelihood ratio (MLR) condition. An alternative is the ability of the agent to destroy or dispose of output costlessly *after* it has been produced (Grossman and Hart 1983, footnote 12).

The condition that yields monotonicity in our model is the strict monotonicity of the effort-cost function, which emerges from the presumption of free disposability of outputs within the technology. This condition is subtly different from either of the two conditions that yield monotonicity in the parametrized distribution framework. In particular, free disposability of outputs does not imply that the agent can costlessly dispose of output after it has been produced. Rather, free disposability of outputs implies that an agent can always choose to commit her time inefficiently if there is a reward for doing so. Because the agent inherits this degree of flexibility from the technology, the principal, in turn, loses at least one degree of freedom in designing his incentive scheme. He cannot make it either monotone-decreasing or constant. Doing so would give the agent an incentive to always produce zero output in each state regardless of the effort level that she commits. She doesn't care about the output, only the reward that she receives for the output. If the reward provides adverse incentives for her to increase output, she can be counted on to exercise her ability to be inefficient.

Lemma 9.2 only shows that high outputs must be matched by high payments. It does not determine which state of nature is the high- or the low-output state. To that end, without loss of generality, we assume that the relative probabilities are such that:

> **Assumption 9.1:** $z_1 \leq z_2$ *in the first-best.*

This motivates:

> **Definition 9.1:** *An output vector* (z_1, z_2) *is monotonic (strictly monotonic) if* $z_1 \leq (<) z_2$.

The solution to the principal's first-best problem requires $z_1 = z_2$ if the technology is not inherently risky (see Chapter 4) for all $z_1, z_2 \geq 0$ (for fixed π_1, π_2).[5] Consider a first-best allocation (z_1, z_2) and payment structure (y_1, y_2) when the effort-cost function is not inherently risky. In that case, the production-risk premium is negative and thus

$$C(z_1, z_2) \geq C(\pi_1 z_1 + \pi_2 z_2, \pi_1 z_1 + \pi_2 z_2).$$

Accordingly, one can always increase (or at least not diminish) the principal's first-best returns by having the agent produce $\pi_1 z_1 + \pi_2 z_2$ in both states instead of the original production vector. When the

5. For brevity, we will use the statement "**z** is (is not) inherently risky." to mean "The technology is (is not) inherently risky at **z**.".

technology is not inherently risky, this reduces the agent's costs, and thus permits the principal to reduce the agent's payments while still achieving the reservation utility.

More generally, the first-best optimum is always inherently risky. There are two cases to consider. First, suppose in the first-best optimum that $z_1 = z_2$. This output vector is trivially inherently risky. The second, by Assumption 9.1, is the case in which $z_1 < z_2$. Now suppose that this state-contingent output vector is not inherently risky. Then, it follows immediately that the principal could employ the same payment structure as for (z_1, z_2) while having the agent produce $\pi_1 z_1 + \pi_2 z_2$ in both states. This would leave the principal's expected return unaffected, but now gives the agent more than the reservation expected utility, thus violating Lemma 9.1.

More importantly, the second-best optimum state-contingent production vector also has to be inherently risky. Suppose to the contrary that there is a second-best optimum $(\mathbf{y}, \mathbf{z})$ in which $\mathbf{z}$ is not inherently risky. Now compare the resulting contract with a contract requiring the agent to produce the state-contingent output vector $(\pi_1 z_1 + \pi_2 z_2, \pi_1 z_1 + \pi_2 z_2)$ and receive $\pi_1 y_1 + \pi_2 y_2$ in both states. This gives the same expected return to the principal as producing $\mathbf{z}$, but at lower cost to the agent, implying that the agent's reservation expected utility is exceeded, again violating Lemma 9.1. Moreover, this second contract satisfies T.2 to T.4 because any contract requiring the agent to produce and receive the same amount in both states trivially meets these constraints. Hence, the contract requiring the agent to produce $(\pi_1 z_1 + \pi_2 z_2, \pi_1 z_1 + \pi_2 z_2)$ must dominate the contract requiring the agent to produce $\mathbf{z}$.

Result 9.1: *First-best or second-best optimality of* $\mathbf{z}$ *implies that* $\mathbf{z}$ *is inherently risky.*

The major import of Result 9.1 is that the search for the optimal second-best and first-best production vectors can be restricted to inherently risky state-contingent production vectors. We now develop the relationship between inherent riskiness and monotonicity further.

For any cost level $c > 0$, denote by $\mathbf{z}^*(c) \in \Re^2_+$:

$$\mathbf{z}^*(c) = \arg\max\{\pi_1 z_1 + \pi_2 z_2 : C(\mathbf{z}) \le c\},$$

and let $z(c)$ represent the implicit solution to the equation $C(z, z) = c$. In words, $(z(c), z(c))$ is the point on the bisector that intersects the

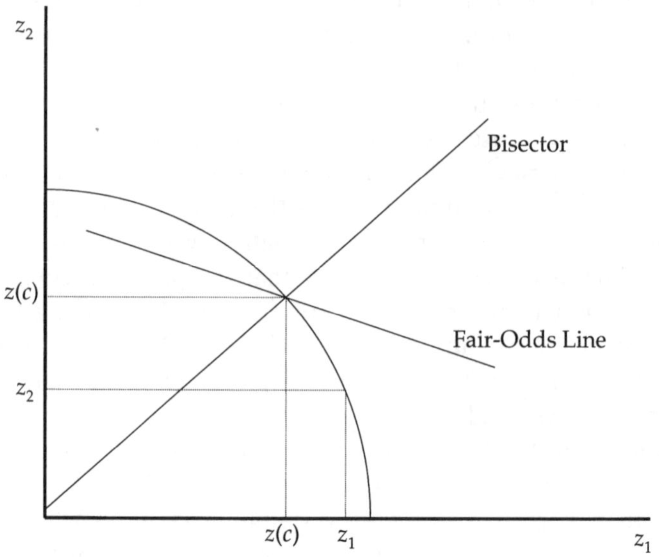

Figure 9.1 Monotonicity and inherent riskiness.

isocost curve given by $\{\mathbf{z}:C(\mathbf{z}) = c\}$. Now suppose that the state-contingent output $\mathbf{z}^*(c)$ is monotonic. That means that the fair-odds line must cut this isocost curve at $(z(c), z(c))$ from below, as illustrated in Figure 9.1. Now consider (z_1, z_2) on the same isocost curve as $\mathbf{z}^*(c)$ but with $z_1 > z_2$. The fair-odds line through (z_1, z_2) must intersect the bisector below the isocost curve, indicating that

$$C(\pi_1 z_1 + \pi_2 z_2, \pi_1 z_1 + \pi_2 z_2) < C(z(c), z(c)) = c = C(z_1, z_2),$$

and that (z_1, z_2) is not inherently risky. A converse analysis applies if $\mathbf{z}^*(c)$ is nonmonotonic. This reasoning yields:

> **Lemma 9.3:** *For any z with z*(C(z)) monotonic (nonmonotonic), a necessary condition for z to be inherently risky is that z be monotonic (nonmonotonic).*

For any cost level c, one might naturally think of the "good" state of nature as the one in which a risk-neutral agent would choose to produce more, given that level of cost. (By Assumption 9.1, the good state of nature at the first-best cost level is state 2.) In these terms, Lemma 9.3 implies that $\mathbf{z}$ can be inherently risky, and thus a potential solution to the principal's problem, only if it is on the same side of the bisector as $\mathbf{z}^*(C(\mathbf{z}))$. That is, solutions to the second-best problem must involve the agent picking the same "good" state of nature as would a risk-neutral producer who faced the same cost level as the agent faces in the second-best case.

The implication of Lemma 9.3 is that any time there are uniquely good and bad states of nature, inherent riskiness will always coincide with monotonicity. In Chapter 4, we outlined two restrictions on the cost structure that ensure the existence of uniquely good and bad states: constant absolute riskiness and constant relative riskiness. Hence, when C exhibits either constant absolute riskiness or constant relative riskiness, Assumption 9.1 then implies that all $\mathbf{z}^*(C(\mathbf{z}))$ must be monotonic. Using Lemma 9.3 then lets us conclude that any $\mathbf{z}$ can only be inherently risky if it is also monotonic. As discussed in Chapter 4, when C is not homothetic or translation homothetic, state 1 may be the bad state for some levels of effort cost and the good state for others. When reversals occur, however, Lemma 9.3 indicates that any inherently risky $\mathbf{z}$ must lie on the same side of the bisector as the output vector $\mathbf{z}^*(C(\mathbf{z}))$ that solves the problem

$$\max\{\pi_1 z_1 + \pi_2 z_2 : C(z_1, z_2) = C(\mathbf{z})\}.$$

For later purposes, we summarize the preceding discussion:

Lemma 9.4: *If* C *exhibits either constant absolute riskiness or constant relative riskiness,* $\mathbf{z}$ *is inherently risky only if it is monotonic.*

9.4 TWO AGENCY-COST FUNCTIONS

Grossman and Hart (1983) recognized that moral-hazard problems can be decomposed into two separate stages. In the first stage, the cost of achieving a particular effort vector on the part of the agent, subject to the participation and incentive constraints, is minimized. In the second stage, the solution to the first-stage cost-minimization problem is used in the choice of the optimal state-contingent output for the principal. A similar decomposition exists here in both the first- and the second-best problem.

9.4.1 Characterizing the Agency-Cost Functions

Formally, the first-best problem can be rewritten in the following form:

$$\begin{aligned} V_{FB}(\pi, \underline{u}) &= \max_{\mathbf{z},\mathbf{y}}\{\pi_1(z_1 - y_1) + \pi_2(z_2 - y_2) : \mathrm{T1}\} \\ &= \max_{\mathbf{z}}\left\{\pi_1 z_1 + \pi_2 z_2 - \min_{\mathbf{y}}\{\pi_1 y_1 + \pi_2 y_2 : \mathrm{T1}\}\right\} \\ &= \max_{\mathbf{z}}\{\pi_1 z_1 + \pi_2 z_2 - Y_{FB}(z_1, z_2; \pi, \underline{u})\}. \end{aligned}$$

We refer to the cost-minimization step in the first-best problem as the *first-best agency-cost problem*, and to its solution, $Y_{FB}(z_1, z_2; \pi, \underline{u})$, as the *first-best agency-cost function*. A similar decomposition exists for the principal's second-best problem:

$$\begin{aligned} V(\pi, \underline{u}) &= \max_{\mathbf{z},\mathbf{y}}\{\pi_1(z_1 - y_1) + \pi_2(z_2 - y_2) : \mathrm{T.1 \text{ to } T.4}\} \\ &= \max_{\mathbf{z}}\left\{\pi_1 z_1 + \pi_2 z_2 - \min_{\mathbf{y}}\{\pi_1 y_1 + \pi_2 y_2 : \mathrm{T.1 \text{ to } T.4}\}\right\} \\ &= \max_{\mathbf{z}}\{\pi_1 z_1 + \pi_2 z_2 - Y(z_1, z_2; \pi, \underline{u})\}. \end{aligned}$$

We refer to the cost-minimization step in the second-best problem as the *second-best agency-cost problem*. It gives the minimum cost to the principal of achieving a particular state-contingent output vector by the agent that will satisfy the participation constraint and the remaining incentive constraints, T.2 to T.4. Because u is strictly concave and strictly increasing, the second-best agency-cost problem can be rewritten after a change in variables as

$$\min_{\mathbf{u}}\{\pi_1 h(u_1) + \pi_2 h(u_2)\}$$

subject to

$$\begin{aligned} &(\mathrm{T}^*.1) \quad \pi_1 u_1 + \pi_2 u_2 - C(z_1, z_2) \geq \underline{u} \\ &(\mathrm{T}^*.2) \quad \pi_1 u_1 + \pi_2 u_2 - C(z_1, z_2) \geq u_1 - C(z_1, z_1) \\ &(\mathrm{T}^*.3) \quad \pi_1 u_1 + \pi_2 u_2 - C(z_1, z_2) \geq u_2 - C(z_2, z_2) \\ &(\mathrm{T}^*.4) \quad \pi_1 u_1 + \pi_2 u_2 - C(z_1, z_2) \geq \pi_1 u_2 + \pi_2 u_1 - C(z_2, z_1), \end{aligned}$$

where $u_i = u(y_i)$, $i = 1, 2$, and $h(u^i) = u^{-1}(y^i)$ is a strictly increasing convex function of u^i.

It is straightforward to verify that, given the structure of an agent's preferences, the agent's participation constraint must be binding in both the first-best and second-best agency-cost problems. We state this as a lemma for future use:

Lemma 9.1a: *In any solution to the first-best agency-cost problem or the second-best agency-cost problem, the agent's participation constraint must hold as an equality.*

Any solution to the second-best agency-cost problem must also satisfy a version of the monotonicity result contained in Lemma 9.2. The proof, here, which is for fixed **z**, is identical to the proof offered earlier for Lemma 9.2. Hence:

Lemma 9.2a: *Any solution,* $\mathrm{u}(z, \underline{\mathrm{u}}) \in \Re^2$, *to the second-best agency-cost minimization problem must satisfy*

$$(\mathrm{u}_1(z, \underline{\mathrm{u}}) - \mathrm{u}_2(z, \underline{\mathrm{u}}))(\mathrm{z}_1 - \mathrm{z}_2) \geq 0,$$

with equality only when both terms on the LHS are zero.

We show in what follows that a solution always exists to the first-best agency-cost problem. In general, however, we cannot show that a solution always exists for the second-best agency-cost problem because the feasible region for the second-best agency-cost problem defined by T*.1 to T*.4 may be empty for fixed **z**. But because h is strictly convex, Jensen's inequality and Lemma 9.1a when applied together imply

$$\begin{aligned}\pi_1 h(u_1) + \pi_2 h(u_2) &\geq h(\pi_1 u_1 + \pi_2 u_2) \\ &= h(\underline{u} + C(z_1, z_2)).\end{aligned}$$

The equality follows from Lemma 9.1a, and the inequality follows from applying Jensen's inequality. If $u_1 \neq u_2$, the preceding inequality is strict. Thus, if the constraint set for the second-best agency-cost minimization problem is nonempty, the principal's objective function must be bounded from below on this set. As a result, for formal purposes, we need to take care of the case when the constraint set is empty. Hence:

Definition 9.2: *For given* $\underline{\mathrm{u}}$, z, *and* $\pi = (\pi_1, \pi_2)$, *the second-best agency-cost function, written* $\Upsilon(\mathrm{z}_1, \mathrm{z}_2; \pi, \underline{\mathrm{u}})$, *is the minimal value of the principal's objective function in the second-best, agency-cost minimization problem if the constraint set is nonempty and is infinity if the constraint set is empty.*

In the first-best agency-cost minimization problem, the principal can always choose a fixed payment equaling $h(\underline{u} + C(z_1, z_2))$ that yields the agent his or her reservation expected utility in each state, and that represents a lower bound to all payments achieving this level of reservation utility. This fact is established by using Lemma 9.1a and the fact that Jensen's inequality implies for strictly convex h that

$$\pi_1 h(u_1) + \pi_2 h(u_2) \geq h(\pi_1 u_1 + \pi_2 u_2) = h(\underline{u} + C(z_1, z_2)).$$

Noting that

$$Y_{FB}(z_1, z_2; \pi, \underline{u}) = h(\underline{u} + C(z_1, z_2)),$$

yields the observation that $Y_{FB}(z_1, z_2) \leq Y(z_1, z_2)$.[6] Because h is strictly convex and strictly increasing and C is strictly convex and increasing in **z**, Y_{FB} is strictly convex and strictly increasing in **z**. Y_{FB} is also strictly increasing and strictly convex in $\underline{u}$.

Recall from the discussion in Chapter 3 that $Y_{FB}(z_1, z_2)$ represents the agent's certainty equivalent for any **y** meeting the voluntary participation constraint, and $Y(z_1, z_2)$ equals the expected value of the agent's payment subject to T*.1 to T*.4. Therefore, again by the discussion in Chapter 3, the risk premium for the payment schedule **y** that implements (z_1, z_2) in the presence of T*.1 to T*.4 equals the difference $Y(z_1, z_2) - Y_{FB}(z_1, z_2)$.

Because the difference between the first-best agency-cost function and the second-best agency-cost function equals the agent's risk premium, this difference is zero whenever the agent's risk premium is zero. This relationship between the first-best and second-best agency-cost functions yields the famous result (Grossman and Hart 1983; Harris and Raviv 1979) that when the agent is risk-neutral, the solutions to the first-best and second-best problems coincide. Moreover, when the agent is strictly risk-averse as we assume (h is strictly convex), the agency-cost function and the first-best cost function will coincide only when all the risk can be removed from the agent's payment stream. Thus:

Result 9.2: $Y(z_1, z_2) = Y_{FB}(z_1, z_2)$ *if and only if* $z_1 = z_2$. *Otherwise,* $Y_{FB}(z_1, z_2) < Y(z_1, z_2)$.

6. In what follows, we shall often suppress $\underline{u}$ and π as arguments of the principal's indirect objective functions where there can be no confusion.

To prove this result, first recall that the first-best agency-cost problem always has a solution, $h(\underline{u} + C(z_1, z_2))$. Consider the case in which $z_1 = z_2$: T*.2 can then be rewritten as

$$u_2 \geq u_1$$

and T*.3 can be rewritten as

$$u_1 \geq u_2,$$

implying that feasible $\mathbf{u}$ satisfy $u_2 = u_1$. Imposing this condition ensures that T*.4 is trivially satisfied and an application of Lemma 9.1a establishes that the second-best agency cost now equals $h(\underline{u} + C(z_1, z_2))$.

Now consider the case in which $z_1 \neq z_2$. The result is trivial when the constraint set for the second-best agency-cost problem is empty. A solution to the first-best agency-cost problem always exists and assumes a finite value, but, by definition, second-best agency cost is infinite in this instance. Now suppose that $z_1 < z_2$. By Lemma 9.2a,

$$u_1(\mathbf{z}, \underline{u}) < u_2(\mathbf{z}, \underline{u}).$$

Hence, the strict convexity of h, Jensen's inequality, and Lemma 9.1a combined imply

$$\begin{aligned}\pi_1 h[u_1(\mathbf{z}, \underline{u})] + \pi_2 h[u_2(\mathbf{z}, \underline{u})] &> h[\pi_1 u_1(\mathbf{z}, \underline{u}) + \pi_2 u_2(\mathbf{z}, \underline{u})] \\ &= h[\underline{u} + C(z_1, z_2)].\end{aligned}$$

A similar analysis applies when $z_1 > z_2$. This completes the proof.

We have already seen that Y_{FB} is strictly increasing and convex in the agent's reservation utility, $\underline{u}$. Thus, increases in $\underline{u}$ increase the principal's first-best agency cost of implementing a given (z_1, z_2) at an increasing rate. We would expect a similar property to hold for $Y(z_1, z_2; \underline{u}, \pi)$, and it does. To see this formally, define $v_i = u_i - \underline{u}$. With this change of variables, the second-best agency-cost-minimization problem can be written

$$\min \pi_1 h(v_1 + \underline{u}) + \pi_2 h(v_2 + \underline{u}),$$

subject to

$$\begin{aligned}
&(\text{T}^{**}.1) \quad && \pi_1 v_1 + \pi_2 v_2 - C(z_1, z_2) \geq 0 \\
&(\text{T}^{**}.2) \quad && \pi_1 v_1 + \pi_2 v_2 - C(z_1, z_2) \geq v_1 - C(z_1, z_1) \\
&(\text{T}^{**}.3) \quad && \pi_1 v_1 + \pi_2 v_2 - C(z_1, z_2) \geq v_2 - C(z_2, z_2) \\
&(\text{T}^{**}.4) \quad && \pi_1 v_1 + \pi_2 v_2 - C(z_1, z_2) \geq \pi_1 v_2 + \pi_2 v_1 - C(z_2, z_1).
\end{aligned}$$

This constraint set is a convex set independent of $\underline{u}$, but the objective function is strictly increasing and strictly convex in $\underline{u}$. Hence, by standard results in optimization theory (for example, Chambers 1988, p. 316), we have:

Result 9.3: *The second-best agency-cost function is increasing and strictly convex in* $\underline{u}$.

9.4.2 A Closed-Form Agency-Cost Function

In this section, we develop a closed-form solution to the second-best agency-cost problem that can be simply computed using graphical techniques. To facilitate our exposition by avoiding the complexities that arise from having reversals of "good" and "bad" states, we shall strengthen our assumptions on C:

Assumption 9.2: C *is positively linearly homogeneous in state-contingent outputs.*

Among other things, Assumption 9.2 guarantees by Lemma 9.4 that any inherently risky $\mathbf{z}$ must also be monotonic. As will become apparent, positive linear homogeneity of C also allows us to show that T*.4 is always a redundant constraint and to demonstrate that the constraint set for the agency-cost problem is nonempty only if the maintained state-contingent output vector is inherently risky. It should be noted that the assumption of strict convexity of C must be modified slightly to allow for positive linear homogeneity of C.

We now consider whether, for given $\mathbf{z}$, the constraint set T*.1 to T*.4 is nonempty, that is, whether the agency-cost function is finite. It turns out that inherent riskiness of the maintained state-contingent output vector for the second-best agency-cost problem is required for this condition to hold. Multiplying T*.2 by π_1 and T*.3 by π_2 and then adding them yields the following necessary condition for the constraint set to be nonempty:

$$[\pi_1 C(z_1, z_1) + \pi_2 C(z_2, z_2) - C(z_1, z_2)] \geq 0. \tag{9.2}$$

Using the positive linear homogeneity to rewrite the left-hand side of (9.2), we obtain

$$\begin{aligned}&\pi_1 C(z_1, z_1) + \pi_2 C(z_2, z_2) - C(z_1, z_2)\\&\quad = C(\pi_1 z_1, \pi_1 z_1) + C(\pi_2 z_2, \pi_2 z_2) - C(z_1, z_2)\\&\quad = (\pi_1 z_1 + \pi_2 z_2) C(1, 1) - C(z_1, z_2)\\&\quad = C(\pi_1 z_1 + \pi_2 z_2, \pi_1 z_1 + \pi_2 z_2) - C(z_1, z_2),\end{aligned}$$

so that (9.2) is satisfied if and only if **z** is inherently risky. Inherent riskiness of **z**, therefore, is necessary for the second-best agency-cost problem to have a solution.

Now suppose that **z** is inherently risky and that T*.2 binds exactly:

$$u_2 - u_1 = \frac{C(z_1, z_2) - C(z_1, z_1)}{\pi_2}.$$

Given that this condition holds, T*.3 will also be satisfied if

$$\frac{C(z_1, z_2) - C(z_1, z_1)}{\pi_2} \leq \frac{C(z_2, z_2) - C(z_1, z_2)}{\pi_1},$$

which is equivalent to (9.2). Hence, for inherently risky **z**, the constraint set defined by T*.2 and T*.3 is nonempty. A sufficient condition for T*.1 to be satisfied is $u_2 \geq u_1 \geq C(z_1, z_2)$, and this is clearly consistent with T*.2, so, for inherently risky **z**, the constraint set defined by T*.1 to T*.3 is nonempty.

The preceding arguments establish:

> **Lemma 9.5:** *Under Assumption 9.2, the constraint set defined by T*.1 to T*.3 is nonempty if and only if z is inherently risky. For inherently risky z, if T*.2 is satisfied exactly, T*.3 is also satisfied.*

Now consider T*.4. Note that T*.2, T*.3, and T*.4 all have the same left-hand side. Hence, multiplying T*.2 by π_2 and T*.3 by $\pi_1 = 1 - \pi_2$, then adding, does not change the left-hand side, but generates a linear combination of the right-hand sides of T*.2 and T*.3. We thus obtain

$$\pi_1 u_1 + \pi_2 u_2 - C(z_1, z_2) \geq \pi_1 u_2 + \pi_2 u_1 - \pi_2 C(z_1, z_1) - \pi_1 C(z_2, z_2).$$

If this condition is satisfied, that is, both T*.2 and T*.3 hold, T*.4 will also be satisfied if

$$C(z_2, z_1) \geq \pi_2 C(z_1, z_1) + \pi_1 C(z_2, z_2).$$

Again, using the linear homogeneity of C establishes that this last condition is satisfied as long as

$$C(z_1, z_1) \geq C(\pi_2 z_1 + \pi_1 z_2, \pi_2 z_1 + \pi_1 z_2). \tag{9.3}$$

Lemma 9.4 ensures that condition (9.3) is satisfied if **z** is inherently risky. So if **z** is inherently risky, we can conclude that the constraint set defined by T*.1 to T*.4 is nonempty.

Summarizing the above, we have:

> **Result 9.4:** *Under Assumption 9.2, for all inherently risky z, the constraint set defined by T*.1 to T*.4 is nonempty. Further, an allocation that satisfies T*.2 exactly satisfies all the incentive constraints to the agency-cost-minimization problem.*

Results 9.1 and 9.4, and Lemmas 9.3 and 9.4 allow us to reason in the following fashion: second-best optimality requires that **z** be inherently risky by Result 9.1; Lemma 9.4 establishes that second-best **z** must be monotonic for C to be positively linearly homogeneous; and, finally, Result 9.4 establishes that for all inherently risky, and hence monotonic **z**, the constraint set for the second-best agency-cost problem is nonempty. Thus, for practical purposes in considering the second-best agency-cost function, we can restrict our attention to those **z** that are inherently risky (and thus monotonic) as long as we maintain Assumption 9.2.

The objective function of the second-best agency-cost problem is strictly convex in the control variables. Having established that the constraint set is convex and nonempty for that problem, it follows immediately that:

> **Corollary 9.4.1:** *Under Assumption 9.2, for all inherently risky z, the second-best agency-cost problem has a unique solution.*

We now proceed to deduce the unique closed-form solution to the agency-cost problem:

> **Result 9.5:** *Under Assumption 9.2, for inherently risky z, any solution to the agency-cost problem satisfies T*.2 exactly.*

Result 9.5, which parallels results by Weymark (1986) for the optimal tax problem, is demonstrated graphically in Figure 9.2. The level curve of the principal's objective function is given by a curve smoothly concave to the origin and tangent to the fair-odds line at the bisector. The principal's preference direction is to the southwest.

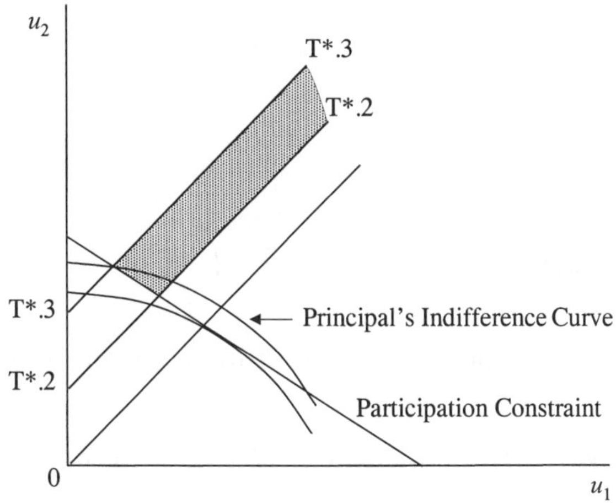

Figure 9.2 The agency-cost problem in utility space.

If T*.3 binds exactly, the set of points meeting T*.3 is given by a line segment parallel to the bisector. The intercept of this line segment on the u_2 axis is $[C(z_2, z_2) - C(z_1, z_2)]/\pi_1$. Now consider the line segment representing the set of points meeting T*.2 exactly. Its intercept on the u_2 axis is given by $[C(z_1, z_2) - C(z_1, z_1)]/\pi_2$. As long as the constraint set defined by T*.2 to T*.4 is nonempty, which inherent riskiness ensures, the intercept of the T*.3 line segment is no lower than the T*.2 intercept. The participation constraint is satisfied by points lying above and to the right of the line segment joining $(C(z_1, z_2)/\pi_1, 0)$ and $(0, C(z_1, z_2)/\pi_2)$. Because the proof of Result 9.4 shows that T*.4 is implied by a convex combination of T*.2 and T*.3, the feasible set, if it is nonempty, is given by the cylinder lying above the participation constraint and between T*.2 and T*.3. At any point other than the intersection between T*.2 and the participation-constraint, agency costs are higher, hence the result.

We are now ready to show, in a fashion similar to Weymark's (1986, 1987) reduction of the hidden-information problem, that the solution to the agency-cost function has a simple closed-form solution. By Result 9.5 and Lemma 9.1a, the equality constraints (T*.1 and T*.2) become a pair of linear simultaneous equations that can be solved for the cost-minimizing levels of u_1 and u_2.

$$\pi_1 u_1 + \pi_2 z_2 = \underline{u} + C(z_1, z_2),$$

$$\pi_2[u_2 - u_1] = C(z_1, z_2) - C(z_1, z_1),$$

or

$$u_1(\mathbf{z}) = \underline{u} + C(z_1, z_1), \tag{9.4}$$

$$u_2(\mathbf{z}) = \underline{u} + C(z_1, z_1) + \frac{C(z_1, z_2) - C(z_1, z_1)}{\pi_2}. \tag{9.5}$$

The preceding derivation is summarized by the main result of this section:

> **Result 9.6:** *Under Assumption 9.2, for inherently risky z, the agency-cost function is given by*
>
> $$Y(z_1, z_2; \pi, \underline{u}) = (1 - \pi_2)h[u_1(\mathbf{z})] + \pi_2 h[u_2(\mathbf{z})],$$

where $u_1(\mathbf{z})$ and $u_2(\mathbf{z})$ are given by (9.4) and (9.5).

The derivation of the agency-cost function is illustrated graphically by the Eucumbene diagram (Figure 9.3)[7]. In this figure, the northeast quadrant contains an isocost curve in (z_1, z_2) space. For positive values of z_1, the southeast quadrant represents the cost of producing a constant output z_1 in each state, that is, producing on the bisector in the northeast quadrant. This permits derivation of $C(z_1, z_2) - C(z_1, z_1)$, which is the difference between the cost of shirking by producing (z_1, z_1) and the cost of producing the desired output (z_1, z_2), which is equal to the cost of production at the point of intersection between the bisector and the isocost curve (z^*, z^*). To illustrate, consider the state-contingent bundle (z_1, z_2) marked in the diagram. Its cost is represented in the southeast quadrant by $C(z^*, z^*)$, and the cost of shirking is given by $C(z_1, z_1)$. The vertical difference, $C(z^*, z^*) - C(z_1, z_1)$, then represents $C(z_1, z_2) - C(z_1, z_1)$.

In the southwest quadrant, the divergence from first-best cost is used to derive second-best agency cost to the principal. The cost of production on the bisector is given by the first-best agency cost $h(\underline{u} + C(z_1, z_2)) = h(\underline{u} + C(z^*, z^*))$. As the production point moves along the isocost curve away from the bisector, $C(z_1, z_2) - C(z_1, z_1)$

7. So-called because it was first drawn by us in the sand on the shoreline of Lake Eucumbene, New South Wales, Australia.

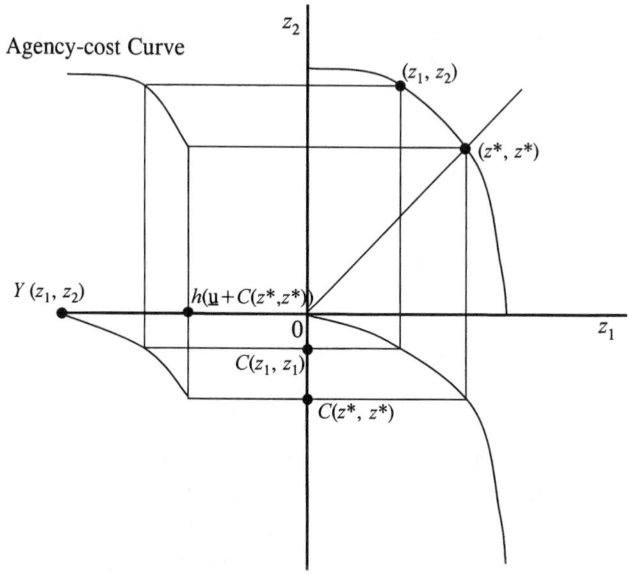

Figure 9.3 Derivation of the agency-cost function.

increases, and, consequently, so does agency cost. Finally, in the northwest quadrant, second-best agency cost is plotted against z_2. (Note that z_1 is determined implicitly by the assumption that the given (z_1, z_2) lies on the isocost curve.)

Results 9.4 to 9.6 can be obtained under weaker conditions on C than Assumption 9.2. However, the agency-cost function given in Result 9.6 is particularly tractable when C is positively linearly homogeneous, so that

$$C(z_1, z_1) = z_1 C(1, 1).$$

Now using the fact that C is convex and h is strictly convex establishes:

Corollary 9.6.1: *For inherently risky* $\mathbf{z}$, *and linearly homogeneous* C, *the agency-cost function* Y *is convex as a function of* $\mathbf{z}$.

Because effort cost is positively linearly homogeneous, and, therefore, exhibits constant relative riskiness, second-best agency cost for any inherently risky $\mathbf{z}$ changes in a simple way in response to a radial expansion of any output vector. (Recall for a technology exhibiting constant relative riskiness, radial changes in the output vector do not change the relative production risk premium.) For $k > 0$,

$$u_i(kz) - \underline{u} = k(u_i(\mathbf{z}) - u), \qquad i = 1, 2,$$

and because h is strictly convex, $h(u_i(kz))$ must be strictly convex in k.

Result 9.7: *For any inherently risky z, and linearly homogeneous* C, $u_i - \underline{u}$ (i = *1,2) is positively linearly homogeneous in z.*

9.5 THE SECOND-STAGE PROBLEM

Corollary 9.6.1 shows that the agency-cost function is strictly convex in **z**. Consequently, the principal's objective function, assuming agency-cost minimization, is strictly concave in **z**. There exists a unique solution to the second-stage second-best problem. Before deriving this solution explicitly, we consider some general results on the solutions to the first-best and second-best problems that don't rely on the assumption of a cost structure exhibiting constant relative riskiness.

9.5.1 General Results on the First-Best and Second-Best Solutions

We start our analysis of the second-stage problem by considering some general implications of decomposition of the first-best and second-best problems. Using Result 9.2, we obtain:

Result 9.8: $V(\pi) = V_{FB}(\pi)$ *if and only if the solution to the first-best problem has* $z_1 = z_2$*, in which case the first-best and second-best solutions coincide. If* $z_1 \neq z_2$ *in the first-best,* $V(\pi) < V_{FB}(\pi)$.

To prove this result, we use the following series of inequalities, valid for any (z_1, z_2):

$$\begin{aligned} \pi_1 z_1^{FB} + \pi_2 z_2^{FB} - Y_{FB}(z_1^{FB}, z_2^{FB}; \pi, \underline{u}) &\geq \pi_1 z_1 + \pi_2 z_2 - Y_{FB}(z_1, z_2; \pi, \underline{u}) \\ &\geq \pi_1 z_1 + \pi_2 z_2 - Y(z_1, z_2; \pi, \underline{u}), \end{aligned}$$

where (z_1^{FB}, z_2^{FB}) denotes the solution to the first-best problem. By the strict convexity of C, the first-best agency-cost function is strictly convex in **z**.[8] Hence, the first-best problem must have a unique solution, and the first inequality can remain weak only if the first-best and the second-best **z** coincide. However, by Result 9.2, the second inequality is weak if and only if $z_1 = z_2$. Therefore, the only way for the first-best and the second-best optimal-value functions to coincide is if the first-best and the second-best state-contingent output vectors coincide and lie on the bisector. This establishes necessity. To go the other way, suppose that in the first-best solution, $z_1 = z_2$. The principal can implement this state-contingent output vector even in the face of T*.2 to T*.4 by guaranteeing the agent a fixed payment in each state, hence the conclusion.

Result 9.8 may be contrasted, for example, with Mirrlees's criticism of the stochastic production-function formulation of the moral-hazard problem, which showed that the principal could always either achieve the first best or get arbitrarily close to it (Mirrlees 1974). In essence, the principal achieved this by specifying a large negative payment whenever output in the worst state of nature fell below that generated by the first-best-effort level, and paying a constant amount whenever output was above this level. The agent, therefore, had an overwhelming incentive to raise output in the worst state. However, as we have seen in Chapters 2, 4, and 6, when production is governed by a stochastic production function, the agent can only do this by increasing effort and, thereby, *raising output in all states of nature*. With the more flexible state-contingent production technology, the agent would respond to such an incentive scheme by simply diverting resources from good states of nature to bad states, and producing in each state the minimum output consistent with receiving the constant positive payment. Thus, the first best would not be achieved by an attempt to impose arbitrarily large fines on the worst outcomes because the producer could always avoid them by reallocating effort.

Another important aspect of state-contingent production technology illustrated by Result 9.8 is the existence of cases of state-contingent production in which it is not merely possible, but optimal to produce the same output in both states, so that, ex post, there is no production uncertainty. Producers whose technology is characterized by a stochastic production function either cannot produce such

8. Under Assumption 9.2, C is not strictly convex as noted before. However, the strict convexity of h, implied by the strict concavity of u, implies that Y_{FB} is strictly convex in this case.

a state-contingent output vector or can do so only by throwing away the difference between good state and bad state output.[9] In the production structure used here, which always allows the agent to produce on the bisector at sufficient cost, Result 9.8 identifies a condition on the technology that is sufficient to remove all moral-hazard contracting problems.

As would be expected on the basis of the analysis in Chapters 4 to 6, generalized Schur-convexity of C is sufficient to ensure that the agent optimally chooses to produce the same output in both states. To see why, notice that in this case, the first-best output pattern involves the agent producing the same output in both states. But as we have already seen, a payment scheme in which the agent produces the same amount in both states in return for a given payment trivially meets T.2 to T.4. Hence, because the principal can do no better than the first best, and the first best is achievable, he implements the first best.

Corollary 9.8.1: $V(\pi) = V_{FB}(\pi)$ *if* C *is generalized Schur-convex.*

As is well known, risk neutrality of the agent (linearity of h, which is ruled out by assumption here) makes moral-hazard problems disappear because the agent is indifferent to risk, and the principal's role as a provider of insurance does not conflict with productive efficiency. A generalized Schur-convex cost structure is another case that makes risk technically unimportant. These cost structures have the property that the first-best solution has equal outputs in both states, so that the principal can always implement the first best by offering the same payment, chosen to satisfy T.1, in both states. (When both outputs and payments are equal in both states, T.2 to T.4 are trivially satisfied.)

The reader should note well, however, that generalized Schur-convex cost structures are not trivially stochastic in the sense that a risk-averse producer will always choose to produce on the bisector. As shown in Chapter 6 (Result 6.10), producers facing price risk and generalized Schur-convex cost structures will generally choose to

9. As Grossman and Hart (1983) observe, if the agent can discard output without the knowledge of the principal, the payment schedule in a solution to the parametrized distribution formulation of the agency-cost problem must be weakly monotonic in reported output. However, this informational structure is different from that considered in this chapter, where the result that the payment schedule must be strictly monotonic in output is derived under the assumption that effort cost is strictly monotonic in output.

produce away from the bisector even in the presence of unbiased futures markets.

By the properties of the first-best and second-best agency cost functions (Result 9.3), we derive:

> **Result 9.9:** $V_{FB}(\pi, \underline{u})$ *and* $V(\pi, \underline{u})$ *are strictly decreasing in the agent's reservation utility* $\underline{u}$.

Hence, any force external to the resolution of the agency-cost problem that makes the agent worse off in his reservation outcome cannot make the principal worse off. In Chapter 10, we shall use the consequences of Result 9.9 to develop a theory of optimal determination of the agent's reservation utility in the framework of agrarian contracting. Before proceeding, it's worth reiterating that Result 9.8, Corollary 9.8.1, and Result 9.9 are general statements about the state-contingent moral-hazard model here considered. That is, *they do not rely on Assumption 9.2.*

9.5.2 The Solution to the Second-Stage Second-Best Problem

Under Assumption 9.2, Lemma 9.2 and Lemma 9.3 imply any potential solution to the second-best problem satisfies $z_2 \geq z_1$. Hence, in developing solutions to the second-best problem, we need only search over state-contingent outputs that lie on or above the bisector in state-contingent output space. This leads immediately to the conclusion:

> **Result 9.10:** *The unique solution to the second-best problem also solves*
>
> $$\max_{z} W^P(z) = \pi_1 z_1 + \pi_2 z_2 - \pi_1 h(u_1(z)) - \pi_2 h(u_2(z))$$
>
> *subject to* $z_1 \leq z_2$, *where* $u_1(z)$ *and* $u_2(z)$ *are given by (9.4) and (9.5).*

Result 9.10 shows that the second-best problem can be solved by maximizing a twice-differentiable function subject to a single linear constraint. Because we need only consider monotonic outputs, this problem can be reduced to a simple nonlinear program in z_1 and α, subject only to nonnegativity constraints, where

$$z_2 = z_1 + \alpha.$$

We can restate the values of u_1 and u_2 in a solution to the agency-cost problem as

$$u_1 = \underline{u} + C(z_1, z_1),$$

$$u_2 = \underline{u} + C(z_1, z_1) + \frac{C(z_1, z_1 + \alpha) - C(z_1, z_1)}{\pi_2}.$$

Substituting these expressions into Result 9.10, denoting the resulting objective function as L, and differentiating with respect to α and z_1 yields the first-order conditions:

$$\frac{\partial L}{\partial \alpha} = \pi_2 - h'(u_2)C_2(z_1, z_2) \leq 0, \qquad \alpha \geq 0, \tag{9.6}$$

$$\frac{\partial L}{\partial z_1} = \frac{\partial L}{\partial \alpha} + \pi_1 - \pi_1(h'(u_1) - h'(u_2))(C_1(z_1, z_1) + C_2(z_1, z_1)) \\ - h'(u_2)C_1(z_1, z_2) \leq 0, \qquad z_1 \geq 0, \tag{9.7}$$

with complementary slackness in both cases.

Now suppose that the optimal production pattern is strictly monotonic, so that $z_1 < z_2$. That is, in the terminology of the literature on adverse selection, *there is a separating rather than a pooling equilibrium*. Then (9.6) holds with equality, so that expression (9.7) can be rewritten as

$$\frac{\partial L}{\partial z_1} = \pi_1 - \pi_1(h'(u_1) - h'(u_2))(C_1(z_1, z_1) + C_2(z_1, z_1)) \\ - h'(u_2)C_1(z_1, z_2) \leq 0.$$

By Lemma 9.1 (using the fact that the solution is strictly monotonic) and the strict convexity of h, $h'(u_1) - h'(u_2) < 0$. Therefore, we conclude that

$$\pi_1 - h'(u_2)C_1(z_1, z_2) \leq 0,$$

and, therefore,

$$\frac{C_1(z_1, z_2)}{\pi_1} \geq \frac{1}{h'(u_2)} \\ = \frac{C_2(z_1, z_2)}{\pi_2}.$$

The last equality follows from (9.6) under the presumption that the solution is strictly monotonic.

Hence, we have proved:

Result 9.11:

(i) A second-best contract structure with strictly monotonic production satisfies

$$\pi_2 - h'(u_2)C(z_1, z_2) = 0.$$

(ii) The optimal contract structure must involve a production pattern such that

$$C_2(z_1, z_2)/\pi_2 \leq C_1(z_1, z_2)/\pi_1 .$$

Result 9.11(i) is perhaps best understood by recalling that, by the implicit function theorem,

$$h'(u_2) = 1/u'(y_2).$$

Therefore, the condition can be rewritten as

$$\pi_2 u'(y_2) - C_2(z_1, z_2) = 0,$$

which would be the first-order condition for a risk-averse agent who is the residual claimant for the output produced.[10] Result 9.11(i), thus, implies that the optimal contract effectively makes the agent the residual claimant in state 2 – the high-output state of nature. The incentive problem is to prevent the agent from shirking by misrepresenting the higher-output state of nature as the low-output state by arranging to always produce z_1. The best way to remove the agent's incentive to shirk in this fashion is to allow her to reap the full marginal benefit from increasing output from z_1 to z_2. Result 9.11(i) ensures that this happens. An interesting implication of Result 9.11(i) is that it rules out all linear payment schemes except for the trivial one where the agent is always made the residual claimant. (Result 9.11[i], however, does not rule out the optimality of contracts that are linear in output, but that have state-contingent side payments.)

10. Result 9.11(i) recalls the optimal income taxation result that the most efficient producers should always face a zero marginal tax for an appropriately designed nonlinear tax schedule (Guesnerie and Seade 1982; Mirrlees 1971). Here the result has a different interpretation but manifests the same basic economic phenomenon.

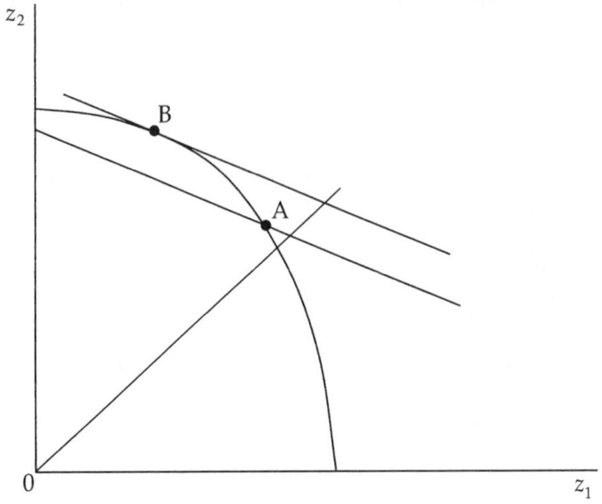

Figure 9.4 Risk aversion and the second-best output.

In the stochastic production-function approach, the riskiness of the output bundle is determined by the effort level. Here, as elsewhere in this book, the riskiness of output is determined independently from the effort level and the scale of output. Result 9.11(ii) shows that, in the absence of the incentive constraints (T.2 to T.4), the principal always prefers a riskier output pattern with a higher expected output for the same level of effort cost. In fact, in the absence of moral-hazard contracting problems, a profit-maximizing principal would simply choose $\mathbf{z}$ to maximize $\pi_1 z_1 + \pi_2 z_2 - C(z_1, z_2)$, and then stabilize the agent's consumption at $h(\underline{u} + C(\mathbf{z}))$. This choice obviously maximizes the residual over and above the payment needed to ensure the agent's reservation utility.

Result 9.11(ii) establishes, however, that the fair-odds line will always cut the isocost curve from below at the second-best production point, say, at point A in Figure 9.4. In the terminology of Chapters 5 and 6, the second-best production point is risk-aversely efficient. Given the same level of effort cost, the risk-neutral principal would always prefer the production bundle B, which is riskier than A, but has a higher expected output. Only the presence of contracting problems prevents the principal from moving the agent to B. That is, if the incentive constraints could be ignored, the principal would always want the agent to divert some existing effort toward production of z_2 instead of z_1.

Summarizing, we have:

Corollary 9.11.1: *In the absence of moral hazard, the principal at the margin would prefer a riskier state-contingent production pattern with a higher expected output.*

Lemma 9.2 establishes monotonicity of the agent's return in observed output. We now show that the principal's net return $\mathbf{z} - \mathbf{y}$ is also monotonic in observed output. If $z_1 < z_2$,

$$\begin{aligned} C_2(z_1, z_2)(z_2 - z_1) &> C(z_1, z_2) - C(z_1, z_1) \\ &= \pi_2(u_2 - u_1) \\ &> \pi_2 u'(y_2)(y_2 - y_1), \end{aligned}$$

where the first inequality follows from the convexity of C, the equality from the fact that T.2 is binding, and the final inequality from the concavity of u. Applying Result 9.11(i) gives:

Corollary 9.11.2: *The optimal contract structure satisfies*

$$(z_2 - z_1) \geq (y_2 - y_1);$$

and

$$(z_2 - y_2) \geq (z_1 - y_1).$$

Corollary 9.11.2 shows that the second-best contract has the agent bear some of the production risk by sharing in the output decrease between state 2 and state 1. Because the payment schedule rises less rapidly than the output schedule, the agent self-insures in the sense of Chapters 7 and 8. That is, the optimal contract exposes the agent to some production risk. Moreover, the second-best production pattern must be consistent with what some strictly risk-averse individual would choose. At the margin, therefore, the agent will always devote more resources to bad-state production than is socially optimal. Inducing the agent to self-insure, as is required for contract efficiency, means that expected output must be decreased below the socially optimal level. Intuitively, it seems quite obvious from the discussion in Chapter 7 (in particular, Result 7.6 from that chapter) that if a condition like Corollary 9.11.2 did not hold for the optimal payment schedule, it would always be to the principal's advantage to

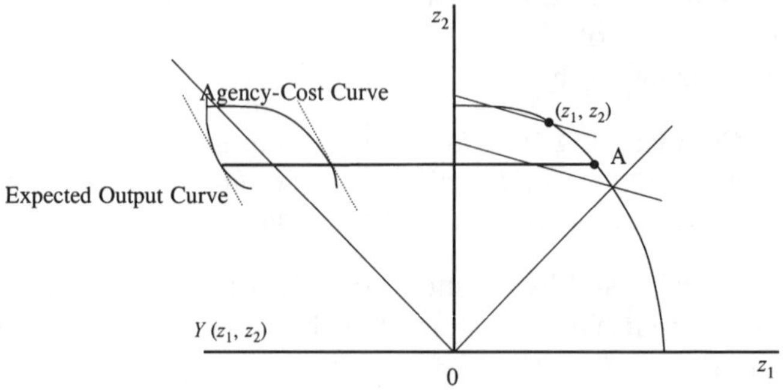

Figure 9.5 The principal's second-stage problem.

require the agent to produce the same amount in both states since the principal's marginal gain from an increase in the good state output would always be negative.

Finally, by using the Eucumbene diagram (Figure 9.3), we can illustrate the solution to the second-stage problem. Figure 9.5 has the agency-cost curve drawn in the northwest quadrant as before. In addition, an expected output curve is plotted. This is obtained by plotting against each z_2, the expected value $\pi_1 z_1 + \pi_2 z_2$ represented by the intersection of the z_2 axis with the inherently risky-odds line through (z_1, z_2). Expected net profit is represented by the horizontal distance between this expected output curve and agency cost. It is maximized (for the cost level represented by the given isocost curve) at the point at which tangents to the agency-cost and expected cost curves are parallel.

9.6 EXTENSIONS AND APPLICATIONS

9.6.1 Extensions

We will briefly sketch a number of extensions to the formal model presented earlier. First, the assumptions of expected-utility preferences for the agent and risk neutrality for the principal could be relaxed. For general preferences, the constraints T.1 to T.4 may be rewritten as

(T.1) $W(y_1, y_2) - C(z_1, z_2) \geq \underline{u}$
(T.2) $W(y_1, y_2) - C(z_1, z_2) \geq W(y_1, y_1) - C(z_1, z_1)$
(T.3) $W(y_1, y_2) - C(z_1, z_2) \geq W(y_2, y_2) - C(z_2, z_2)$
(T.4) $W(y_1, y_2) - C(z_1, z_2) \geq W(y_2, y_1) - C(z_2, z_1)$,

or, assuming that T.1 holds with equality,[11]

(T.1) $W(y_1, y_2) - C(z_1, z_2) = \underline{u}$
(T.2) $W(y_1, y_1) - C(z_1, z_1) \leq \underline{u}$
(T.3) $W(y_2, y_2) - C(z_2, z_2) \leq \underline{u}$
(T.4) $W(y_2, y_1) - C(z_2, z_1) \leq \underline{u}$.

Subject to appropriate regularity conditions on W, the argument presented before to show that a cost-minimizing solution will have T.2 binding remains valid. The main advantage of the expected-utility representation used here is the possibility of deriving an explicit solution for u_1 and u_2, and therefore a closed-form solution for the agency-cost function.

The assumption of risk neutrality for the principal could be relaxed to allow for either a net-returns objective function $W^p(\mathbf{z} - \mathbf{y})$ or a separable objective function $W^p(\mathbf{z}) - g^p(\mathbf{y})$. The first approach allows for the replacement of the first-best solution derived here with one based on Borch's risk-sharing rule. The second approach is interesting primarily because the principal's problem has the same functional form as the agent's. This suggests the possibility of a model incorporating a hierarchy in which individuals act as both principals and agents.

The information structure used in the moral-hazard model could be modified in a number of ways. If the agent receives partial information about the state of nature prior to contracting, the model incorporates problems of adverse selection. A simple adverse-selection model might be set up as follows. Suppose that agents choose a state-contingent production vector, then observe a signal[12] that gives infor-

11. For general preference structures, this may not be true.
12. In a state-space representation of uncertainty, a signal or message is an event, that is, a subset of the space of states of nature. To represent a signal about production prospects, it is necessary to consider a state space finer than the two-element space {1, 2} considered here. In this finer state space, the conditions relevant to production are events, which may still be denoted 1 and 2. Observation of a given signal or message determines the conditional probability of events 1 and 2.

mation about the relative probabilities of states 1 and 2, and then contracts with the principal. The value of the signal corresponds to the agent's information about his "type," which plays a central role in standard adverse-selection models. The parallel with standard adverse-selection models is exact if the principal cannot observe the signal but can verify the state of nature ex post. More interesting, perhaps, is the possibility of a model incorporating both adverse-selection and moral-hazard effects, which arise if the principal is uninformed about the state of nature both ex post and ex ante. Further variations arise if information arrives before production decisions are made. A variety of monitoring problems may be represented by supposing that the principal can, at a cost, receive information about the state of nature.

Finally, the average level of the agent's payment in the model presented here is determined by an exogenous reservation utility. A number of alternatives may be considered. If a minimum-payment constraint (rather than a reservation utility constraint) is binding, a model similar to that found in the literature on efficiency wages will emerge. The reservation utility may be determined within the model as the highest utility the agent can achieve by consuming the bundle (z_1, z_2) instead of contracting with the principal. Alternatively, if principals act competitively, the equilibrium requirement for zero expected profits may be used in conjunction with a labor supply curve to determine an endogenous utility level for agents.

In the next chapter, we consider yet another possibility, namely, that the principal engages in exploitative or coercive activity to limit the agent's outside opportunities and thereby reduce reservation utility. Our analysis is predicated on the finding that the principal's objective function is strictly decreasing in the agent's reservation utility. Hence, if the principal could costlessly decrease the agent's reservation utility, he would do so because it would offer him a net gain.

A final extension of the present model would be to examine the agency problem under the assumption that the agent's cost structure exhibits constant absolute riskiness instead of constant relative riskiness.

9.6.2 Applications

Moral-hazard models have been applied to problems including insurance, sharecropping, wage determination, and constitutional design.

In all cases, state-contingent production plays a crucial but often unrecognized role. Significant policy implications are likely to arise from recognition of the possibility that agents can reallocate effort to improve outcomes in some states of nature at the cost of accepting worse outcomes in other states. The more flexible the agent's productive technology, the more constrained is the principal in designing an incentive-compatible contract. Rather than briefly survey a wide range of potential applications,[13] we will set out an agenda for a particularly challenging task – economic modeling of crime.

Consider potentially criminal activities as commitments of effort $\mathbf{x}$ that produce state-contingent benefits to the criminal $\mathbf{z}$, effects on society $\mathbf{q}$, and other outcomes $\mathbf{m}$ that may be used as evidence by police and courts. Assuming that the external effects $\mathbf{q}$ reduce welfare, we may describe such activities as antisocial. Individual i will undertake antisocial activity if the returns from doing so exceed the reservation utility $\underline{u}_i$ associated with the best alternative option. The problem for society has several interrelated parts.

Prevention and mitigation strategies may be used to reduce either the benefits from undertaking antisocial activity or the damage done by such activity. Such strategies may be modeled as changes to the individual's production possibility set. For example, locks increase the effort required to break into houses and cars. Seat belts and airbags reduce the damage resulting from crashes caused by unsafe driving. (We focus on the external damage caused by the unsafe driving of others.) More generally, most interdictive policies are, at least partially, predicated on the principle of raising the criminal's cost of engaging in criminal activity. In our framework, these can be modeled directly in terms of the criminal's technology.

Sanctions or rewards may be designed to induce individuals to refrain from antisocial choices. That is, given the observation of some subset of ($\mathbf{z}$, $\mathbf{q}$, $\mathbf{m}$) and perhaps some information about the state of nature, the problem is to design a set of sanctions or rewards $\mathbf{y}$. In most developed societies, there is a distinction between civil law, including regulation, in which most sanctions and rewards are monetary, and criminal law, in which sanctions such as imprisonment may be imposed. An important problem is to provide an explanation for

13. In Quiggin and Chambers (1998b), we present a detailed application of this model to the problem of point-source pollution control.

the existence of this distinction and for the fact that some activities (for example, pollution) are regarded in some contexts as civil wrongs, and in other contexts as criminal wrongs.

The optimal sanction structure will in general be monotonic; that is, the more severe the crime, the more severe the punishment. Otherwise, potential criminals will act on the reasoning that "I may as well be hung for a sheep as a lamb." This point seems obvious enough, but is obscured in much of the existing literature in which individuals are presumed to face a choice set consisting of only two elements (Commit crime, Don't commit crime). Under this assumption, the strategy of imposing a maximum penalty with low probability often appears to be optimal. However, this "public execution of parking violators" prescription arises from the unrealistic assumptions of the model concerning the agent's range of choices and is not a good guide to policy.

Society must also make decisions about the allocation of resources to the collection of evidence and about the rules of inference required in determining a verdict. There is a large literature on the latter question, but it has not normally been placed in the context of a general model of economic choice. In particular, the costs of Type I and Type II errors are normally treated as exogenous, rather than as being determined within the model. More fundamentally, this literature normally takes as given a central principle of the criminal justice system – the requirement for judges or juries to make a determination "Guilty or Not Guilty" before any criminal sanction is imposed. An important corollary is that since findings of guilt are assumed to be "beyond reasonable doubt," the severity of the sentence is not supposed to be affected by any residual doubts. In reality, practices such as plea-bargaining erode such sharp distinctions. An important problem for an economic analysis of crime and punishment should be to explain such phenomena.

Last but not least, it is necessary to focus on the reservation utility $\underline{u}_i$. In the next chapter, we consider the possibility that principals may achieve higher profit levels by actions that reduce the attractiveness of alternative options. In the case of crime, the opposite is true. An improved outcome, with lower levels of crime, will be achieved if more attractive alternatives, such as secure and well-paying jobs are available, thereby increasing $\underline{u}_i$.

10 Endogenous Reservation Utility: Agency and Exploitation

In Chapter 9, the agent's reservation utility is taken as exogenous to the principal. In effect, this assumption implies that principals are, in the words of Braverman and Stiglitz (1986), ". . . expected-utility takers." In this, our final chapter, we will illustrate the power of the moral-hazard model developed in Chapter 9 by applying it to examine the determination of the agent's reservation utility and the possibility of exploitation of the agent by the principal through extra-contract means.

One of our consistent criticisms of the parametrized distribution formulation is that it does not lend itself to interesting comparative-static analyses. In Chapter 9, we showed how our reformulation of the moral-hazard problem could be used to conduct an array of comparative-static experiments. In this chapter, we demonstrate the point even more forcefully by using the results of Chapter 9 to develop a theory of equilibrium determination of the agent's reservation utility. Then we show how that equilibrium reservation utility, the principal's cost, and the agent's expected output respond to changes in the cost of exploiting the agent and in the market price of the output produced by the agent.

In our introductory chapter, we emphasized that the state-contingent formulation permitted the application of standard economic analyses to decision making under uncertainty. In particular, we emphasized there and in Chapters 4 and 5 that standard duality principles apply to such problems. This chapter returns to that point and underlines it by showing how principal–agent problems, given the agency-cost function developed in Chapter 9, can be analyzed using arguments familiar from duality theory that imply interesting and important comparative static results.

The assumption of an alternative (presumably competitive) market, to which the agent has free access and with which the principal effectively competes is plausible in many instances, but in others it isn't. A particularly compelling example comes from the literature on agrarian contracting, which uses principal–agent models to formulate an economic theory of peasant 'exploitation' by landlords. To make the discussion in this chapter more concrete, therefore, we use the metaphor of a peasant–landlord contracting problem to discuss the equilibrium determination of the agent's reservation utility.

In existing models, principals (landlords) certainly "exploit" any monopsony power vested in them by their position as the residual claimant, but they still must offer the agent (peasant) her next best alternative. Consequently, the equilibrium contracts, as in Chapter 9, are constrained Paretian-efficient. Apart from distributional concerns, they resemble contracts that would emerge in a competitive market where the landlord has no ability to exploit the peasant. Directly unproductive profit-seeking (DUP) activity, in which valuable economic resources are diverted from productive activity to enhancing the landlord's ability to exploit the peasant, is not countenanced by these models.[1]

Because exploitative investment is a DUP activity, a principal–agent formulation of agrarian contracting in the presence of such investment must encompass two forms of market imperfection: the landlord's exploitative activity and the asymmetric-information (moral-hazard) problem underlying the principal–agent formulation of the agrarian contracting problem. Second-best theory suggests that removing only one of these imperfections may not improve social welfare. In particular, removing moral hazard need not improve social welfare. *With extra-contract exploitative investment by the landlord, moral hazard may play a positive social role by limiting the landlord's ability to exploit the peasant.* One obvious case occurs when, in

1. A number of writers have discussed the asymmetric access to coercive mechanisms that the landlord class historically has had in agrarian economies (Basu 1986; Binswanger, Deininger and Feder 1993; Boserup 1979; Chwe 1990). The contribution of this chapter is a model of the interaction between asymmetric access to coercive mechanisms, and asymmetric information.

the absence of moral hazard, the landlord's exploitative investment reduces social welfare below what would occur if the peasant and the landlord did not contract and the landlord committed nothing to exploitation. In such a case, the presence of moral-hazard problems severe enough to prevent contracting would improve welfare.

Among other results, we show that the level of peasant exploitation is increasing in the value of the crop grown and decreasing in the cost of exploitation. Finally, we develop the social-welfare properties of the agrarian contracting–exploitation problem. We exhibit instances when moral hazard plays a positive social role by limiting the landlord's incentive to exploit the peasant.

10.1 THE MODEL

A risk-neutral landlord and a risk-averse peasant tenant are contracting over the conditions required for the peasant to farm a given plot of land for the landlord. The contract includes any borrowing or lending between the peasant and the landlord as well as wage payments for farming the land. The landlord is the residual claimant for the crop grown and has the right to specify the contract terms. The landlord has access to a competitive market in which the crop can be sold at the going rate of p. As in Chapter 9, crop production is uncertain, and there is hidden action because the landlord cannot observe the peasant's allocation of effort or the state of nature. Ex post output is observable and contractible. Unlike in Chapter 9, however, by an appropriate expenditure of effort through political or other extra-contract channels, the landlord can affect the peasant's next best alternative, that is, the peasant's reservation utility. The peasant takes this next best alternative as given, and in considering whether to adopt the contract offered by the landlord only compares the offered contract with this alternative.[2] Contracting takes place before uncertainty is resolved, and before the peasant commits any effort. After

2. Another approach would be to assume that landlords, and peasants also contract over the peasant's alternative, with the peasant, perhaps, paying a fee to avoid adverse actions by the landlord. This violates the intent and the spirit of our problem, which is to consider whether the landlord might usefully pursue extra-contract means to exploit the peasant. To focus on this aspect of the problem, we explicitly assume that the peasant and the landlord cannot contract over the alternative itself.

the contract is concluded, the peasant commits effort prior to the resolution of uncertainty. Then uncertainty is resolved, and the landlord receives the output and makes the payment to the peasant on that basis. Both parties to the contract can commit, and the contracts, once agreed upon, are enforceable at zero cost.

The production model is the same as that used in Chapter 9. There are two states of nature and a single stochastic output – the agricultural crop for which the landlord is the residual claimant. The information structure is as follows. Only the peasant observes the conditions under which production takes place, that is, only the peasant can observe which state of nature occurs and what input levels are committed. The landlord cannot observe the peasant's effort but, being the residual claimant, can observe and has the rights to the output that occurs. Both the landlord and the peasant know the technology and each other's preferences. They also share common a priori beliefs about the probability with which each state of nature will occur.

As in Chapter 9, the peasant's ex post preferences are additively separable in the returns and the vector of inputs committed to production. To simplify, we assume that the utility of returns exhibits the logarithmic, constant relative risk-aversion form. Hence,

$$w(y, \mathbf{x}) = \ln y - g(\mathbf{x}).$$

Here, as in Chapter 9, y is the peasant's consumption, and g is a strictly increasing and strictly convex function of the effort vector, $\mathbf{x}$. The peasant is not directly concerned about output.

The peasant's effort-cost function is denoted by $C(\mathbf{z})$. $C(\mathbf{z})$ is convex, strictly increasing, twice continuously differentiable, and positively linearly homogeneous in $\mathbf{z}$. Relative probabilities are such that a risk-neutral individual would always consider state-2 to be the good state of nature in the sense that

$$\frac{C_2(z\mathbf{1})}{\pi_2} \leq \frac{C_1(z\mathbf{1})}{\pi_1},$$

where $\mathbf{1}$ is the two-dimensional unit vector.

For given $\mathbf{y}$ and $\mathbf{z}$, the peasant's maximum expected utility is, therefore,

$$\pi_1 \ln y_1 + \pi_2 \ln y_2 - C(\mathbf{z}).$$

We will denote the peasant's reservation utility by $\underline{u}$, which is subject to the landlord's choice, but which the peasant takes as given.

To preserve generality and model simplicity, the exact mechanism by which the landlord sets the reservation utility is not specified. We only presume that the landlord does have the ability to determine $\underline{u}$. That ability, however, is economically limited because the landlord must commit resources to affect $\underline{u}$. For example, if the peasants had the alternative of working as wage laborers, the landlord might be able to exert political influence to have earnings taxes imposed on wage laborers. But exerting political influence necessarily has a positive opportunity cost, if only in terms of the cost of the landlord's time committed to moral and other types of suasion. To formalize, suppose that the peasant's reservation utility in the absence of landlord intervention is u^o: The landlord is assumed to incur cost, measured by $Af(\underline{u})$, to lower the peasant's reservation utility below u^o, where $A > 0$, and f: $[\underline{\underline{u}}, u^o] \to \Re_+$ is a decreasing and convex function satisfying $Af(u^o) = 0$ and $Af'(u^o) = 0$, where $\underline{\underline{u}}$ denotes a minimum feasible level of utility. In what follows, we shall often refer to A, rather loosely, as the landlord's cost of exploitation.

The agrarian contract between the peasant and the landlord takes the same form as in Chapter 9. The landlord nominates for each state of nature a payment y_i and asks the peasant to report both the unobservable state and the observable output z_i to receive that payment. If the peasant is to receive y_i, she must report that state i occurred and the observable output must be z_i. We refer to $[(y_1, z_1), (y_2, z_2)]$ as the contract.

Specifying a state-contingent payoff-production contract creates an incentive problem, however, because the landlord cannot observe the peasant's effort or which state of nature occurs. Only the peasant has this information. Therefore, the peasant may find it advantageous to misrepresent which state of nature actually occurs unless the landlord designs a contract that makes doing so irrational. Thus, by the results in Chapter 9, any contract that the landlord can implement must satisfy the following constraints:

$$\begin{aligned} &\pi_1 \ln y_1 + \pi_2 \ln y_2 - C(z_1, z_2) \geq \ln y_1 - C(z_1, z_1), \\ &\pi_1 \ln y_1 + \pi_2 \ln y_2 - C(z_1, z_2) \geq \ln y_2 - C(z_2, z_2), \\ &\pi_1 \ln y_1 + \pi_2 \ln y_2 - C(z_1, z_2) \geq \pi_1 \ln y_2 + \pi_2 \ln y_1 - C(z_2, z_1). \end{aligned} \tag{10.1}$$

An immediate consequence of Result 9.1 and Lemma 9.4 in Chapter 9, the properties of the peasant's effort-cost function, and our assumption that state 2 is the good state of nature is:

Lemma 10.1: *Any contract satisfying (10.1) must also satisfy:*

$(y_1, z_1) < (y_2, z_2)$, *or*
$(y_1, z_1) = (y_2, z_2)$.

We can now state the landlord's problem formally. The landlord chooses $(\underline{u}, z_1, z_2, y_1, y_2)$ to

$$\max\{\pi_1(pz_1 - y_1) + \pi_2(pz_2 - y_2) - Af(\underline{u})\}$$

subject to

$$\pi_1 \ln y_1 + \pi_2 \ln y_2 - C(z_1, z_2) \geq \underline{u},$$
$$\pi_1 \ln y_1 + \pi_2 \ln y_2 - C(z_1, z_2) \geq \ln y_1 - C(z_1, z_1),$$
$$\pi_1 \ln y_1 + \pi_2 \ln y_2 - C(z_1, z_2) \geq \ln y_2 - C(z_2, z_2),$$
$$\pi_1 \ln y_1 + \pi_2 \ln y_2 - C(z_1, z_2) \geq \pi_1 \ln y_2 + \pi_2 \ln y_1 - C(z_2, z_1).$$

These constraints are explained more fully in Chapter 9. Briefly, the first inequality represents the peasant's *participation constraint*. Even though there is extra-contract exploitation on the part of the landlord, or "extortion," the peasant chooses where to commit effort. So although the landlord can affect the reservation utility, he cannot determine where the peasant works. The last three inequalities, of course, correspond to (10.1). A standard result (Lemma 9.1, Chapter 9) for additively separable utility structures is:

Lemma 10.2: *For given* $\underline{u}$, *the landlord specifies a contract that yields the peasant exactly his or her reservation utility.*

Because the landlord chooses the peasant's reservation utility, Lemma 10.2 implies that ultimately the landlord also chooses the peasant's welfare level.

10.1.1 The Agency-Cost Function

As in Chapter 9, we solve the landlord's problem in stages. In the first-stage agency-cost problem, the landlord chooses (y_1, y_2) to

$$\min\{\pi_1 y_1 + \pi_2 y_2\}$$

subject to

$$\pi_1 \ln y_1 + \pi_2 \ln y_2 - C(z_1, z_2) \geq \underline{u},$$
$$\pi_1 \ln y_1 + \pi_2 \ln y_2 - C(z_1, z_2) \geq \ln y_1 - C(z_1, z_1),$$
$$\pi_1 \ln y_1 + \pi_2 \ln y_2 - C(z_1, z_2) \geq \ln y_2 - C(z_2, z_2),$$
$$\pi_1 \ln y_1 + \pi_2 \ln y_2 - C(z_1, z_2) \geq \pi_1 \ln y_2 + \pi_2 \ln y_1 - C(z_2, z_1).$$

Applying Result 9.6 in Chapter 9 gives:

Lemma 10.3: *If* **z** *is monotonic and inherently risky, the second-best agency-cost function is given by the twice-differentiable function*

$$Y(z_1, z_2; \pi_2, \underline{u}) = exp(\underline{u}) m(z_1, z_2; \pi_2),$$

where

$$m(z_1, z_2; \pi_2) = (1 - \pi_2)\, exp(C(z_1, z_1)) + \pi_2\, exp\left(\frac{C(z_1, z_2)}{\pi_2} - \frac{1-\pi_2}{\pi_2} C(z_1, z_1)\right).$$

Corollary 10.1: *If z is monotonic and inherently risky, then (a)* Y *is strictly increasing and strictly convex in* $\underline{u}$, *with* $Y_u = Y$, *and (b)* Y *is increasing in* z_2 *and convex in z.*

Corollary 10.1(a) shows why the landlord should commit resources to reducing the tenant's reservation utility: As the peasant's reservation utility falls, the landlord's cost of getting the peasant to adopt any state-contingent output vector falls. Hence, the landlord always gains from a costless reduction in the peasant's reservation utility. For each unit that the peasant's reservation utility falls, the landlord can reduce the peasant's utility in each state by a like amount, thus lowering each state-contingent payment to the peasant.

The fact that agency cost takes the multiplicative form exp $(\bar{u})$ $m(z_1, z_2; \pi_2)$ reflects the constant, relative risk-aversion property of the logarithmic utility function assumed here. Consequently:

Result 10.1: *If* **z** *is monotonic and inherently risky, an increase in* $\underline{u}$ *leads to equiproportionate increases in* $exp(\underline{u})$, y_1, y_2, *and* Y.

The peasant's certainty equivalent for the state-contingent payment scheme (y_1, y_2) (first-best agency cost) is $\exp(C(z_1, z_2) + \underline{u})$ and its expected value is $Y(z_1, z_2; \pi_2, \underline{u}, t)$. Hence, the peasant's risk premium for the payment scheme (y_1, y_2) is

$$\exp(\underline{u})\left(\pi_2\left(\exp\left(\frac{C(z_1, z_2)}{\pi_2} - \frac{1-\pi_2}{\pi_2}C(z_1, z_1)\right) - \exp(C(z_1, z_1))\right)\right).$$

Result 10.1 and this recognition yield:

Corollary 10.2: *If* $\mathbf{z}$ *is monotonic and inherently risky, an increase in* $\underline{u}$ *leads the landlord to offer the peasant a payment scheme with a higher risk premium. The increase in the risk premium is proportional to the increase in exp(*$\underline{u}$*).*

10.2 AN OPTIMAL AGRARIAN CONTRACT FOR AN "EXPECTED-UTILITY" TAKER

In this section, we solve the second-stage of the landlord's problem, and in so doing solve the standard optimal agrarian contract. By Lemma 10.1, we can restrict attention to $\mathbf{z}$ that are monotonic and inherently risky. The second-stage problem is formally stated as the following concave program:

$$V(\underline{u}, p, \pi) = \max_{\mathbf{z}}\{p(\pi_1 z_1 + \pi_2 z_2) - Y(z_1, z_2; \pi_2, \underline{u})\}.$$

However, a little manipulation reveals that

$$V(\underline{u}, p, \pi) = \exp(\underline{u})\upsilon\left(\frac{p}{\exp(\underline{u})}, \pi\right),$$

where

$$\upsilon\left(\frac{p}{\exp(\underline{u})}, \pi\right) = \max_{z_1, z_2}\left\{\frac{p}{\exp(\underline{u})}(\pi_1 z_1 + \pi_2 z_2) - m(z_1, z_2; \pi_2)\right\}.$$

Standard comparative-static manipulations determine how expected crop size and expected landlord cost (the tenant's expected payment) respond to changes in p and $\underline{u}$. Let $q = p/\exp(\underline{u})$, and

$$\mathbf{z}(q) \in \arg\max\left\{\frac{p}{\exp(\underline{u})}(\pi_1 z_1 + \pi_2 z_2) - m(z_1, z_2; \pi_2)\right\}.$$

By definition:

$$qE[\mathbf{z}(q)] - m(\mathbf{z}(q); \pi_2) \geq qE[\mathbf{z}(q^\circ)] - m(\mathbf{z}(q^\circ); \pi_2),$$

and

$$q^{\circ}E[\mathbf{z}(q^{\circ})]-m(\mathbf{z}(q^{\circ});\pi_2)\geq q^{\circ}E[\mathbf{z}(q)]-m(\mathbf{z}(q);\pi_2),$$

where E is the expectations operator over π. Adding these inequalities and rearranging obtains:

$$(q^{\circ}-q)(E[\mathbf{z}(q^{\circ})]-E[\mathbf{z}(q)])\geq 0.$$

A similar manipulation also reveals that

$$\left(\frac{1}{q}-\frac{1}{q^{\circ}}\right)(m(z_1(q^{\circ}),z_2(q^{\circ});\pi_2)-m(z_1(q),z_2(q);\pi_2))\geq 0.$$

These two inequalities imply:

> **Result 10.2:** *For given* $\underline{u}$, *the expected value of the landlord's optimal output vector* (E[*z(q)*]) *is nondecreasing in the crop price* (p) *and nonincreasing in the peasant's reservation utility; and the peasant's expected payment (agency cost) is nondecreasing in* p.

The landlord responds to an increase in p by asking the peasant to produce a higher expected output, which necessarily requires a greater effort. To induce the peasant to increase effort, the landlord must offer the peasant a higher expected payment. Similarly, an increase in reservation utility increases agency cost proportionally for all state-contingent output pairs. Faced with this increased cost, the landlord reduces expected crop size.

As an aside, it is interesting to note that V and Y are convex conjugates (Rockafellar 1970), so that a dual relationship between them also exists. Because this is true, it immediately follows that:

> **Result 10.3:** *For given* $\underline{u}$*: (a)* $V(\underline{u}, p, \pi)$ *is decreasing and concave in* $\underline{u}$ *with* $V_u = -Y$*; and (b)* $V(\underline{u}, p, \pi)$ *is nondecreasing and convex in* p *with* $V_p(u, p, \pi) = E[z(q)]$.

Result 10.3 is established by elementary maximization arguments. For (a), note that the landlord's objective function is decreasing in $\underline{u}$ by the properties of the agency-cost function. Hence, $V(\underline{u}, p, \pi)$ must be decreasing as well. Corollary 10.1 establishes that the landlord's objective function is strictly concave in $\underline{u}$ and concave in $\mathbf{z}$. Standard results in optimization theory, for example, Chambers (1988, Lemma 14, p. 316) then imply that the indirect objective function is also concave in $\underline{u}$. This establishes (a) after applying the envelope theorem to obtain the derivative property.

Moving on to (b), notice that $p^o > p$ implies that $q^o > q$ for fixed $\underline{u}$. Now suppose that the crop price increases from p to p^o but that the landlord has the same ex post output vector implemented as at p. The landlord's expected profit increases by $(p^o - p)E[\mathbf{z}(q)]$. The landlord will only rationally change the ex post output vector if it increases expected profit even further. Convexity follows from an argument well known in the duality literature (McFadden 1978). Consider $p^* = \mu p + (1 - \mu)p^o$ for $0 < \mu < 1$. It follows that

$$\begin{aligned} &pE\mathbf{z}(p) - Y(z_1(p), z_2(p); \pi_2, \underline{u}) \\ &\quad \geq pE(\mathbf{z}(p^*)) - Y(z_1(p^*), z_2(p^*); \pi_2, \underline{u}), \end{aligned}$$

and

$$\begin{aligned} &p^{o}E\mathbf{z}(p^{o}) - Y(z_1(p^{o}), z_2(p^{o}); \pi_2, \underline{u}) \\ &\quad \geq p^{o}E(\mathbf{z}(p^*)) - Y(z_1(p^*), z_2(p^*); \pi_2, \underline{u}). \end{aligned}$$

Multiply the first expression by μ, the second expression by $(1 - \mu)$, and add them together to establish convexity. To establish the derivative property, apply the envelope theorem.

The first part of Result 10.3 is particularly important because it establishes:

> **Corollary 10.3:** *The landlord's optimal expected payment to the peasant (agency cost) is nondecreasing in the peasant's reservation utility.*

If the peasant's reservation utility rises, the landlord must respond by offering the peasant a higher expected payment to encourage her to decline the alternative. Or put another way, the landlord would always find it in his interest to try to costlessly reduce the peasant's reservation utility.

By Corollary 10.1, the objective function for the second-stage problem is concave. As in Chapter 9, define $\alpha \geq 0$ by

$$z_2 \equiv z_1 + \alpha.$$

The resulting necessary and sufficient first-order conditions for z_1 and α in the landlord's optimization problem are

$$p - Y_1(z_1, z_2, \underline{u}, \pi) - Y_2(z_1, z_2, \underline{u}, \pi) \leq 0, \qquad z_1 \geq 0,$$
$$p\pi_2 - Y_2(z_1, z_2, \underline{u}, \pi) \leq 0, \qquad \alpha \geq 0$$

in the notation of complementary slackness.

The first of these conditions is a state-arbitrage result for the landlord (see Chapters 5 and 6). It implies that the landlord optimally designs the contract so that the peasant increases **z** to the point where there is no marginal increase in the landlord's expected profit from increasing both state-contingent outputs by the same positive amount. For an interior solution, a one unit increase in both state-contingent outputs breaks even at the margin. The second condition is more transparent if it is rewritten as

$$p\pi_2 - \exp(u_2)C_2(z_1, z_2) \leq 0,$$

which is the first-order condition for setting z_2 for a risk-averse peasant who is the residual claimant for the crop (e.g., see Chapter 9, Result 9.11). Therefore, the optimal agrarian contract effectively makes the peasant the residual claimant in state 2. As in Chapter 9, the reason is also apparent; the incentive problem is to induce the peasant to choose the state-contingent output vector (z_1, z_2) and not (z_1, z_1). One way to do this is to make the peasant the residual claimant for all marginal increases in the high-state output.

If $\alpha > 0$,

$$p(1 - \pi_2) - Y_1(z_1, z_2, \underline{u}, \pi) \leq 0,$$

implying that z_1 also should be increased to the point where the landlord can make no positive expected profit by increasing it further. It does not imply, however, that the peasant should be made the residual claimant of state-1 output as can be verified by computing Y_1 using Lemma 10.3. If the peasant were the true residual claimant for the state-1 output, optimality would require instead that

$$p(1 - \pi_2) - \exp(u_1)C_1(z_1, z_2) = 0.$$

Summarizing, we have the following special case of Result 9.11 in Chapter 9:

> **Result 10.4:** *Under the stated conditions, an interior "expected-utility taking" optimal contract satisfies:*

$$(a)\ p\pi_2 - exp(u_2)C_2(z_1, z_2) = 0$$

$$(b)\ \frac{Y_1}{\pi_1} = \frac{Y_2}{\pi_2}.$$

10.3 THE PROFIT-MAXIMIZING LEVEL OF PEASANT EXPLOITATION

The final stage of the landlord's optimization problem is the choice of the optimal level of peasant exploitation. Given preceding developments, this problem can be formulated mathematically as the following concave program:

$$W(p, \pi; A) = \max_{\underline{u}}\{V(\underline{u}, p, \pi) - Af(\underline{u})\}.$$

We first determine whether exploitation, which we now define as the landlord choosing $\underline{u} < u^o$, is profitable for the landlord. The assumption that the marginal cost of exploitation is negligible at u^o and Result 10.3 ensure that

$$V_u(u^o, p, \pi) - Af'(u^o) < 0,$$

implying that some exploitation is always optimal. Letting

$$\bar{u}(A) \in \arg\max\{V(\underline{u}, p, \pi) - Af(\underline{u})\},$$

arguments similar to those used to establish Result 10.1 imply

$$(A^o - A)(f(\bar{u}(A^o)) - f(\bar{u}(A))) \geq 0,$$

which by the fact that f is monotonic in $\bar{u}$ implies

$$(A^o - A)(\bar{u}(A^o) - \bar{u}(A)) \geq 0.$$

As the cost of exploiting peasants grows, the level of peasant exploitation falls, that is, the peasant's reservation utility rises. Using this latter fact with Result 10.2 yields:

> **Result 10.5:** *The landlord exploits the peasant; the level of peasant exploitation is nonincreasing in the cost of exploitation* (A)*, and the expected value of the crop is nonincreasing in the cost of exploitation* (A)*.*

The second part of Result 10.5 follows because Result 10.2 establishes that, for given $\underline{u}$, the expected value of the crop is nonincreasing in the peasant's reservation utility. Hence, anything that increases the peasant's reservation utility and that has no direct impact on expected crop size (for example, an increase in A) also decreases expected crop size. Consequently, as intuition would suggest, landlords respond to increases in the cost of exploitation by downsizing the agricultural operation and allowing the peasant access to more attractive nonagrarian alternatives.

Corollary 10.3 and Result 10.5 give:

> **Corollary 10.4:** *The expected payment to the peasant (agency cost) is nondecreasing in* A.

As the cost of exploitation falls, the landlord increases exploitation while reducing the peasant's payment.

A unique maximum, which is completely characterized by the first-order conditions, exists for this problem. From the discussions of the agency-cost function and the "expected-utility taking" problem and standard results in optimization theory:

> **Result 10.6:** *(a)* $W(p, \pi_2; A)$ *is nonincreasing and convex in* A*; and (b)* $W(p, \pi_2; A)$ *is nondecreasing and convex in* p *with* $W_p(p, \pi_2; A)$ *equal to the expected crop size.*

The derivative property and the fact that $W(p, \pi_2; A)$ is convex in p imply that increases in the market price lead the landlord to design a contract that requires the peasant to increase the average output produced. Naturally, we expect this increase in expected output to be associated with an increase in effort on the part of the peasant and an increase in exploitative activities by the landlord. By the first-order conditions to this problem,

$$V_u(\underline{u}, p, \pi) - Af'(\underline{u}) = 0$$

from which

$$\underline{u}_p = \frac{-V_{up}(\underline{u}, p, \pi)}{V_{uu}(p, \underline{u}, \pi) - Af''(\underline{u})}.$$

By Result 10.3 and our assumptions on the cost of exploitation, the denominator of this last expression is negative. Hence, the whole expression is negative if $V_{up}(\underline{u}, p, \pi) < 0$, and positive if this last inequality is reversed. Using Result 10.3(a),

$$V_u(\underline{u}, p, \pi) = -Y(z_1, z_2; \underline{u}, \pi),$$

from which

$$V_{up}(\underline{u}, p, \pi) = -\frac{dY}{dp}(z_1, z_2; \underline{u}, \pi)$$

for fixed $\underline{u}$. Result 10.2 establishes that the peasant's expected payment is nondecreasing in p. Combining that result with this expression establishes:

> **Result 10.7:** *The peasant's reservation utility (exploitation) is nonincreasing (nondecreasing) in the crop price.*

Landlords respond to more favorable market opportunities for the crop by increasing their exploitative activities. At the same time, they force the peasant to expand the average crop size. As the crop price rises, the landlord wants the tenant to produce more of the crop on average. To make the tenant more amenable to doing so, the landlord increases his exploitative activities. In interpreting Results 10.5 and 10.7, one should recall that Lemma 10.2 establishes that the landlord always forces the peasant to the reservation utility level. Thus, Results 10.5 and 10.7 are direct statements about the peasant's welfare. *As the cost of exploitation rises, the peasant's welfare rises, but as the crop price rises the peasant's welfare falls.*

We now examine the effect a change in p has on the expected payment to the peasant. Our interest is in calculating

$$\frac{dY(z_1(p), z_2(p); \pi_2, \underline{u}(p))}{dp}.$$

Result 10.3(a) now implies

$$\begin{aligned}\frac{dY}{dp} &= -V_{up}(\underline{u}, p, \pi) + Y\underline{u}_p \\ &= \underline{u}_p(Y + V_{uu}(p, \underline{u}, \pi) - Af''(\underline{u})).\end{aligned}$$

By Result 10.7, $\underline{u}_p$ is positive so that the sign of the overall effect will be determined by the term in parentheses. Direct calculation reveals that

$$V_{uu} = -Y - \frac{Y_2}{\pi_2}\left(\pi_1 \frac{\partial z_1}{\partial \underline{u}} + \pi_2 \frac{\partial z_2}{\partial \underline{u}}\right).$$

The term in parentheses on the right-hand side of this expression equals the effect on expected crop size of an increase in the peasant's reservation utility from the expected-utility-taking problem. By Result 10.1, this term is negative. Substituting, we have

$$\frac{dY}{dp} = \underline{u}_p \left(-\frac{Y_2}{\pi_2} \left(\pi_1 \frac{\partial z_1}{\partial \underline{u}} + \pi_2 \frac{\partial z_2}{\partial \underline{u}} \right) - Af''(\underline{u}) \right). \tag{10.2}$$

Hence, we conclude that when f is a linear function, the landlord's expected payment to the peasant must decrease with the crop price since the peasant's reservation utility is forced down as a result of the increase in the crop price. Result 10.3(a) implies that $V_{uu} \leq 0$. Therefore,

$$-\frac{Y_2}{\pi_2} \left(\pi_1 \frac{\partial z_1}{\partial \underline{u}} + \pi_2 \frac{\partial z_2}{\partial \underline{u}} \right) \leq Y,$$

whereas the first-order condition for the landlord's profit-maximizing problem requires

$$-V_u(\underline{u}, p, \pi) - Af'(\underline{u}) = 0.$$

Applying the envelope theorem to the expected-utility-taking problem establishes that

$$V_u = -Y$$

on using Corollary 10.1(a). Now combining these last three results, we have established that

$$-\frac{Y_2}{\pi_2} \left(\pi_1 \frac{\partial z_1}{\partial \underline{u}} + \pi_2 \frac{\partial z_2}{\partial \underline{u}} \right) \leq -Af'(\underline{u}).$$

Now if $(-f''/f') > 1$, it follows that

$$-Af' < Af''.$$

These last two inequalities establish that the parenthetical term in (10.2) above is negative. Hence, payments must rise because we have already established that reservation utility falls.

Summarizing this discussion, we have:

> **Result 10.8:** *If* f($\underline{u}$) *is linear, an increase in the crop price results in a decrease in the peasant's expected payment (agency cost). When* $-f''/f' > 1$*, an increase in the crop price results in an increase in the peasant's expected payment (agency cost).*

More intuitively, when p increases, two things happen. The expected size of the crop increases as the landlord takes advantage of the increased opportunities for profit in the crop market. At the same time, as Result 10.7 shows, the landlord also increases his exploitation of the peasant. As expected crop size increases, the landlord wants the peasant to commit more effort for a given level of exploitation, which tends to increase the landlord's payment to the peasant. However, as exploitation rises, Corollary 10.3 implies that the landlord can pay the peasant less and still keep her employed in crop production. This latter "exploitation effect" diminishes the peasant's expected payment. If the landlord's marginal cost of exploitation is low and constant, the landlord's desired level of exploitation rises rapidly as the crop price increases. The increased exploitation effect dominates and pushes down the total expected payment to the peasant. However, when the marginal cost of exploitation rises sufficiently rapidly, an increase in the crop price leads to only a small change in exploitation, and the direct effect encouraging a larger expected crop size dominates.

The striking conclusion is that, with rising output prices, expected payment to the peasant may rise even though exploitation increases. This happens when the landlord wants the peasant to work much harder for a given level of reservation utility, but increased exploitation is costly at the margin. Result 10.8, therefore, is consistent with the well-known, and somewhat controversial, empirical results reported by Fogel and Engerman (1972) that suggest that slaves engaged in the production of cotton were better fed than free farm workers, but were nevertheless worse off because of more intensive exploitation.[3] An issue raised in our model, and touched on by Fogel and Engerman, is whether slaveowners, in fact, pushed exploitation to its profitable limit. We conjecture that slaveowners experienced great difficulty in increasing their degree of exploitation beyond the levels achieved under the plantation system. This view is supported by the observation of extensive use of piece-rate and other incentive systems by masters willing to exact the most extreme and barbaric forms of coercion when such coercion was profitable.

3. Of course, alternative theoretical explanations (e.g., efficiency-wage concerns) for this phenomenon have been offered. Our intent is not to debate those explanations, but to point out that an exploitation explanation is also consistent with the same body of data.

More generally, the changes in the pattern of slavery associated with increasing demand for cotton were along the lines predicted by the model presented here for increases in p. As cotton became more valuable, increased efforts were devoted by individual slaveowners and slave-state politicians to preventing escapes and strengthening the power of masters over slaves. At a casual level, one might also note that the oppressive rule of southern slavery had engendered large-scale and organized attempts to liberate slaves by transporting them clandestinely to the free North. Given the presence of such organized institutions as the Underground Railroad, any significant increase in exploitation would be associated with increased cost of tracking down and returning "run slaves."

10.4 EXPLOITATION, AGENCY, AND SOCIAL WELFARE

So far, little has been said about the welfare consequences of exploitative activity on the part of the landlord. Obviously, exploitative activity hurts peasants, but a general assessment of the welfare consequences of exploitative activity requires a comparison of landlord gains and peasant losses. A simple criterion to use in making welfare judgments about exploitation, via the Kaldor compensation test, is to determine whether the landlord could successfully bribe peasants to produce the landlord's desired output (under exploitation) in the absence of exploitation. The payment that landlords would have to make to bribe peasants in this fashion is

$$Y(z_1, z_2; \pi_2, u^o) - Y(z_1, z_2; \pi_2, \underline{u})$$

where $\mathbf{z}$ and $\underline{u}$ are evaluated at the landlord's solution to the exploitation problem. The landlord can only afford this bribe if

$$W(p, \pi_2; A) \geq Y(z_1, z_2; \pi_2, u^o) - Y(z_1, z_2; \pi_2, \underline{u})$$

or

$$p(\pi_1 z_1 + \pi_2 z_2) - Y(z_1, z_2; \pi_2, u^o) - Af(\underline{u}) \geq 0 \tag{10.3}$$

where $\mathbf{z}$ and $\underline{u}$ are again evaluated at the landlord's solution to the exploitation problem.

We are interested in evaluating (10.3) under two different assumptions about the informational structure of the model. First, we consider the case when no informational asymmetry is present, so that the landlord and peasant can contract directly on $\mathbf{z}$. In this case, $Y(z_1, z_2; \pi_2, u^o)$ in expression (10.3) is replaced by $\exp(C(z_1, z_2) + u^o)$. (The reader can easily verify that $Y(z_1, z_2; \pi_2, u^o)$, in the absence of informational asymmetries, reduces to $\exp(C(z_1, z_2) + u^o)$.) In what follows, we report an example that shows that this version of expression (10.3) may be negative when evaluated at the landlord's most preferred $\mathbf{z}$ and $\underline{u}$.

Next, we consider the case in which the landlord cannot observe the state of nature or the peasant's effort so that expression (10.3) is evaluated using the agency-cost function derived before. For given $\mathbf{z}$, we observe that the level of exploitation chosen by the landlord will always be higher when information is asymmetric. To see why, note that the first-order condition for the landlord for given $\mathbf{z}$ when information is asymmetric using Corollary 10.1(a) is

$$-Y(z_1, z_2; \pi_2, \underline{u}) = Af'(\underline{u}),$$

and when information is symmetric, the first-order condition is

$$-\exp(C(z_1, z_2) + \underline{u}) = Af'(\underline{u}),$$

which implies that $\underline{u}$ is greater under symmetric information than under asymmetric information because $Y(z_1, z_2; \pi_2, \underline{u}) - \exp(C(z_1, z_2) + \underline{u})$ is the peasant's nonnegative risk premium for fixed $\underline{u}$. (This result can be recognized as a corollary to Result 9.2 in Chapter 9.) It, therefore, follows that both the landlord and peasant will be worse off when information is asymmetric. (Recall that the landlord can never achieve a greater level of profit under asymmetric information than symmetric information because of the presence of the constraints represented by (10.1).) Summarizing:

> **Result 10.9:** *For given* $\mathbf{z}$, *the landlord always receives a lower profit and awards the peasant a lower reservation utility when information is asymmetric than when information is symmetric.*

One obvious case in which the information asymmetry leads to a socially superior outcome is that in which expression (10.3) is negative in the symmetric case, but in which the information asymmetry is so severe that there does not exist any incentive-compatible contract yielding the landlord a positive profit. More generally, it is possible that the asymmetric case will yield a positive profit and a net social welfare gain, whereas the symmetric case will generate either a smaller social welfare gain or a social welfare loss. An example illustrates each of these cases.

Example 10.1: *We consider the case where the cost function takes the simple linear form*

$$C(z_1, z_2) = c_1 z_1 + c_2 z_2,$$

so that the full-information first-best-cost function is

$$Y_{FB} = exp(\underline{u} + c_1 z_1 + c_2 z_2).$$

The requirement that $c_2/\pi_2 < c_1/\pi_1$ *gives* $c_2/\pi_2 < c_1 + c_2$. *Cost minimization implies that only* z_2 *is produced in the full-information first-best case. The first-order condition for a utility-taking landlord at* $\underline{u}$ *is*

$$c_2\, exp(\underline{u} + c_2 z_2) = \pi_2$$

or

$$z_2 = (log(\pi_2) - log(c_2) - \underline{u})/c_2,$$

for which agency cost is

$$exp(\underline{u} + c_2 z_2) = exp(log(\pi_2) - log(c_2)) = \pi_2/c_2.$$

The landlord's return for given $\underline{u}$ *is*

$$\pi_2 z_2 - \pi_2/c_2 - f(\underline{u}) = (log(\pi_2/c_2) - \underline{u} - 1)\pi_2/c_2 - f(\underline{u})$$

A necessary and sufficient condition for the existence of a contract yielding positive social welfare is that $log(\pi_2/c_2) - u^{o} - 1 > 0$ *or* $\pi_2/c_2 > exp(u^{o} + 1)$. *Note that even when this condition is not satisfied, there may exist contracts profitable to the landlord involving positive exploitation costs. The profit-maximizing exploitation condition is*

$$f'(\underline{u}) = -\pi_2/c_2.$$

This may be consistent with arbitrarily severe exploitation over a range in which f *is approximately linear with* $f'(\underline{u}) > -\pi_2/c_2$. *The landlord's bribe required to compensate the peasant for exploitation is*

$$(exp(u^{o}) - exp(u(A)))exp(c_2 z_2)$$

and is convex in u^o*. Hence, the welfare loss to the peasant from exploitation and the net loss to society (in the Kaldor–Hicks sense) may be arbitrarily large. In particular, there may be a welfare loss relative to the case in which the landlord and peasant do not contract, so that the landlord receives zero and the peasant receives* u^o*, the outside option in the absence of exploitation.*

We now consider the private-information case. The solution to the agency-cost problem is

$$u_1 = \underline{u} + (c_1 + c_2)z_1$$
$$y_1 = exp(\underline{u})exp((c_1 + c_2)z_1),$$
$$u_2 = \underline{u} + (c_1 + c_2)z_1 + c_2/\pi_2(z_2 - z_1)$$
$$y_2 = exp(\underline{u})exp((c_1 + c_2)z_1 + c_2/\pi_2(z_2 - z_1)).$$

So

$$\frac{\partial Y}{\partial z_2} = c_2 exp(\underline{u})exp((c_1 + c_2)z_1 + c_2/\pi_2(z_2 - z_1)),$$
$$\frac{\partial Y}{\partial z_1} = exp(\underline{u})(c_1 + c_2)exp((c_1 + c_2)z_1) - \frac{\partial Y}{\partial z_2}.$$

An interior optimum for the principal's problem will exist only if $\partial Y/\partial z_2 = \pi_2$, $\partial Y/\partial z_1 = \pi_1$*. Suppose* $\partial Y/\partial z_2 = \pi_2$ *and* $z_1 = 0$*. We require* $\partial Y/\partial z_1 = \pi_1$*, or*

$$exp(\underline{u})(c_1 + c_2) \leq 1.$$

Assuming that this condition holds, the first-order conditions will be satisfied at an interior optimum with

$$exp((c_1 + c_2)z_1) = 1/exp(\underline{u})(c_1 + c_2)$$

or

$$z_1 = [-log(c_1 + c_2) - \bar{u}]/(c_1 + c_2),$$
$$c_2 exp(u)exp((c_1 + c_2)z_1 + (c_2/\pi_2)(z_2 - z_1)) = \pi_2,$$

or

$$[c_2/(c_1 + c_2)]exp((c_2/\pi_2)(z_2 - z_1)) = \pi_2,$$
$$z_2 - z_1 = \frac{\pi_2}{c_2} log(\pi_2(c_1 + c_2)/c_2).$$

The landlord's profit for given $\underline{u}$ *is*

$$
\begin{aligned}
P &= z_1 + \pi_2(z_2 - z_1) - exp(\underline{u})exp((c_1 + c_2)z_1 \times \\
&\quad (1 + exp)(c_2/\pi_2)(z_2 - z_1)) - f(\underline{u}) \\
&= \frac{-log(c_1 + c_2) - \underline{u}}{(c_1 + c_2)} + (\pi_2^2/c_2)log\left(\frac{\pi_2(c_1 + c_2)}{c_2}\right)1/ \\
&\quad (c_1 + c_2)(1 + \pi_2(c_1 + c_2)/c_2) - f(\underline{u}).
\end{aligned}
$$

The profit-maximizing exploitation condition is (for an interior solution)

$$
f'(\underline{u}) = \frac{-1}{c_1 + c_2},
$$

and hence the equilibrium level of $\underline{u}$ *will be higher than in the full-information problem. In particular, we may consider a case in which* $-1/(c_1 + c_2) > f'(u^o) > -\pi_2/c_2$ *and* f *is approximately linear over a wide range. Then no exploitation will take place in the private-information case, but the social loss from exploitation may be arbitrarily large in the full-information case.*

The reason this happens is that the contractual problems arising from the information asymmetry are so difficult to resolve that they effectively hinder the landlord's attempts at exploiting the peasant. As the landlord's ability to exploit the peasant grows, one, therefore, might conjecture that it will become increasingly likely that information asymmetries underlying the hidden-action problem will play a more prominent social role in limiting losses from exploitative behavior. Consider, for example, the polar case in which the landlord's marginal cost of exploiting the peasant is very low and constant. At the margin, the landlord is almost always assured of making a gain from investing in exploitative activity, and the landlord will try to push the peasant to minimum subsistence. Now if no information asymmetry is present, the landlord can also expropriate all the surplus that the peasant produces above his or her subsistence level – the ultimate Marxian solution. And, in this same case, suppose that it was completely infeasible for the landlord to monitor or observe the peasant's behavior. Even though the landlord has the ability to drive the peasant to the brink of bare subsistence, his inability to negotiate a solution to the agency problem, and thus to profitably contract, negates his exploitative ability.

10.5 EXTENSIONS

The model presented could be extended in a number of directions. First, the logarithmic expected-utility objective function could be replaced by any objective function with constant relative-risk aversion. Second, technology could be made endogenous, with landlords allocating effort between productive activity and exploitation, modeled as reducing $\underline{u}$. More interestingly, the individual interaction described here could be extended to a model of class conflict between landlords and peasants acting collectively, subject to the usual free-rider problems.

Epilog

We hope that the arguments made in the Introduction and the 10 substantive chapters have convinced the reader that the end of this book represents a beginning. Our parting claim is that we have only scratched the surface of what can be achieved using state-contingent production models. Uncertainty is a key aspect of everyday life, and few, if any, technologies are wholly deterministic. Sadly, but largely because of the cumbersome models that have been employed, theoretical and empirical analysis of stochastic production problems has made little progress for almost two decades. Beyond the spate of theoretical contributions that sprang from Sandmo's pathbreaking contribution, little of consequence has been done. Our immodest goal in writing this book has been to start the project of rescuing stochastic production analysis from that moribund state.

In doing so, we have tried to start from the beginning with the most basic concept of a state of nature and then work forward through the specification of a state-contingent technology to its direct economic ramifications. Our guiding principle has been the presumption, often eschewed by theorists in this area, that modern methods of economic analysis, such as duality theory, have much to offer in the analysis of stochastic production problems. Economic principles are not, as has sometimes been suggested, suspended when uncertainty is introduced. To counter this latter view, we have spent a fair amount of time demonstrating the obvious fact that producers facing a stochastic technology will minimize cost and optimize in a straightforward fashion. This was done for two reasons: first, to put productive decision making under uncertainty on the same footing as nonstochastic production analysis; and second, to counter the logical errors that had led researchers, misled by the pathological properties of the stochastic production-function specification, to question the legitimacy of even these most basic economic precepts.

Once this (in hindsight, obvious) point had been made, we moved on to the perhaps not obvious, but still transparent, implications of these basic facts. It turns out that this simple recognition can be pushed remarkably far in several areas. A complete theory of the firm, for very general preferences, lies ready to hand, and with it comes an equally complete theory of hedging and speculative behavior, a theory of production insurance, and ventures into the problems of agency that have received so much attention in recent years. Our concluding hope is that researchers more skilled than us will push these modest developments to the intellectual heights that the original contributions of Arrow, Debreu, Hirshleifer, and Yaari merit.

References and Selected Bibliography

Allais, M. (1953). Le comportement de l'homme rationel devant le risque: critique des axioms et postulates de l'ecole Americaine. *Econometrica* 21(4): 503–46.

Anderson, R. W., and J. P. Danthine. (1981). Cross Hedging. *Journal of Political Economy* 89(6): 1182–96.

(1983). The Time Pattern of Hedging and the Volatility of Futures Prices. *Review of Economic Studies* 50: 249–66.

Arrow, K. (1953). *Le rôle des valeurs boursiers pour la repartition la meillure des risques*. 53. CNRS, Paris. Cahiers du Seminair d'Economie.

(1965). Aspects of the theory of risk-bearing. Yrjo Jahnsson Lecture, Helsinki.

Basu, K. (1986). One Kind of Power. *Oxford Economic Papers* 38: 259–82.

Binswanger, H. P., K. Deininger, and G. Feder. (1993). Power, Distortions, Revolt, and Reform in Agricultural Land Relations. *World Bank Policy Research Working Papers*.

Blackorby, C., and D. Donaldson. (1978). Measures of Relative Equality and Their Welfare Significance. *Journal of Economic Theory* 18: 59–80.

(1980). A Theoretical Treatment of Indices of Absolute Inequality. *International Economic Review* 21: 107–36.

Borch, K. (1962). Equilibrium in a Re-insurance Market. *Econometrica* 30: 424–44.

Boserup, E. (1979). *The Conditions of Agricultural Growth: The Economics of Agrarian Change Under Population Pressure*. New York: Aldine.

Braverman, A., and J. E. Stiglitz. (1986). Landlords, Tenants and Technological Innovations. *Journal of Development Economics* 23: 313–32.

Chambers, R. G. (1988). *Applied Production Analysis: A Dual Approach*. Cambridge: Cambridge University Press.

(1989a). Concentrated Objective Functions For Nonlinear Tax Models. *Journal of Public Economics* 39: 365–75.

Chambers, R. G. (1989b). Insurability and Moral Hazard in Agricultural Insurance Markets. *American Journal of Agricultural Economics* 71(3): 604–16.
Chambers, R. G., Y. Chung, and R. Färe. (1996). Benefit and Distance Functions. *Journal of Economic Theory* 70: 407–19.
Chambers, R. G., and R. Färe. (1998). Translation Homotheticity. *Economic Theory* 11: 629–41.
Chambers, R. G., and J. Quiggin. (1992). A State-Contingent Approach to Production under Uncertainty. Working Paper, College Park: University of Maryland.
(1996). Nonpoint Source Pollution Control as a Multi-Task Principal–Agent Problem. *Journal of Public Economics* 59(1): 95–116.
(1997). Separation and Hedging Results with State-Contingent Production. *Economica* 64(254): 187–209.
(1998). Cost Functions and Duality for Stochastic Technologies. *American Journal of Agricultural Economics* 80: 288–95.
Chew, S. H. (1983). A generalization of the quasilinear mean with applications to the measurement of income inequality, and decision theory resolving the Allais paradox. *Econometrica* 51: 1065–92.
Chwe, M. (1990). Why Were Workers Whipped? Pain in a Principal–Agent Model. *Economic Journal* 100: 1109–21.
Danthine, J. P. (1978). Information, Futures Prices, and Stabilizing Speculation. *Journal of Economic Theory* 17: 79–98.
Debreu, G. (1952). A Social Equilibrium Existence Theorem. *Proceedings of the National Academy of Sciences* 38: 86–93.
(1959). *The Theory of Value*. New Haven: Yale University Press.
De Finetti, B. (1974). *Theory of Probability*. New York: Wiley.
Färe, R. (1988). *Fundamentals of Production Theory*. Berlin: Springer-Verlag.
Färe, R., and S. Grosskopf. (1994). *Cost and Revenue Constrained Production*. Berlin: Springer-Verlag.
Färe, R., and T. Mitchell. (1992). Output Scaling in a Cost-Function Setting. *Journal of Productivity Analysis* 3: 417–25.
Färe, R., and D. Primont. (1995). On Inverse Homotheticity. *Bulletin of Economic Research* 47: 161–6.
Feder, G., R. E. Just, and A. Schmitz. (1980). Futures Markets and the Theory of the Firm under Price Uncertainty. *Quarterly Journal of Economics* 94: 317–28.
Fogel, R. W., and S. L. Engerman. (1972). *Time on the Cross: The Economics of American Negro Slavery*, 1st ed. Boston: Little, Brown.
Grossman, S., and O. Hart. (1983). An Analysis of Principal–Agent Problems. *Econometrica* 51: 7–46.
Guesnerie, R., and J.-J. Laffont. (1984). A Complete Solution of a Class of Principal–Agent Problems with an Application to the Control of the Self-Managed Firms. *Journal of Public Economics* 25: 329–70.
Guesnerie, R., and J. Seade. (1982). Nonlinear Pricing in a Finite Economy. *Journal of Public Economics* 17: 157–79.

Hadar, J., and W. Russell. (1969). Rules for Ordering Uncertain Prospects. *American Economic Review* 59(1): 25–34.

Hanoch, G., and H. Levy. (1969). The Efficiency Analysis of Choices Involving Risk. *Review of Economic Studies* 36: 335–46.

Hardy, G., J. Littlewood, and G. Pólya. (1952). *Inequalities*, 2nd ed. Cambridge: Cambridge University Press.

Harris, M., and A. Raviv. (1979). Optimal Incentives with Imperfect Information. *Journal of Economic Theory* 20: 231–59.

Hart, O., and B. Holmstrom. (1987). The theory of contracts. In T. F. Bewley, (Ed.), *Advances in Economic Theory*, pp. 711–55 Cambridge: Cambridge University Press.

Hirshleifer, J. (1965). Investment Decisions Under Uncertainty: Choice-Theoretic Approaches. *Quarterly Journal of Economics* 79(4): 509–36.

(1966). Investment Decisions Under Uncertainty: Applications of the State-Theoretic Approach. *Quarterly Journal of Economics* 80(2): 52–77.

Hirshleifer, J., and J. Riley. (1992). *The Analytics of Uncertainty and Information*. Cambridge: Cambridge University Press.

Holmström, B. (1979). Moral hazard and observability. *Bell Journal of Economics* 10: 74–91.

Holmström, B., and P. Milgrom. (1987). Aggregation and Linearity in the Provision of Intertemporal Incentives. *Econometrica* 55: 303–28.

(1991). Multitask Principal–Agent Analyses: Incentive Contracts, Asset Ownership, and Job Design. *Journal of Law, Economics and Organization* 7: 25–52.

Holthausen, D. M. (1979). Hedging and the Competitive Firm Under Price Uncertainty. *American Economic Review* 69: 989–95.

Kreps, D. (1990). *A Course in Microeconomic Theory*. Princeton: Princeton University Press.

Krug, E. (1976). *Stochastic Production Correspondences*. Meisenhaim am Glam: Verlag Anton Hain.

Landsberger, M., and I. Meilijson. (1990). A Tale of Two Tails: An Alternative Characterization of Comparative Risk. *Journal of Risk and Uncertainty* 3(1): 65–82.

Luenberger, D. G. (1992). Benefit Functions and Duality. *Journal of Mathematical Economics* 21: 461–81.

(1995). *Microeconomic Theory*. New York: McGraw-Hill.

(1996). Welfare from a Benefit Viewpoint. *Economic Theory* 7: 445–62.

Machina, M. (1982). "Expected Utility" Analysis without the Independence Axiom. *Econometrica* 50(2): 277–323.

(1987). Choice under Uncertainty: Problems Solved and Unsolved. *Journal of Economic Perspectives* 1(1): 121–54.

Machina, M. J., and D. Schmeidler. (1992). A More Robust Definition of Subjective Probability. *Econometrica* 60: 745–80.

Malmquist, S. (1953). Index Numbers and Indifference Surfaces. *Trabajos de Estatistica* 4: 209–42.

Marshall, A., and I. Olkin. (1979). *Inequalities: Theory of Majorization and Its Applications*. New York: Academic Press.
McFadden, D. (1978). Cost, Revenue, and Profit Functions. In M. Fuss, and D. McFadden, (Eds.), *Production Economics: A Dual Approach to Theory and Applications*. Amsterdam: North Holland.
Milne, F. (1995). *Finance Theory and Asset Pricing*. Oxford: Oxford University Press.
Mirrlees, J. A. (1971). An Exploration in the Theory of Optimum Income Taxation. *Review of Economic Studies* 38: 175–208.
(1974). Notes on Welfare Economics, Information and Uncertainty. In M. Balch, D. McFadden, and S. Wu, (Eds.), *Essays on Economic Behaviour under Uncertainty*. Amsterdam: North-Holland.
Nelson, C., and E. Loehman. (1987). Further Toward a Theory of Agricutural Insurance. *American Journal of Agricultural Economics* 69: 523–31.
Newbery, D., and J. Stiglitz. (1981). *The Theory of Commodity Price Stabilisation – A Study in the Economics of Risk*. Oxford: Oxford University Press.
(1982). Risk Aversion, Supply Response, and the Optimality of Random Prices: A Diagrammatic Analysis. *Quarterly Journal of Economics* 97(1): 1–26.
Peleg, B., and M. Yaari. (1975). A Price Characterisation of Efficient Random Variables. *Econometrica* 43: 283–92.
Pratt, J. W. (1964). Risk Aversion in the Small and the Large. *Econometrica* 32: 122–36.
Quiggin, J. (1981). Risk Perception and Risk Aversion among Australian Farmers. *Australian Journal of Agricultural Economics* 25(2): 160–9.
(1982). A Theory of Anticipated Utility. *Journal of Economic Behavior and Organization* 3: 323–43.
(1991). Comparative statistics for Rank-Dependent Expected Utility Theory. *Journal of Risk and Uncertainty* 4(4): 339–50.
(1992). *Generalized Expected Utility Theory: The Rank-Dependent Model*. Amsterdam: Kluwer Academic.
Quiggin, J., and R. G. Chambers. (1998a). Risk Premiums and Benefit Measures for Generalized Expected Utility Theories. *Journal of Risk and Uncertainty* 17: 121–38.
(1998b). A State-Contingent Production Approach to Principal–Agent Problems with an Application to Point-Source Pollution Control. *Journal of Public Economics* 70: 441–72.
(2000). Increasing and Decreasing Risk Aversion for Generalized Preferences. Working Paper, College Park: University of Maryland.
Radner, R. (1968). Competitive Equilibrium under Uncertainty. *Econometrica* 36: 31–54.
Raviv, A. (1979). The Design of an Optimal Insurance Policy. *American Economic Review* 69: 84–96.
Rockafellar, R. T. (1970). *Convex Analysis*. Princeton: Princeton University Press.
Rolfo, J. (1980). Optimal Hedging Under Price and Quantity Uncertainty: The Case of a Cocoa Producer. *Journal of Political Economy* 88: 100–16.

Ross, S. (1973). The Economic Theory of Agency: The Principal's Problem. *American Economic Review* (Papers and Proceedings) 63: 134–9.

Rothschild, M., and J. Stiglitz. (1970). Increasing Risk: I. A Definition. *Journal of Economic Theory* 2: 225–43.

Samuelson, P. (1947). *Foundations of Economic Analysis*, Cambridge: Harvard University Press.

Sandmo, A. (1971). On the Theory of the Competitive Firm under Price Uncertainty. *American Economic* Review 61: 65–73.

Savage, L. J. (1954). *Foundations of Statistics*, New York: Wiley.

Schmeidler, D. (1989). Subjective Probability and Expected Utility without Additivity. *Econometrica* 57: 571–87.

Segal, U., and A. Spivak. (1990). First-Order versus Second-Order Risk-Aversion. *Journal of Economic Theory* 51(1): 111–25.

Segerson, K. (1988). Uncertainty and Incentives in Nonpoint Pollution Control. *Journal of Economics and Environmental Management* 15: 87–98.

Shavell, S. (1979). On Moral Hazard and Insurance. *Quarterly Journal of Economics* 93: 541–62.

Shephard, R. W. (1953). *Cost and Production Functions*. Princeton: Princeton University Press.

(1970). *Theory of Cost and Production Functions*. Princeton: Princeton University Press.

Spence, M., and R. Zeckhauser. (1971). Insurance, Information, and Individual Action. *American Economic Review* 61(2): 380–7.

Townsend, R. M. (1978). On the Optimality of Forward Markets. *American Economic Review* 68: 54–66.

Von Neumann, J., and O. Morgenstern. (1944). *Theory of Games and Economic Behavior*. Princeton: Princeton University Press.

Weymark, J. (1986). A Reduced-Form Optimal Nonlinear Income Tax Problem. *Journal of Public Economics* 30: 199–217.

(1987). Comparative Static Properties of Optimal Nonlinear Income Taxes. *Econometrica* 55: 1165–85.

Yaari, M. (1969). Some Remarks on Measures of Risk Aversion and Their Uses. *Journal of Economic Theory* 1: 315–29.

(1987). The Dual Theory of Choice under Risk. *Econometrica* 55: 95–115.

Index